OTHER CRIMINAL JUSTICE PUBLICATIONS

Published by
THE W. H. ANDERSON COMPANY
646 MAIN STREET
CINCINNATI, OHIO 45201

Criminal Justice
National Advisory Board

POLICE

IN THE

COMMUNITY

Being a Volume of the
Criminal Justice Text Series

by

Charles P. McDowell B.S., M.P.A., Ph.D.

Cincinnati

The W. H. Anderson Company

COPYRIGHT © 1975

By

THE W. H. ANDERSON COMPANY

Second Printing— April, 1976

Library of Congress Catalog Card Number: 75-20976

ISBN No. 0-87084-557-8

Not houses finely roofed or
the stones of walls well-builded,
nay, nor canals and dockyards,
make the city, but men able to
use their opportunity.

ALCAEUS

Contents

Chapter

Contents

Preface

The issues and problems involved in police-community relations can only be assessed from the perspective of specific police departments within specific cities. The police are themselves a part of the urban kaleidoscope: adding to the overall picture and at the same time they mirror the context in which they operate. To understand the police is to understand them within their working context. A study of the police within a city is necessarily a study of that city itself. Greater justice could be done in a book which demonstrated the relationships among certain areas—specifically, relationships between the police and certain other pieces within the urban kaleidoscope. The information contained in this book will be of value to the student of police-community relations; however, the burden is upon the student to interpret its data in the light of his own particular community context. The book will give the reader an enhanced ability to critically examine his own community and the police department within the total community context.

There are many people the author must thank for a variety of reasons. Dr. Glenn W. Rainey of Eastern Kentucky University contributed the materials in Chapter 10, and his insights into the problem of police corruption add a significant dimension to the book. A debt is acknowledged to Dr. Carl Matthews, President Emeritus of North Texas State University and to Dr. Merl E. Bonney, Emeritus Distinguished Professor of Psychology, of North Texas State University. Much is owed to my colleagues and friends in the police profession, and it is hoped that this book will in some way positively facilitate their work. Finally, a thank you to my wife Cindy, for without her thoughtful comments, proofreading skills, and patience this book would not have been written.

C. P. McDowell
Little Rock, Arkansas

1

Historical Development
of the Police

The police are such a common sight in most cities that it would be reasonable to assume that most people tend to take them for granted. Of course individual experiences and variations in lifestyle will play a role in the perspective from which the police are viewed; yet, the police are accepted by virtually all elements of society as a normal part of the urban mosaic. Although various individuals and groups may have different expectations of the police, none question the legitimacy of the police as an agency of society.

However, the police have not always been a part of the urban scene. In fact, the police—at least as we know them—are a relatively recent addition to cities. The police have evolved into their present form as society itself has changed and matured. It has been this development of *society as a whole* which has created the need for the police and which has shaped their organizational structure and their functions. The police are but one means of social control, and it was necessary for society to develop to a certain point before the role requirements of the police were themselves shaped. Perhaps a brief "backward glance" will clarify this point.

Social Control

Social control refers to the various means whereby the behavior of the individual is regulated so that the prevailing social norms are adhered to.[1] In pre-industrial societies, in which the kinship system was dominant, social control was basically a family responsibility. In such a situation the individual was dependent upon the good will and acceptance of the family and tribe for his security and support. If a person offended his or another family, it became the responsibility of the parties directly involved to resolve the problem. Thus in the ancient societies based on this model, justice was an individual problem. The only time the community as a whole became involved in the control of an individual's deviant behavior was when the offender did something which was believed to threaten the safety of the community as a whole or which would offend the gods (which could have serious consequences for the whole community).

---

[1] See for example Arnold W. Green, *Sociology: An Analysis of Life in Modern Society*, 5th ed. (New York: McGraw-Hill Book Company, 1968), especially chapter twenty-one "The Law and Social Control"; see also Hazel B. Kerper, *Introduction to the Criminal Justice System* (St. Paul, Minn.: West Publishing Co., 1972), pp. 3–4.

With the rise of mercantile capitalism during the middle ages (at which time there also developed more refined concepts of the individual ownership of property) informal social controls began to give way to more formal controls which were generally administered by the church and the feudal lords. However, the nature of and the need for social controls was still seen as being largely vested in the family, so long as religious or political boundaries were not crossed. The subtle changes in the nature of social organization and the means of social control were noted by the German sociologist Ferdinand Toennies in his formulation of the concepts of "Gemeinschaft" and "Gesellschaft." Gemeinschaft denotes a communal setting based on interactional relationships which are bound together by sentiment. There are several types of social relationships which are basically gemeinschaft in nature, such as kinship units or groups of people who have lived close together over a long period of time. Also included would be groups with a similar outlook, as in the case of members of a religious order. The term gemeinschaft thus describes groups of people welded together in close interpersonal ties and represents a close sense of community.[2]

Gesellschaft, on the other hand, is an interactional system which is characterized by individualism and mutual distrust. Toennies believed that in a gesellschaft setting everyone is alone and isolated, and that there exists a general state of social tension. In the gesellschaft setting individuals tend to be competitive and there is a continuous struggle for personal gain and advantage as well as an absence of mutual concern. Toennies felt that industrialization was leading society towards gesellschaft-type relationships.

It should be readily apparent that in a gesellschaft type of society, social controls would have to be taken out of the family and placed in a larger, yet "neutral" setting. Since society as a whole is considered the victim of criminal acts rather than simply the person most directly harmed, it is but a short step to conclude that the agency charged with social control must therefore be a public agency. However, before the need to employ gesellschaft types of controls presented itself, it was necessary for society to go from a basically rural, agrarian type of society to an urbanized, industrial society. This came about during the Industrial Revolution.

The Industrial Revolution

The industrial revolution was actually a series of revolutions in science, technology, and agriculture which took place from about the middle of the eighteenth century to the middle of the nineteenth century.[3] Although the

[2] Melvin L. DeFleur, William V. D'Antonio and Lois B. DeFleur, *Sociology: Man in Society*. (Glenview, Illinois: Scott, Foresman and Company, 1971), p. 87.
[3] See for example *The New Cambridge Modern History, Volume IX*, (Cambridge:

industrial revolution started in England, it quickly spread to other western nations, including the United States. The consequences of the industrial revolution radically changed life for western man, and its full impact is still a matter of study and debate by contemporary scholars. Although the term "industrial revolution" is used, perhaps among the most important advancements were those which were made in agriculture, for in a sense the more directly "industrial" changes were in part a consequence of agricultural innovations.

Agricultural Advances. Up to the early 1700's there had been few improvements in agricultural methods in England since the Middle Ages; the medieval three-field system was still employed wherein one third of the land was allowed to lie fallow because adequate grain crops could not be produced from land used more than two years in succession. Also, farmers used the large open fields (commons) which surrounded the villages without using fences or hedges.[4] Farm production was just adequate to meet the demands of the population, but there was no surplus for export. Then in the 1730's Jethro Tull, a wealthy farmer, discovered that if the ground was properly prepared and the seed planted in rows (instead of "broadcasting") that farmers using cultivators could use less seed and grow more grain. Another pioneer was Lord Charles Townsend, who experimented with crop rotation and found that by planting certain root crops the soil would be restored and at the same time livestock could be fed by the crop. This was a highly significant move, for it meant that the age-old practice of slaughtering the livestock in the fall could be abandoned and that not only could the productivity of the land be greatly increased but that livestock could be sustained year round, thus increasing the supply of meat and milk.

Increases in agricultural productivity also brought about the enclosure of the common lands, which were systematically divided up and placed under more intensive cultivation. Although this greatly increased agricultural output, it also displaced large numbers of freemen who in turn went to the cities—and who found employment in the bourgeoning industries.[5]

Industrial Advances. While farmers were converting the land from one of a subsistence economy to one which was capable of producing large surpluses, corresponding changes were being wrought in the more purely

The University Press, 1965); Thomas S. Ashton, *The Industrial Revolution, 1760–1830,* (London: Oxford University Press, 1958); or Phyllis Deane, *The First Industrial Revolution,* (Cambridge: The University Press, 1965).

[4] Goldwin Smith, *A History of England,* (New York: Charles Scribners' Sons, 1949, 1957), p. 493.

[5] *Ibid.*

industrial realm, or as Smith has said, "Englishmen were applying mechanical power to industry on a scale never known before. Production was increased. New economic, social, and political problems were created for all western civilization." [6] England's basic industries (wool, cotton, iron, and steel) were refined and enhanced during this period.

In 1733 John Kay invented the "flying shuttle" which doubled the output of cotton and wool weavers, and in 1764 the "spinning jenny" was invented by James Hargraves. These and other technical developments soon took the production of this class of goods out of homes and concentrated them in factories (prior to the advent of the industrial revolution the textile industry furnished raw materials to artisans and then collected and marketed the finished product. The new power looms rendered this means of production obsolete). The textile industry of course experienced a major forward impetus with the invention of the cotton gin by Eli Whitney in 1793, and the mass production of textiles served as the opening salvo of what was to become an extensive factory system in England and the United States.

In 1705 an inventor by the name of Thomas Newcomen developed a formidable "fire-engine," a steam driven engine which consumed some thirteen tons of coal a day! In 1769 James Watt improved upon Newcomen's engine and produced a relatively efficient steam engine which was soon employed in cotton factories. It also came to play a major role in the iron and steel industries. Iron factories had been using wood as their fuel in the smelting process, and England's forests were becoming depleted.[7] The steam engine was combined with the use of coal in the production of iron, thus producing the blast furnaces which enabled the iron masters to produce large quantities of high grade iron. This was rapidly followed by the discovery of a means of making the cast iron more malleable so that wrought iron could be produced, and finally the Bessemer process enabled the foundries to produce large quantities of steel.

Every where production increased; displaced farmers entered the textile mills and the iron forges; more people could be fed by fewer farmers and great surpluses could be developed which underscored trade and commerce. Colonial empires were founded, industry grew, and an entirely new mercantile class blossomed: "Men drove bargains and smashed obstacles. They seized un-imagined opportunities. They made things of beauty and beastliness. The wens of England's great cities sprawled ugly and dark; they enslaved the workers and the factory owners at the same time. Industrial capitalism became huge, efficient, and impersonal." [8] Out

[6] *Ibid.*, pp. 497–498.
[7] *Ibid.*, p. 499.
[8] *Ibid.*, p. 500.

of this revolution came great cities with teeming, dense populations. And out of these cities came the need for a more formal and centrally directed form of social control: the police.

History of the Police *

The face of America has changed since colonial days from a collection of predominantly rural and independent jurisdictions to an industrialized urban nation. Yet in several respects law enforcement has not kept pace with this change. As America has grown and policing has become correspondingly complex, the existing law enforcement system has not always been altered to meet the needs of a mechanized and metropolitan society.

Over the years, the proliferation of independent and, for the most part, local policing units has led to an overlapping of responsibilities and a duplication of effort, causing problems in police administration and in the coordination of efforts to apprehend criminals. America is a nation of small, decentralized police forces.

Other problems have plagued the police over the years. Forces have lacked an adequate number of sufficiently qualified personnel. Unattractive salaries and working conditions, and a general lack of public support have hindered police development. And the need for harmonious police-community relations has been a persistent problem, one which, unfortunately, has not been widely recognized until recently. Community relations problems are nothing new; they have existed since American cities were divided into subsocieties by virtue of different ensuing waves of immigrants from western, and later eastern, Europe, who started settling in urban centers before the turn of this century.

To understand better the prevailing problems that police agencies face today, it is helpful to examine their development in England as well as in the United States; for there are many weaknesses in the existing system that stem from practices developed in the rural colonies and from the colonial philosophy of law enforcement.

Early History of English Law Enforcement

France and other continental countries maintained professional police forces of a sort as early as the 17th century. But England, fearing the oppression these forces had brought about in many of the continental countries, did not begin to create police organizations until the 19th century. Moreover, England, in its early history, did not maintain a permanent army of paid soldiers that could enforce criminal laws when not engaged in guarding the country's borders against invaders. The cost of developing a force specifically for peace-keeping duties was believed to be too high for the royal purse.

* Taken from one report of the President's Commission on Law Enforcement and the Administration of Justice, *Task Force Report—The Police.* (Washington, D.C.: Government Printing Office, 1967), p. 3–7.

Private citizens could do the job cheaper, if given a few shillings reward for arrests. This simple law enforcement expedient, which had begun with Alfred the Great (870–901), can be recognized as the forerunner of American police agencies.

Primarily, the system encouraged mutual responsibility among local citizen's associations, which were pledged to maintain law and order; [6] it was called the "mutual pledge" system. Every man was responsible not only for his own actions but also for those of his neighbors. It was each citizen's duty to raise the "hue and cry" when a crime was committed, to collect his neighbors and to pursue a criminal who fled from the district. If such a group failed to apprehend a lawbreaker, all were fined by the Crown.

The Crown placed this mutual responsibility for group police action upon 10-family groups. Each of these was known as a "tithing." From the tithing, there subsequently developed the "hundred" comprised of 10 tithings. From this developed the first real police officer—the constable.[7] He was appointed by a local nobleman and placed in charged of the weapons and equipment of each hundred.

Soon, the "hundreds" were grouped to form a "shire," a geographical area equivalent to a county.[8] A "shire-reeve"—lineal antecedent of tens of thousands of sheriffs to come—thus came into being, appointed by the Crown to supervise each county. The constable's breadth of authority remained limited to his original "hundred." The shire-reeve was responsible to the local nobleman in ensuring that the citizens enforced the law effectively. From his original supervisory post, the sheriff soon branched out to take part in the pursuit and apprehension of lawbreakers.

It was during the reign of Edward I (1272–1307), that the first official police forces were created in the large towns of England. These were called the "watch and ward," and were responsible for protecting property against fire, guarding the gates, and arresting those who committed offenses between sunset and daybreak. At the same time the constable became the primary law enforcement officer in all towns throughout England.

In 1326, to supplement the "shire-reeve" mutual pledge system, Edward II created the office of justice of the peace. The justices, originally noblemen, were appointed by the Crown to assist the sheriff in policing the county. This led in time to their taking on local judicial functions, in line with the primary duty of keeping the peace in their separate jurisdictions.

The constable, who retained the responsibility of serving as a major official within the pledge system, meanwhile gained in importance. He became an

---

[6] J. Daniel Devlin, "Police Procedure, Administration and Organization" (London: Butterworth & Co., 1966), p. 3.
[7] Supra, note 5 at p. 49.
[8] Ibid.

assistant to the justice, responsible for supervising the night watchmen, inquiring into offenses, serving summonses, executing warrants, and taking charge of prisoners.[9] It was here that the formal separation between judge and police officer developed.

As law enforcement increasingly became the responsibility of the central government in 14th century England, the justice, as the appointee of the King, exercised a greater degree of control over the locally appointed constables. By the end of the century the constable no longer functioned independently as an official of the pledge system. Rather, he was obliged to serve the justice. This essentially set the justice-constable patterns for the next 500 years. The "justice [remained] the superior, the constable the inferior, conservator of the peace"[10] until the second quarter of the 19th century.

Meanwhile, over these years, the local pledge system continued to decline. Community support languished. And with considerable reason.[11]

What was everybody's business became nobody's duty and the citizens who were bound by law to take their turn at police work gradually evaded personal police service by paying others to do the work for them. In theory constables were appointed annually, but in fact their work was done by deputies or substitutes who so acted year after year, being paid to do so by the constables. These early paid police officers did not rank high in popular estimation as indicated in contemporary references. They were usually ill-paid and ignorant men, often too old to be in any sense efficient.

But as the local pledge system was declining, innovations in policing were cropping up in the emerging cities of the 17th and 18th centuries. Those first law enforcement officers were increasingly assisted by a paid night-watch force. Although these nominally were responsible for guarding the cities against thieves and vandals, apparently they were not effective. Reportedly they did little more than roam the streets at night, periodically calling out the condition of the weather, the hour, and the fact that "all was well."

Industrialization of England

While England remained essentially a rural country, the dominance of the justice of the peace in law enforcement machinery aroused little formal opposition. But with the advent of the Industrial Revolution at the end of the 1700's families by the thousands began traveling to factory towns to find work. Inevitably, as the cities grew, established patterns of life changed and

[9] Supra, note 6 at p. 6.
[10] Royal Commission on the Police, "Royal Commission on the Police 1962, Final Report" (London: Her Majesty's Stationery Office), p. 12.
[11] Supra, note 6 at p. 7.

unprecedented social disorder resulted. Law enforcement became a much more complex enterprise.

Government and citizens alike responded to this need for better law enforcement. A number of fragmented civic associations, such as the Bow Street Horse and Foot Patrol, were formed to police the streets and highways leading out of London and the Government passed statutes creating public offices, later to be known as police offices. Each of these housed three paid justices of the peace, who were authorized to employ six paid constables. These new posts thus helped to centralize law enforcement operations within a small area.

By the beginning of the 19th century nine police offices had been established within the metropolitan area of London, but there was little apparent effort to coordinate their independent law enforcement activities. This was reportedly due to the fact that each office refused to communicate with another for fear that the other might take credit for detecting and apprehending an offender.

In London especially, these weaknesses combined to make the police forces seemingly powerless to combat crime. Highwaymen on the road, thieves lurking in the cities, daily bank robberies, juvenile delinquency—all presented major law enforcement problems.[12] However, out of this difficult situation emerged a unique remedy to discourage thieves from attacking citizens; in the early 1800's gaslights were introduced on the streets of London.

Many of the experiments in law enforcement before 1820 failed "because no scheme could reconcile the freedom of action of individuals with the security of person and property."[13] In 1822, Sir Robert Peel, England's new Home Secretary, contended that, while better policing could not eliminate crime, the poor quality of police contributed to social disorder. Seven years later he introduced and guided through Parliament an "Act for Improving the Police In and Near the Metropolis." This led to the first organized British metropolitan police force. Structured along the lines of a military unit, the force of 1,000 was the first one to wear a definite uniform. The men were commanded by two magistrates, later called commissioners, who were given administrative but not judicial duties. Ultimately, the responsibility for equipping, paying, maintaining, and to a certain degree supervising the "bobbies," as they later became known, was vested in the Home Secretary. Because he was made accountable to the Parliament "for the exercise of his authority over the Metropolitan police, it could [thus] be said that the new force was under the ultimate control of a democratically elected Parliament."[14]

Availability of competent manpower, then as today, became an immediate

[12] Supra, note 5 at p. 59.
[13] Supra, note 6 at p. 10.
[14] Supra, note 6 at p. 16.

problem. It was difficult to recruit suitable men to serve in the "new police," for the salaries were poor and the commissioners selective. And there were other harassments. Parliament objected to appropriating Government funds to maintain a police force. The radicals were afraid of tyranny. The aristocracy, though willing to accept the protection of such a force, was disgruntled because the commissioners refused to abide by the traditional rules of patronage in making appointments.

Nevertheless, the London metropolitan police proved so effective in suppressing crime and apprehending criminals that within 5 years the provinces, which were experiencing increasing crime problems and violent riots, asked London for policing help.[15] Shortly after, Parliament enacted a series of police reform bills. Among them, one empowered justices of the peace in 1839 to establish police forces in the counties; and in 1856 another required every borough and county to have a police force.

As regular police forces developed, the justices of the peace voluntarily relinquished their law enforcement duties and confined themselves to deciding questions of law. Before this change occurred, the police had served as the agents of the powerful justices and had consequently used the justices' authority to carry on investigation of those in custody. When the justices relinquished their law enforcement powers, the legislature gave no consideration as to what, if any, investigative responsibilities should be transferred to the police. As a result, the statutes for law enforcement officers that remain on the books today contain little recognition of the broad discretion that police continue to exercise.[16]

Law Enforcement in the American Colonies

American colonists in the 17th and 18th centuries naturally brought to America the law enforcement structure with which they were familiar in England. The transfer of the offices of constable and sheriff to rural American areas—which included most colonial territory—was accomplished with little change in structure of the offices. Drawing upon the pattern of the mutual pledge system, the constable was made responsible for law enforcement in towns, while the sheriff took charge of policing the counties. The Crown-appointed Governors bestowed these offices on large landowners who were loyal to the King. After the revolution, sheriffs and constables tended to be selected by popular elections, patronage then being on the wane.

In many colonial cities the colonists adopted the British constabulary-nightwatch system. As early as 1636 Boston had nightwatchmen, in addition to a military guard. New York and Philadelphia soon developed a similar

[15] Christopher Hibbert, "The Roots of Evil" (London: Weidenfield and Nicolson, 1963), pp. 125–128.
[16] Edward J. Barrett, Jr., "Police Practices and the Law—From Arrest to Release or Charge," California Law Review, March 1962, 50: 17–18.

nightwatch system. The New York nightwatchmen were known as the "Rattle-watch," because they carried rattles on their rounds to remind those who needed reminding of their watchful presence.

Urbanization in the United States

As American towns grew in size and population during the first half of the 19th century, the constable was unable to cope with the increasing disorder. As in England years before, lawlessness became more prevalent: [17]

> New York City was alleged to be the most crime-ridden city in the world, with Philadelphia, Baltimore and Cincinnati not far behind. . . . Gangs of youthful rowdies in the larger cities . . . threatened to destroy the American reputation for respect for law. . . . Before their boisterous demonstrations the crude police forces of the day were often helpless.

Again, as in England, many American cities began to develop organized metropolitan police forces of their own. Philadelphia was one of the first. In 1833 a wealthy philanthropist left a will that provided for the financing of a competent police force in Philadelphia. Stimulated by this contribution, the city government passed an ordinance providing for a 24-man police force to work by day and 120 nightwatchmen. The force was unfortunately shortlived, for the ordinance was repealed less than 2 years later.

In 1838, Boston created a day police force to supplement the nightwatch, and other cities soon followed its lead. Crime, cities were finding, was no respecter of daylight. There were certain inherent difficulties, however, in these early two-shift police systems. Keen rivalries existed between the day and night shifts, and separate administrations supervised each shift. Recognizing the evils of separate police forces, the New York Legislature passed a law in 1844 that authorized creating the first unified day and night police, thus abolishing its nightwatch system. Ten years later Boston consolidated its nightwatch with the day police.

Following the New York model, other cities developed their own unified police forces during the next decade. By the 1870's the Nation's largest cities had full-time police forces. And by early 1900's there were few cities of consequence without such unified forces. These forces gradually came under the control of a chief or commissioner, often appointed by the mayor, sometimes with the consent of the city council and sometimes elected by the people.

These first formal police forces in American cities were faced with many

[17] Arthur Charles Cole, "The Irrepressible Conflict, 1859–1865," A History of American Life in 12 Volumes, vol. VIII, Arthur M. Schlesinger, Sr., and Dixon Ryan Fox, editors (New York: The Macmillan Co. 1934), pp. 154–155.

of the problems that police continue to confront today. Police officers became the objects of disrespect. The need for larger staffs required the police to compromise personnel standards in order to fill the ranks. And police salaries were among the lowest in local government service, a factor which precluded attracting sufficient numbers of high standard candidates. It is small wonder that the police were not respected, were not notably successful, and were not known for their vitality and progressiveness. Moreover, the police mission in the mid-1800's precluded any brilliance: [18]

The aim of the police departments was merely to keep a city superficially clean and to keep everything quiet that [was] likely to arouse public [ire].

Many of the problems that troubled these first organized metropolitan police forces can perhaps be traced to a single root—political control. As one authority has explained: [19]

Rotation in office enjoyed so much popular favor that police posts of both high and low degree were constantly changing hands, with political fixers determining the price and conditions of each change . . . The whole police question simply churned about in the public mind and eventually became identified with the corruption and degradation of the city politics and local governments of the period.

In an attempt to alleviate these problems, responsible leaders created police administrative boards to replace the control exercised over police affairs by mayors or city councils. These boards were given the responsibility of appointing police administrators and managing police affairs. Unfortunately, this attempt to cure political meddling was unsuccessful, perhaps because the judges, lawyers, and local businessmen who comprised the administrative boards were inexpert in dealing with the broad problems of the police.

Another attempt was made at police reform during the close of the 19th century. Noting that poor policing tended to occur mainly in urban areas, the State legislatures, which were dominated by rural legislators, required that police administrators be appointed by authority of the State. Thus State control became an alternative to local control of law enforcement. This move brought little success, for many problems had not been anticipated: [20]

[18] Arthur M. Schlesinger, Sr., "The Rise of the City, 1878–1898," A History of American Life in 12 Volumes, vol. X, Arthur M. Schlesinger, Sr., and Dixon Ryan Fox, editors (New York: The Macmillan Co., 1934), p. 115.
[19] Bruce Smith, Sr., "Police Systems in the United States" (2d rev. ed., New York: Harper and Bros., 1960), pp. 105–106.
[20] Id. at p. 186.

For one thing, the theory of state control . . . was not uniformly applied. It was primarily directed at the larger cities, by legislatures seeking to [perpetuate] rural domination in public affairs.

In spite of increased state control, the large city continued to pay for its police service, and police costs rose. One reason was that police boards were not even indirectly responsible to the local taxpaying public which they served. In cases where the State and city governments were not allied politically, friction increased. It increased further when the State-appointed administrator instituted policy out of harmony with the views of the majority of the city population. It was not until the first decades of the 20th century that cities regained control of police forces in all but a few cases.[21]

After these sincere attempts at reform during the last half of the 19th century, police forces grew in size and expanded in function. However, there was very little analysis of the changes in society that made expansion necessary nor of the effect such changes would work upon the role of the police. Civil service proved helpful, spreading to local police agencies and alleviating some of the more serious problems of political interference. The concept of merit employment, which some reformers had been proposing, was embraced by some forces.

One of the most notable police advancements of the 1900's was the advent of police training schools, even though on a somewhat modest basis. In the early 1900's, the new policeman learned chiefly in the school of experience: [22]

. . . Thus, for the most part the average American city depends almost entirely for the training of its police recruits upon such casual instruction as older officials may be able and willing to give.

In numerous areas, however, it was not until the 1940's and notably in the 1950's that police departments established and, in many cases, greatly expanded their recruit training programs.

State and Federal Law Enforcement Agencies

Although a State police force, known as the "Texas Rangers," was organized in 1835 to supplement Texas' military forces, modern State police organizations did not emerge until the turn of the century. In 1905, the Governor of Pennsylvania, in the absence of an effective sheriff-constable system, created the first State force. Its initial purpose was to cope with a public dispute between labor and management. Soon such continuing factors as the inadequacy of local policing by constables and sheriffs and the inability

---

[21] Id. at pp. 186–187. State control of urban police continues to exist in certain cities in Missouri, Maryland, Massachusetts, Maine, and New Hampshire.

[22] Elmer D. Graper, "American Police Administration" (New York: The Macmillan Co., 1921), pp. 109–110.

or unwillingness of city police forces to pursue lawbreakers beyond their jurisdictional limits convinced State legislatures of the need for Statewide police forces.[23]

The majority of State departments were established shortly after World War I to deal with the increasing problem of auto traffic and the accompanying wave of car thefts. Today all States except Hawaii have some form of State law enforcement body. While some State agencies are restricted to the functions of enforcing traffic laws and protecting life and property on the highways, others have been given general policing authority in criminal matters throughout the State.

The role of the Federal Government in law enforcement has developed in a sporadic and highly specialized manner. Federal law enforcement actually started in 1789, when the Revenue Cutter Service was established to help prevent smuggling. In 1836, Congress authorized the Postmaster General to pay salaries to agents who would investigate infringements involving postal matters. Among the more important law enforcement responsibilities later recognized by Congress were internal revenue investigation and narcotics control. Congress authorized a force of 25 detectives in 1868 and increased the number in 1915. In 1924, J. Edgar Hoover organized the Federal Bureau of Investigation in the Justice Department.[24]

With the expansion of interstate movement of people and goods, and Federal involvement in all aspects of life, the responsibilities of Federal agencies have increased significantly within the last few years. These Federal agencies are responsible to departments of the National Government. The Treasury Department's Secret Service is, for example, charged with the protection of the President and with investigating counterfeiting and forgery of Federal documents. Civilian departmental agencies, with the sole exception of the FBI, function under civil service regulations.[25]

The manpower and jurisdiction of the FBI have increased greatly since its establishment. Some of the statutes that have been responsible for this expansion are the National Stolen Property Act, the Federal Kidnapping Act, the Hobbs Act (extortion), the Fugitive Felon Act, the White Slave Act, the National Bank Robbery Act, Federal interstate gambling laws, and the Dyer Act. The last brings within the FBI's jurisdiction automobiles stolen and taken across the border of a State. Recent passage of strong Federal legislation has enhanced the FBI's role in the enforcement of civil rights.

Modernization

Serious study of police reform in America began in 1919. The problems exposed then and those faced by police agencies today are similar in many

[23] Supra, note 19 at pp. 147–150.
[24] Supra, note 5 at pp. 67–68.
[25] John Coatman, "Police" (London: The Oxford University Press, 1959), p. 50.

respects. For example, in 1931 the Wickersham Commission noted that the average police chief's term of office was too short, and that his responsibility to political officials made his position insecure. The Commission also felt that there was a lack of competent, efficient, and honest patrolmen. It said that no intensive effort was being made to educate, train, and discipline prospective officers, or to eliminate those shown to be incompetent. The Wickersham Commission found that with perhaps 2 exceptions, police forces in cities above 300,000 population had neither an adequate communications system nor the equipment necessary to enforce the law effectively. It said that the police task was made much more difficult by the excessively rapid growth of our cities in the past half century, and by the tendency of different ethnic groups to retain their language and customs in large cities. Finally, the Commission said, there were too many duties cast upon each officer and patrolman. The Missouri Crime Commission reported that in a typical American city the police were expected to be familiar with and enforce 30,000 Federal, State, or local enactments!

Despite the complexity of these problems, many hopeful improvements have occurred in the past few decades. Some cities, counties, and States have taken great strides in streamlining their operations through reorganization and increased use of technology and the use of modern techniques to detect and apprehend criminal offenders. Others are on the threshold of modernization. But many departments remain static. And it is these that obviously constitute a burden on the machinery of justice, and are detrimental to the process of achieving a truly professional police service.

Appendix A
The Development of Crime
in Early English Society *

The purpose of this paper is to trace the development of crime and criminal law in England from 400 A.D. to 1200 A.D. This period of history was selected for two reasons. First, early Saxon laws were recorded, and thus the changes which occurred in the legal structure over a period of years can be traced and analyzed; and second, it was during this period of English history that the tribal law of the Saxons gave way to the common law system which is now basic to Anglo-American law. Whatever social forces produced the common law system had to be present during this period. It is the intent of the writer to analyze these legal changes in terms of changing social conditions.

The method used was that of institutional legal history.[1] A basic assumption of sociological jurisprudence is that law is related to institutional history and change. The social changes that occurred in England during the period studied produced crime and criminal law as we know them today.

PART I

Anglo-Saxon Social Structure

The Iberians and Celts. The earliest settlers of Britain were the Iberians and the Celts. These people were organized along tribal lines, and there is no evidence of a social structure other than the tribal structure. They were bound together by the "legal and sentimental ties of kinship as the moral basis of society." [2] Trevelyan estimates that the Celts and Iberians were in the iron age. Agricultural practices were very crude. Pigs and cattle were kept as a part of their economic life, along with hunting, fishing, herding, weaving, and metal work.[3]

Between 55 B.C. and 400 A.D. the Romans occupied Britain, but for the exception of roads, walls, and town sites the Romans never did Latinize the Celts. Celtic tribalism still survived beyond the city walls.[4]

The Anglo-Saxons. Caesar and Tacitus describe the Anglo-Saxons as tribal units occupying the territory of North Germany. They had an iron-age culture:

* SOURCE: Clarence Ray Jeffery, "The Development of Crime in Early English Society," *Journal of Criminal Law, Criminology and Police Science*, vol. 47, pp. 647–666, March-April, 1957. By permission of the author and publisher.
[1] Jeffery, C. Ray, *Crime, Law, and Social Structure.* Jour. Crim. Law, Criminol. and Pol. Sci. vol. 47, 4 (1956).
[2] Trevelyan, G. M. *History of England*, New York: Doubleday and Co., vol. I, p. 25.
[3] *Ibid.*, pp. 26–28
[4] *Ibid.*, p. 43.

they utilized metals for tools and war weapons; they grew corn; they herded cattle.[5] They had a very crude and extensive type of agricultural system. These tribes possessed a very loose type of military organization and were quite warlike.[6] The consanguine family was the important social unit; the blood-tie was the important social relationship. The primitive fusion of institutional functions in the kinship group is undoubtedly the most important characteristic of this social arrangement.

Each tribe was in theory a group of kinsmen. The tribe performed the economic, political, religious, and familistic functions performed by separate and distinct institutional structures in a modern society. The tribe was the land-owning unit, and the land was cultivated by a group of kinsmen who formed plough-teams and who cultivated the land in an open-field system. Political control was in the hands of the armed warriors who met in the folk-moot or tribal council to elect a king or to pass laws. The king was elected from a given hereditary line, and he was the king of a tribe, never of a territorial unit. "The notion of a territorial influence was never for a moment involved in it." [7] The conjugal family unit was less important than the kinship group. "In general the mores of this period were bound up with the assumption that everyone belonged to a localized kinship group to which he is answerable." [8] "The tie which united these smaller pastoral communities was simply that of kindred." [9]

The Feudal System

Disintegrating Tribalism. The change that was taking place in English social structure has been characterized as "disintegrating tribalism." [10] "But even before the migrations to Britain, tribalism was yielding to individualism, and kinship was being replaced by the personal relation of warrior to his chief, which is the basis of aristocracy and feudalism." [11]

The whole economic and political structure of society was undergoing a great change. If by any two words we could indicate the nature of this elaborate process we might say that "tribalism" was giving place to "feudalism." [12]

Even before their invasion of Britain these Teutonic tribes had developed the *comitatus,* a military leader and his followers. They were bound to one another by a code of honor, and the relationship between a military leader

---

[5] Stubbs, William, *The Constitutional History of England,* Oxford: Clarendon Press, 1891, vol. I, p. 15 ff.

[6] *Ibid.,* p. 16 ff.

[7] Kemble, John M., *The Saxons in England,* London: Bernard Quartich, 1879, vol. I, p. 137. See also Trevelyan, *op. cit.,* p. 50.

[8] Queen, Stuart A. and Adams, John B., *The Family In Various Cultures,* New York: J. P. Lippincott Co., 1952, p. 175.

[9] Stubbs, *op. cit.,* p. 15.

[10] Gibbs, Marion, *Feudal Order,* New York: Henry Schuman, Inc., 1953, p. 10 ff.

[11] Trevelyan, *op. cit.,* p. 51.

[12] Maitland, F. W. and Montague, F. C., *A Sketch of English Legal History,* New York: Putnam and Sons, 1915, p. 10.

and his followers was a personal one. The military leader supplied certain necessities and the warriors shared in the booty whenever a raid was carried out.[13] This military system was replacing the familistic system. The social class system even before the invasions included an *eorl,* a military leader; the *ceorl,* his follower and the *laet,* a slave or conquered man.[14]

The British invasions, between 400 and 600 A.D., accentuated this transition from a tribal state to a feudal state. These invasions were of two different types. First came bands of warriors, the *comitatus,* without women and children; followed by kinship groups, farmers with their families.[15] These "war bands were one of the features of disintegrating tribalism." [16] The warriors settled the land which they were granted as rewards for their military service. Later on the kinship groups settled the land. "They were not so much territories as communities of tribesmen who felt themselves bound together by common customs and blood-ties; sometimes one or two hundred families, sometimes considerably more." [17] Each patriarchal family unit was allotted a share of land, called a *hide,* from which it gained economic subsistence.[18] At the beginning of Saxon history in England we find a distinction between the military man and the agricultural man, a distinction which was to play an important role in the development of feudalism in England.

Feudalism. In his discussion of feudalism Ganshof makes a distinction between two different but related meanings of the term "feudalism." As a *society* feudalism refers to a system of personal dependence, with a military class occupying the higher levels in the social scale, and with a subdivision of rights in real property corresponding to this system of personal dependence. As a *legal* system feudalism means a body of institutions creating obligations of service and duty—a military service on the part of the vassal and an obligation of protection on the part of the lord with regard to the vassal.[19]

Land System. The feudal system began in England with the invasions. The conquering warriors were granted land by their chiefs as a reward for military service. The land settlement pattern was mixed, that is, it included both military and family units. The granting of land to a follower by a chief was called a *beneficium* or benefit. The recipient of the land was able to cultivate it for his own use, to use it as a benefit free from obligations of

---

[13] Kemble, *op cit.,* vol. I, pp. 163–184.
[14] Vinogradoff, Paul, *The Growth of the Manor,* London: George Allen and Unwin, 1904, pp. 123–124.
[15] Trevelyan, *op. cit.,* p. 56.
[16] Gibbs, *op. cit.,* p. 17.
[17] *Ibid.,* p. 19.
[18] *Ibid.,* p. 20.
[19] Ganshof, F. L., *Feudalism,* New York: Longmans, Green and Co., 1952, p. xv.

service and taxation.[20] Land held in *alod,* an original grant of land to a military follower, was held free of service and rent. Land held in *fief* or *feud* was held in return for service and rent. Land grants were originally made for services rendered, as in the case of the invasions; however, by the ninth century the process was reversed. Service was now rendered in return for a benefice.[21] By the tenth century all land in England was bookland, land held in *fief.* A grant of land by a lord to a vassal came to be known as a *fief* or *feud,* and these terms replaced the term *beneficium.*[22] Land was now under the control of private landlords, and any man who occupied the lord's land owed the lord services. This concept of landownership replaced the system found during the tribal state of Saxon history when the tribe owned the land and each man as a tribesman shared in this ownership.

Vassalage. There was a legal union between vassalage and the benefice since the land relationship created by the grant also created a personal relationship between lord and vassal.[23] *Commendation* was the legal process by which a freeman placed himself under the protection of a lord in return for his services. The act of *commendation* was the way in which the personal tie between men replaced the kinship tie which was disintegrating as a result of the migrations and population growth. An act of *manumission,* usually performed on the altar of a church, freed the serf from his lord. A serf could also be freed by joining the holy orders, being knighted, or by fleeing to a free town and remaining there for a period of a year and a day.[24]

The tenure system, or system of service, developed as an expression of the *fief.* The most common service was knight's service, or military service. In this way military service was connected to the occupation of land. A distinction was made between the man who owed military service and the man who owed other types of services, especially agricultural services.[25] A *thegn* was a man with five hides of land who owed military service to a lord. He was liable for the *trinoda necessitas;* the *fyrd* or military expedition, the repairing of military fortifications, and the repairing of roads and bridges.[26]

The *ceorl* was a freeman with one hide of land. He paid a fee to his lord, but performed no services. The *geneat* was free from week work. The *gebur* was bound to the land and he did week work, work of an uncertain nature required every day of the week. The man who did week work was in a servile position because his services could be demanded every day by the lord. The more specific the demands on a man, the freer he was in this feudal arrange-

[20] *Ibid.,* p. 11.
[21] *Ibid.,* p. 47; p. 237.
[22] *Ibid.,* p. 96.
[23] *Ibid.,* p. 37 ff.
[24] Pollock, Frederick, and Maitland, F. W., *The History of English Law before the Time of Edward I,* Cambridge: University Press, 1932, vol. I, pp. 427–429.
[25] Gibbs, *op. cit.,* p. 55.
[26] Stubbs, *op. cit.,* p. 208–210.

ment.[27] As the kinship system disintegrated the *ceorl* sought protection from economic want and from the Danes during the Danish invasions of the ninth and tenth centuries. In return for security he would perform services for his lord.[28] By the time of Aethelstan (925) a law required that every man have a lord. "... the manorial system arises at the end of the Old-English period mainly in consequence of the subjection of a labouring population of free descent to a military and capitalistic class ..." [29]

The practice of a man seeking lordship increasingly provided an alternative social discipline. For a good lord gave his man the material support which a father gave his sons, and the social protection which the kindred gave its members.[30]

Besides military and agricultural services several other types of tenure emerged. Tenure by frankalmoin was held by ecclesiastical groups in return for prayers and saying masses. Tenure by serjeanty was personal service, such as carrying a lord's sword or working in his kitchen. Tenure by socage was a personal tenure involving gifts to the lord on special occasions, such as birthdays and holidays.[31]

Political Unification. The political unification of these militaristic-tribalistic settlements came about as a result of three forces: (1) civil wars among local military leaders, (2) the Danish invasions of the tenth century, and (3) the acceptance of Christianity as the religion of the land.[32] By the tenth century England was united into six or eight large Kingdoms or Earldoms.

The constitutional system of the Saxon tribes was organized around the tribe and the chief. The tribal chief was replaced by a king. The king was a landlord, a military leader. The Saxon invasions plus tribal warfare produced in England a number of such local kings. The concept of kingship changed from a tribal to a territorial concept. The king was elected by the *witan,* usually from a given royal family.[33]

The tribal council was replaced by the *witenagemot,* or the *witan,* a meeting of the large landlords of the community. The *witan* declared law, elected kings and granted land to lords and churchmen.[34]

Within a kingdom the local subdivisions were known as *shires,* and each *shire* was ruled by an *ealdorman.* The *shire* was a political, military, and fiscal unit of government, and the *shire-moot* was an important feudal court. The

[27] Gibbs, *op. cit.,* p. 55 ff. See also Vinogradoff, *The Growth of the Manor, op. cit.,* pp. 232–233.
[28] Stenton, Frank, *Anglo-Saxon England,* Oxford: Clarendon Press, 1950, pp. 463–464.
[29] Vinogradoff, *The Growth of the Manor, op. cit.,* p. 235.
[30] Gibbs, *op. cit.,* p. 21.
[31] Pollack and Maitland, *op. cit.,* vol. I, pp. 282–295.
[32] Stubbs, *op. cit.,* vol. I, p. 187 ff.
[33] Kemble, *op. cit.,* vol. II, p. 142. See also M. M. Knappen, *Constitutional and Legal History of England,* New York: Harcourt, Brace and Co., 1942, p. 28.
[34] Kemble, *op. cit.,* vol. II, pp. 195–221.

hundred was a smaller unit than the *shire,* controlling the judicial and agricultural affairs of several agricultural villages.[35]

Village and Manor. With the disintegration of the kinship settlements the
local agricultural village came into prominence. These villages were centers
for administering agricultural policy, as well as centers of trade and commerce. The manor was the official residence of the lord. It included his house
and land. It also represented the agricultural system based on tenure. It included the agricultural classes who worked the land. An open-field system
of cultivation was used, along with certain areas designated as pasture land,
waste land, and forest land. The manor was also a military and political unit.
Each unit furnished so many men for the *fyrd.* The manorial court maintained
the judicial control of the manor.[36]

Christianity

Trevelyan has stated that "the change of religion was the first great step
forward of the English people." [37] "Anglo-Saxon Christianity transmuted Anglo-
Saxon society." [38] When the Saxons invaded Britain Celtic Druidism still existed in the isolated regions of northern England. However Britain was soon
converted to Christianity. By 597 Aethelbert, the king of the Kentians, had
married a Christian woman and had accepted Christianity himself. The Pope
sent Augustine to England to effect a conversion, and by 735 there were two
archbishoprics in England. The Germanic warlords allowed the Church to exist
and eventually became its converts because it was useful to them.[39]

Christianity and the State. The Church furnished the Teutonic tribes with
their only contact with Roman civilization. The Church furnished a model for
the state system that was to come. The political unity of England was in a
large part due to the spiritual unity of the people under one God and one
Pope.[40] The Church also furnished the people with a new moral and social
philosophy. A new philosophy of human nature and society emerged. Man
was basically weak and immoral. He was born with original sin as a result
of his fall from Eden. The purpose of life on earth was salvation, and the body
of the church offered to man the means to this salvation. The State was viewed
as an agent of God. ". . . the authority of the secular power in administering
justice and punishing crime is derived from God." [41] The purpose of the State

[35] Stubbs, *op. cit.,* vol. I, pp. 104–108. See also Kemble, *op cit.,* vol II, pp. 125–149.
[36] Vinogradoff, *The Growth of the Manor, op. cit.,* p. 296 ff. See also Frederic Seebohm,
The English Village Community, and F. W. Maitland, *Domesday Book and Beyond.*
[37] Trevelyan, *op. cit.,* p. 74.
[38] *Ibid.,* p. 79.
[39] Gibbs, *op. cit.,* p. 29.
[40] Trevelyan, *op. cit.,* p. 90. See also Stubbs, *op. cit.,* vol. I, p. 266.
[41] Carlyle, R. W., and Carlyle, A. J., *A History of Medieval Political Theory in the West,*
London: William Blackstone and Sons, 1915, vol. III, p. 101.

was to control these sinful individuals during their stay on earth. The major philosophical issue of this period was the question of the nature of the power of the State, the relation between sacred and secular power. The Church claimed prior control over the prince through the Pope because all power was derived from God. Christianity prepared man for the acceptance of a secular ruler, and the rapid growth of the State is in no small measure a reflection of this Christian notion of society. Christianity taught people to accept their position on earth as God-given. Man should worry about the hereafter, not the here-and-now.[42]

Christianity and Feudalism. The Church was more than a spiritual force; it was a feudal system with its land grants, laws, courts, and secular officials. The bishops were great landlords. The priests and bishops were members of the *witan;* they sat on the hundred-moot and the shire-moot. It was the Church who first taught the kings to use written charters and wills to alienate land.[43] The Church supported the feudal system which was emerging in England at this time. "The Church, in elaborating the legal and learned aspects of daily life, was thereby promoting the feudal system based on territorialism, the sharp distinction of classes, and the increasingly unequal distribution of wealth and freedom." [44]

The fundamental social cleavage in England, as on the continent, was formed by exploitation of peasants by landlords. A section of these landlords were soldiers, another section priests; with sword and cross they protected the people, or so it was said to justify their privileged position in society.[45]

Catholic discipline, as defined and sanctioned by the law of the Church, the canon law, was created in the feudal period. So we need not be surprised that it was well adapted to the needs of a class divided society. Nothing more sharply differentiates feudalism from tribalism and the society of our own time.[46]

What we have written so far may suggest that the effects of conversion to Christianity, including the psychological effects, worked themselves out at two levels; the economic and political. In England, as in many other parts of Europe, the formation of ecclesiastical estates was part of a wider movement —the extension and improvement of agriculture and the subjection of the peasantry to the power of landlords.[47]

At this time there was no separation of Church and State. The Church was an important part of the feudal system. A new system of social order and

[42] *Ibid.,* vol. III, p. 170.
[43] Knappen, *op. cit.,* p. 42.
[44] Trevelyan, *op. cit.,* p. 94.
[45] Gibbs, *op. cit.,* p. 7.
[46] *Ibid.,* p. 9.
[47] *Ibid.,* p. 42.

control emerged "when Christianity and territorial feudalism were beginning to lay new restraints on the individual...." [48]

The Norman Invasion

When William became King of England in 1066, the Saxon era of English history ended and the Norman began. There were few changes in the social structure already described. The land tenure system was accentuated and extended by William. He proclaimed himself to be the "supreme landlord" of all England, and all men who held land held *his* land.[49] The Domesday Survey was a complete survey of the tenure system. This survey attached all men to the soil and reduced all social relationships to a land tenure system. It redistributed the land to Norman nobles who replaced the Saxons as the new upper class. The principle of *nulle terre sans seigneur,* no land without its lord, was now universal in England.[50] The new class system had the Norman noble at its apex with the Saxon population in various agricultural positions. The thegn became a Norman knight; the ceorl became a villein. Villeins, bordarii, cotters—agricultural classes—were of Saxon descent.[51] The separation of the military and agricultural classes was now complete. "Between the two epochs (tribalism and the state) stands feudalism as an attempt to connect military organization directly with the agricultural husbandry." [52]

After the breakdown of the tribal and clan organization, and before the rise of the State, feudalism was the only method by which a helpless population could be protected, war efficiently conducted, colonization pushed forward, or agriculture carried on with increased profits. For it was a process of differentiating the functions of warrior and husbandman.[53]

The split between the Church and State came after the Norman invasion. William attempted to gain control of ecclesiastical affairs whenever he could. The Triple Concordat limited the authority of the Pope. Under William the lay and ecclesiastical courts of law were separated. The controversy and struggle between Church and State continued through the reigns of William Rufus, Henry I, and Stephen. It came to a head during the reign of Henry II with the Becket controversy.[54]

After the death of William the Conqueror the nobles and churchmen gained power at the expense of the crown. It was a period of civil war and peasant

[48] Trevelyan, *op. cit.,* p. 97.
[49] Stubbs, *op. cit.,* vol I, p. 274 ff.
[50] Trevelyan, *op. cit.,* p. 172.
[51] Vinogradoff, Paul, *English Society in the Eleventh Century,* Oxford: Clarendon Press, 1908, p. 213.
[52] *Ibid.,* p. 213.
[53] Trevelyan, *op. cit.,* p. 124.
[54] Stenton, *op. cit.,* pp. 650–651.

uprisings, especially during the reign of Stephen. At this time nobles and bishops reached the height of their power.[55]

PART II

Anglo-Saxon Legal System

Tribal Law. The Anglo-Saxon legal system was originally a system of tribal justice. The old legal codes were recorded from the time of Aethelbert on (570) so that a complete record of the changes which occurred in the legal system is available.[56] Aethelbert followed the Roman practice of recording the laws. These laws are a record of Anglo-Saxon tribal custom, based on the principle of kinship. There is no evidence of borrowing from the Roman legal system. Whenever a migration or invasion occurred the laws were recorded so as to make them familiar to all. The family or kinship group, not the State, was regarded as the injured party.[57]

All crime was crime against the family: It was the family that was regarded as having committed the crimes of its members; it was the family that had to atone, or carry out the blood-feud. In time, money payments were fixed as commutations for injury; but, even as late as the twelfth century, Welsh blood-feuds were fought. . . .[58]

The feud was a kinship matter. If a slaying occurred within a family group no feud took place. The offender was either ignored or exiled. Feuds occurred only between kinship groups.[59]

Feudal Law

Wer, Wite, and Bot. As feudalism and Christianity changed the organization of Saxon society, the blood-feud was replaced by a system of compensations: the *wer*, *wite*, and *bot*. The *wer* or *wergild* was a money payment made to a family group if a member of that family were killed or in some other way injured. The *bot* was a general payment of compensation for injuries less than death. The *wite* was a public fine payable to a lord or king. The only punishment referred to is outlawry, or *friedlos*. A man who was an outlaw could be

[55] Poole, A. L., *From Domesday Book to Magna Carta: 1087–1216*, Oxford: Clarendon Press, 1951, pp. 178–192.

[56] The following books contain collections of the early laws of the Saxons: B. Thorpe, ed., *Ancient Laws and Institutes of England*, London: Commission of Public Records, 1840. F. L. Attenborough, *The Laws of the Earliest English Kings*, Cambridge: University Press, 1922. George Rightmire, *The Law of England at the Norman Conquest*, Columbus: Herr Printing Co., 1932. A. J. Robertson, *The Laws of the Kings of England from Edmund to Henry I*, Cambridge, University Press, 1925.

[57] *Select Essays in Anglo-American Legal History*, Boston: Little, Brown and Co., 1907, vol. I, pp. 35–37.

[58] Traill, H. D., *Social England*, New York: Putnam and Sons, 1899, vol. I, p. 5.

[59] Seebohm, Frederic, *Tribal Custom in Anglo-Saxon Law*, London: Longmans, Green and Co., 1902, pp. 20–31.

slain by anyone without fear of reprisal or feud. Anyone offending the folk-peace could be placed outside this peace, or be made peaceless. Imprisonment was a punishment unknown to the Saxons.[60]

Like the blood-feud, the *wergild* contained within it the idea of collective responsibility. The clan as a group was responsible for the offenses of its members, and for the collection and payment of the *wer*.[61] Gradually the *wer* replaced the feud. By Alfred's time (871) the feud could be resorted to only after compensation had been requested and refused.[62] A law of Aethelred's made it a breach of the king's peace to resort to the feud before demanding compensation. (Aethelred IV.4.) The collective responsibility of the kin was gradually destroyed and absorbed by other groups.

If a breach of peace be committed within a "burh" let the inhabitants of the "burh" go get the murderers, or their nearest kin, head for head. If they will not go, let the ealdorman go; if he will not go, let the king go; if he will not go let the ealdordom lie in "peacelessness." (Aethelred 11.6.)

Henceforth, if anyone slay a man, he shall himself bear the vendetta, unless with the help of his friends he pay compensation for it within twelve months to the full amount of the slain man's wergild, according to the inherited rank.

1. If, however, his kindred abandon him and will not pay compensation on his behalf, it is my will that, if afterwards, they give him neither food nor shelter, all the kindred, except the delinquent, shall be free from the vendetta. (Edmund 11.1.)

The authorities must put a stop to the vendettas. First, according to public law, the slayer shall give security to his advocate and the advocate to the kinsman of the slain man, that he, the slayer, will make reparation to the kindred.

1. After this it is incumbent upon the kin of the slain man to give security to the slayer's advocate that he, the slayer, may approach under safe conduct and pledge himself to pay the wergild. (Edmund 11.2.)

And no monk who belongs to a monastery anywhere may lawfully either demand or pay compensation incurred by vendetta. He leaves the law of the kindred behind when he accepts the monastic rule. (Aethelred VIII.25)

As feudalism developed in England between 700 and 1066, the lords and bishops replaced the kinship group as the recipients of the *wer* and *wite*. The *wer* was now determined by the amount of land owned by a man, his feudal rank, rather than by his rank in the family.

[60] Pollock and Maitland, *op. cit.,* vol. II, pp. 450–451.
[61] Kemble, *op. cit.,* vol. I, pp. 231–236.
[62] Law of Alfred: 42.

If anyone grants one of his men freedom on the altar, his freedom shall be publicly recognized, but the emancipator shall have his heritage and wergild. (Wihtred 8.)

If anyone slays a foreigner, the king shall have two-thirds of his wergild, and his relatives one-third. (Ine 23.)

If an Englishman living in penal slavery absconds, he shall be hanged, and nothing shall be paid to his lord. (Ine 24.)

He who begets an illegitimate child and disowns it shall not have the wergild at its death, but its lord and the king shall have it. (Ine 27.)

At this time no distinction is made between intentional and unintentional slayings, or between private and public wrongs.

If one kills another unintentionally by allowing a tree to fall on him the tree shall be given to the dead man's kindred, and they shall remove it within 30 days from the locality. (Alfred 13.)

If a beast injures a man, its owner must hand over the beast to the injured man or come to terms with him. (Alfred 24.)

If a man has a spear over his shoulder, and anyone is transfixed thereon, he shall pay the wergild without the fine. (Alfred 36.)

If a bone is laid bare, 3 shillings shall be paid as compensation. (Aethelbert 34.)

If a bone is damaged, 4 shillings shall be paid as compensation. (Aethelbert 35.)

If a shoulder is disabled, 30 shillings shall be paid as compensation. (Aethelbert 38.)

Today we would view such a schedule of payments as belonging to the law of tort, personal injuries for which compensation may be due at law. An insurance policy provides exactly the type of protection provided above by the early Saxon law. Whether or not we call this law criminal law or tort law depends upon the way we use these terms. This is not criminal law as we know it today. Even in the case where the king or lord inherited a wergild it was in the spirit of being an heir, and is not analogous to a criminal action. A man can fall heir to a suit at civil law, but a man cannot fall heir to a criminal law suit, nor can he collect damages and compensation as a result of a crime.

Some crimes were "botless," that is, no compensation was allowed. In such a case the feud had to be resorted to. Secret murder was a "botless" crime.[63]

We can watch a system of true punishments—corporeal and capital pun-

[63] *Select Essays in Anglo-American Legal History, op. cit.,* vol. I, p. 100.

ishments—growing at the expense of the old system of pecuniary mulcts, blood-feud, and outlawry; but on the eve of the Norman Conquest mere homicide can still be atoned for by payment of the dead man's price or "wergild," and if that be not paid, it is rather for the injured family than for the state to slay the slayer.[64]

The Mund and the King's Peace. In the *wite* we see the germ of the idea that a wrong is not simply the affair of the injured party and his kin, but rather it involves a breach of a *mund* of a king, or bishop.[65] Early Germanic justice was based on a folk-peace, a peace of the community. This idea gave way to the *mund.* A *mund* was the right a king or lord had to protect a person or area. At first the *mund* was restricted to special persons and areas; gradually it was extended to include the king's court, army, servants, hundred-court, and finally the four main highways in England. It was now referred to as the "king's peace." [66] The kings, lords, and bishops now received the compensation rather than the kinship group. They had a *mund* which had to be protected.

Other Teutonic tribes had a legal system similar to that of the Saxons. The Welsh tribes had a *galanas,* or murder fine, that was allowed in lieu of the bloodfeud. Among the Irish tribes the *eric,* or a death fine for homicide, was shared by the kin. The Frankish law book, *Lex Salica,* described the same system of feuds and compensation for the Frankish tribes in France.[67]

The Administration of Justice. The Teutonic tribes placed the administration of justice in the hands of local tribal councils, popular assemblies known as folk-moots. As feudalism replaced tribalism these folk-moots were replaced by hundred-moots and shire-moots. The hundred-moot, the court of the hundred, was gradually restricted to lords, stewards, priests, reeves, and four men from each township. It also contained a body of twelve men who heard arguments, which committee later emerged as our petit jury.[68] The shire-moot was attended by ealdormen, bishops, lords, and shire-reeves. In these courts precedence was given to the pleas of the Church, or kings, and complaints involving individuals, pleas known as "common pleas." [69]

In later Saxon history an important development in the hundred was the tithing. The tithing represented a local grouping of ten men who stood as surety for one another. If one of them broke the law, the other nine would make good the harm. The tithing was based on the notion that every man ought to have a lord. Only lordless men belonged to a tithing since men with a lord had a surety." As long as the family remained strong, and the duty of

[64] Traill, *op. cit.,* vol. I, p. 172.
[65] Holdsworth, W. S., *A History of English Law,* Boston: Little, Brown and Co., 1923, vol. II, p. 47.
[66] Pollock and Maitland, *op. cit.,* vol. I, p. 44; vol. II, pp. 453–454.
[67] Seebohm, *Tribal Custom in Anglo-Saxon Law, op. cit.,* pp. 32–145.
[68] Rightmire, *op. cit.,* pp. 19–26.
[69] *Ibid.,* pp. 16–20.

giving up or paying for an offending member and avenging an injured member was acknowledged and carried out, the place of general police was fairly filled; but as population growth, migration, and new ideas loosened family ties, the kings began to substitute local mutual responsibility of freeholders arranged in little groups. . . ." [70] "This was the way, apparently, that a substitute was found in the towns for the absent kindreds." [71]

In these courts the responsibility for initiating a trial was placed with the injured party, who in turn summoned the defendant to court. There was no prosecuting official.[72] Proof was by compurgation or ordeal. If compurgation were used, the parties involved secured the aid of oath-helpers who swore to the truthfulness of the charge. These oath-helpers were originally kinsmen; later on, they were members of the tithing. The number of oath-helpers needed depended upon the rank of the parties and the seriousness of the offense. Trial by ordeal included the hot iron ordeal, the hot and cold water ordeal, and the dry bread or *corsnaed* ordeal.[73] The ordeal was administered with the aid of a priest. Just prior to the Norman invasions a new trial procedure, the jury of presentment, came into existence. It was composed of twelve men who presented facts to the court. It resembled the grand jury of today in many respects.[74]

Sac and Soc. The administration of justice is inseparable from the exercise of jurisdiction. Jurisdiction was now based on a land tenure system, and was related to the feudal system. Those people on the land of a lord or king are in his *mund,* under his protection, and therefore, in his jurisdiction. The right to jurisdiction was given to lords along with a grant of land in grants called *sac* and *soc.* These words, when added to a grant of land, meant that the grantee could hold private court for his subjects and keep the returns therefrom. Such justice was a profitable business for lords and bishops.[75]

By the time of Canute (1016) most of the hundred-moots had passed into the hands of private lords. The manorial court developed as an important aspect of the legal system. Justice was now in the hands of the landlords. "The man who had land judged the man who had not. . . ." [76]

The Church and the Law. There was no separation of lay and ecclesiastical courts until the time of William, which meant that most of the court business was of an ecclesiastical nature. The church accepted the system of compensation and compurgation, assigning various values to its own ranks. The bishops and priests sat on the various courts, and they held grants of *sac* and *soc.* Excommunication was used as a punishment for secular as well as

[70] Traill, *op. cit.,* vol. I, p. 138.
[71] Seebohm, *Tribal Custom in Anglo-Saxon Law,* op. cit., p. 413.
[72] *Essays in Anglo-Saxon Law,* Boston: Little, Brown and Co., 1905, pp. 185–205.
[73] Attenborough, *op. cit.,* note on Law of Ine, 37.
[74] Stubbs, *op. cit.,* vol. I, pp. 125–128.
[75] *Ibid.,* pp. 119–121.
[76] *Ibid.,* pp. 207–208.

sacred offenses.[77] A church law provided benefit of clergy, which meant that people within the sanctity of the church could not be subject to the feud. The Church also demanded compensation for itself for many offenses. "The judicial matters of the Church were apparently transacted in the ordinary *gemots* of the hundred and of the shire." [78] The following laws are selected to illustrate the ecclesiastical nature of these Saxon codes.

Men living in illicit union shall turn to a righteous life repenting their sins, or they shall be excluded from the communion of the Church. (Wihtraed 3.)

If a servant, contrary to his lord's command, does servile work between sunset on Saturday and sunset on Sunday, he shall pay eighty sceattas to his lord. (Wihtraed 9.)

In the first place, we command that the servants of God heed, and duly observe, their proper rule. (Ine 1.)

A child shall be baptized within thirty days. If this is not done, the guardian shall pay forty shillings compensation. (Ine 5.)

If anyone is liable to the death penalty, and he flees to a church, his life shall be spared and he shall pay such compensation as he is directed to pay by legal decision. (Ine 5.)

If anyone withholds Peter's Pence, he shall pay *lahslit* in a Danish district, and a fine in an English district. (Edward and Guthrum, 5.1.)

We enjoin upon every Christian man, in accordance with his Christian profession, to pay tithes, and church dues, and Peter's Pence, and plough-alms. (Edmund 1.)

He who has intercourse with a nun, unless he makes amends, shall not be allowed burial in consecrated ground any more than a homicide. (Edmund 1.)

Priests know full well that they have no right to marry. (Aethelred V.9.)

[Every Christian man shall make amends for] horrible perjuries and devilish deeds, such as murder, homicide, theft, robbery, gluttony, covetousness, greed, and intemperance, fraud, and various breaches of the law, violation of holy orders, and of marriage, and misdeeds of any kind. (Aethelred V.25.)

Norman Law

One of the first acts of William the Conqueror was to claim that he was the guardian of the laws of Edward. The Saxon legal system was accepted in its

---

[77] Thomas Oakley, *English Penitential Discipline and Anglo-Saxon Law in Their Joint Influence,* New York: Columbia University Studies in History, Economics, and Public Law, 1923, p. 86.

[78] *Ibid.,* p. 139.

entirety.[79] A few changes were introduced by the Normans. William separated the lay and ecclesiastical courts, so that from this time on two distinct legal systems existed: state law and canon law.[80]

The differentiation of the functions of lay and spiritual courts was a lone step towards a higher legal civilization. Without it neither Church nor State could have freely developed the law and logic of their position.[81]

William required all freemen to swear fealty to him as King of England.[82] The practice of Englishry and the murder-fine were introduced. Any man found dead under suspicious circumstances was deemed to be a Frenchman unless Englishry were proven, and the district in which the body was found had to pay a murder-fine.[83] The frankpledge replaced the tithing in order to enforce the law of Englishry. Trial by battle replaced the trial by ordeal. The lords grew in power through grants of *sac* and *soc;* they controlled the administration of justice. The kings were too weak to centralize the control of judicial functions in their own hands.[84] The law of Henry I was still the law of *wer, wite,* and *bot.* The central problem of Henry I's time was: "Who in the myriad of possible cases has *sake* and *soke,* the right to hold court for the offender and to pocket the profits of jurisdiction?" [85]

PART III

The Emergence of Crime and Criminal Law in England

It was during the reign of Henry II (1154–1189) that the old tribal-feudal system of law disappeared and a new system of common law emerged in England. A comparison of the laws of Henry I and Henry II reveals that a revolution occurred in the legal field. The former described a system of *wer, bot,* and *wite;* the latter described a system of writs, procedures, and common law.[86]

In this period we are at a turning point in the history of English law. We still see traces of old tribal divisions and old tribal rules—divisions and rules which an unmitigated feudal system would have modified but perpetuated. But we can see also that a strong centralized court, in touch with the main currents of the intellectual life of Europe, is beginning to make some general rules for all England.[87]

The sources of this new law were the Constitutions of Clarendon, the

[79] Maitland and Montague, *op. cit.,* p. 27.
[80] Episcopal Laws of William I.
[81] Trevelyan, *op. cit.,* p. 176.
[82] Ten Articles of William I.
[83] Holdsworth, *op. cit.,* vol. II, p. 150.
[84] Maitland, F. W., *Domesday Book and Beyond,* Cambridge: University Press, 1897, pp. 80–96.
[85] Pollock and Maitland, *op. cit.,* vol. I, p. 106.
[86] *Ibid.,* vol. II, p. 458.
[87] Holdsworth, *op. cit.,* vol. II, p. 173.

Constitutions of Northampton, and the records of the Curia Regis. These records, known as Pipe Rolls, were kept by Glanvil and Bracton, court officials. Glanvil's work, *"A Treatise on the Laws and Customs of England Compared in the Time of Henry II,"* was a record of the proceedings of the Curia Regis, and it revealed a system of writs, which were necessary in order to be admitted to court. The important legal question now is: "What writ do I need to gain admittance to the King's court?" No mention is made here of tribal justice, or wergilds and bot.[88]

The Court System. During the reign of Henry I the Curia Regis was a court of the nobility. Between 1166 and 1178 great changes occurred in the Curia Regis. It came to be a court of common law for the common man. It gave the peasant the right to a court hearing, a right he had been denied by the manorial court. Thus developed a court of common law as a result of the growth of a strong centralized government. As Henry II gained control of the government from the feudal lords, he also gained control of the administration of the justice. The peasant now looked to the king, not his lord, for justice. Henry opened Westminster Hall, where the Court of King's Bench met, to all who possessed the proper writ. In 1285 the Statute of Westminster II provided that jury cases could be tried in local communities rather than at Westminster.[89]

In time the King's Court came to be several courts. The Court of Common Pleas heard minor pleas without the presence of the king being required. The Court of the Exchequer heard tax and fiscal cases. The Court of the King's Bench was held in the presence of the king to hear difficult and important cases. After 1268 the king did not have to be present in court personally. An official acted in the name of the Crown. The Court of Chancellory issued royal writs. A system of royal justice emerged. This is a system of common law, law common to all England and available to all men.[90]

The hundred court and the shire court continued in existence for several centuries; however, as the common law developed these courts declined in importance, and finally disappeared. In 1278 Edward made an attempt to gain jurisdiction over all land through the Quo Warranto Inquest, an inquest into the titles held to jurisdiction by various lords.[91] As the Crown grew in strength it reserved to itself the right to hold court and dispense justice. Federal justice was absorbed and replaced by royal justice.

The shire-reeve, or sheriff, before the time of Henry II, had been an important judicial official in the county. Henry, through an Inquest of Sheriffs, subordinated this office to the Crown, and after his time the sheriff was a

[88] *Ibid.*, pp. 188–190.
[89] Maitland, F. W., *The Constitutional History of England,* Cambridge: University Press, 1931, pp. 61–64. See also Maitland and Montague, *op. cit.,* p. 36.
[90] Knappen, *op. cit.,* pp. 166–168.
[91] Trevelyan, *op. cit.,* pp. 256–257.

minor official who represented the interests of the Crown in local counties. This was an important step in the extension of royal control and justice into the various counties.[92]

Henry II also made use of itinerant justices, called justices in *eyre*. These men travelled about England, holding court sessions in the various hundreds and shires. They declared law in the name of the king. A jury of twelve men would present the facts to the judge whenever he was in their particular hundred.[93]

Trial by oath and ordeal was replaced by trial by battle and trial by jury. The Fourth Lateran Council of 1215 forbade the clergy to participate in trial by ordeal, which meant that alternatives had to be used. During the time of Henry II a defendant was allowed the alternative of a jury trial or trial by battle. Many men refused to accept a jury trial because if they were convicted their property escheated to the king's treasury rather than going to their families. Many were forced to accept a jury trial by means of the *peine forte et dure,* a system of torture whereby heavy stones were placed on a man's chest until he consented to a jury trial or died. It was not until the Abraham Thornton case in 1818, in which the defendant used the ordeal, that Parliament abolished the ordeal.[94]

A new writ, the writ of trespass, came into existence to replace trial by appeal. It allowed a litigant to collect damages. Indictment was now by jury, and charges were brought by the Crown. Private appeals were no longer allowed. The initiation of criminal trials was in the hands of the Crown.[95] "The new procedure, though accusatory, was a true criminal procedure and the king prosecuted, and every indictment alleged that the accused had offended against the peace of our lord, the king, his crown and dignity." [96]

The King's Peace. By the time of Henry II the King's peace extended to all persons and all places in England. The special *munds* of the lords and bishops were devoured by the king's peace. The king was now a territorial king and his peace extended throughout the land. The king was now the source of law. He had jurisdiction in every case. The State, and not the family or the lord, now was the proper prosecutor in every case.[97]

Crime and Criminal Law. "Sometime in the twelfth century this ancient system of *writ* and *bot* disappeared, leaving in its place the beginnings of a common law of crime." [98]

[92] Stubbs, *op. cit.,* vol. I, pp. 649–652.
[93] Knappen, *op. cit.,* pp. 170–172. See also Stubbs, *op. cit.,* vol. I, pp. 652–654.
[94] Maitland and Montague, *op. cit.,* pp. 60–63. See also Traill, *op. cit.,* p. 293.
[95] Holdsworth, *op. cit.,* vol. II, p. 364.
[96] *Ibid.,* vol. II, p. 621.
[97] Pollock and Maitland, *op. cit.,* vol. II, pp. 463–464. See also Maitland, *Constitutional History of England, op. cit.,* p. 107.
[98] Walsh, William, *Outlines of the History of English and American Law,* New York: New York University Press, 1923, p. 371.

On no other part of our law did the twelfth century stamp a more permanent impress of its heavy hand than on that which was to be criminal law of after days. The change that it made will at first sight seem to us immeasurable. At the end of the period we already see the broad outlines which will be visible throughout the coming ages. . . . We go back a few years . . . and we are breathing a different air. We are looking at a scheme of *wer,* blood-feud, *bot* and *wite.*[99]

In that most revolutionary of all centuries, under the influence of the East, of the idealism induced by the Crusades, of the reality of the Christian story brought home by nearer knowledge of the Holy Land, of the re-discovery of Roman law, of a world enlarged by contact with a greater civilization, all forms of thought were in process of revision; great minds were questioning accepted beliefs and customs; the Western world suddenly ceased to regard murder, arson, rape, and theft as regrettable torts which should be compensated by payment to the family—such and other offenses came to be regarded not only as sins for which a penance was required by the Church, but as crime against society at large to be prosecuted by the community through its chief; the ever-recurring blood-feud was gradually discredited in men's minds. The transfer of the receipt of payment from the kinsfolk to the king disinclined men to favor violence.[100]

The State Takes the Place of the Kinsmen—The very core of the revolutions in law and finance that took place in Henry's reign was the transfer of the initiative in criminal matters from the kindred of the injured man . . . to the king as public prosecutor.[101]

Pleas of the Crown—The king's jurisdiction finally ousted the communal courts and tended to control the courts of the barons, because the king . . . could give a hearing which, if not as speedy, was very likely to be more impartial than the court presided over by local great men.[102]

By 1226 an agreement between the criminal and the relatives of a slain man would not avail to save the murderer from an indictment and a sentence of death. The state no longer allowed a private settlement of a criminal case.[103] During Glanvil's time pleas were for the first time divided into civil and criminal.[104] By adding the words *de pace domini regis infracta* to a plea any offense could be made a plea of the crown.[105]

Blackstone defined a crime as a public offense.

The distinction of public wrongs from private, of crimes and misdemeanors

---

[99] Pollock and Maitland, *op. cit.,* vol. II, p. 448.
[100] Jeudwine, J. W., *Tort, Crime and the Police in Medieval England,* London: Williams and Norgate, 1917, p. 84.
[101] *Ibid.,* p. 85.
[102] *Ibid.,* pp. 110–111.
[103] Holdsworth, *op. cit.,* vol. II, p. 257.
[104] Pollock and Maitland, *op. cit.,* vol. I, p. 165.
[105] Reeves, John, *History of the English Law,* Philadelphia: M. Murphy Co., 1880, vol. I, p. 384.

from civil injuries, seems principally to consist of this: that private wrongs, or civil injuries, are an infringement or privation of the civil rights which belong to individuals, considered merely as individuals; public wrongs, or crimes and misdemeanors, are a breach and violation of the public rights and duties due to the whole community, considered as a community, in its social aggregate capacity ... treason, murder, and robbery are properly ranked among crimes; since besides the injury done the individual, they strike at the very being of society; which cannot possibly subsist where actions of this sort are suffered to escape with impunity.[106]

A new doctrine of criminal responsibility was emerging, the doctrine of *mens rea* or intent. Murder was now divided into murder with malice aforethought and murder without malice aforethought. Malice aforethought can be dependent upon other conditions, such as infancy, lunacy, drunkenness, and so forth. The psychiatric view of personality development clashed with this legal view of free will and moral responsibility. A major issue in criminal law today is: "How can a man be guilty of a crime, possess mens rea, if his actions are determined by sociological and psychological conditions?"

The notion of natural crime, a crime against a law of nature rather than against a legal law, was present in the criminal law at its inception. This led to the definition of crimes as *mala in se,* acts bad in themselves, and *mala prohibita,* acts which are crimes because they are prohibited by positive law. This led to the current confusion in criminology between anti-social behavior and anti-legal behavior.[107]

Criminal law is related to acts which, if there were no criminal law at all, would be judged by the public at large much as they are judged at present. If murder, theft, and rape were not punishable by law, the words would still be in use and would be applied to the same or nearly the same actions.[108]

Which has occasioned some to doubt how far a human legislature ought to inflict capital punishment for *positive* offences; offences against the municipal law only, and not against the law of nature. ... With regard to offences *mala in se,* capital punishments are in some instances inflicted by the immediate *command* of God Himself to all mankind; as, in the case of murder. ...[109]

The English common law is based on the assumption that there is a higher moral order which is a part of the law of nature and from which positive laws are derived.

Throughout the Middle Ages the Law of Nature, identified by Gratian with the law of God, was regarded by the canonists and civilians as the reason-

---

[106] Blackstone, William, *Commentaries on the Laws of England,* 8th ed., Oxford: Clarendon Press, 1778, Book IV, p. 5.
[107] Jeffery, *op. cit.*
[108] Stephen, J. F., *A History of the Criminal Law of England,* London: Methuen and Co., 1883, vol. II, p. 75.
[109] Blackstone, *op. cit.,* Book IV, p. 9.

able basis of all law...in English law not so much is heard of the law of nature....As a matter of fact, the work done elsewhere by the law of nature was done in England by "reasons."...Similarly this appeal to reason and expediency has led in later law to talk about the distinction between *malum prohibitum* and *mala in se*. . . .[110]

Church and State. Although Church and State had been separated under William, the separation was not complete. The practice of "benefit of clergy" had existed for some time. All clerks of the court had a right to be tried in an ecclesiastical court. Henry II attempted to overcome the abuses of this practice when in the Constitutions of Clarendon he provided that criminous clerks were to be sentenced in lay courts. Thomas Becket, the archbishop, opposed the sentencing of clerks in a lay court, and after a bitter struggle Becket was slain. The immediate effect of Becket's death was to postpone the issue until a later date, but gradually the Church lost its right to punish crime through the use of force.[111] The Church could punish offenders of the canon law through excommunication and a system of penances, but this was a spiritual rather than a secular jurisdiction.

This does not mean, however, that State and Church developed separately and independently of one another. They functioned as an interdependent system. The moral code of the Church was made an important part of the common law. The legal system borrowed a great deal from the Church in those areas concerning marriage, sexual practices, morals, wills, property rights, and so forth.

The notion of crime contains within it the notion of sin, for which punishment is required. The concept of *mens rea* was derived from the Christian view of sins of the mind. Sin can be punished individually, not collectively, so that the individual and not the clan or family is responsible. Only individuals have a soul that can be saved; social groups do not possess souls, and for that reason tribal responsibility gave way to the Christian notion of individual responsibility.

The concept of crime thus developed as it did as a result of this interaction of the Church and State. However, it was the State, not the Church, that became the agent for punishing sin.

Although the religious might preach that it was a sin to kill, the conception of killing as an offence against the community is co-existent only with the conception of the power and the will of the State to enforce penalties for offences against the community. So long as overlords of the tribes, whether the king of Ireland or the king of France, contented himself with collecting

[110] Holdsworth, *op. cit.,* vol. II, pp. 603–604.
[111] Poole, *op. cit.,* pp. 197–212.

customary dues and took no notice of wrongs as between individuals... crime as such did not exist.[112]

Kemble has summarized this social change when he stated: "And thus, by slow degrees, as the State itself became Christianized, the moral duty became a legal one." [113] Before a moral offense is a crime it has to become a legal offense.

The transition from tribalism to feudalism to territorialism was complete. The State was not yet complete in all its aspects, but territorialism as we know it was emerging from feudalism. This is especially true in the case of criminal law. The *wer, wite,* and *bot* had disappeared, and in their place a new system of common law emerged.

The State replaced the family as the agent of social control.

The main fact in the development of the State, manifesting itself roughly from the end of the twelfth century, is that the citizens are protected by a central power... with its national councils and courts. Between the two epochs stands again the doctrine, and to a certain extent, the practice of feudalism.[114]

In the end the king or the parliament, or both, came to be directly related to all individuals who compose the State, and in their authority the local and personal authorities and jurisdictions of feudalism were finally lost.... The royal justice at last absorbs all feudal justice ... but it was not feudalism that triumphed, but territorialism.[115]

CONCLUSIONS

Social Structure and Social Change in England

The pattern of social change in England from 400 to 1200 was a change from tribalism to feudalism to nationalism. The *land-tie* replaced the *blood-tie* as the basis for social order.

During the tribal period there was a fusion of institutional functions in the kinship unit. This body was the political, economic, family, religious, and ecological unit. By 1200 separate institutions existed in these several areas. Political authority was now in the hands of landlords. By the time of Henry II the king emerged as the supreme landlord in this feudal hierarchy. Economic organization shifted from a hunting, fishing, and pastoral economy, where the kinship group was the economic unit, to an agricultural economy, where the feudal manor was the economic unit. Each man occupied land belonging to his lord, rather than to his kin, and he was attached to this land through a personal-legal relationship known as the tenure system. Status

---

[112] Jeudwine, *op. cit.,* p. 89.
[113] Kemble, *op. cit.,* vol. II, p. 516.
[114] Vinogradoff, *English Society in the Eleventh Century, op. cit.,* p. 213.
[115] Carlyle and Carlyle, *op. cit.,* vol. III, p. 20.

was now based on this tenure system. Feudalism was based on a division of men into two classes: military and agricultural. Religion was now controlled by a professional hierarchy of priests and bishops who acted as both church officials and landlords. Christianity was an important aspect of the feudal system. The conjugal family did not perform the many functions performed by the tribal family. This shift from an institutional family to a companionship family is a familiar theme in sociological literature today.[116]

A new social structure emerged in England, and as a result of these changes a new legal system came into existence. During the tribal period the legal system was in the hands of the tribal group, and justice was based on the blood-feud. As tribalism gave way to feudalism, the feud was replaced by a system of compensations. Justice passed into the hands of landlords. There was no separation of lay and ecclesiastical courts until the time of William. State law and crime came into existence during the time of Henry II as a result of this separation of State and Church, and as a result of the emergence of a central authority in England which replaced the authority of the feudal lords. Henry replaced feudal justice with state justice by means of justices in eyre, the king's peace, a system of royal courts, and a system of royal writs. Common law emerged as the law of the Crown available to all men. The myth that the common law of England is the law of the Anglo-Saxons is without historical foundation.[117] The family was no longer involved in law and justice. The State was the offended social unit, and the State was the proper prosecutor in every case of crime. Justice was now the sole prerogative of the State. "Custom passes into law." This shift occurred historically when a political community separate from the kinship group emerged as a part of the social organization. A comparison of tribal law and state law reveals these basic differences.

Tribal Law	State Law
1. Blood-tie	Territorial-tie
2. Collective responsibility	Individual responsibility
3. Family as unit of justice and order	State as unit of justice
4. Feud or compensation	Punishment

The basic thesis presented in sociological and anthropological literature concerning law and society is that the development of law has been from tribal law to State law. This idea is developed in one way or another by Maine, Weber, and Hoebel.[118] The growth and development of English law from Saxon tribal law to State law supports Maine's thesis that there has

[116] Burgess, Ernest W., and Locke, Harvey J., *The Family, from Institution to Companionship,* New York: American Book Co., 1953.
[117] Radin, Max, *The Law and You,* New York: Mentor Book, 1948, p. 103.
[118] Jeffery, C. Ray, *Crime, Law and Social Structure,* Jour. Crim. Law, Criminol. and Pol. Sci. 47, 4 (1956).

been a transition from kinship authority to territorial authority. It likewise supports Weber's thesis that a change from traditionalistic to rationalistic authority occurred when the State emerged as the unit of social order.

In this paper I have attempted to make the sociology of law the subject of study rather than the criminal. One of the basic difficulties in criminological research is that very little use is made of such basic sociological concepts as institution, history, social change, social organization, and social theory. This orientation is clearly seen in a statement from Sutherland and Cressey that "criminal behavior is not affected directly or significantly by variations in the form of the general social institutions—economics, government, religion, and education. . . ." [119] Group behavior is affected by the institutional structure within which it occurs. But more to the point, the system of social control used to judge behavior as legal or illegal is functionally interrelated with the social institutions: political, economic, familial, and educational. As sociologists we should be interested in sociological jurisprudence. A theory of crime depends upon an institutional study of law and society.

[119] Sutherland, Edwin H., and Cressey, Donald R., *Principles of Criminology,* 5th ed., New York: J. P. Lippincott, 1955, p. 217.

2

Roles of the Urban Police

The police departments in large cities deal with a wide range of problems. Some of the problems confronting police officers are directly concerned with violations of law, whereas others relate more to personal problems of individual citizens. In addition, the police are very frequently called upon to preserve peace and maintain a general sense of good order. Each of these problem areas has gradually become refined into a specific role which the police have become expected to perform. In addition, since the police are so highly visible and since they represent so many different things to different people, the police have become highly symbolic as well. An examination of the broad role areas of the police should serve to clarify the nature of the police function.

Law Enforcement

In order to provide for the common welfare of its citizens, the government has enacted laws which seek to protect the health, welfare and morals of the people. In the United States, the police powers of government are carried out by the states and their respective political subdivisions through the enactment of state and local laws. Each state has a criminal code and local governments may add further laws (in the form of ordinances) to them. The violation of these laws and ordinances poses a threat to all citizens, because such violations diminish the prospects of safety and security to which all citizens are intitled.

Violations of the law call for some agency to identify the violators and to remand them to the courts for adjudication. This responsibility has been vested in the police and is one of their most fundamental responsibilities. Just exactly how the police have performed this role has been the subject of considerable controversy, yet their basic responsibility in this area remains unquestioned.

Since the police frequently encounter violent persons in their performance of this role, they must themselves be trained and equipped to deal with violence, even to the extent of engaging in violent actions themselves when the circumstances so dictate. As will be seen later, this association of violence with the enforcement of the law has created a psychological environment with respect to law enforcement which has had an important impact on both the police and the citizens they serve.

The law enforcement function poses several difficult dilemmas for the police. In the first place, citizens generally have no complaint when the police investigate reported crimes or when they arrest offenders. However, when the police attempt to discover crimes which have not been reported or when they seek to keep crimes from occurring, then there often develops a difference of opinion between the citizen and the police as to the propriety of their conduct.[1] This is all the more so when the police attempt to intervene in situations where no apparent crime has been committed (as in the case of "field interrogations" of persons who appear to be suspicious).[2]

Second, the police in cities of any size almost universally engage in "preventive patrol." It is believed that by having large numbers of officers visibly present on the streets, the opportunity for crime will be diminished thus deterring would-be offenders and in some cases would actually permit catching them in the act. This particular tactic has produced mixed results; some people are in fact arrested in the act, yet even the most intensive patrolling cannot interdict or prevent crimes which are committed inside private dwellings or out of view, or those which are committed out of anger or as a consequence of mental incompetency.

The police are seldom credited for crimes which they have prevented because it is difficult to determine what actually would have happened had the police not acted. On the other hand, the commission of a crime, especially one in which the offender is not detected, indicates to many people that the police are unable to adequately carry out their role of enforcing the law. Thus the high visibility of the police, coupled with their difficulty in consistently enforcing the law have provided a basis for criticism of the police as law enforcement agents.

In carrying out the role of enforcing the law, the police have been left largely to their own ingenuity, which has been limited, among other things, by the rule of law. That is, in enforcing the law the police are not themselves above the law. They must therefore restrict their enforcement tactics to those which are not legally prohibited. For example, evidence must be obtained by legal means, arrests must be valid, and statements and confessions taken from suspects must not be extracted under duress.

Even where violations of the law have taken place, the role of the police in enforcing the law may remain unclear or ambiguous. For example, police intervention in landlord-tenant disturbances or in marital arguments often place the police in the highly undesirable position of

[1] Albert J. Reiss, Jr., *The Police and the Public*, (New Haven: Yale University Press, 1971), pp. 45–47. Reiss discusses the need for police to establish their authority in situations in which they intervene. This of course can involve tactics which are distasteful to the people who are on the receiving end of the police services, whether the incident be one involving criminal conduct or simply peace-keeping.

[2] Charles A. Reich, "Police Questioning of Law-Abiding Citizens," in Arthur Niederhoffer and Abraham S. Blumberg, eds., *The Ambivalent Force: Perspectives on the Police*, (San Francisco: Rinehart Press, 1973), pp. 244–251.

being used not to impartially enforce the law but to lend the weight of authority to one side of an argument.

One of the most significant problems in the law enforcement role is that of determining which laws to enforce and how vigorously to enforce them. The sheer number of laws in the United States is staggering: there are over 2,800 federal crimes and an even larger number of crimes exist at the state and local levels. Given the manpower and technical limitations which characterize most police departments, the police must establish some kind of system of priorities so that they can target the offenses they will attempt to deal with.

The offenses which tend to receive the highest general priorities are crimes against the person, such as murder, robbery, and rape. Next in importance come the offenses against property and public order, such as thefts, traffic violations, and public drunkenness. Citizens frequently differ in opinion on the seriousness of an offense as well as the priorities placed on them by the police, especially when the offense is minor in scope. Many a patrolman has heard a speeder say "Why mess with me? Why don't you spend your time catching crooks?"

It is clear that although the law enforcement function is a legitimate role of the police, in actual practice the carrying out of that role is frequently a difficult and unrewarding task.

Peacekeeping and Public Service

In spite of the apparent mandate of the police to enforce laws, some writers have contended that the policeman's role is defined more by his responsibility for maintaining order than by his responsibility for enforcement of the law. Skolnick has modified this position somewhat in his statement that "The police in a democratic society are required to maintain order and to do so under the rule of law." [3]

Bittner addressed himself to this point when he said that there appear to be two more or less independent domains of police activity: one involves police conduct in affairs which will later be brought under the scrutiny of the courts, and the other involves activities which will not be subject to any outside review. [4] These two domains spell the difference between "law officers" and "peace officers."

A policeman's peacekeeping role is not as clear as his law enforcement role, although the two actually serve the same end. In many cases an

[3] Jerome H. Skolnick, *Justice Without Trial*, (Totowa, New Jersey: Littlefield, Adams & Co., 1966), p. 6.

[4] Egon Bittner, "The Police on Skid-Row: A Study in Peacekeeping," in William J. Chambliss, *Crime and the Legal Process*, (New York: McGraw-Hill Book Company, 1969), p. 137.

officer may find it expedient to resolve a problem without resorting to an arrest (or an arrest may not be legally justified). This might be the case in many types of minor disturbances such as marital squabbles or neighborhood arguments.

Actually, the police are called upon to perform a wide range of peace-keeping or service activities. Many of these events are non-criminal in nature, or if they involve some kind of criminal act, it might be very minor in scope. These types of activities include auto accidents, lost children, family disturbances, barking dogs, abandoned cars, and so on. Although these are relatively insignificant incidents, they are none the less important to the parties involved.

In fulfilling this peacekeeping/service role, two important factors are worth noting: (1) the police are generally mobilized by citizens, and (2) they are often asked to do things that could perhaps be done as well or better by some other non-police agency. With respect to the first point, Reiss has reported observational studies of police activity in high crime rate areas of three cities which reveal that 87 percent of all patrol mobilizations were initiated by citizens.[5] This means that the bulk of the police activities recorded were *reactive* in nature; that is, they were responses made to specific requests or notifications. It may therefore be seen that the police frequently provide service in response to demand, although they have little way of knowing exactly what kind of service will be expected of them until they arrive at the site of the demand.

Very often the services they provide do not call for the intervention of a police officer per se. However, it appears that the potential the police possess in their capacity as law enforcement agents is not what entirely controls the legitimacy of their peacekeeping and service activities. Rather, as Reiss has indicated, their legitimacy derives from the fact that they were called.[6] Thus the police come because they have been asked to come, and their right to act once they arrive derives as much from the fact that they were called as it does from any powers installed upon them by the law.

The police have accepted the peacekeeping/service role with relatively little opposition. Of course it should be remembered that the police are frequent participants in general peacekeeping and service events in spite of the fact that they would often prefer not to be. Such continuing experiences might even condition officers to an acceptance of these duties.

The second factor in police response to service demands (that they provide services which could often be performed as well or better by other agencies) is actually in large part a function of the fact that the police are

[5] Reiss, *op. cit.*, p. 11.
[6] *Ibid.*, p. 64.

mobilized by citizens. People call the police because they know they will come. The police are available at any time of the day or night, and they are free. In addition, when the police arrive, they will do *something*. In fact, the mere presence of the police is frequently enough to alter the situation. When the police speak, they speak with authority (in situations which are sometimes ambiguous and confusing). Even if one questions the particular approach the police take, few question their right to do so. As for the police officers themselves, they come into contact with so much service and peacekeeping activity that before long they develop the ability to deal with such problems with relative ease. Even in those situations where they recognize the fact that there is nothing they can do themselves, they can and do refer citizens to other agencies for help.

It has already been mentioned that the police must discriminate to some extent with respect to the laws that they will enforce. This also holds true to the extent of the services that they will perform, and for the same reason: there are so many demands on a policeman's time that he must be selective in how he will spend that time. Police officers tend to base their performance on past experience. This is especially so in those cases where there is more room for latitude. In actual practice this means that serious felonies such as murders, rapes, and aggravated assaults (especially where there has been an injury) are handled by the police with considerable formality. The reason for this is the greater likelihood that the case will be brought before a court and that the officer's role in the matter will be subject to review.

On the other hand, misdemeanors and lesser offenses are frequently of such little overall importance (other than to the parties involved) that they are handled informally. Many police officers will try to deal with a minor infraction by some means other than arrest. This is often desirable for several reasons. First, if the problem can be informally resolved, then that obviously ends the matter. Second, if an arrest can be avoided, then the officer will not have to cope with the paper work which normally accompanies an arrest, nor will he have to devote the time and effort to administratively processing a prisoner. Third, if the problem can be resolved informally, then there is a greater likelihood that hostile feelings among the parties will be lessened.

The selective emphasis employed by the police in their task-environment is normally discussed under the heading of "police discretion."[7]

[7] See for example Michael Banton, *The Policeman and the Community*, (London: Tavistock, 1964), pp. 6–7; Wayne LaFave, *Arrest: The Decision to Take A Suspect into Custody*, (Boston: Little, Brown and Company, 1965); and James G. Fisk, "Some Dimensions of Police Discretion," in Jack Goldsmith and Sharon Goldsmith, eds., *The Police Community*, (Pacific Palisades, California: Palisades Publishers, 1974), pp. 63–83.

The existence of police discretion has been widely recognized, although its legitimacy has not been universally accepted.[8] Part of the problem lies in the fact that police officers "have *not* been delegated discretion *not* to invoke the criminal law process." [9] But, by the same token, full enforcement of the law is impossible, thus creating an insoluble dilemma. Added to this are the ambiguity of many laws, the imposition of departmental regulations, and limitations on police manpower, to name but a few of the major constraints. James Q. Wilson sees much of the problem of police discretion as being a function of who (police or citizen) initiates the police action, and whether that action is directed at enforcing the law or maintaining order.[10]

Although this wide latitude in decision-making has many benefits, it also serves as a source of some difficulty as well. For example, it has been shown that the police tend to impose more rigorous standards of law enforcement on some groups than on others.[11] This discretionary enforcement of the law and the differential means by which police deal with different groups has been the subject of considerable discussion in recent years.

Another problem related to the discretionary nature of police role performance is that within their task-environment the police must deal with a wide range of people, and they may not always correctly understand all of those with whom they must deal, or they may inaccurately perceive community sentiment.[12] If police officers feel ill at ease around such minorities as blacks, chicanos, or Indians, it may very well be easier for them to assess a problem situation in a strictly legalistic context than to attempt to employ a wider degree of discretionary latitude. Thus, for example, an officer who is unfamiliar with the cultural folkways (or language) of Mexican-Americans, may well be more likely to invoke an arrest than to attempt to unravel a problem in a disturbance-type situation.[13]

[8] Herman Goldstein, "Police Discretion: The Ideal Versus the Real," *Public Administration Review,* 23 (September 1963).

[9] Joseph Goldstein, "Police Discretion Not To Invoke the Criminal Justice Process: Low Visibility Decisions in the Administration of Justice," in George F. Cole, ed., *Criminal Justice: Law and Politics,* (Belmont, California: Wadsworth Publishing Co., Inc., 1964), p. 134.

[10] James Q. Wilson, *Varieties of Police Behavior: The Management of Law and Order in Eight Communities,* (New York: Atheneum, 1971), p. 85.

[11] See Jerome H. Skolnick, *Justice Without Trial: Law Enforcement in Democratic Society,* (New York: John Wiley & Sons, Inc., 1966), especially chapter 4, pp. 71–90.

[12] Thomas J. Crawford, "Police Overperception of Ghetto Hostility," *Journal of Police Science and Administration* 1:2 (June 1973), pp. 168–174.

[13] See also Janet B. Sawyer, "Social Aspects of Bilingualism in San Antonio, Texas," and Edward T. Hall and Mildred R. Hall, "The Sounds of Silence," both in Virginia R. Clark, Paul A. Escholz, and Alfred F. Rosa, editors, *Language,* (New York: St. Martin's Press, 1972), pp. 430–437 and 459–471, respectively.

Because of the latitude the police have in the manner in which they carry out their responsibilities, it often appears that different cities have different "styles" of policing. From his studies of the police departments in eight different cities, Wilson defined three styles of community policing.[14] The first is the "watchman" style. This type of police department is one which places a stronger emphasis on order maintenance than on law enforcement. Specific offenses are judged "less by what the law says about them than by their immediate and personal consequences, which will differ in importance depending on the standards of the relevant group—teenagers, Negroes, prostitutes, motorists, families, and so forth." [15] Wilson points out that in the watchman style department "Patrolmen are locally recruited, paid low salaries, expected to have second jobs, given the very minimum in initial training and almost no in-service training, and not rewarded for having or getting higher education." [16]

The second style is the "legalistic" police department. In this style, the emphasis is on law enforcement more than order maintenance. "The police will act, on the whole, as if there were a single standard of community conduct—that which the law prescribes." [17] Legalistic departments also value technical efficiency and stress officer productivity. This style of policing displays the police as ministerial agents of laws for which they are not responsible, yet which they are obliged to enforce.

Wilson's third style is the "service" style of police department. In this category, the police take seriously all requests for "either law enforcement or order maintenance (unlike police with a watchman style) but are less likely to respond by making an arrest or otherwise imposing formal sanctions (unlike police with a legalistic style)." [18] Such a department is keenly conscious of the need for community relations and for treating the public with courtesy.

The reasons that a police department adopts a particular style are many and complex; yet the need to balance order maintenance and enforcement activities is a problem with which virtually all departments must come to grips. How they do this, and what external constraints they must cope with, are among the factors which make most police departments relatively unique.

Symbolic Utility

In the preceding sections, the active roles that the police play were discussed. In addition, the police have come to play a largely passive yet

[14] James Q. Wilson, *op cit.*
[15] *Ibid.*, p. 141.
[16] *Ibid.*, p. 151.
[17] *Ibid.*, p. 172.
[18] *Ibid.*, p. 200.

highly important role: they are a symbol. This is significant in that if the police are perceived as being a certain type of organization, they will most likely be responded to on that basis. In addition, their symbolic role will condition not only what the citizen expects of the police, but also what the police expect of themselves. Niederhoffer clearly recognized this when he said that:

> The policeman is a 'Rorschach' in uniform as he patrols his beat. His occupational accouterments—shield, nightstick, gun, and summons book—clothe him in a mantle of symbolism that stimulates fantasy and projection. Children identify with him in the perennial game of 'cops and robbers.' Teenagers in autos stiffen with compulsive rage or anxiety at the sight of the patrol car. To people in trouble the police officer is a savior. In another metamorphasis the patrolman becomes a fierce ogre that mothers conjure up to frighten their disobedient youngsters. At one moment the policeman is hero, the next, monster.[19]

The meaning of any symbol is social in origin; that is, the meaning of a symbol is given to it by those who use it.[20] In general, there seem to be two kinds of symbols. The first includes those which are referential and are denotative in nature; they are words that have a specific reference (e.g., "book," or "chair"). Through the use of referential symbols people are able to refer to a class of objects. The other type of symbol includes those which are expressive, or connotative. They are used to evoke associations that are diffuse and open-ended rather than specific and limited. However, not all symbols are used as either strictly denotative or connotative:

> Many symbols carry affective connotations but are used without explicit recognition of their affective natures; that is, they are used for their sense rather than for their literal meaning. They express emotion and they arouse emotion, and they are often used to induce an attitude rather than to convey information.[21]

As Stone and Farberman have pointed out, while the relationship between an object and its representative designation is arbitrary, it is,

[19] Arthur Niederhoffer, *Behind the Shield: The Police in Urban Society*, (Garden City, New York: Doubleday/Anchor Books, 1969), p. 1.
[20] Leonard Broom and Philip Selznick, *Sociology*, (New York: Harper & Row, Publishers, 1973), p. 57.
[21] Eugene L. Hartley and Ruth E. Hartley, *Fundamentals of Social Psychology*, (New York: Alfred A. Knopf, 1959), p. 112.

nonetheless, established and maintained through consensus.[22] Thus the meaning of a symbol need not coincide with objective reality. As a consequence, and in spite of the large amount of time devoted by the police to peacekeeping activities, the general public still apparently has a tendency to view the police as agents of legalistic control: as enforcers of the law—"crime fighters." The President's Commission on Law Enforcement and the Administration of Justice has reported that partially as a result of the news and entertainment media

> ... the police have come to be viewed as a body of men continually engaged in the exciting, dangerous, and competitive enterprise of apprehending and prosecuting criminals.[23]

Of course the police do perform such a role, although it does not consume the bulk of their time. In order for them to be able to carry out this role, they must have certain skills and abilities. These skills and abilities have in turn given rise to suspicion in some quarters that the police are a group of men engaged in a "tainted" occupation; or, as Bittner has suggested:

> Because they are posted on the perimeters of order and justice in the hope that their presence will deter the forces of darkness and chaos, because they are meant to spare the rest of the people direct confrontations with the dreadful, perverse, lurid, and dangerous, police officers are perceived to have powers and secrets no one else shares.[24]

If this view is correct, one might easily presume that many citizens can interpret those "secrets" and "powers" as not only being necessary in the "war on crime" but as also being tools which can be of value in dealing with problems of a lesser and more personal nature—like making an intoxicated husband calm down and behave. If the policeman becomes a symbol of the *enforcement function* alone, then a significant gap will develop between what the police are in reality and what they are believed to be. The police must make every effort to correctly assess the symbolic role they play in the various segments of their respective communities and to maintain congruence between the reality of the symbols and the police themselves. In this respect, it must be borne in mind that any

[22] Gregory P. Stone and Harvey A. Farberman, *Social Psychology Through Symbolic Interaction*, (Waltham, Massachusetts: Xerox College Publishing, 1970), p. 90.

[23] President's Commission on Law Enforcement and the Administration of Justice, Nicholas deB. Katzenbach, Chairman, *Task Force Report: The Police*, (Washington, D.C.: Government Printing Office, 1967), p. 13.

[24] Egon Bittner, *The Functions of the Police in Modern Society*, (Washington, D.C.: Government Printing Office, 1970), p. 6.

2

symbol derives its meaning from those who perceive the symbol: "Inherently the universe is meaningless and totally indifferent to the existence of man... the universe presents itself as an occasion for man's creative capacities. It awaits his investiture of identity, meaning, value, sentiments, and rules." [25] Because the police as a symbol are vested with the meanings the community attaches to them, policing is a function of the specific communities in which it takes place. For this reason "Priorities regarding the police role are largely established by the community the police agency serves." [26]

The roles and goals of the police are vitally important issues, for they will have a direct impact on the quality of life in the urban environment. This issue is of sufficient importance that the National Advisory Commission on Criminal Justice Standards and Goals, appointed by the Justice Department's Law Enforcement Assistance Administration, has set the following standards with respect to the police function: [27]

Every police chief executive immediately should develop written policy, based on policies of the governing body that provides formal authority for the police function, and should set forth the objectives and priorities that will guide the agency's delivery of police services. Agency policy should articulate the role of the agency in the protection of constitutional guarantees, the enforcement of the law, and the provision of services necessary to reduce crime, to maintain public order, and to respond to the needs of the community.

1. Every police chief executive should acknowledge that the basic purpose of the police is the maintenance of public order and the control of conduct legislatively defined as crime. The basic purpose may not limit the police role, but should be central to its full definition.

2. Every police chief executive should identify those crimes on which police resources will be concentrated. In the allocation of resources, those crimes that are the most serious, stimulate the greatest fear, and cause the greatest economic losses should be afforded the highest priority.

3. Every police chief executive should recognize that some government services that are not essentially a police function are, under some circumstances, appropriately performed by the police. Such

[25] Stone and Farberman, *op cit.*, p. 89.
[26] National Advisory Commission on Criminal Justice Standards and Goals, Russell W. Peterson, Chairman, *Police*, (Washington, D.C.: Government Printing Office, 1973), p. 13.
[27] *Ibid.*, pp. 12–13.

48

services include those provided in the interest of effective government or in response to established community needs. A chief executive:

a. Should determine if the service to be provided has a relationship to the objectives established by the police agency. If not, the chief executive should resist that service becoming a duty of the agency;

b. Should determine the budgetary cost of the service; and

c. Should inform the public and its representatives of the projected effect that provision of the service by the police will have on the ability of the agency to continue the present level of enforcement services.

d. If the service must be provided by the police agency, it should be placed in perspective with all other agency services and it should be considered when establishing priorities for the delivery of all police services.

e. The service should be made a part of the agency's police role until such time as it is no longer necessary for the police agency to perform the service.

f. In connection with the preparation of their budgets, all police agencies should study and revise annually the objectives and priorities which have been established for the enforcement of laws and the delivery of services.

4. Every police agency should determine that scope and availability of other government services and public and private social services, and develop its ability to make effective referrals to those services.

The standards set forth by the National Advisory Commission lend clear recognition to the complex interrelationship between the police, the law, and the community. It would be impossible to say that the police could only enforce the law or even that they must consistently and regularly enforce all laws and enforce them in an even fashion.

The police must deal with such a wealth of intangibles in the urban setting that to strictly delineate their roles would be impossible. The police are but one element of the community as a whole, and what they do and how they do it must be determined by the community.

Appendix A
The Police Role in an Urban Society *

One of the most critical issues facing the United States today is the definition of the police role in a modern and urban democratic society. Until that role is defined, both for the present and the future, we shall never effectively resolve the pressing problems with which we are confronted—a very grim prospect indeed.

The 1960's were years of great fear, discord, and strife; yet we know that this may be only a prologue to events that would occur in the decade we have now entered. We are all haunted by the possibilities inherent in the violence, hatred, and fear that beset our society; and we are equally aware of the great responsibility that falls to the police service for preventing these possibilities from becoming reality. Here we pause fearfully. For if the police service of the 1970's responds to the challenges and the responsibilities of this decade as it did in the last decade, failure is assured. We cannot escape the conclusion that in the 1960's the police were severely tried and found to be desperately wanting. The nation has survived this failure, but the record of the police in the 1960's has made success in the 1970's more imperative but less attainable.

As the first and activating element of the criminal justice system, the police are confronted with a multiplicity of problems, many of which are shared in common with the entire system, which is in deep difficulty. But central to these problems is a single basic issue, concerning the administration of the police service; to lose sight of this is to obscure the real crisis of policing today. In turn, any solution to this problem can only come about through a resolution of the police role or roles.

Friend of All, Armed Nemesis of Some

Historically, the roles of police, even though not carefully or accurately articulated, were nonetheless generally understood and accepted. Quite obviously, this is most definitely not the case in contemporary America. Youth, ethnic groups, academicians, political leaders, businessmen, and lay citizens all have divergent, disparate views of those historic police roles. This lack of consensus has created an atmosphere in which sharp conflict over the rationale for police action flourishes, and consequently bitter debate rages throughout a community or even the nation. These debates are sometimes so acrimonious that the only result is a tearing of the social fabric that holds a community or nation together.

History has left us a bewildering hodgepodge of contradictory roles that the police are expected to perform. We may well ask, for example, are the

* SOURCE: Bernard I. Garmire, "The Police Role in an Urban Society," *The Police and the Community*, Robert F. Steadman, ed. Baltimore: The John Hopkins University Press, 1972. Copyright ©, The Committee for Economic Development. By permission of the publisher.

police to be concerned with peacekeeping or crime fighting? The blind enforcers of the law or the discretionary agents of a benevolent government? Social workers with guns or gunmen in social work? Facilitators of social change or defenders of the "faith"? The enforcers of the criminal law or society's legal trash bin? A social agency of last resort after 5:00 p.m. or mere watchmen for business and industry?

Actually, the police are expected to do all those things and become all things to all people, at once the confessor and the inquisitor, the friend of all yet the armed nemesis of some. Supermen, not men, could do all these things; but, the theory of supermen was practiced three decades ago, and the civilized world is the less for it.

In sum, the public had developed such high expectations of its police that those expectations moved beyond reality to something that could be better described as faith. As the public came to have faith in the police to do all things, the police came to have faith that they could do all things; when disillusionment set in, the singers lost faith in the song, in each other, and in themselves.

If we are to restore any semblance of faith in the police by the public— and the police themselves—we must begin first by defining the police role very carefully so that it does not distort reality. The historical definition of the police role eventually achieved this regrettable result by fostering the belief that police, because they were present and visible twenty-four hours a day, could function as a gigantic surrogate service agency to the community handling all the needs of the people all of the time.

To establish credibility or faith in the police service requires that the police role be delineated so that there are reasonable expectations about what the police should do and can do. Once we know what the police are to do, then we can address the three critical problems of police recruitment, training, and leadership. As matters stand now, we do not know what we are recruiting men for, what kind of training and education they ought to have, or what kind of leadership we ought to be developing—because we don't know where we want to lead them in the first place.

The result of this failure is that the police perform two conflicting basic roles that cannot be integrated administratively in any single agency. Yet operationally, individual police officers are assigned those very same conflicting roles and are expected to master them psychologically so that, in the street, they can perform each with proficiency as the occasion demands. These two roles are community service and law enforcement.

I define the community-service role as one in which the police provide essentially a social service to the community; i.e., intervening in domestic quarrels, handling those who are under the influence of alcohol or drugs, working with dependent and neglected children, rendering emergency medical or rescue services and generally acting as a social agency of last resort—

particularly after 5:00 p.m. and on weekends—for the impoverished, the sick, the old, and the lower socioeconomic classes.

An example of the community-service roles is the family fight. What is needed here are the skills and resources of a marriage counselor, a psychiatrist, or a social worker. It does not serve the interests of either the state or the man and the wife to make an arrest. Nor does it serve the interests of the state or the family simply to suppress the noise level of the quarrel or to prevent an assault by invoking the threat of arrest and jail.

I define the law-enforcement role as one in which the police enforce criminal laws. This is the role for the crime fighter and the thief catcher. In this role, the primary tasks are criminal investigation, collection of evidence, interrogation of suspects, arrests of suspects, maintenance of order and safety, combatting organized crime, suppression of disturbances and riots, and, generally, the hard core enforcement of criminal laws.

The commission of a robbery in which the victim was brutally assaulted clearly falls within the law-enforcement role. In this case, law-enforcement and criminal-investigation skills are required to identify the suspect and to bring him before the court.

Police agencies and police officers are attempting to fill both roles, and I submit that they are not properly trained, equipped, or capable of performing *either* role with any degree of success, let alone both of them. Even if the numbers of policemen were vastly increased, even if their training were improved, and even if their resources were expanded, I still submit that they could not perform both roles—so sharply do they conflict and so different are the skills required. One person simply cannot reasonably be expected to master both roles intellectually and jump psychologically from one to another in an instant's notice. Furthermore, the law-enforcement role of police is so strongly perceived by some citizens that they totally reject the idea that police could or should fill a community-service role even if they were capable of doing so.

Here is the kind of thing that we expect of today's police officer:

At 9:00 p.m. he responds to a robbery in progress and upon arrival exchanges gunshots with a suspect.

At 10:00 p.m., after he has made a report of the incident, he receives a call of a violent family brawl. He is white, they are black, and the suspect with whom he just exchanged gunfire an hour earlier was black. The officer is expected to handle their marital problems effectively and dispassionately, but he also has to return to radio service quickly because it is Saturday night and two other calls are waiting for him. Need more be said? Do we really believe that one man can do this night after night, month in and month out? Granted, the officer is not fired upon or assaulted every night. But the potential is there and he knows it: witness the frequent news reports concerning the ambushes, sniping, and other offenses directed against police. Is it not time that we took notice of the realities of policing and admit that one man or one group of men cannot intellectually and psychologically do all this?

In order to consider this question, the Miami police department collaborated with the Psychiatric Institute Foundation to study police response to stress. This study was financed by the Law Enforcement Assistance Administration (LEAA). The results of this study, which are described in the following chapter, suggest that the multiplicity of roles that officers must fill contributes significantly to police fatigue and stress. My own personal experience of thirty-three years in the police service in all ranks strongly affirms this finding.

Such studies must be regarded only as a beginning; we must explore much more fully the possibilities of developing a psychiatric set of standards for police work, which in turn poses this basic question: What are the roles police perform and what are the criteria and measurement methods to identify those applicants who are best suited to perform each role or a combination of roles? We must examine the hypothesis that there is a constellation of psychological factors that makes some persons better suited for one kind of police role than another. We must determine what makes a good community-service worker, a good crime fighter, and a good administrator; we must discover, if possible, ways of finding persons who can perform adequately in two or more different roles.

Two Agencies Under Civilian Control

What is implicit in the foregoing analysis is a drastic reorganization of the administration of the police function, as suggested at the outset of this chapter. The police service must be reorganized both structurally and functionally so that it conforms in a rational way to the realities of the roles to be performed. I will outline here one organizational scheme for accomplishing this.

The contemporary police organization should be divided into two agencies under one department, one concerned with the law-enforcement function, the other with the community-service function. The community-service agency would operate on a twenty-four-hour basis and would be satisfied by people who are psychologically best suited for this function as well as specifically educated and trained to perform it. There would be no need for them to operate in uniform, and, depending on the locality generally, no need for them to be armed. They may or may not have full powers of arrest.

The law-enforcement agency would function as criminal investigators, thief catchers, and so forth, and it likewise would be composed of people psychologically attuned to the law-enforcement role and for it. In essence, they would be performing the police functions of patrol and investigation; they would, of course, be armed and possess full police powers.

Administering both agencies at the departmental level would be a professional staff composed of public administrators directly responsible to the elected or appointed head of government. The public administrators would not necessarily be policemen. Indeed, they should be chosen for their administrative expertise—not just for their law-enforcement or community-service expertise. The overhead or staff agencies should be predominantly staffed by civilians possessing required skills in such areas as planning, budgeting, personnel administration, and systems analysis. I wish to emphasize the importance of developing and maintaining civilian control over both the law-enforcement and community-service agencies.

The highest career professional in each agency would be a director, who reports to the public administrator. The director would have only a small administrative staff because the bulk of the staff services would be provided and controlled at the departmental level, further strengthening the concept of civilian control. In short, the law-enforcement and community-service agencies would be strictly line or operating agencies.

Additionally, a citizen advisory board should be established composed of persons appointed and elected to that board. The members should represent and be drawn from all elements of the community. This would be a board charged not with investigating civilian complaints against the department on with the far more important responsibility of advising the department on problems, means, and goals. The board should deliberately seek to provide policy input and feedback.

It is clear that fewer personnel would be needed in the law-enforcement function than in the community-service function. Numerous studies have indicated that the greater part of a police officer's time—perhaps two-thirds—is spent in the service role rather than the enforcement role. But if we truly attempt to provide adequate community services, we must expect to increase our personnel and financial commitments in this area. It will not be possible simply to take a police department and divide it into the two agencies without increasing both personnel and financing. I would estimate that total resources will have to be increased by 20 to 25 per cent in order to implement the new system.

I would recommend such an increase *only* if it were to be employed in establishing the new organizational complex—not if it were to be invested in the present police system. It is time that we recognized the tremendous inefficiencies that exist in the policing function. Until the police structure and function are rationalized in this country, such an investment would amount to throwing good money after bad.

It must be admitted that the new system as proposed here perhaps raises more questions than it answers. The intent is to propose a conceptual model for a new system, not to settle all the myriad details. If the concept has merit, then the details and attendant problems can be worked out during the research and testing phase.

One specific element that should be mentioned is traffic control. Even though untold resources have been diverted from the police forces in an effort to combat the traffic problem, the results have been rather meager. The basic question is whether traffic control is indeed properly a function of police, or whether traffic offenders should be handled in a criminal or quasi-criminal process. The answer may well be in handling traffic cases through a separate administrative system, with an educational and training process substituted for fines or imprisonment. For those who persistently violate the traffic codes, penalties under a point system might well be invoked, with the worst offenders being denied their driving privileges. In fact, the entire mechanism of traffic control should be removed from the criminal justice system and handled as a transportation or social-service matter. It might appropriately fall under the community-service arm of a reorganized police force.

The Need for Outside Help

No matter what new models for the reform and reorganization of the police function are chosen, it is hardly realistic to expect that the initiative for these moves are to come solely, or perhaps even mainly, from within the police forces themselves. The average police department is too ingrown, too stagnant, to undertake this kind of vigorous, sweeping action. Nor, in a sense, is it fair to place the whole burden of reform on the shoulders of the police. For the development of truly efficient police forces, organized along the functional lines suggested in this chapter, requires the creation of new governmental structures; such an endeavor lies outside either the scope or the competence of the police.

An outstanding example of such a problem—one of the most persistent and frustrating problems confronting our municipalities and states—is the Balkanization of the police forces. There are approximately 40,000 police agencies ranging in size from one man to 30,000 men. It is not necessary to elaborate on the disadvantages of such a fractured system; they are too well known. Perhaps only cities of 50,000 or more should be allowed their own police agencies; the state should police the smaller cities and the rural areas. In the metropolitan areas there should be consolidation of the smaller police agencies. If this were done, the number of police agencies could be reduced from 40,000 agencies to roughly 400-plus agencies—with clear gains in terms of effectiveness and efficiency.

The consolidation of police agencies, accompanied by a rationalization of police structure and function, could be the first step down the long road toward the reform of the police system and the resolution of its problems. But very clearly a move of such magnitude will require the combined exertions and the cooperation of many government agencies at all levels, from

2

federal through local, as well as assistance from agencies in the private sector. This likewise applies to many other badly needed reforms, which are unlikely to come through the efforts of the police alone. One such vitally important initiative is the loosening up of the present rigid parochialism of police department bureaucracies that promotes and perpetrates mediocrity and inefficiency. We must open avenues for lateral entry into police agencies, providing for movement of those with integrity and expertise from department to department, as well as some sort of a retirement system which could be transferred from place to place. Again, there is a vital need for some national system for the rating of police agencies for their effectiveness and efficiency. This would be a great improvement òver the Uniform Crime Reporting system as it exists today; needless to say, the magnitude of such a system is such that only the federal government is capable of bringing it into being.

What is of the utmost importance is that a start be made—now—in implementing the concepts discussed in this chapter. Initial steps that could be taken to bring about a coordination of efforts to this end are:

First, the police service must break down its institutional version of the Berlin Wall and seek assistance and advice from nonpolice organizations, such as foundations and agencies in the psychiatric, social work, and similar fields.

Second, the federal government and foundations are in an admirable position to induce two or three municipal governments to experiment with the concepts through cash grants to support the costs and to evaluate the results.

Third, both organizations can support research and educational and training programs designed to prepare police agencies for conversion to the new system.

Fourth, private industry can assist by providing funding programs to encourage development of the new system, and, through the exercise of community leadership, it can encourage municipal and state governments to modernize and rationalize their police systems.

A recent observation by William A. Westley is apropos here. "The police," he writes, "must be given the advantage of sophisticated knowledge of social organizations which is now transforming industry and other community institutions in ways appropriate to the requirements of modern society."[1]

But even were this to be accomplished successfully, I do not believe that this will make policemen and the police service objects of love and endearment; it is not in the nature of men—particularly Americans—to give such affection to those representatives of authority who directly control their lives.

[1] William A. Westley, "Learning to Love the Police," *The New York Times* (November 15, 1971), p. 41. © 1971 by The New York Times Company. Reprinted by permission. Westley is director of the Industrial Relations Center, McGill University, Quebec, Canada, and author of *Violence and the Police: A Sociological Study of Law, Custom, and Morality* (Cambridge, Mass., MIT Press, 1970).

And, no matter how we describe the activities of the police, the business of police is policing. The most that we can hope for, police-community relations or public relations notwithstanding, is respect for the police as professionals, confidence in their integrity, and public conviction that the police will perform their mission.

3

Social Classes, Status, Changing Trends

Introduction

The American city is a place of great diversity. Its physical make-up offers a blend of new and old, rich and poor, and gradations of attractiveness which range from one extreme to the other. People who reside in these cities likewise represent considerable variation along such dimensions as race, ethnicity, mode of dress and style of speech, levels of education, amount of income, type of employment, preferences in entertainment, types of residence, political and social attitudes and in many other ways.

A cursory examination of a city will reveal that its people vary systematically in where and how they live, in the way they are treated by others and how they treat others. Urban life is not by any means the same for all residents, though they may share many superficial characteristics in common. Many factors come together to determine the life style and location where a person lives within the city, and these factors determine one's "position" in society. We will explore some of the more obvious social differences among groups of people as they relate to the police function and sphere, and demonstrate the dynamics of the interrelationship by drawing upon generalities for the purposes of demonstrating some of the elementary dimensions involved.

Social Class

American society like other societies outside of the United States contains inequalities in its social structure. The term "inequality" is used to indicate *variability:* the considerable differences to be found among social groupings of citizens. Groupings are discussed under the heading of *social stratification*, which is often analyzed through the use of an arbitrary classification of classes.

In a society based on democratic ideals of equality, it is difficult to visualize a stratified class structure. However, even though the United States does not have a system of nobility which confers rank and title upon certain specially chosen citizens, as is found in many other countries, the United States does have a system of social classes and to deny this fact invites a seriously distorted picture of the American social struc-

3

ture. Although we vary in many ways, it is generally possible to group us into specific categories. One of the most obvious criteria used to classify people is on the basis of income. Ely Chinoy, a noted sociologist, has defined a social class as being "... a number of persons sharing a common position in the economic order."[1]

The use of an economic index to determine social classes is directly related to other significant life style "indicators" such as education, employment, and type and location of residence. Social class distinctions are often difficult to delineate and can be misleading. Sociologists have studied class relationships in a wide variety of settings. "Community" studies have developed a general consensus that on a nation-wide level there exists a social structure of basically five classes. On a local or regional basis this classification may vary somewhat; however, the five basic classifications provide a good tool for sociological analysis.

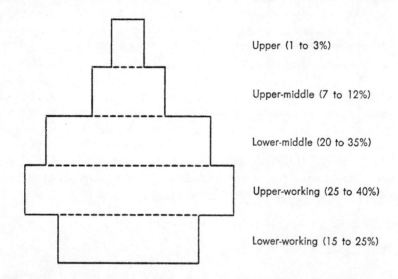

Figure 1. A national view of the social-class structure. The percentages presented are derived from a number of studies of the social structure made in communities ranging from 5,000 to 500,000 in population; the percentage ranges show how a given class varies in size.

From Robert J. Havighurst and Bernice Neugarten, Society and Education, 3d ed., fig. 1.3, p. 19. © Copyright 1967 by Allyn and Bacon, Inc., Boston. Reprinted by permission.

[1] Ely Chinoy, Society, second edition. (New York: Random House, 1967), p. 171.

Why are considerations of social class important? Research in a number of fields has shown that as one's class position increases: [2]

—Infant mortality rates decrease.

—Life expectancy increases.

—Chances for survival in wartime in the armed forces increases.

—Number of visits to a doctor increases.

—The amount of yearly and lifetime income increases.

—The desire to improve one's self remains constant.

—The status of one's occupation increases.

—The likelihood of living in a "status" house in a "status" neighborhood increases.

—The level of education increases.

—Facility in symbolic communication increases.

—Accuracy of role-taking ability increases.

—Selection of dating and marriage partners from the same level remains constant.

—Age of first marriage increases.

—Likelihood of marriage being broken by divorce, separation, or desertion decreases.

—Likelihood of being a virgin at marriage increases.

—Likelihood of parents treating children in a warm, permissive manner and using praise and reasoning rather than physical punishment in socialization increases.

—Likelihood of voting in a presidential election increases.

—Extent of knowledge about political issues increases.

—Likelihood of identifying one's self politically as a Republican increases.

—Likelihood of belonging to voluntary associations increases.

[2] Glenn M. Vernon, *Human Interaction*. New York: Ronald Press Company, 1965, pp. 240–242.

—Likelihood of playing a leadership role in a church increases.

—Likelihood of having associates who are described as "close friends" increases.

—Even though the likelihood of engaging in antisocial acts remains somewhat constant, the likelihood of becoming an official delinquent as a result thereof decreases.

—Likelihood of receiving "justice" in the courts of the land increases.

—Likelihood of endorsing principle of deferred gratification increases.

—Status anxiety remains somewhat constant except at upper-upper level.

In order to understand the city as a complex social system, it is therefore necessary to have at least a basic comprehension of the interrelated dynamics of the class structure. The class structure will vary somewhat from one geographical area to the next, however for purposes of analysis we will discuss the subject according to the class structure shown in figure 1. There are a number of dimensions which serve as the basis for making class distinctions; according to another noted sociologist Kahl, they include: [3]

—Prestige

—Occupation

—Possessions, wealth, and income

—Social interaction

—Class consciousness

—Value orientations

—Power

Each of the five basic classes gravitate differently with these dimensions, and it is these variables of collective differences which makes one social class distinctive from another.

Upper Class (1–3%). The upper class is defined as being composed of persons who typically enjoy considerable prestige within their community; that is, they are generally respected individuals. Their names are usually well known throughout much of the community and perhaps

[3] Joseph A. Kahl, *The American Class Structure.* (New York: Holt, Rinehart, & Winston, Inc., 1957).

nationally. Members of the upper class are usually wealthy and consequently, to define this class in terms of occupation or where they work is difficult. Their occupation might be proprietary; that is, they may be the owners of a business or many businesses, and their work may be the management of substantial investments. Among the very elite upper-upper class, the wealth held is inherited and the individual represents the current generation of a family tradition of wealth.

There are however occupations which enjoy high prestige in their own right. This prestige is not simply a function of how much income is produced, but also includes such factors as personal independence, responsibility, work site and conditions. Among the occupations which have high prestige ratings are: jurists; physicians; scientists; certain public officials; university professors; diplomats; attorneys; and others.[4] Members of the upper class characteristically work in occupations which confer prestige, and control economic assets of almost staggering proportions: the top 5 per cent of the families in the nation receive 19 per cent of the national income.[5] *Fortune* magazine has conservatively estimated that 153 of these persons had individual wealth in excess of $50 million.[6]

Members of the upper class reflect a pattern of differential contact in their social interaction, that is, they tend to socialize with their peers. Characteristically they generally use their wealth to assure selective interaction. For example they may belong to exclusive clubs and send their children to private schools. Members of the upper class usually live in "the best part of town" in residences which provide a maximum of material comfort and privacy.

Generally members of this class are aware of their status and are careful not to publicly damage their reputations by their activities. Class consciousness is particularly acute on the part of the upper-upper class, which is composed of well established line families—as opposed to the lower-upper class, which is composed of the "new rich." Class consciousness manifests itself in a sense of an obligation to the class of which the individual is a member to maintain reputation and status.

Value orientations of the upper class, according to Kahl, are summed up in the term "graceful living."

The upper class, in short, can be described as a group who believe in tradition, in continuity of behavior with the past; they emphasize

[4] Robert W. Hodge, Paul M. Seigel and Peter H. Rossi, "Occupational Prestige in the United States, 1925–1963," *American Journal of Sociology*, 70 (November 1964), pp. 286–302.

[5] Abraham S. Blumberg, ed., *Law and Order: The Scales of Justice*, second edition. (New Brunswick, New Jersey: Transaction Books, 1973), p. 6.

[6] Arthur M. Louis, "America's Centimillionaires," *Fortune*, 77 (May 1968), pp. 152–157.

familism and lineage, which is cemented by the family fortune as something inherited from the past or to be passed along in the future; they favor the skills of graceful living. . . .[7]

Their financial and social status allows members of the upper class to typically enjoy considerable power within their communities—and frequently at the national level. They command resources which give them an important leverage in determining community affairs in that their individual opinions are sought and respected. As a collective group the upper class has been described as a "power elite," and studies of the power structure of communities consistently disclose the fact that the upper class wields considerable power.

Their socialization process and their very low visibility determines why members of the upper class seldom come into direct contact with the police, either as complainants or offenders, except in the area of traffic violations. When the upper class citizen does come into contact with the police: ". . . high status offenders are the recipients of the respect and deference that citizens—including the police, prosecutor, judge, and jurors—have been conditioned to accord their equals or social superiors."[8]

The American sociologist, Reckless, has noted that "studies which emphasize class structuring of behavior in American society definitely show that the upper classes are practically free from official action by police and courts. . . ."[9] Although members of the upper class are seldom arrested, this does not mean they seldom commit crimes. Criminal acts do occur, and "such infractions mainly involve falsification of reports, evasion of taxes, misuse of funds, and outright but covered-up theft."[10] Reckless believes that "If the practices of politicians and businessmen in America were subject to ready reporting, the upper-class rates of crime would increase enormously."[11]

Their offenses like the life style they lead are of the type which involve extremely low visibility and involve victims who are unlikely to be aware of their victimization.

The Upper-Middle Class (7–12%). Havighurst and Neugarten describe the upper-middle class in the following terms:

About half of the adult members of this class have climbed to their present status from lower beginnings. Hence this class seems to be

[7] Kahl, *op. cit.*, p. 192.
[8] Stuart L. Hills, *Crime, Power, and Morality.* (Scranton: Chandler Publishing Co., 1971), p. 20.
[9] Walter C. Reckless, *The Crime Problem,* fourth edition. (New York: Appleton-Century-Crofts, 1967), p. 110.
[10] *Ibid.*, p. 111.
[11] *Ibid.*

made up largely of active, ambitious people. The men are business executives and professional men; the women are active in home-making, club work, PTA, and civic organizations. The members of this class do not have aristocratic family traditions. Although some are interested in building up such traditions, the typical comment is 'we do not care about our ancestors. It isn't *who* you are, but *what* you are.' [12]

The upper-middle class is composed of individuals who enjoy a degree of local prestige, from their occupations and or as a result of their active civic participation; however, they are not generally known outside of their community. These individuals typically have a prestigious occupational status, as either a member of a profession or a business executive.

They are self-sufficient and enjoy various degrees of wealth. They will tend to live in "good" residential neighborhoods and enjoy considerable material comfort. Their social interaction tends to include contact with their peers in business and professional associations as well as during the course of civic activities. Generally, they are not class conscious but they are aware of their status in the community.

The primary value orientation of the upper-middle class, according to Kahl, is career:

The upper-middle class believe in themselves and in the American way of life, and they are devoted to their careers. They stress planning for the future and not too much regard for the past; they stress activity, accomplishment, practical results; they stress individualistic achievement within the framework of group cooperation and collective responsibility.[13]

Individuals of the upper-middle class may exercise limited amounts of power, although their primary source of power comes through cooperative efforts, such as through the local bar association or various business associations. In such an indirect fashion members of the upper-middle class can exert considerable influence in community affairs and politics. What they lack in the way of individual personal power, they can compensate for through access to individuals who do have such power.

In the area of criminal conduct, Reckless feels that "the middle class in America is probably most free of crime and probably enjoys a condition of living and activity which most insulates them against criminal

[12] Havighurst and Neugarten, *op. cit.*, p. 23.
[13] Kahl, *op. cit.*, p. 201.

3

activity." [14] He notes that "The middle class watches its step." [15] When upper-middle class citizens *do* violate the law (except for traffic violations), it is likely to take the form of a "white collar crime." A most prominent of such cases was the so-called "Heavy Electric" case of 1961, where twenty-nine corporations and forty-five senior executives were prosecuted in criminal court for illegally conspiring to rig bids, fix prices, and control the market on heavy electrical equipment valued at over $175,000,000 annually. The companies involved were fined almost $2,000,000, and seven of the executives were sent to jail for thirty days. Twenty-seven executives were given suspended sentences.[16] The unusual aspect of this case was not in the punishments, but that the case was brought into the criminal justice system at all.

Members of the upper-middle class preserve the security of their world through cooperation, respect, and understanding. They generally accord the police a high degree of legitimacy, although seldom call upon them. The presence of a marked police car parked in an upper-middle class neighborhood is apt to generate considerable conversation, speculation, and even embarrassment.

The Lower-Middle Class (20–35%). Members of the lower-middle class, according to Havighurst and Neugarten, tend to be "at the national average," [17] from various points of view, including prestige. Occupationally, this class typically includes white collar clerical workers, small businessmen, and sales personnel, among others. Their financial status tends to be below that of the upper-middle class. The financial posture of the lower-middle class has become rather precarious in recent years, and many families in this class have found it necessary for both husband and wife to work in order to maintain the standard of living to which they strive.

Families in the lower-middle class usually live in "respectable" residential neighborhoods, and their residences are likely to be a modest single-family dwelling, a duplex, or in an apartment. Much of the social interaction of the lower-middle class takes place generally through the medium of fraternal organizations or church activities. Members of this class tend to identify themselves as middle class, and place a premium on their self-sufficiency and respectability.

As individuals they have relatively little power to influence their

[14] Reckless, *op. cit.*, p. 112.
[15] *Ibid.*
[16] Gilbert Geis, "White Collar Crime and the Heavy Electrical Equipment Antitrust Case of 1961," in Geis, ed., *The White Collar Criminal.* (New York: Atherton Press, 1968), pp. 139–151.
[17] Havighurst and Neugarten, *op. cit.*, p. 25.

community environment. They generally fail to take advantage of collective efforts to bring about community and political changes. Perhaps this is due to the fact that individuals of the lower-middle class lead relatively orderly and stable personal lives, and thus feel no overbearing compulsion to effect social changes.

Lower-middle class citizens as a group view the police in a positive light.[18] Their concern for respectability leads them to support the police, and generally believe that the police do a "good job." A large proportion of police officers come from the lower-middle class, with the job of police patrolman being an excellent example of lower-middle class occupation.

The Upper Working Class (25–40%). The upper-working class may well be the largest single class within American society in terms of its absolute numbers. The average city will most likely contain more upper-working class citizens than any other single social category. The term "working class" is very appropriate to describe the upper-working class as they constitute the bulk of the *labor* force. This includes such groups as skilled and semi-skilled workers who are employed in production industries. As individuals, they command no influence within the community as a whole, perhaps due to the fact that their occupations require relatively little skill, training, or education. This class has made significant gains in recent years in terms of income, however. Upper working-class families tend to live in small houses, or possibly mobile homes, or multiple family dwellings. Their neighborhoods tend to be crowded, with homes built close together causing problems of on-street parking of family cars and trucks.

Members of the upper-working class are not typically social joiners; in general they tend to prefer spending their spare time "around the house" or visiting with friends or neighbors. They are not personally class conscious, but do tend to be concerned about those whom they view as being "beneath" them—especially ethnic and racial minorities, and this concern often takes the form of outright prejudice.

The principal value orientation of this class is generally simply that of "making it," in economic terms. This is apt to be no small task in a world that is usually seen as hostile and highly competitive. Ability to exercise power is extremely limited to this class and they view the exercise of community and political power under a sentiment of "It's not what you know that counts but who you know."

Significantly this class is differentiated by a different group of social mores from those typically found in the upper class and the middle class.

[18] Phillip H. Ennis, *Criminalization in the United States: A Report of a National Survey.* President's Commission on Law Enforcement and the Administration of Justice, Field Survey II. (Washington, D.C.: Government Printing Office, 1967), pp. 52–72.

3

There is less emphasis on the principle of deferred gratification or planning for the future. Upper-working class individuals are more apt to be "now" oriented, taking their pleasures and opportunities as they find them. This contrasts with the upper and middle class willingness to delay gratification in favor of constructing a more solid future. Commonly found among upper-working class people is a kind of pride which demands that the individual not "back down" or that he not "take any unnecessary guff off anyone." There generally exists a greater willingness to resolve conflict by direct confrontation rather than through mediation, including the use of personal violence.

The police have considerable contact with members of the upper-working class and members of this class tend to generally accept the police as a perfectly proper and legitimate aspect of their life-space, whether or not individuals of this class have a positive or negative feeling towards the police. The police are often called to deal with family disturbances, loud neighbors, missing children, and to investigate the many burglaries, thefts, acts of vandalism and other matters involving police interaction which take place in upper-working class neighborhoods.

The Lower-Working Class (15–25%). The members of the lower-working class are at the bottom of the system of social stratification, in that they do not have prestige, and tend to be stigmatized. Occupationally they comprise the unskilled and untrained, and are chronically unemployed or underemployed. They have little in the way of possessions or wealth, and reside in the least desirable areas of a city. Welfare recipients and a disproportionately large number of the ethnic and racial minorities are of this class. They are not respected in general by members of the other classes and their social opportunities are minimal. The lower-working class constitutes the most impoverished, disenfranchised, and least autonomous segment of American society. Families in this class typically suffer from multiple problems, such as broken homes, poor health, and inadequate living conditions, among other deprivations.

Members of the lower-working class and the police are in constant contact with one another, and statistics on crime and delinquency consistently point to a relationship between the condition of poverty and crime. The exact nature of the poverty-crime relationship is complex. In a materialistically oriented society such as ours, many people who live in a state of material and social impoverishment, respond to this deprivation with various forms of criminal deviance.

Although crime occurs at all levels of our society, it appears to be most commonly associated with the lower-working class, and consequently, the enforcement activities of the police are concentrated in lower-working class areas.

Evidence indicates that in the consumer realm especially the poor are systematically exploited and illegal practices directed against them are more the rule than the exception. The poor are not able to cope with this problem,[19] and this climate has produced serious consequences. Berelson and Steiner point out that:

A deep-seated distrust of authority figures pervades... the lowest class... from childhood to old age. Suspicion is directed toward police, clergymen, teachers, doctors, public officials, public health nurses, and social workers... politicians are believed to operate a machine designed to exploit poor people... institutions for care of the disabled and the ill are believed to run for money and one has to have 'pull' to get into them... Hostility against official representatives of society is linked to convictions that they are being exploited. Some believe that they have to live in the slums because the state is taking advantage of them.[20]

The hostility and frustration of the lower-working class is often manifested in overt violence. The lower-working class lives in a social/psychological environment which includes a reliance on luck and which calls for the person to be willing to demonstrate his masculinity and to vigorously defend himself using violence when necessary. Little stock is placed in the protection of the individual's personal public reputation as it is in the other classes. Some theorists conclude that among the lower-working class there is to be found a "subculture of violence":

There is little doubt that... the 'subculture of violence' is concentrated in segments of the American population having little power —among adolescents rather than adults, in the working class rather than in the middle class, among deprived minority groups rather than white protestant Anglo-Saxons.[21]

The higher crime rates associated with low economic status prompts the police to engage in a more intense patrol of the lower-working class neighborhoods. Residents of these neighborhoods make more demands for police services than do the residents of other neighborhoods. Increased police patrol is used first, as a deterrent to would-be offenders and second, as a response to the high frequency of calls for service.

[19] See for example David Caplovitz, *The Poor Pay More.* (New York: The Free Press, 1963).
[20] Bernard Berelson and Gary A. Steiner, *Human Behavior.* (New York: Harcourt, Brace, and World, Inc., 1964), p. 456.
[21] Jackson Toby, "Violence and the Masculine Ideal: Some Quantitative Data," *The Annals*, 364 (March 1966), p. 22.

Many of the offenses committed in lower-working class areas tend to be "high visibility" type offenses, such as public drunkenness and disorderly conduct. The crowded living conditions, and perhaps boredom, bring residents of lower class neighborhoods out of doors. The street becomes the family room, the alley becomes the den, and the neighborhood bar becomes the recreation room. Problems occur, and because of high visibility, the police are able to intervene, often times without having been called. Many serious confrontations result because of the lower-working class suspicion of the police which often leads them to resent police entry into affairs into which they have not been invited. Reiss has noted: "... citizens who behave antagonistically toward the police are more likely to be treated in a hostile, authoritarian, or belittling manner by the police than citizens who behave with civility or who extend deference." [22] The result of this interaction has been a longstanding cycle of animosity between the police and the residents of these neighborhoods. Based on investigations and numerous interviews following the major riots of the 1960's, it was learned that members of the lower-working class expressed three intensely felt grievances: objections to certain police practices, unemployment and underemployment, and inadequate housing.[23]

Although members of the lower-working class frequently call upon the police for their assistance and peacekeeping roles, they also realize that they are themselves recipients of police law enforcement efforts. Minorities, whom the police have not understood or typically cared to understand, view the police as an army of occupation sent into poor neighborhoods to enforce middle-class standards. The police are exposed to a panorama of human degradation in their dealings with this strata of society, for they see their clientele at their worst. The police who deal with the bottom of the social strata often come to view them as the slag heap of humanity and accordingly afford them little respect. Minorities are over represented in lower class populations, consequently the antipathy the police feel towards the lower end of this class often becomes flavored with racial or ethnic bias.

Status

Status can be defined into two general categories, *ascribed* and *achieved*. *Ascribed* status is a function of those things over which the

[22] Albert J. Reiss, Jr., *The Police and the Public.* (New Haven: Yale University Press, 1971), p. 53.
[23] *Report of the National Advisory Commission on Civil Disorders,* Otto Kerner, Chairman. (Washington, D.C.: U.S. Government Printing Office, 1968), p. 111.

individual has no control, such as sex, race, ethnicity, etc. *Achieved* status, is that which has been acquired by the individual. Achievement can alter status; for example, through education one can become a member of a profession and in so doing alter his class membership. Certain ascribed status cannot be changed, such as race or sex. These "master" statuses which label the individual in such a fashion, make it almost impossible for him to effect significant personal change in his social environment—a problem keenly noted by black attorneys and physicians.

The significance of one's status is that it is *ranked*, with some people enjoying a higher status than others. This ranking based upon social position, determines the manner in which the individual will be treated by others. One of the chief determinants of one's status is occupation, which is intimately related to one's class. Class and status, in fact, are mutually supporting, as pointed out by Chinoy:

> Persons who occupy a common rank tend, on the whole, to associate with one another, particularly in more narrowly 'social' activities, rather than with persons of higher or lower status ... To the extent that they set themselves off from others, limit participation in certain social activities to those of similar prestige, and establish and maintain social relationships with one another, they can be said to constitute a *status group*.[24]

Status denotes place in the social pecking order, and derives primarily from class membership, occupation, race, education, and income. In our society we have developed numerous symbols which can be used to reflect the status of the individual. Type and location of residence, style of clothing, size of automobiles, etc. One's status determines his peers, as well as his social superiors and inferiors. Status in America, in spite of the massive changes wrought in recent decades, is largely controlled and defined by "... a white, Anglo-Saxon, male, Protestant culture in many respects." [25]

Police who have traditionally been drawn from the upper-working class and the lower middle class, have tended to show deference to members of the middle class and those above, and to expect the deference of those classes below them.[26] There is considerable evidence

---

[24] Chinoy, *op. cit.*, p. 175.

[25] Everett C. Hughes, *The Sociological Eye: Selected Papers on Institutions and Race*. (Chicago: Aldine-Atherton, Inc., 1971), p. 146.

[26] Herbert A. Bloch and Gilbert Geis, *Man, Crime and Society*. (New York: Random House, 1962), pp. 386–388.

3

to indicate that the status-based perspective has played a large role in the quality of justice administered in this country. The police who necessarily must exercise discretion in the enforcement of the law, have been traditionally guided by considerations and influences of class and status. Allegations of a double standard of justice in the cities—an allegation for which there has been considerable supporting evidence, has a great deal to do with the interaction dynamics of the class structure of the United States.

Changing Trends

It must be emphasized that "the notion of social-class position as a generalized summary of various statuses no longer 'fits' reality in this country as closely as it once did." [27] Various social classes formerly widely separated from one another by relatively distinctive life-styles, have broken down as a consequence of the advent of mass communications, transportation, increased industrial productivity, and the development of consumer affluence. The availability of free public education and the rise of higher education, including low cost state colleges and community colleges, have further served to narrow the gap between the classes. The occupational structure of the nation has generated a high degree of mobility, social and geographical, which has altered the distinctness of class lines.

One of the most important of the forces for change has been the great expansion of occupational opportunity. Green has noted, "the most striking modern trend in status is away from class and in the direction of occupation. The usual interest people have in the newcomer does not center on his background, but what he does for a living." [28] With the fast pace of technological progress, industry and government have broken away from their earlier "elitism" in hiring and have become more interested in talent and ability rather than on the strength of having gone to the "right" college or university. A new meritocracy has developed in which the individual's family and social background have become increasingly less important. People are recognized for what they do rather than who they are or who their parents were. With the burgeoning job market over the long run, more people are moving around the country to take advantage of employment opportunities, and this has had an impact in breaking up old, long-standing patterns of residency in the city.

[27] Arnold W. Green, *Sociology: An Analysis of Life in Modern Society*, fifth edition. (New York: McGraw-Hill Book Co., 1968), p. 200.
[28] *Ibid.*, p. 232.

In spite of the limitations on the use of class as a cubby-hole for labeling people, and despite the fact that class distinctions are becoming increasingly vague, the concept of class is still of importance to those who wish to understand the city. American cities developed physically along lines consistent with the traditional class distinctions. The upper class had its own residential areas, as did the working class etc., and to an extent this is still the case. Who one is, what he does for a living, the amount of power he has, his patterns of social interaction, and his value orientations are still related to where he will live in the city, how he will be treated by others, and how he will relate to other institutions in the city, and how those institutions will relate to him.

Although the distinct status dimensions, such as occupation, education, and ethnicity, are becoming less important in general, police officers still deal with groups of people who vary systematically from one another on the basis of class and status. Individual police officers must realize that these varied groups will have different concerns and anxieties and that the police play a significantly different role with each class.

Appendix A
The Many Faces of Crime*

Crime has many faces.

White-collar crime converts billions of dollars annually in tax evasion, price-fixing, embezzlement, swindling and consumer fraud.

Organized crime reaps hundreds of millions in gambling, loansharking, drug traffic, extortion and prostitution, corrupting officials and resorting to force, including murder when necessary, to accomplish its purposes.

Crime in the streets, as we have come to call it, encompassing a wide variety of crimes against people and against property—robbery, mugging, burglary, larceny, theft and looting—produces millions of hard-earned dollars for its perpetrators.

Crimes of passion, emotion overwhelming reason, include most murders, rapes and assaults. Conduct once deemed immoral and made criminal —gambling, prostitution, alcohol and drug abuse, profanity, abortion, homosexuality, fornication and obscenity—is a pervasive face of crime accounting for hundreds of thousands of arrests annually.

Violations of regulations designed to protect the public health, safety and convenience—traffic control, building codes, fire ordinances, minimum standards of quality, mandatory safety precautions, misrepresentation—involve highly antisocial conduct in mass society causing hundreds of thousands of deaths each year.

Revolutionary crime and illegal conduct intended to alter institutions impose rioting, mob violence, unlawful confrontation, arson and trespass on a weary society. Terrorist actions—sniping, bombing and ambushing—common in parts of the world, are an ever increasing risk in America.

Corruption in public office—bribes, payoffs, fixes, conflicts of interest— occurs in every branch of government, legislative, executive, judicial, administrative, and at every level, federal, state and local.

Police crime—wrongful arrest, brutality and blackmail—is not unknown.

Types and methods of crime are as varied as human behavior in our complex and changing society. Persons capable of crime act within the range of their opportunity, their conduct shaped by their situation. Bankers rarely rob banks. There are easier, safer, more successful ways of obtaining money. The poor do not fix prices. They do not even have the price. But among those capable of crime each finds his own way.

It is the crimes of poor and powerless people that most enrage and frighten the affluent, comfortable and advantaged majority. Riots, muggings, robbery

* SOURCE: Ramsey Clark, "The Many Faces of Crime" in *Crime in America*, New York: Simon and Schuster, 1970. © 1970 by Ramsey Clark. Reprinted by permission of Simon and Schuster.

and rape are loathsome not only because they are inherently irrational and inhumane but because they and their causes are so foreign to the experience of people with power that they are incomprehensible. If opportunities open to the poor offered more rational and humane avenues to the ends sought by crime, these means would be utilized. It is the inhumane and irrational condition of the poor that finally causes some among them to commit such crimes.

Few people think analytically when they consider the problem of crime. It is an emotional subject. First to mind come crimes we have experienced. Then we think of crimes we sense with greatest horror—those we fear most. As a result we ignore many types of crime. We are aware of the crimes decried in the headlines but remain unaware of most crimes. Comparatively rare occurrences in the world of crime become so notorious that they form our basic impression, even knowledge, of crime. But to conceive of crime as only an inhuman murder or rape or a filling station robbery is like viewing measles as a mere skin blemish. The real danger is beneath the surface. It is fever and damage to body tissue. It is mutation of basic human qualities that may be transmitted to the next generation. The simplistic diagnosis of crime leads to the wrong prescription: all that is necessary is to control a few individuals. But crimes are interrelated. Society cannot hope to control violent and irrational antisocial conduct while cunning predatory crime by people in power continues unabated.

Any nation that wishes to prevent crime must be conscious of the whole range of criminal activity.

Each type of crime exists because we are what we are. Our national character and condition create capabilities for crime, cause us to suffer them and inhibit commitment to their control. Different crimes are related in their causes and in the motivations of those who commit them. For these reasons prevention and control of nearly all categories of crimes will be achieved by the same social reforms and law enforcement practices.

To think of controlling street crime while organized crime flourishes is to ignore their clear connections. Narcotics supplied by the professionals nourish thefts, burglaries and sometimes robberies and muggings by the addicted driven to buy more drugs. To believe crimes of violence can be controlled while property crimes are widespread is to assume a discipline in a mind capable of crime which experience does not reflect. The values that permit theft from an empty car are unlikely to prevent armed robbery of a bus driver. Where white-collar crime is accepted, burglary, larceny and theft must be expected. If a poor man capable of crime had custody of the company books, he would rarely burglarize when he could embezzle. Embezzlement is easier and safer and if the perpetrator is caught, the penalties are relatively insignificant. Nothing so vindicates the unlawful conduct of a poor man, by his light, as the belief that the rich are stealing from him through overpricing and sales of defective goods or that middle class employees abscond with cash receipts.

The crimes to which we pay least attention are those committed by people of advantage who have an easier, less offensive, less visible way of doing wrong. White-collar crime is usually the act of respected and successful people. Illicit gains from white-collar crime far exceed those of all other crime combined. Crime as practiced among the poor is more dangerous and less profitable. One corporate price-fixing conspiracy criminally converted more money each year it continued than all of the hundreds of thousands of burglaries, larcenies or thefts in the entire nation during those same years. Reported bank embezzlements, deposits diverted by bank employees, cost ten times more than bank robberies each year. Bank robberies are always known because by definition bank employees are present and money is taken by force. Bank robbery is nearly always reported because insurance cannot be claimed unless it is. Embezzlement, on the other hand, is frequently not reported when restitution is possible or if the amount involved is small. Sometimes embezzlement is not discovered.

White-collar crime is the most corrosive of all crimes. The trusted prove untrustworthy; the advantaged, dishonest. It shows the capability of people with better opportunities for creating a decent life for themselves to take property belonging to others. As no other crime, it questions our moral fiber.

To the victims the consequences of white-collar crime are often more dire than those that follow theft, burglary or robbery. White-collar crime can dig deeper than the wallet in the pocket to wipe out the savings of a lifetime. The thief takes only what is in the purse or the dresser drawer at the moment of his crime. The embezzler may reach beyond to destroy the equity of a family, ruin a whole firm, or render corporate stock valueless.

Naturally we dread violent crime most—murder, rape, assault and robbery. To many these are the world of crime, and all else is insignificant. But they are only the most extreme manifestations of our capability to injure others. They tell us that people can be conditioned to the ultimate insensitivity—the capacity to take or damage life.

Violent crime springs from a violent environment. Mental illness, addiction, alcoholism, widespread property crime, the prevalence of guns, police brutality and criminal syndicates, all contribute to its dimension. Rioting is followed by weeks of arson and violent skirmishing. Children are deeply disappointed that they missed the excitement of participation and seek another chance, as earlier generations regretted being too young to fight in World Wars I and II. Disturbances on the city streets cause resonant vibrations among inmates in jails and penitentiaries who riot and damage prison property. Campus unrest both reflects and adds to general unrest. The youngest see it all and learn.

The motives of most crimes are economic. Seven of eight known serious crimes involve property. Many crimes against persons, such as robbery, mugging, kidnaping and sometimes assault and murder, are incidental to a property crime. Their main purpose is to obtain money or property.

Property crimes cost billions annually. From kids stealing candy bars to multimillion-dollar frauds, they manifest a lack of concern for other people. This insensitivity largely reflects attitudes developed through social experience. While the contributory factors are many and varied, the capability for crime develops in early childhood when character is forming. Children living in places where people have no rights that they are capable of enforcing will rarely have a regard for rights of others. Since legal rights tend to reflect important values of society, such individuals have little regard for things society considers important. To know that police take bribes, the church treasurer ran off with the building fund, the construction contractor swindled your father out of the cost of new roofing, and three of your friends make more in a night stripping cars than you make in a week washing them is not conducive to respect for law. Some finally rationalize that they would be fools to play it straight when everyone they know is on the make. The next step may be rolling a drunk. For suburban youth living in materialistic abundance the motivations for rapidly increasing property crime are different, diverse and more difficult to identify. Neglect, anxiety, family breakup, emptiness, the loneliness of the individual in huge high schools and lack of identity contribute. Faceless youngsters of affluent families steal cars, burglarize suburban homes and commit acts of malicious destruction most often because nothing else in their lives seems important.

When police crime occurs, it too brutalizes. Where police protection is purchased, it corrupts. Anyone who experiences such things or believes that they happen will have little confidence in law or its enforcement. Where can he turn? If he lives in a world of brutality, he will be brutal. If he lives in a world of corruption, he will be corrupt. The black rage of the ghetto results from an accumulation of inhuman experiences. It evolves from frustration to despair to rage. This is the ultimate product of our inhumanity. Decades ago in the South people we now say suffer black rage were called "bad niggers." Their lives often ended with lynching. We have come to see the same rage among all of our disadvantaged people of every race. We succeed in driving the last drop of pity from some.

Many crimes reflect merely the gap between our preachment and our practice. They expose the dimension of national hypocrisy. We professed to prohibit the production, transportation and sale of alcoholic beverages when we knew their widespread use would continue. The harm that comes from such self-deception is difficult to underestimate. How much respect can there be for the integrity of the law? How is equal justice possible? Only a handful of the known offenders ever felt the sanction of the Prohibition laws. Criminal empires were created because the profits were high and legitimate businesses would not compete. Relationships between police and the communities they served were seriously impaired—the respect and confidence essential to effective law enforcement destroyed. Police, however professional, can never hold the respect of the people when they must endeavor to enforce laws that the public will not obey.

In our turbulent times, when youth seriously questions the purpose, the integrity and the effectiveness of our laws, we must have the courage to face honestly and answer truthfully such difficult issues as the continued prohibition of marijuana and other mild stimulants and depressants, gambling, prostitution, abortion, and sexual relations between consenting adults. Nothing is worth while for the individual, or for his society, unless his own actions are honest. The failure to face and answer such issues is as dishonest as the false answer. The consequence in the lives of millions is immense.

There are still many, nurtured on the Puritan ethic, who believe drink and debauchery are so much more alluring to the multitudes than justice and rectitude that they conceive of goodness as merely self-denial. They insist that the law prohibit those who would not deny themselves. But prohibition is impossible. Forces more powerful than the fear of police are at work. If society really intends to control gambling, drugs and prostitution, it must work to educate, to humanize, and to civilize.

Laws that cannot be enforced corrupt. Partial enforcement of laws against known violators is inherently unequal except in the most sensitive and skillful hands, and usually even then. We become a government of men rather than of laws, where men choose who will be arrested and who will remain free for the same infraction. Those arrested are bitter, while those permitted to continue unlawful activity corrupt others and themselves. The watching public is cynical.

Political campaign financing is a classic illustration of the hypocrisy we will tolerate. At the federal level, and generally at the state, a major portion of the funds for political campaigns is raised in violation of law. Federal law says that not more than $3 million shall be spent by a presidential nominee in pursuit of that office. National parties have spent many times that amount in recent elections. Estimates of the total cost of the presidential campaigns of 1964 and 1968 exceed $100 million each. The Federal Corrupt Practices Act limits candidates for the United States House of Representatives to $10,000 and for the Senate to $25,000. Candidates have spent more than $1 million seeking a Senate seat. It is impossible for a major candidate with opposition to comply with such unrealistic limits. Evasion is forced, because the practicalities and prior practice leave no choice. The losers are the law and the people.

Criminal codes must be simplified. Unenforceable laws, antiquated laws, laws that are inconsistent with the moral standards of the public or the economic facts of life must be repealed. New laws and new techniques of control relevant to the needs of the day must take their place. Only then can society look at crime with a straight face. Only then can the law be an effective instrument of public policy.

Of the many faces of crime, the most tragic is never recognized by many. The rubble it leaves in wasted human lives exceeds many times over all the injury of violent crime. Assaults, rapes, even murders are counted in the thousands and tens of thousands. But millions fall victim to the cruelest of all crimes, which takes its toll in miserable, empty and wasted lives. It is the crime of power over impotence—the crime of a society that does not insure equal protection of the laws. It is crime against people who have no rights— the crime of a society which seeks to maintain order without law. From it grows most crime of violence and much property crime.

It is the crime of failing to provide fire escapes, condoning faulty wiring and other fire hazards, permitting overcrowding in unsanitary tenements infested with rats, all in violation of ordinances with criminal penalties. It is the illegal sale of rotten meat and impure bread at excessive prices—and racial discrimination in employment in violation of federal statutes and state fair employment practices acts.

It is the willful violation of basic constitutional rights. The United States Supreme Court in 1954 declared racially segregated schools inherently un-equal. That most fundamental of rights has been denied to more than 95 per cent of a whole generation of black students in the public schools of the eleven states that were the Confederacy—a majority of the black school children of the nation. Does government have a greater duty to prevent a physical assault than the theft of an education? Would you rather have your child brutally beaten or deprived of his chance for a good education? Poor young blacks wind up suffering both. The cost to America of this one huge crime of deprivation is immeasurable.

Our society permits conditions to exist in which laws cannot be enforced. Gambling, narcotics, prostitution, extortion and loansharking are open and notorious. Police see it and know it. Areas of our cities are so dangerous that neither life nor what little property people who live there have is safe. The basic solution for most crime is economic—homes, health, education, employment, beauty. If the law is to be enforced—and rights fulfilled for the poor—we must end poverty. Until we do, there will be no equal protection of the laws. To permit conditions that breed antisocial conduct to continue is our greatest crime. We pay dearly for it.

4

Urban Population Factors
and the Police

Since the police concern themselves with events that typically involve people, it is important for them to understand population factors as they in turn reflect the urban environments in which they must work. This chapter will deal with such population factors as size and density; density and race; the age/sex distribution; daytime versus nighttime population shifts; intracity social patterns and crime; and, census tracts and their uses. The relevance of these concepts to the functions of the police will be discussed.

When the size of a city is mentioned, what is generally referred to is its population rather than the area included within its legal boundaries. However, if one considers size on the basis of population alone, then certain other considerations must also be taken into account. The failure to do so could produce distortions of such a magnitude as to invalidate the concept.

The designation "city" normally refers to a political subdivision of a State and alludes to a defined area over which a municipal corporation has been established and for which local government services are provided. In other words, the legal city is the one which the municipal police department serves. However, the population of the legal city may be quite misleading when one simply considers the "size" of the city. The city may actually be part of an *urbanized area,* which consists of a central city (or cities) and the surrounding closely settled territory. In that case a city's police department will not only have its own base population to cope with, but will also be influenced by the population of the surrounding areas. Or, a city may be part of a Standard Metropolitan Statistical Area (SMSA). The SMSA is a designation devised by the Bureau of the Census and it basically involves two considerations. First, it includes a city (or cities) of specified population—usually 50,000 —which constitutes the central city and which identifies the county in which it is located as the central county. Second, it includes economic and social relationships with contiguous counties which are metropolitan in character, so that the periphery of the specific metropolitan area may be determined. In fact, a SMSA may even cross state lines (Such as the St. Louis, Missouri/Illinois SMSA).

The city of Houston, Texas is a good illustration of these relationships. Houston was ranked as the sixth most populous *city* in the 1970 census, with a population of 1,232,022.[1] However, the *urbanized area* of Houston showed it to be the thirteenth most populous urbanized area in the United States, with a population of 1,677,863.[2] Houston is also the central city of a Standard Metropolitan Statistical Area, and is ranked as the thirteenth most populous SMSA with 1,985,096 persons.[3] Finally, Houston is the county seat of Harris County, Texas, which is the seventh most populous county in the United States, with a population of 1,741,912.[4]

It can be easily seen that to think of Houston solely in terms of the population of the *legal city* alone is to invite a distorted picture of that area's population structure. Yet on the other hand, the Houston Police Department is restricted in its policing activities to the corporate city of Houston, for its jurisdiction is limited to the legal city. Table 1 shows the twenty largest population centers in the United States according to three different definitions.

One of the factors most closely related to the population of a city is its *population density*. The population density of a city generally refers to the number of persons per square mile of *land area*. The use of land area as a base makes sense because the total city area would also include lakes and rivers and to include them would deflate the actual population density.

Population densities vary enormously from one city to another, and there are a number of factors which account for this variation. In the first place, density will be affected by the extent to which population increase and area expansion have kept pace. What this means is that some cities have been able to expand their corporate boundaries to accommodate their expanding populations; that is, such cities have grown outward from their original boundaries and have incorporated what would otherwise be suburban areas. On the other hand, some cities have been locked in because their legal boundaries are fixed due to the fact that they are surrounded by incorporated areas and cannot expand their boundaries. In this latter case, the central city may be surrounded by other, smaller incorporated cities but the suburban cities may provide much of the labor force for the central city. In such a case the population of the legal city does not accurately reflect the total number of people who impact on the central city, and population growth within the central city automatically increases that city's population density.

Another factor affecting population densities within a city would be site limitations which restrict land use. For example, extremely rugged

[1] *County and City Data Book, 1972,* United States Department of Commerce, Bureau of the Census. Washington, D.C.: U.S. Government Printing Office, 1972.

[2] *Ibid.*

[3] *Ibid.*

[4] *Ibid.*

TABLE 1

The Twenty Largest Population Centers in the United States
in 1970 According to Three Different Designations*

CITY			URBANIZED AREA			SMSA		
Rank	City	Population	Rank	Area	Population	Rank	SMSA	Population
1	New York City	7,895,563	1	N.Y.C.-Northeastern N.J.	16,206,841	1	NYC	11,575,740
2	Chicago	3,369,357	2	Los Angeles-Long Beach	8,351,266	2	Los Angeles/Long Beach	7,040,697
3	Los Angeles	2,809,813	3	Chicago-Northwestern Ind.	6,714,578	3	Chicago	6,977,611
4	Philadelphia	1,949,996	4	Philadelphia, Pa./N.J.	4,021,066	4	Philadelphia Pa/NJ	4,822,245
5	Detroit	1,513,601	5	Detroit	3,970,584	5	Detroit	4,203,548
6	Houston	1,232,022	6	San Francisco/Oakland	2,987,850	6	San Francisco/Oakland	3,108,026
7	Baltimore	905,787	7	Boston	2,652,575	7	Washington D.C.—Md.-Va.	2,861,638
8	Dallas	844,401	8	Washington D.C.—Md-Va.	2,481,489	8	Boston	2,753,700
9	Washington, D.C.	756,510	9	Cleveland	1,959,880	9	Pittsburgh	2,401,362
10	Cleveland	750,879	10	St. Louis, Mo./Ill.	1,882,944	10	St. Louis Mo./Ill.	2,363,346
11	Indianapolis	746,302	11	Pittsburgh	1,846,042	11	Baltimore	2,071,016
12	Milwaukee	717,372	12	Minneapolis/St. Paul	1,704,423	12	Cleveland	2,063,729
13	San Francisco	715,674	13	Houston	1,677,863	13	Houston	1,985,031
14	San Diego	697,027	14	Baltimore	1,579,781	14	Newark	1,859,096
15	San Antonio	654,153	15	Dallas	1,338,684	15	Minneapolis/St. Paul	1,813,587
16	Boston	641,071	16	Milwaukee	1,252,457	16	Dallas	1,556,324
17	Memphis	623,530	17	Seattle/Everett	1,238,107	17	Seattle/Everett	1,424,611
18	St. Louis	622,236	18	Miami, Fla.	1,219,661	18	Anaheim/Santa Anna/ Garden Grove	1,420,676
19	New Orleans	593,471	19	San Diego	1,198,323	19	Milwaukee	1,403,887
20	Phoenix	581,562	20	Atlanta	1,172,778	20	Atlanta	1,390,247

SOURCE: County and City Data Book, 1972. U.S. Department of Commerce, Bureau of the Census. Information reflects 1970 census data.

terrain or marshy land that would not be conducive to residential construction would therefore force the city's population into a smaller space and accordingly increase the density of the population. Also, older cities frequently have narrow streets and small lot sizes, which bring more people into closer physical proximity thus increasing the density. There are other factors which also play a role, such as constructions patterns (row houses, for example increase density) and variations in the proportions of land used for residential as opposed to commercial use.

Population density is apparently related to the size of the urban place. Table 2 shows that there was a significant correlation between the rank orders of the twenty most populous cities on the basis of their populations and population densities. In addition, the Census Bureau has reported that among urban places, the number of inhabitants per square mile decreased as the size of the place decreased. In other words, as total size decreases, so does the density of the population.

The Federal Bureau of Investigation has reported that one of the conditions that affects the volume and type of crime includes the "density and size of the community population and the metropolitan area of which it is a part." [5] As the F.B.I. statement implies, the significance of population density is relative to the specific area under consideration. However, high population densities are often associated with crowding. Obviously, the higher the density per square mile, the more the residents will be crowded together. High densities in urban centers are also typically associated with closer proximity to the downtown business area, higher frequency of multistory apartments, walk-up apartments, and row houses. These characteristics are in turn generally associated with lower income and lower socioeconomic status, higher rates of unemployment, and a greater demand for police services.

Population Density and Race

The most dense populations in urban centers have in recent decades also come to be associated with the concentration of blacks, especially in eastern and western cities. This is because the black population in the United States has become increasingly more urbanized and more metropolitan than has the white population. The Kerner Commission has reported that "Almost all Negro population growth is occurring within metropolitan areas, primarily within central cities" and that "... central cities are steadily becoming more heavily Negro, while the

---

[5] *Crime in the United States: Uniform Crime Reports, 1972*, United States Department of Justice, Federal Bureau of Investigation, Washington, D.C.: U.S. Government Printing Office, 1973, p. vii.

TABLE 2
A Correlation Matrix
of The Twenty Most Populous American Cities
Correlating Rank Order of Selected Variables, 1970†

	POPULATION	POPULATION DENSITY	PERCENT OF POPULATION BLACK	RATIO OF POLICE TO CITIZENS	PERCENT OF FAMILIES WITH LESS THAN $3000 INCOME	RATIO TO POPULATION OF SERIOUS CRIMES REPORTED TO POLICE
POPULATION	1.00	.55**	.28	.35	.18	.14
POPULATION DENSITY	.55**	1.00	.26	.78**	.05	.25
PERCENT OF POPULATION BLACK	.28	.26	1.00	.56**	.57**	.47*
RATIO OF POLICE TO CITIZENS	.35	.78**	.56**	1.00	.29	.44*
PERCENT OF FAMILIES WITH INCOMES LESS THAN $3000	.18	.05	.57**	.29	1.00	.35
RATIO TO POPULATION OF SERIOUS CRIMES REPORTED TO POLICE	.14	.25	.47*	.44*	.35	1.00

†Based on 1970 population data, Bureau of the Census.

*P > .05
**P > .01

4

urban fringes around them remain almost entirely white." [6] According to the Bureau of the Census, on the basis of data gathered from the 1970 census, 58.2 percent of the Negro population was found to reside in central cities and 74.3 percent of the Negro population resided in Standard Metropolitan Statistical Areas. This inner city black population represented a 50.6 percent increase from 1950 to 1960, and a 32.1 percent increase from 1960 to 1970.

The inward migration of blacks into the cities has brought about a racial transition in many central city neighborhoods, resulting in an exodus of whites from the central cities and producing a concentration of blacks. It has been this massive inward migration of poor blacks into the central cities, and the flight of the whites out of them, that has produced the racial ghettoes with high population densities and high crime rates (the 1972 Uniform Crime Reports indicated that 53.7 percent of the arrests for violent crimes involved black suspects, and that blacks accounted for 31.5 percent of those arrested for property crimes).[7] These conditions have also produced a general aura of despair and insecurity in the urban ghettoes.

In general, it has been found that crime rates in large cities tend to be much higher than those in other areas; furthermore, within these cities the crime rates are higher in disadvantaged black areas than anywhere else. Specifically, within the larger cities the highest actual *risk* areas are the older neighborhoods which encircle the downtown business district.

With respect to crime rates in these areas, the Kerner Commission has pointed out that:

> Two facts are crucial to an understanding of the effects of high crime rates in racial ghettoes: most of these crimes are committed by a small minority of the residents, and the principal victims are the residents themselves.
> ... the majority of law abiding citizens who live in disadvantaged Negro areas face much higher probabilities of being victimized than residents of most higher income areas, including almost all suburbs. For nonwhites, the probability of being raped is 3.7 times higher among nonwhite women, and the probability of being robbed is 3.5 times higher for nonwhites in general.[8]

It should also be pointed out in passing that high crime rates have

[6] *Report of the National Advisory Commission on Civil Disorders*, Otto Kerner, Chairman. Washington, D.C.: U.S. Government Printing Office, 1968, p. 118.
[7] *Uniform Crime Reports, op. cit.*, p. 130.
[8] *National Advisory Commission on Civil Disorders, op. cit.*, pp. 134–135.

consistently been associated with these dense inner areas, regardless of the race or ethnic character of the residents. The high crime rates among urban blacks may not be attributed to them because they are black, but rather because urban blacks tend to enjoy far fewer advantages than their white urban and suburban counterparts. For example, according to census data, the average of the median salaries for the white families in the twenty most populous American cities in 1970 was $10,592. The average of the median salaries for the black families in the same cities was $6,926, or about 35 percent less.

Because of the higher crime rates and the frequency of calls for service, the police typically engage in a more aggressive patrol of high population density areas, as was noted in chapter 3. Because of their responsibility for maintaining order and insuring public safety, the disruptive conditions typical of crowded areas often bring the police into sharp conflict with the residents. In the case of black ghettoes, the police have come (in many cities) to symbolize white dominance, racism, and economic repression. Occasionally the police do in fact reflect such attitudes, and when this is the case it only serves to widen the existing gap between the lower class minority citizen and the policeman.

The relationship between crime and population density has been widely debated. It has been shown that crime rates tend to be highest in the inner city and that they diminish as one moves out towards the suburbs. It has also been shown that population densities tend to follow the same pattern. However, such a relationship is more *apparent* than it is actually *causal*. High density alone would no doubt provide more opportunity for many types of crimes, but the key seems to be the *quality* of the density. As Harries has pointed out,

> It would seem that conventional measures of population density (persons per acre or persons per acre of residential land) are quite inadequate as predictors of criminal environments. A 'crowding index,' such as person per room, is apparently a much better measure since it approximates human reactions to space and is more likely to help us predict areas of social pathology.[9]

Where large numbers of people are crowded together under conditions which strain the human capacity for effective adjustment and adaptation, there may indeed be good grounds to anticipate conflict, disorder, violence and an increased need for the presence of the police.

Highly populated urban locations have been associated with increased

[9] Keith D. Harries, *The Geography of Crime and Justice.* New York: McGraw-Hill Book Company, 1974, p. 83.

4

needs for police services and hence with larger police departments. Table 3 shows the ratio of police to citizens in the 20 most populous American cities.

TABLE 3

Population, Number of Police Personnel,
and Ratio of Police to Citizens in
the Twenty Most Populous American
Cities*

CITY	RANK	POPULATION	NUMBER OF POLICEMEN	RATIO OF POLICE TO CITIZENS
New York	1	7,895,563	31,671	1 – 249
Chicago	2	3,369,357	12,961	1 – 260
Los Angeles	3	2,809,813	6,806	1 – 413
Philadelphia	4	1,949,996	7,780	1 – 251
Detroit	5	1,513,601	5,159	1 – 293
Houston	6	1,232,022	1,794	1 – 687
Baltimore	7	905,787	4,082	1 – 222
Dallas	8	844,401	1,635	1 – 516
Washington, D.C.	9	756,510	5,055	1 – 150
Cleveland	10	750,879	2,464	1 – 305
Indianapolis	11	746,302	1,090	1 – 685
Milwaukee	12	717,372	2,088	1 – 344
San Francisco	13	715,674	1,820	1 – 393
San Diego	14	697,027	920	1 – 758
San Antonio	15	654,153	912	1 – 717
Boston	16	641,071	2,798	1 – 229
Memphis	17	623,530	1,089	1 – 573
St. Louis	18	622,236	2,220	1 – 280
New Orleans	19	593,471	1,454	1 – 408
Phoenix	20	581,562	943	1 – 617

*Based on 1970 census data

The number of police officers to citizens in the twenty largest cities ranges from 1–150 in Washington, D.C. to 1–758 in San Diego. However, Washington, D.C. has the fifth most dense population in the twenty most populous cities while San Diego ranks 17 out of the twenty. As can be seen in table 2, there was a correlation of .78 between the rank order of the twenty largest American cities (on the basis of population) with respect to population density and the ratio of police to citizens. This high relationship suggests that other factors being considered, the more dense the population of a city the more likely it is to have a larger police department.

From a pragmatic point of view, those areas of the city which have the densest populations are also likely to be areas which contain the ingredients for crime and delinquency and which also call for the increased presence of the police.

Age and Sex Structure of the Population

The F.B.I. has reported that "when only the serious crimes are considered, 19 percent of all arrests in 1972 were for persons under the age of 15 and 44 percent were under 18 years of age." [10] They further reported that "male arrests outnumbered female arrests by almost 6 to 1 in 1972." [11] The Uniform Crime Reports thus clearly indicate that crime is associated with young males more than with any other group.

This in turn would lead to the logical hypothesis that cities with lower median ages would have higher crime rates. However, this hypothesis is difficult to substantiate, because other factors also affect crime rates, and it is the combination of such factors interacting together which would give the best predictor of crime.

When the status of being young and being male is also associated with lower socioeconomic status, crowded living conditions, lower levels of education and diminished opportunities because of racial or ethnic status, then it is reasonable to predict higher arrest rates and higher rates of official delinquency.

The staffing and deployment of personnel within police departments should concern itself with these as well as other factors when the department is developing its various strategies. Perhaps the police department will reach a point of diminishing returns by simply adding patrolmen to work areas in which large numbers of youths live in crowded, counterproductive circumstances. The actual need may be for a combination of police and other services. This philosophy is echoed by the National Advisory Commission on Criminal Justice Standards and Goals in their Standard #3.1, which recommends that:

> Youth services bureaus should be established to focus on the special problems of youth in the community. The goals may include diversion of juveniles from the justice system; provision of a wide range of services to youth through advocacy and brokerage, offering crisis intervention as needed; modification of the system through program coordination and advocacy; and youth development.
>
> 1. Priorities among goals should be locally set.
> 2. Priorities among goals (as well as selection of functions) should be based on a careful analysis of the community, including

[10] *Uniform Crime Reports, op. cit.,* p. 34.
[11] *Ibid.*

4

an inventory of existing services and a systematic study of youth problems in the individual community.

3. Objectives should be measurable, and progress toward them should be scrutinized by evaluative research.[12]

Daytime/Nighttime Population Shifts

The Census Bureau counts people where they sleep. In fact, the actual physical distribution of people as reflected in a population map would probably be most accurate at around 3:00 a.m. when most people are home in bed.

The significance of this is that the population of a city is physically mobile and just exactly where the people are will tend to be a function of the time of day. Some of the ways in which the daytime population distributes itself were studied by Wier, who studied the daytime population of Winnipeg, Canada.[13]

Wier divided the daytime population into four groups. The first group was residential and consisted of housewives, small children, and domestic help. The second group, which he classified as "institutional," was composed of people in hospitals, nursing homes, schools and colleges, and other institutional settings. The third category contained the employed and was composed of people working in specific locations, primarily in the industrial and business areas of the city. The fourth and final group contained transients, such as shoppers, travelers, pedestrians, and those driving in their automobiles. Although the purpose of Wier's study was one of the methodology of data collection, it indicated the ways in which people spatially distribute themselves during the day.

The periodic shifts in population pose various kinds of problems for the police. Perhaps the most obvious problem is a direct function of the actual *movement* of the population: traffic. Traffic volumes vary by time of day, with particular density in the mornings and evenings as people go to and from their places of employment.

The police frequently experience increased demands for their services in the evening hours when the bulk of the labor force is not at work and when they are pursuing personal interests. Family quarrels, disturbances, and general peacekeeping calls tend to be sufficiently high during the evening hours that a number of cities have found it in their interest to

[12] National Advisory Commission on Criminal Justice Standards and Goals, *Community Crime Prevention.* Washington, D.C.: U.S. Government Printing Office, 1973, p. 70.
[13] Thomas R. Wier, "A Survey of the Daytime Population of Winnipeg," *Queen's Quarterly,* Vol. 67, No. 4 (Winter 1961).

create a "fourth watch" to deal with the increased volume of activity (such a watch works from about six in the evening until two in the morning). The problem for the police is that they must schedule their patrol and traffic activities at those times and in those places where the demand for them will be the greatest. This is known as the "proportional distribution" of the patrol force, and is based in part on the location and mobility of the population.

Exactly where the police are to be deployed (that is, the actual beats they work), should therefore be based on the percentage of the police problems found within a given area:

> The selected crimes, arrests, and calls for services should be separated by hour of the day and day of the week within each reporting district, grid map, or census tract. The reporting district totals for each shift should then be weighted by the average number of minutes required to handle each of these activities on the various shifts.[14]

This procedure thus keys the response of the police into the demand for their services and measures them in such a fashion as to take into consideration population densities and movements.

Intracity Social Patterns

An urban area does not display a consistent and uniform social landscape: cities represent an array of lifestyles, socioeconomic statuses, ethnic classifications, and residency distributions. These differences become apparent to the casual observer as he drives through a city and notes the different kinds of neighborhoods through which he passes. This is the social geography of the city, and actually amounts to a series of subcommunities within the city.

The most obvious aspect of the intracity social pattern lies in the visible spectrum. Generally, as one moves away from the central city, one passes through areas of multi-occupant buildings (apartment houses and older homes which have been chopped up into apartments), apartments situated near or over shops, and duplexes. These somewhat crowded areas gradually thin out and are replaced by zones that tend to be more exclusively residential in nature and which contain a higher proportion of single family dwellings and are situated on larger lots.

[14] National Advisory Commission on Criminal Justice Standards and Goals, *Police.* Washington, D.C.: U.S. Government Printing Office, 1973, p. 70.

4

The outer residential areas often include off-street parking, fewer commercial establishments, and tend to offer a more aesthetic appearance to the viewer.

These neighborhoods also represent gradations in other respects. For example, Pyle has shown a close correspondence among certain health factors (such as tuberculosis, infant mortality, and VD) and residency in densely populated, lower socioeconomic inner city areas.[15]

Rates of mental illness have also been linked with specific geographic patterns indicating that some types of mental disorder are consistently associated with certain types of neighborhoods within the city.

Sociologists have also shown that crime and delinquency rates are related to geographic patterns within the city. One of the earliest and best known studies describing crime and urban ecology was that conducted by Clifford Shaw and Henry McKay in Chicago.[16] Shaw and McKay mapped delinquency rates and were thus able to study the distribution of delinquency within the city. In their study of Chicago and other cities, they were able to correlate crime and delinquency with such factors as substandard housing, poverty, foreign nativity, and mobility.

Social patterns and crime were also studied by Calvin Schmid in a study of Seattle.[17] He found that the central segment of the city contained 15.5 percent of the city's population; yet over a three year period, 47 percent of the offenses known to the police occurred there. Schmid also found a difference in the types of crimes committed in different areas of the city; in fact, he found that "The spatial patterning of the different types of crime shows a striking variation in incidence from one part of the city to another." [18] He thus noted that skid-row ranked highest for such crimes as vagrancy, disorderly conduct, and drunkenness. On the other hand, the Central Business District ranked highest in shoplifting and check frauds. Schmid also showed that in Seattle the areas of highest educational status ranked relatively low in crime, but that the areas of lowest educational status displayed a relatively high crime rate. He subjected a complex wealth of sociological and population data to factor analysis, which is a mathematical technique used in reducing a large number of variables to a small number of independent factors. In so doing, he discovered a number of factors which cast interesting light on social and demographic relationships.

[15] George F. Pyle, Some Examples of Urban Medical Geography. Unpublished M.A. Thesis (University of Chicago, 1968).
[16] Clifford R. Shaw and Henry McKay, Juvenile Delinquency and Urban Areas. Chicago: University of Chicago Press, 1942.
[17] Calvin S. Schmid, "Urban Crime Areas: Part I," and "Urban Crime Areas: Part II," American Sociological Review, 25, 1960, pp. 527–542 and 655–678.
[18] Ibid., p. 531.

One factor (low social cohesion and low family status) was found to be associated with "older, declining, lower status" neighborhoods.[19] These neighborhoods contained, among other things, a high proportion of women in the labor force (and hence not at home with small children), low levels of education, high rates of unemployment, a high percentage of older persons, high population mobility, and lack of home ownership. Also associated with this Factor were "relatively high crime rates for automobile theft, theft from automobile, indecent exposure, shoplifting, non-residential robbery, and check fraud."[20]

Another Factor (Low Social Cohesion—Low Occupational Status) emphasized the attributes which are often associated with low occupation and low status. Such neighborhoods contained larger proportions of laborers and unemployed persons as well as a high proportion of Negroes and foreign born whites. They tended to reside in older housing (constructed prior to 1920). This group tended to have a low degree of social solidarity but not as much of a lack of family life as those families falling within the first Factor. In terms of crime, this group was associated with fighting, robbery, non-residential burglary, and disorderly conduct.

The third Factor (Low Family and Economic Status) reflected a pattern which included a large proportion of unmarried and unemployed males and high rates of unemployment. This was a skid-row syndrome and produced a crime picture which included drunkenness, vagrancy, lewdness, petty larceny, and fighting.

Another Factor isolated was that of race. This factor indicated a "significant association of the Negro population and non-residential robbery and non-residential burglary."[21] This latter relationship indicated a specific relationship between concentrations of Negroes and non-residential robbery and burglary; however, this simply serves to underscore repeated findings that the higher official crime rate for Negroes is the result of the wider distribution among blacks of the characteristics associated with lower class status and with crime.

The reasons that some crimes are committed in higher numbers in some parts of the city rather than in others are many, but one example would be opportunity. For instance, there are more goods to shoplift in the Central Business District, and the commercial nature of the Central Business District makes it much more vulnerable to certain types of fraud and theft. The crowded areas which surround the downtown zone concentrate large numbers of people close together and provides opportunities for burglaries, thefts, and robberies.

[19] *Ibid.*, p. 535.
[20] *Ibid.*
[21] *Ibid.*, p. 538.

Another circumstance which combines with opportunity to enhance the likelihood of crime is frustration. This includes frustration at the inability to use legitimate means to acquire things one desires because of low income and low education. The frustration which results from living in inadequate housing under unpleasant circumstances can also produce hostility. These frustrations may erupt into aggressive acts against property or against the person, as the opportunity presents itself. This is not to say that a person in such circumstances is not responsible for his conduct; it merely points out that where and how one lives and works can have a significant impact on how he behaves.

The police do not shape the demography of the community. Indeed, they must equip, organize, and deploy themselves because of it. The ways in which people in the various parts of the city live and interact call forth various kinds of responses from the police. Low crime rate areas tend to emphasize more service activity on the part of the police, whereas the areas which typically have the highest crime rates accordingly produce more demands for law enforcement. The fact that the police must react according to the demands of the intracity social patterns has from time to time given rise to the impression that there is a double standard in the quality of the administration of justice, as was noted in the last chapter. Although this is true to a certain extent, these differences also reflect different needs for different kinds of police services. Because of this variety of intracity social patterning, the National Advisory Commission on Criminal Justice Standards and Goals (in their report on Community Crime Prevention) has made these recommendations on police services.

> Allocation of personnel and mobile equipment for police protection should be based on at least the following factors relating to the needs of a particular area:
> a. Size of the land area;
> b. Density and nature of the population (especially youth);
> c. Reported incidence of total offenses in the area;
> d. Physical environment (street and open space lighting); and,
> e. Traffic patterns.[22]

It is important to also note that the National Advisory Commission on Criminal Justice Standards and Goals has emphasized the great need for the effective delivery of *all* social services. This approach is far-sighted in nature because it leans toward correcting situations which contribute to criminal deviance as opposed to simply "policing" the community.

[22] National Advisory Commission on Criminal Justice Standards and Goals, *Community Crime Prevention, op. cit.,* pp. 37–38.

Census Tract Data

Police planners require information if their plans and projections are to have meaning. They obviously need data pertaining to the offenses handled by the police, but they also need data concerning the community which must be policed. In many cities a wealth of information is currently available—and very frequently overlooked. This is the data gathered by the Bureau of the Census. The Bureau of the Census collects information on a number of units, one of the most significant of which is the *census tract*.

Census tracts are areas within large cities which have been established for statistical purposes. A tract is formulated as a cooperative effort between a local committee and the Bureau of the Census. The original concept was first proposed in 1906 by Dr. Walter Laidlaw of New York City. Dr. Laidlaw was convinced of the need for data pertaining to homogeneous subdivisions of the city so that neighborhoods could be effectively studied. The idea gradually grew, and tract statistics from the 1970 census have been published for 241 areas. All of the Standard Metropolitan Statistical Areas (with the exception of those developed as a result of the 1970 census) have been tracted.

Census tracts are generally constructed so that they are relatively uniform with respect to population characteristics, economic status, and living conditions. Although the average census tract has about 4,000 residents, the total number within a tract can be much larger or much smaller. Census tracts are established with the idea of keeping them relatively permanent so that changes in population and housing over a period of time can be studied and plotted.

The information given in Appendix A is extracted directly from Appendix B of the 1970 *Census Tracts* published by the Bureau of the Census. It gives the definitions and explanations of the subject characteristics enumerated in the census tract reports.

The demographic and social information gathered by the Bureau of the Census can be of considerable value to the police. The police can correlate their offense/offender/victim data (which is gathered in the process of responding to offenses which become known to the police) with the information gathered by the Census Bureau. In this way, census tracts can be used for the mapping of demands for police service, and within the census tracts themselves correlations may be established between demands for police service and specific social or demographic variables. This should reveal in fairly clear detail what kinds of demands for police services may be expected from the various parts of town, and should provide a good predictive basis for the allocation of police manpower.

Perhaps one of the most interesting possible uses of this type of information would be in the construction of police beats and districts. Most large police departments divide the city into large districts which are in turn broken down into beats. Each beat is an area patrolled by one or more police officers during a tour of duty. Although officers often leave their beat during the course of a shift, it is none the less the basic working territory. Beat allocations are determined in a number of ways, but most frequently on the basis of service demands and the geographic layout of the city. Smaller beats tend to be those with the greatest demands for police services. If, however, the police department in a large city would divide its beats according to census tracts (or the subdivisions within them, such as the enumeration district or block) then the officers working those beats would have a wealth of social and demographic information directly associated with the areas they must patrol.

Appendix A
Definitions and Explanations of Subject Characteristics*

Census Data: Population Characteristics

Age

The age classification is based on the age of the person in completed years as of April 1, 1970, and was determined from the reply to questions on age and on month and year of birth.

Race

Data are shown for two racial categories, white and Negro. The category "white" includes persons who indicated their race as white, as well as persons who did not classify themselves in one of the specific race categories on the questionnaire but entered Mexican, Puerto Rican, or a response suggesting Indo-European stock. The category "Negro" includes persons who indicated their race as Negro or Black, as well as persons who did not classify themselves in one of the specific race categories on the questionnaire but who had such entries as Jamaican, Trinidadian, West Indian, Haitian, and Ethiopian. All other racial categories, such as American Indian, Japanese, and Chinese, are included in the total but not shown separately. The classification by race shown for occupied housing units refers to the race of the head of the household occupying the unit.

Nativity, Parentage and Country of Origin

The category "native" comprises persons born in the United States, the Commonwealth of Puerto Rico or an outlying area of the United States, or at sea. Also included in this category is the small number of persons who, although they were born in a foreign country, have at least one native American parent. The category "foreign-born" includes all persons not classified as native. The category "native of native parentage" comprises native persons both of whose parents are also natives of the United States. "Native of foreign or mixed parentage" comprises native persons one or both of whose parents are foreign born.

The category "foreign stock" includes the foreign-born population and the native population of foreign or mixed parentage. In this report, persons of foreign stock are classified according to their country of origin. Natives of foreign parentage whose parents were born in different countries are classified according to the country of birth of the father. Natives of mixed

* SOURCE: *1970 Census of Population and Housing: Census Tracts.* Washington, D.C.: U.S. Government Printing Office (1972), Appendix B.

parentage are classified according to the country of birth of the foreign-born parent.

Spanish Heritage

In the census tract reports, separate tables are presented for the population of Spanish heritage, which is variously identified in the reports for different areas: in 42 States and the District of Columbia it is identified as "Persons of Spanish language"; in five Southwestern States, as "Persons of Spanish language or Spanish surname"; and in the Middle Atlantic States, as "Persons of Puerto Rican birth or parentage." Similarly, separate housing statistics are presented for housing units in these categories, identified on the basis of the classification of the household head occupying the unit. The specific definitions involved in identifying these population groups are given below.

Spanish Language

Persons of Spanish language comprise persons of Spanish mother tongue (see definition below) and all other persons in families which the head or wife reported Spanish as his or her mother tongue. A housing unit is classified as occupied by persons of Spanish language if the head or his wife reported Spanish as his or her mother tongue.

Spanish Surname

In five Southwestern States (Arizona, California, Colorado, New Mexico, and Texas) persons with Spanish surnames are identified. Separate statistics are presented, in these States, for persons of Spanish language combined with all additional persons of Spanish surname. These additional persons are shown in the category "Other persons of Spanish surname."

Puerto Rican Birth or Parentage

The population of Puerto Rican birth or parentage includes persons born in Puerto Rico and persons born in the United States or an outlying area with one or both parents born in Puerto Rico. Statistics for this group are shown for areas in New York, New Jersey, and Pennsylvania.

Spanish Mother Tongue

Mother tongue is defined as the language spoken in the person's home when he was a child.

Household

A household includes all the persons who occupy a group of rooms or a single room which constitutes a housing unit (see definition of housing unit, below). The average population per household is obtained by dividing the population in households by the number of household heads.

The population per household for Negroes and persons of Spanish heritage, may not in all cases be a true representation of the household size for these groups. For example, some persons of a given group may be roomers or domestic employees living with household heads of a different ethnic classification.

Relationship to Head of Household

Four categories of relationship to head of household are recognized in this report:

1. *Head of household.*—One person in each household is designated as the "head," that is, the person who is regarded as the head by the members of the household. However, if a married woman living with her husband was reported as the head, her husband was considered the head for the purpose of simplifying the tabulations. Two types of household heads are distinguished—the head of a family and a primary individual. A family head is a household head living with one or more persons related to him by blood, marriage, or adoption. A primary individual is a household head living alone or with nonrelatives only.

2. *Wife of head.*—A woman married to and living with a household head, including women in common-law marriages as well as women in formal marriages.

3. *Other relative of head.*—All persons related to the head of the household by blood, marriage, or adoption except "wife of head."

4. *Not related to head.*—All persons in the household not related to the head by blood, marriage, or adoption. Roomers, boarders, lodgers, partners, resident employees, wards, and foster children are included in this category.

Group Quarters

Persons in living arrangements other than households are classified by the Bureau of Census as living in group quarters. Group quarters are located most frequently in institutions, rooming houses, military barracks, college dormitories, fraternity and sorority houses, hospitals, monasteries, convents, and ships. A house or apartment is considered group quarters if it is shared by the person in charge and five or more persons unrelated to him, or, if there is no person in charge, by six or more unrelated persons.

Inmate of Institution

Inmates of institutions are persons under care or custody at the time of enumeration in homes, schools, hospitals or wards for juveniles, the physically handicapped, or the mentally handicapped; homes or hospitals for mental, tuberculosis, or other chronic disease patients; homes for unwed mothers; nursing, convalescent, and rest homes; homes for the aged and dependent; and correctional institutions.

Family

According to 1970 census definitions, a family consists of a household head and one or more other persons living in the same household who are related to the head by blood, marriage, or adoption; all persons in a household who are related to the head are regarded as members of his (her) family. A "husband-wife family" is a family in which the head and his wife are enumerated as members of the same household. Not all households contain families, because a household may be composed of a group of unrelated persons or one person living alone. The mean size of family is derived by dividing the number of persons in families by the total number of families.

Own Children and Related Children

This report shows statistics on families by presence of "own" children and "related" children of specified ages. A child under 18 years old is defined as an "own child" if he or she is a single (never married) son, daughter, stepchild, or adopted child. The number of children "living with both parents" includes stepchildren and adopted children as well as sons and daughters born to the couple. "Related children" in a family include all persons under 18 related to the head except "wife of head." The "mean number of related children" is derived by dividing the total number of related children of the specified age in families by the number of families having children of that age. In table P-1 the number of own children under 18 years of age is divided by "persons under 18 years" to obtain the "percent of total under 18 years."

Unrelated Individuals

An unrelated individual, as defined in this report, may be any of the following: a household head living alone or with nonrelatives only, a household member not related to the head, or a person living in group quarters who is not an inmate of an institution.

Marital Status

The marital status classification refers to the status at the time of enumeration. Persons classified as "married" consist of those who have been married only once and those who remarried after having been widowed or divorced. Persons reported as separated (living apart because of marital discord, with or without a legal separation) are classified as a subcategory of married persons. Persons in common-law marriage are classified as married, and persons whose only marriage had been annulled are classified as never married. All persons reported as never married are shown as "single."

Children Ever Born

In this report, statistics on the number of children ever born are presented for women 35 to 44 years old who have ever been married. Respondents were instructed to include children born to the woman before her present marriage, children no longer living, and children away from home, as well as children born to the woman who were still living in the home.

School Enrollment

School enrollment is shown for persons 3 to 34 years old. Persons were included as enrolled in school if they reported attending a "regular" school or college at any time between February 1, 1970, and the time of enumeration. Regular schooling is that which may advance a person toward an elementary school certificate or high school diploma, or a college, university, or professional degree. Schooling that was not obtained in a regular school and schooling from a tutor or through correspondence courses were counted only if the credits obtained were regarded as transferable to a school in the regular school system. Persons were included as enrolled in nursery school only if the school included instruction as an important and integral phase of its program. Schooling which is generally regarded as not "regular" includes that given in nursery schools which simply provide custodial day care, in specialized vocational, trade, or business schools, in on-the-job training, and through correspondence courses.

Elementary school, as defined here, includes grades 1 to 8, and high school includes grades 9 to 12. If a person was attending a junior high school, the equivalent in terms of 8 years of elementary school and 4 years of high school was recorded. In general, a "public" school is defined as any school which is controlled and supported primarily by a local, State, or Federal government agency.

Years of School Completed

The data on years of school completed were derived from the answers to the two questions: (a) "What is the highest grade (or year) of regular school he has ever attended?" and (b) "Did he finish the highest grade (or year) he attended?" Persons whose highest grade of attendance was in a foreign school system, or in an ungraded school whose highest level of schooling was measured by "readers," or whose training was received through a tutor were instructed to report the approximate equivalent grade in the regular United States school system. A person was reported as not having completed a given grade if he dropped out or failed to pass the last grade attended.

Residence In 1965

Residence on April 1, 1965, is the usual place of residence five years before enumeration. The category "same house" includes all persons five years old and over who did not move during the five years as well as those who had moved but by 1970 had returned to their 1965 residence. The category "different house" includes persons who, on April 1, 1965, lived in the United States in a different house from the one they occupied on April 1, 1970, and for whom sufficient information concerning the 1965 residence was collected. These persons were subdivided into three groups according to their 1965 residence in or outside a standard metropolitan statistical area: "in central city of this SMSA," "in other part of this SMSA," and "outside this SMSA." The category "abroad" includes those with residence in a foreign country or outlying area of the United States in 1965.

Reference Week

The data on employment status and place of work relate to the calendar week preceding the date on which the respondents completed their questionnaires or were interviewed by enumerators. This week is not the same for all respondents because not all persons were enumerated during the same week.

Employment Status

Employed persons comprise all civilians 16 years old and over who were either (a) "at work"—those who did any work at all as paid employees or in their own business or profession, or on their own farm, or who worked 15 hours or more as unpaid workers on a family farm or in a family business; or (b) were "with a job but not at work"—those who did not work during the reference week but had jobs or businesses from which they were temporarily absent due to illness, bad weather, industrial dispute, vacation, or other personal reasons. Excluded from the employed are persons whose only activity consisted of work around the house or volunteer work for religious, charitable, and similar organizations.

Persons are classified as unemployed if they were civilians 16 years old and over and: (a) were neither "at work" nor "with a job, but not at work" during the reference week, (b) were looking for work during the past 4 weeks, and (c) were available to accept a job. Persons who did not work at all during the reference week and were waiting to be called back to a job from which they had been laid off are also included as unemployed.

The "civilian labor force" consists of persons classified as employed or unemployed in accordance with the criteria described above. The "labor force" includes all persons in the civilian labor force plus members of the Armed Forces (persons on active duty with the United States Army, Air Force, Navy, Marine Corps, or Coast Guard). All persons 16 years old and over who are not classified as members of the labor force are defined as "not in labor force." This category consists mainly of students, housewives, retired workers, seasonal workers enumerated in an "off" season who were not looking for work, inmates of institutions, disabled persons, and persons doing only incidental unpaid family work (less than 15 hours during the reference week). Of these groups, students and inmates are shown separately in selected tables.

Place of Work

Place of work refers to the geographic location at which civilians and Armed Forces personnel not on leave carried out their occupational or job activities during the reference week. For the purposes of this report, these locations were defined with respect to the boundaries of the standard metropolitan statistical area as "inside SMSA" and "outside SMSA." Locations within the SMSA, were subdivided into the central business district of the central city, the balance of that county, or, if outside that county, the specific county of the SMSA.

The central business district (CBD) is usually the downtown retail trade area of the city. As defined by the Bureau of the Census, the CBD is an area of very high land valuation characterized by a high concentration of retail business offices, theaters, hotels, and service businesses, and with a high traffic flow. CBD's consist of one or more census tracts and have been defined only in cities with a population of 100,000 or more. In order to be counted as working in the CBD, the respondent had to give the exact address (street name and number) of his place of work. Since some respondents did not do this, the number of persons working in the CBD is usually understated by an unknown amount.

The exact address (number and street name) for the place of work was asked. Persons working at more than one job were asked to report the location of the job at which they worked the greatest number of hours during the reference week. Salesmen, deliverymen, and others who work in several places each week were requested to give the address at which they began work each day, if they reported to a central headquarters. For cases in which daily work was not begun at a central place each day, the person was asked to report the exact address of the place where he worked the most hours last week. If his employer operated in more than one location (such as a grocery store chain or public school system), the exact address of the location or branch where the respondent worked was requested. When the number or

4

street name could not be given, the name of the building or the name of the company for which he worked was to be entered.

Means of Transportation to Work

Means of transportation to work refers to the chief means of travel or type of conveyance used in traveling to and from work on the last day the respondent worked at the address given as his or her place of work. The "chief means" referred to the means of transportation covering the greatest distance if more than one means was used in daily travel. "Worked at home" was marked by a person who worked on a farm where he lived or in an office or shop in his home.

Occupation, Industry, and Class of Worker

The data on these three subjects in this report are for employed persons 16 years old and over and refer to the job held during the reference week. For persons employed at two or more jobs, the data refer to the job at which the person worked the greatest number of hours.

Income in 1969

Information on money income received in the calendar year 1969 was requested from persons 14 years old and over. "Total income" is the algebraic sum of the amounts reported separately for wage and salary income, nonfarm net self-employment income, farm net self-employment income, Social Security or railroad retirement income, public assistance or welfare income, and all other income. The figures represent the amount of income regularly received before deductions for personal income taxes, Social Security, bond purchases, union dues, medicare deductions, etc.

"Wage or salary income" is defined as the total money earnings received for work performed as an employee at any time during the calendar year 1969. It includes wages, salary, pay from Armed Forces, commissions, tips, piece rate payments, and cash bonuses earned. "Nonfarm net self-employment income" is defined as net money income (gross receipts minus business expenses) received from a business, professional enterprise, or partnership in which the person was engaged on his own account. "Farm net self-employment income" is defined as the net money income (gross receipts minus operating expenses) received from the operation of a farm by a person on his own account, as an owner, renter, or sharecropper.

"Social Security or railroad retirement income" includes cash receipts of Social Security pensions, survivors' benefits, permanent disability insurance payments, and special benefit payments made by the Social Security Administration (under the National old-age, survivors, disability, and health insurance programs) before deductions of health insurance premiums.

"Medicare" reimbursements are not included. Cash receipts from retirement, disability, and survivors' benefit payments made by the U.S. Government under the Railroad Retirement Act are also included. "Public assistance income" includes cash receipts of payments made under the following public assistance programs: aid to families with dependent children, old-age assistance, general assistance, aid to the blind, and aid to the permanently and totally disabled. Separate payments received for hospital or other medical care are excluded from this item. "Income from all other sources" includes money income received from sources such as interest; dividends; net income (or loss) from property rentals; net receipts from roomers or boarders; veteran's payments; public or private pensions, periodic receipts from insurance policies or annuities; unemployment insurance benefits; workmen's compensation cash benefits; net royalties; periodic payments from estates and trust funds; alimony or child support from persons who are not members of the household; net gambling gains; nonservice scholarships and fellowships; and money received for transportation and/or subsistence by persons participating in special governmental training programs, e.g., under the Manpower Development and Training Act.

Receipts from the following sources were not included as income: money received from the sale of property (unless the receipt was engaged in the business of selling such property); the value of income "in kind" such as food produced and consumed in the home or free living quarters; withdrawal of bank deposits; money borrowed; tax refunds; exchange of money between relatives living in the same household; gifts and lump-sum inheritances, insurance payments, and other types of lump-sum receipts.

Although the income statistics cover the calendar year 1969, the characteristics of persons and the composition of families refer to the time of enumeration (April 1, 1970). For most families, however, the income reported was received by persons who were members of the family throughout 1969.

The median income is the amount which divides the distribution into two equal groups, one having incomes above the median and the other having incomes below the median. For families and unrelated individuals the median income is based on the distribution of the total number of families and unrelated individuals, including those with no income.

The mean income is the amount obtained by dividing the total income of a particular statistical universe by the number of units in that universe. Thus, mean family income is obtained by dividing total family income by the total number of families. For the six types of income the means are based on families having those types of income.

Care should be exercised in using and interpreting mean income values in the statistics for small areas or small subgroups of the population. Since the mean is strongly influenced by extreme values in the distribution, it is especially susceptible to the effects of sampling variability, misreporting, and processing errors. The median, which is not affected by extreme values, is, therefore, a better measure than the mean when the population base is small. The mean, nevertheless, is shown in this report for most small areas and small subgroups because, when weighted according to the number of cases, the means can be added to obtain summary measures for areas and groups other than those shown in this report.

Poverty Status in 1969

Families and unrelated individuals are classified as being above or below the poverty level, using the poverty index adopted by a Federal Interagency Committee in 1969. This index provides a range of income cutoffs or "poverty thresholds" adjusted to take into account such factors as family size, sex and age of the family head, the number of children, and farm-nonfarm residence. The poverty cutoffs for farm families have been set at 85 percent of the nonfarm levels. These income cutoffs are updated every year to reflect the changes in the Consumer Price Index. The poverty threshold for a nonfarm family of four was $3,743 in 1969.

Appendix B
Issues in Community Relations:
Field Operations *

The Role of Field Operations

The police have nearly all of their contact with citizens through patrol operations, and the bulk of their resources are devoted to that function. The police/community relationship is made on the streets—it is made by officers on patrol. Consequently, the police administrator who wants to improve community relations must take a hard look at his patrol procedures and activities.

Good patrol work is community service. Most police-citizen contact is initiated by the citizen, and thus provides the officer an opportunity to be of service to someone in the community. The citizen's expectations are often complex and even unfathomable: he may have fears about an intruder, and thus needs to have his fears allayed; he may be angry at the noise of the party next door, and thus wants redress; he may be frantic with bullies who have beaten his child, and thus feels a need for legal revenge. By using good judgment, by showing concern, and by attempting to provide service, the patrolman can lay the foundation of a good police/community relationship. The officer must understand that although the call may not be especially exciting or unusual, it is likely to represent a significant event in the life of the citizen. The patrolman will undermine community relations if he belittles the importance of that request, if he is belligerent, or if he treats the citizen's claim for service with less than full concern.

If this were the full extent of police service, it would be relatively easy to maintain satisfactory police community relations. In many contacts with citizens, however, police are asked to arbitrate between conflicting claims and to take action on one side or the other. There may be differences about what happened and what ought to be done. The officer must negotiate, arbitrate, and somehow satisfy all parties to the dispute that he has acted in a fair and equitable manner. In such situations, difficult as they are, the patrolman frequently has been asked to intervene. In other instances—such as field interrogation or stop and frisk situations—an officer is intervening where his presence is not desired. Especially in the case of a "victimless crime," the police officer may find the legitimacy of his presence vigorously questioned.

If the department is to enjoy good community relations, its officers must

* Taken from "Prescriptive Package" *Improving Police/Community Relations*, by Robert Wasserman, Michael P. Gardner and Alana S. Cohen of the Governor's Committee on Law Enforcement and Criminal Justice, Commonwealth of Massachusetts. This project was supported by a grant awarded by the Law Enforcement Assistance Administration, U.S. Department of Justice through the National Institute of Law Enforcement and Criminal Justice. June 1973, pp. 24–31.

be sensitive to the impact their actions will have on the neighborhood they serve. This is a matter of supervision and of training. It is also a matter of the department's willingness to hold officers accountable for their actions. A fundamental reason for the strain in police/community relations appears to be departmental failure to adopt a community policing orientation. Citizen attitudes are too often considered unimportant to police policy makers—in fact, those attitudes may be dismissed as irrelevant to the "professional" decisions that police administrators must make. Criticism is frequently rejected out-of-hand as resulting from "anti-police" bias. And, all too often, patrol activities are evaluated in terms of arrest figures and crime rates: tactics initiated to reduce crime may be measured only by their short-term effects, ignoring their impact on police/community relations.

This disregard for community opinion is often most acute in those high-crime, low-income areas of the city where many members of minority groups reside. Too many departments make a practice of assigning their worst officers to these areas as a kind of "punishment duty." Unfortunately, this practice also punishes the community segments most in need of effective police services and greatly aggravates the police/community relationship.

A community-oriented approach to policing is not a simple matter. It requires measurements which do not now exist—measurements which will reflect the community's opinions about the quality and sensitivity of police service. It also requires an ability to satisfy, insofar as possible, citizen expectations that may vary from area to area.

Establishing a Positive Relationship

Accountability and Responsibility

Patrol officers and supervisors should be evaluated in part by how well they develop the confidence of the community. This is especially important in those sections which, historically, have had poor relations with the department. Many departments have taken steps in recent years to ensure that community-oriented measures of effectiveness are included in the evaluation process. In Baltimore (Maryland), for example, interviews are conducted with citizens who recently have had contact with the police. The citizens—who are selected on a random basis—are asked how well the police officers served them. Other departments, ranging from Simi Valley (California) to Holyoke (Massachusetts), are likewise giving more consideration to community reactions to specific patrol tactics. The methods include neighborhood meetings, "rap sessions," and the monitoring of citizen complaints and commendations.

Where feasible, patrol officers should be permanently assigned to a particular area of the community and (with their supervisors) should be given prime responsibility for all police functions in that area. Accountability is the essence of a sound delegation of authority. It is also a means of encouraging positive police performance. Most "team policing" experiments in recent years have relied heavily on this principle of geographic accountability. In Holyoke (Massachusetts), New Orleans (Louisiana), Dayton and Cincinnati (Ohio), Los Angeles (California), and New York City, officers have been assigned to particular areas and given responsibility for both the quality of policing and for community relations in those areas. The actual level of responsibility, of course, varies significantly. Smaller communities like Holyoke and Dayton have been able to place most of the responsibility on patrol officers, whereas New York and Los Angeles have continued to rely on more centralized authority.

The Role of the Patrol Officer

The patrol officer must accept direct responsibility for providing services in ways that improve the police/community relationship. He can be guided in this task by positive supervision and various modifications in his duties. For example, permitting the patrol officer to conduct investigations increases both his status and his responsibility. When investigation is separated from patrol, the beat officer tends to see himself as a small cog in the police bureaucracy, rather than as a professional responsible for solving the problems of clients. Expanding his investigative responsibilities gives him an added opportunity to provide service that can lead to improved police/community relations. Such a step also gives citizens the feeling that the officer on patrol is not merely performing a perfunctory role.

Dayton, Holyoke, Cincinnati, and New Orleans have had varying degrees of success in transferring broader investigative responsibility to the patrol officer. Each has tried to expand the patrolman's duties by permitting him to follow up the preliminary investigations of crime occurring within his district. The officer is generally given broad discretion regarding when and how specialized units (such as detectives) will be called into these investigations. In the case of homicides, serious assaults, or other particularly serious or complicated matters, it has been agreed that technical experts should be involved from the beginning. A successful program of this type generally requires some additional training for the patrol officer in investigative techniques, constitutional limitations, and related matters. Manpower scheduling must also be designed to provide the officer with sufficient time to complete his follow-up investigations. Where workloads are heavy, the officer will have to be equally imaginative in scheduling patrol activities, in order to maximize use of the available time. This has been a significant problem, particularly in Dayton, where fiscal austerity has reduced the size of the department at a time when calls for service have increased substantially. Despite such problems and some increased costs, practically all of the departments are sufficiently satisfied with progress to continue the team-policing effort. In fact, some communities, including Cincinnati and Holyoke, are now expanding their programs. *After a two-year trial in a single patrol sector, Holyoke is now converting its entire department to the model of geographic accountability and unified investigative and patrol functions. Dayton is planning a similar move.

Neighborhood Identification

Patrol sectors should be based on definable neighborhood boundaries, and a given neighborhood should not be split into more than one patrol sector. One of the advantages of geographically-organized patrol is the officer's ability to take account of varying needs and desires in different areas of the city. Such differences often follow neighborhood lines. The New Orleans Urban Squad, for example, patrols two large housing projects which form distinct communities. Similarly, the Holyoke experiment began in a well-defined, low-income area with a substantial number of Spanish-speaking residents. The area is separated from the rest of the city by a canal and an industrial section. In Dayton, the original team-policing area involved a more diverse neighborhood, but the residents viewed it as a distinct community; it was bounded by a river and a highway, called by a single name, and represented by several community organizations.

Advisory Councils

The departments should encourage the establishment of neighborhood or community councils composed of community leaders willing to meet regularly with members of the patrol unit. Membership on the advisory council might be by invitation or even by community election. Neither method provides a foolproof way of obtaining citizens who will represent viewpoints other than their own, or of selecting individuals genuinely interested in police problems. Consequently, an effort must be made to strike a balance of viewpoints and to find people willing to meet and work on community problems. The function of neighborhood councils is to explore community problems, needs, and priorities, as well as departmental strengths and inadequacies. The goal is to improve police services and increase community-police cooperation. The councils should receive departmental support, perhaps including part-time clerical assistance, a telephone-answering ser-

* There has been a good deal of experimentation in the kind of training introduced and in the approach to such issues as manpower scheduling. Dayton has relied on an extensive formal training program, while New York and Cincinnati have used a more informal "group process" approach. Cincinnati has turned over all manpower scheduling responsibilities (within the experimental patrol district) to the sergeant on the beat. Other departments, not having gone quite so far, have greatly expanded the discretion of the local units.

vice with a highly publicized number, and some compensation for council members. The police officers, of course, should be able to carry out council-related business as part of their official duties. The programs previously cited have all included neighborhood meetings or advisory councils. Even departments that have not made major revisions in the patrol function have found neighborhood advisory councils to be helpful. Miami (Florida) recently initiated a major effort in this regard, and other cities, such as Cambridge (Massachusetts), have begun small-scale programs utilizing neighborhood advisory committees. It is important that the officers responsible for policing a neighborhood be a part of the neighborhood council. Their attendance at meetings should be encouraged, since this will contribute to increased communication and understanding. This tactic has been used with considerable success in Cambridge, where officers assigned to the Riverside-Cambridge port area regularly attend community meetings. Their willingness to become involved in community affairs has resulted in reduced community tensions.

To be successful, the department must be sincere in its desire to involve the community. It must communicate this desire, it must be willing to commit adequate resources, and it must clearly set forth the limitations of committee authority. Perhaps no factor contributes more to the demise of such committees—or to a deterioration of both police and community attitudes—as misunderstandings about the advisory group's authority. In one large city, a community relations project was virtually destroyed because it became embroiled in the issue of community control. Members of the advisory committee demanded more power than the department was prepared to relinquish, and much bitter feeling resulted. The need for advance planning and a clear and early communication of project aims and limitations is paramount.

Most departments have insisted that such committees have an advisory function only. Quite understandably they have been unwilling to turn important management functions, patrol assignments, transfers, and complaint reviews over to an untested neighborhood panel. Generally, these efforts have had better results than those in departments where the role of such committees has been intentionally or unintentionally vague. At least one department, however, has given the committee veto power over the assignment of a team-policing District Commander, and has suffered no apparent harm from that decision. Dayton (Ohio) decided that if its team-policing program were to work, the District Commander would have to have full community support. The Chief of Police nominated a well-respected lieutenant; the advisory council was impressed with the officer and backed him unanimously. Careful planning by the department (and a shrewd assessment of the feeling of the council) thus resulted in a major advancement in confidence between the department and the community.

4

Police Auxiliaries

A number of police departments have developed volunteer police auxiliary units to alleviate problems of inadequate manpower. A useful variation of this approach is being tested in Dayton, where a large and enthusiastic auxiliary program has organized volunteers into neighborhood teams. An individual can belong only to the auxiliary unit within his own neighborhood, and can patrol only in that neighborhood. This arrangement has facilitated community acceptance of the program, and has helped screen out volunteers whose motives might be questionable.

Open Community Meeting

Patrol officers and advisory councils should schedule regular public meetings with prepared agendas and time for general discussion. In this way, viewpoints not represented in council meetings are likely to be heard. Several departments, including those in Los Angeles and Cincinnati, have experienced success with this type of program. Care should be taken that community needs and priorities are reflected in the agenda, and that such meetings are not used exclusively for pre-packaged departmental presentations.

Task-Oriented Patrol

During periods when officers do not have a heavy service-call demand and are primarily on preventive patrol, they might well undertake specific tasks such as contacting troubled families or talking with tenant groups, landlord merchants, and others. Crime prevention, the adequacy of alarm systems and locks, fears or concerns about particular crimes . . . are all appropriate subjects. Patrolmen should be encouraged to develop specialties, and departments should provide opportunities for training and proper application of skills. A few departments have experimented with this task-oriented form of patrolling, although none has reported any significant success. In at least one department, the program faltered due to a lack of supervisory leadership. However, almost all departments report that some of their officers become bored with long periods of inactivity and seek additional special tasks. Often, such officers are remarkably successful in creating new opportunities for contact between police and the community. During his regular tour of duty, for example, one patrolman in Randolph (Massachusetts) developed and implemented an entire community relations program, including classroom visits and speaking engagements. Every department should identify such officers and encourage their initiative. In Novato, California, different patrol officers spend their lunch hour each week in the community's junior and senior high schools. Advance publicity, an informal setting, cooperative officers and growing student enthusiasm have made the program a success.

Crime prevention offers one of the most promising areas for such special endeavors. The service may be provided on a centralized basis, but—in order to maximize the community relations benefits—it should rest largely with the regular neighborhood patrol officers.

Ride-Along Programs

Patrol officers and advisory councils should encourage public participation in "ride-along" programs so that citizens may observe the complexities of police work. Officers should make a special point of inviting hostile or critical community members to participate. Ride-along programs have been said to be of limited value, primarily because of lack of community participation. The failures, however, appear to be largely related to lack of preparation or follow-through: departments that have made a concerted effort to encourage participation have found ride-along programs to be worthwhile. Public response in Washington (D.C.), Syracuse (New York), Menlo Park (California), Montgomery County (Maryland), Cambridge (Massachusetts), and many other communities has been very encouraging. Menlo Park, for example, has concentrated on involving young blacks in its program, and has found that participation is greater when groups of three juveniles ride in a single patrol car. This is probably because they are more comfortable with friends in an alien environment, and because they feel less likely to be mistaken for informers or arrested suspects. Another technique under consideration by a number of departments is linking the ride-along program to the social studies curriculum of the local junior high or high school. Novato (California) routinely asks participants in its ride-along program to evaluate the experience, the officer they rode with, and the department as a whole. Several improvements in operations have resulted from the response.

The Patrol Officer as Referral Agent

Officers should not neglect community services in the belief that the police function is restricted to crime control. The community supports the operation of the department twenty-four hours a day; it is entitled to whatever services the department can reasonably render during that time. These include order-maintenance or conflict-management duties, provision of certain emergency services, and other specialized government tasks. (A service-oriented patrol force may also increase its impact on crime, by stimulating community cooperation and participation in general police activities.)

San Diego (California) is planning to assign officers to develop profiles of the neighborhood they police. The profiles will include the social services and other resources available to the community, the patterns of crime and calls for service, and identification of community leaders and block representatives. This information will be gathered from census and other data, and by meeting with individuals and groups on a block-by-block basis. The information will be used to enable the officers to make better use of the formal and informal community resources available to help them. Patrol officers should be aware of the social services available in their communities, and, after dealing with the immediate situation, should refer persons in need of assistance to the appropriate agency. This has been done with some success in New York City as part of a special family crisis-intervention project. Other departments have developed formal and informal relationships with social service agencies and have encouraged their officers to make referrals to them. Officers should also be aware of the rights of individuals in domestic disputes, landlord-tenant conflicts, consumer-fraud complaints, and other civil situations. Rights and procedures may then be explained to the disputants. In some situations patrol officers may take an even more active role; Oakland (California) has had highly favorable response to its Landlord-Tenant Complaint Program, and has recently expanded the program because of its popularity, especially among low-income residents. The department receives many calls each day from persons inquiring about their rights. The dispatch officer or an officer working in the Conflict Management Bureau explains the relevant sections of California law, and advises the caller to consult an attorney for any legal action. When a dispute cannot be simply resolved, officers may arbitrate or otherwise help to move the conflict out of the street and into the courtroom or to the negotiating table.

The Patrol Officer as Mediator

Patrol officers must learn conflict-management techniques that will defuse hostility. Officers are often thrust into a controversy by opposing interest groups. Downtown merchants may want the police to force juveniles off the sidewalks in front of their premises, while the juveniles complain that they have no other meeting place. Patrol officers should encourage negotiation in such circumstances, rather than rely exclusively on the coercive power of the police. Some of the techniques that may prove useful are open meetings, negotiation, or arbitration before a citizens advisory council, and a careful explanation of the patrol officers' role.

Field Interrogation

The department with the active participation of patrol officers and community representatives, should re-evaluate field interrogation policies and other police-initiated citizen contacts. The benefits of widespread field interrogation must be weighed against the negative community reactions. Patrol officers should be instructed to use the technique only after careful consideration of alternative methods, such as continued surveillance. Under no circumstances should field interrogation techniques be employed as a means of harassing "known criminals" or other groups or individuals regarded as deviant. Field interrogation probably should be used only in specific instances of reported or suspected crime or in response to particularly suspicious behavior. Supervisors should monitor field interrogation practices and ensure that their officers conduct the necessary interrogations courteously and efficiently. Finally, the officers should provide all individuals they interrogate with cards bearing their name and badge number.

The value of field interrogation in crime control is in doubt, especially when the interrogation is not directed at specific reported or suspected crime but is for general information gathering purposes. There may be instances when it is necessary to increase field interrogation to meet a particularly serious crime problem or to allay citizen fears. Before doing so, however, the department should discuss the situation with community representatives and explain why the practice is to be employed. At least one department has successfully taken this approach. It wanted a great increase in field stops in a predominantly black section of the city; a meeting with community leaders was held to explain the growing crime problem, and those in attendance then toured the area in patrol cars while the officers explained their field interrogation techniques. The meeting then reconvened at police headquarters. The meeting did not result in unanimous support for the program, but it did develop substantial support for the program, greater understanding, and increased respect for the police. San Diego (California) has launched a major experiment to test the usefulness of field interrogation as a crime-fighting technique. The department plans to stop all field interrogations in one section of the city, while substantially increasing the number of stops in another section. Controls have been devised to ensure that constitutional rights will not be violated. By comparing the results in these two sectors and in a control sector, the department should be able to measure the effect of field stops—both on crime and on community relations.

Sensitivity to Crowd Dynamics

Patrol officers and supervisors should be sensitive to the risk of attracting large crowds at incidents. One of the primary sources for such gatherings is the assembly of several police cars in a particular area. Efforts should be made to remove superfluous police cars as quickly as possible, since nothing dissipates a crowd as effectively as eliminating the attraction. The gathering of crowds frequently results in bitter and destructive police-citizen encounters. Members of the crowd are likely to be agitated, and officers will understandably be concerned about physical danger and problems of interference. Consequently, early removal of the attraction and rapid return to a normal situation are extremely important. The department should also establish—and supervisors enforce—strict guidelines regarding the use of sirens, flashers,

4

and high-speed driving. Use of these emergency techniques must be kept to an absolute minimum. Abuse of them can endanger police and public safety, provoke fear, and attract unnecessary attention to police activities.

Personnel Assignments

Personnel assignments should take the potential community relations impact into account. Officers who have difficulty controlling their emotions, who cannot endure verbal abuse, or who exhibit strong racial or class bias should not be assigned to sectors where the community relationship is tense or deteriorating. They should be placed in less sensitive sectors, removed from the street, or (if their problems are serious enough), removed from the department. At times, individuals in a community will become especially hostile toward a particular patrol officer. This is usually a response to the officer's inability to handle personal relationships, although it may simply reflect animosity toward an authority figure. If the hostility persists, the department should transfer the officer, since he is not able to perform his general assignment satisfactorily. This is not a surrender to unreasonable community demands; it is an appropriate response to a serious personnel and patrol problem.

Mobility of Manpower

The department should experiment with new methods for transporting patrol personnel. Most rely on the basic one-or-two-man radio car for patrol purposes, perhaps with some walking beats in commercial or business districts. For a number of years, increased use of walking beats has been a standard proposal for encouraging better community contact. Although the principle is sound, the restricted mobility and limited coverage of a foot patrolman presents a number of disadvantages. Baltimore (Maryland) has developed an interesting compromise with the use of five-speed bicycles in selected areas. Mobility is increased and contact with citizens is not significantly restricted. Berkeley (California) and Baltimore have also found bicycle patrol an effective burglary-prevention technique. It permits silent patrol down alleys, along narrow or one-way streets, and into other areas not easily accessible to motor patrol. Another technique being tried by some departments is the assignment of one of the officers in a two-man car to a walking beat for at least part of his tour of duty. This increased flexibility permits greater mobility, as well as back-up support in case of an emergency.

SUMMARY

The suggested decentralization of administration need not constitute an abdication of command control or responsibility. In fact, by decentralizing operations and increasing accountability, top command should be able to

improve overall departmental control. Departmental leadership must be attentive to patrol developments however, and, must ensure that innovative practices remain within the scope of the department. Before major programs or changes are begun in a patrol sector, they should be thoroughly discussed with top command. Advisory committees can and should remain advisory—unless, as in Dayton, a decision is made to realign the power structure. Some departments may believe that their manpower is inadequate or their overtime funds too scarce to permit officers to assume extra community duties. Each department must assess its own ability to handle such activities without cost increases. Beyond that, it must decide how much the police/community relationship is worth. In many departments, manpower resources could be allocated more efficiently. Excessive use of two-man cars, superfluous patrol coverage between 2 a.m. and 8 a.m., unnecessary use of patrolmen as clerk-typists and dispatchers, and other similar practices may contribute to inefficient manpower allocation. With good management and planning, it is possible that ample time can be found for community-related activities. Some overtime will probably be necessary, and imaginative use of available funds can provide rewards and incentives to those officers demonstrating a commitment to improved police/community relations. The "pay incentive" system is one of the most successful aspects of New Orleans' Urban Squad program. The rewards are such that officers are careful to retain the community-oriented spirit of the effort, so as not to jeopardize their involvement in the program.

These recommendations range from relatively minor matters to some which would require a basic reorganization of preventive patrol. All are aimed at improved police/community relations, and all seek to complement a basic goal of the patrol force: improved patrol accountability and capability. The techniques set forth have been operationally tested in a number of cities. The department wishing to improve relationships between its patrol force and the community should at least experiment with some of these measures. Without a willingness to innovate, chances for improvement and ultimate success will no doubt be limited.

5

Metropolitan Growth, Challenges, and Police Response

The American city has been in a continual state of development and change. Some of the change has been orderly and constructive, while other aspects of it have been violent and disruptive. Why cities are located exactly where they are, and why they have developed in the ways they have has been the result of many specific forces. A basic understanding of cities in general and of the departments that police them must therefore include at least a brief overview of this developmental process.

The logic of metropolitan growth described in Appendix A (See p. 142, herein) has led to the formulation of several theories dealing with urban growth processes. The most prominent among these theories will be discussed briefly so that the reader might further appreciate the dynamics involved in the growth of urban centers.

Concentric Zone Theory

The Concentric Zone theory, which was developed by Ernest W. Burgess of the University of Chicago, attempted to provide a descriptive framework for the spatial organization of urban land use. Burgess, who was a sociologist, developed his concept of "concentric zones" in the 1920's as a part of his study of land use in Chicago.[1]

Burgess hypothesized that given the proper circumstances (a uniform land surface, universal accessibility, and free competition for space), land use in an urban area would arrange itself in a series of concentric circles. The circles and their land use patterns were found by Burgess to describe the circumstances typical of a number of cities.

Zone 1, the innermost circle, is the *Central Business District* and is the focal point of the city's commercial, social, economic, and civic activities. It contains the large retail houses, office buildings, hotels, financial institutions, and theaters. If the city is large enough zone 1 might even have separate districts for specific functions, as in the case of New York City's finance district (Wall Street), retail commerce (5th Avenue, for instance), and entertainment district (Times Square). In smaller cities these func-

---

[1] Ernest W. Burgess, "Urban Areas," in T. V. Smith and L. D. White, eds., *Chicago: An Experiment in Social Science Research* (Chicago: University of Chicago Press, 1929), pp. 113–138.

5

tions tended to intermingle so that a general "downtown" pattern was found to exist. In terms of population, zone 1 is densely populated during the day, but is virtually uninhabited at night except for transients and hotel residents. As has already been noted, crime is high in zone 1, perhaps because of the sheer availability of opportunity for certain types of offienses.

Zone 2, which surrounds the Central Business District, is the *zone in transition*. In its earlier days, this zone contained many of the finer residences and residential neighborhoods. These were the homes of the more affluent people who worked in the city and who desired comfortable, convenient homes close to their places of work. In horse-and-buggy days this meant that one could not live too far from town; certainly not nearly as far out as was made possible by the automobile. However, as the commercial and business district of the downtown area expanded, they began to encroach upon this residential neighborhood. In some cases residential "islands" remained, but for the most part the affluent citizens moved further away from the center of the city. Many of the older homes have since become chopped up into apartments and rooming houses and high population density housing has been added to the area (tenement houses, multi-story walk-up apartments, and even row houses). Because this zone lacks the centralized character of the central business district (it tends to be a belt surrounding it), and because it contains so many residences, it has tended to attract cheap commercial establishments, many of which cater to the needs of low income, transient residents. Hence the zone in transition contains warehouses and storage facilities to service the central business district, rooming houses, cheap hotels and flophouses, pawn shops, liquor stores, used furniture stores and commercial enterprises involved in light industry. Zone 2 is likely to be fairly dense in its population but the residents are apt to be low-income, low status families and individuals. Here one finds high concentrations of ethnic minorities, decrepit homes, unsightly streets, and evidence of social deterioration. This zone is also high in social problems, such as broken homes, vice, and delinquency. If the city has a skid-row, it will most likely be situated in the zone in transition. In previous decades this zone was inhabited by incoming immigrants and others who lacked the wherewithal to deal successfully with society. Those people who are able to generally try to move out of this zone into a better area. Those who cannot leave become part of what David Matza has called the "dregs," which are the core of those in "Disreputable poverty ... persons spawned in poverty and belonging to families who have been left behind by otherwise mobile ethnic populations."[2]

2 David Matza, "The Disreputable Poor," in Richard Bendix and Seymore M. Lipset, eds., *Class, Status and Power* (New York: The Free Press, 1966), pp. 289–302.

The zone in transition gradually blends in with and gives way to zone 3, which is the *zone of workingmen's homes*. This third ring, according to Burgess, is made up of residents of upper working class status and includes a large number of laborers and factory employees. The residents are often people who have moved out of zone 2 but who wish to remain close to the central part of the city. In the earlier decades of this century, zone 3 was where second generation immigrants were frequently found. It represents a life style reflecting more stability and better income than is to be found in zone 2, but one in which social and economic want are not unknown.

Zone 4 is the *zone of better residences*. Burgess originally saw zone 4 as a residential zone. In this circle, workers who had obtained sufficient financial independence have relocated within it. It is an area of higher per capita income and the homes located within zone 4 are better than those in the zones closer to the center of the city. The owners of these homes tend to be businessmen, salesmen, professional people and other middle class workers. The zone contains local retail establishments, but of the type which typically furnish goods and services to residential areas, such as grocery stores, drug stores, cleaning establishments and so on. This zone is the typical residential belt which surrounds large cities and which is not too far from the center of the city but which at the same time is sufficiently removed from the downtown (and surrounding areas) to provide a more comfortable life-style.

Zone 5 is the *commuter's zone*. It includes the suburban areas and the most affluent residential neighborhoods. The residential tracts within this zone tend to be spatially isolated from one another and tend to be situated along lines of rapid travel which extend outward from the city.

In Burgess' conceptualization, the concentric zones of the city are not static but undergo change as the city grows. The inner zones intrude on those which surround them, pushing the outer zones even further out. This effect has been likened to the movement of the ripples in a pond when a rock is thrown in.

Although this scheme of land use accurately reflects many American communities, Burgess has not been without his critics. However, it is important to realize that Burgess developed his concentric zone theory in the early part of this century and that considerable change has taken place since then. For example, the massive development of the transportation industry has had a significant impact on city development. More people can now live further and further away from the city and yet not be hindered in their access to it. At the same time, the growth of satellite cities—the so-called "bedroom" communities—has also affected the nature and use of the central city. As has already been noted, the influx of large numbers of blacks into the cities has been responsible for the flight from the city of many whites, thus altering the tax base of the city and adding to the general concentration of social problems (this point is discussed below). As these developments have taken place, the very nature of the city has begun to change; however, the pattern of land use described by Burgess was a function of circumstances which now no longer exist as they did in earlier decades. However, in many of the older cities where the land use patterns did correspond with Burgess' formulation, one may still find a rough order of concentric zones, much as Burgess originally described them.

Sector Theory

As opposed to Burgess' concentric zone theory, Sector theory takes the position that residential land use in cities assumes the forms of "wedges" or sectors which extend outward from the center of the city and which tend to follow transportation lines. However, sector theory, as it was originally developed by Homer Hoyt, only dealt with *residential* land use, whereas Burgess also considered non-residential land use patterns as well.

Hoyt was an economist in the Division of Economics and Statistics of the Federal Housing Administration, and in 1934 he carefully examined data pertaining to individual blocks in 142 small and medium sized American cities. He added supplemental data from New York, Chicago, Philadelphia, Washington, D.C., and Detroit. One of Hoyt's principal discoveries was that rent very closely related to other housing characteristics and could therefore be used as an index for assessing the structure of residential areas. Hoyt found that: [3]

> ...rent areas in American cities tend to conform to a pattern of sectors rather than of concentric circles. The highest rent areas of a city tend to be located in one or more sectors of the city. There is a gradation of rentals downward from these high rental areas in all directions. Intermediate rental areas, or those ranking next to the highest rental areas, adjoin the high rent area on one or more sides, and tend to be located in the same sectors as the high rental areas. Low rent areas occupy other entire sectors of the city from the center to the periphery.

The high rent area of a city usually was initially located near the central business district, out of convenience for the businessmen who

[3] *The Structure and Growth of Residential Neighborhoods in American Cities,* U.S. Federal Housing Authority (Washington, D.C.: Government Printing Office, 1939), p. 70.

worked there. Their homes were located on the side of the city away from the industrial or warehouse districts which served the central business district. These homes were in turn bounded by the intermediate-rental areas, thus forming a gradation. As the higher income (upper class) families migrated, their movement was away from the city, and their movement tended to draw the growth of the city in the same general direction, thus giving rise to the development of the city by "sectors."

The movement of the high-rent areas, according to Hoyt, was guided by a number of factors, including: [4]

1. High-grade residential growth tends to proceed from the given point of origin, along established lines of travel or toward another existing nucleus of buildings or trading centers.

2. The zone of high-rent areas tends to progress toward high ground which is free from the risk of floods and to spread along lake, bay, river, and ocean fronts, where such water fronts are not used for industry.

3. High-rent residential districts tend to grow toward the section of the city which has free, open country beyond the edges and away from "dead end" sections which are limited by natural or artificial barriers to expansion.

4. The higher priced residential neighborhood tends to grow toward the homes of the leaders of the community.

5. Trends of movement of office buildings, banks, and stores pull the higher priced residential neighborhoods in the same general direction.

6. High-grade residential areas tend to develop along the fastest existing transportation lines.

7. The growth of high-rent neighborhoods continues in the same direction for a long period of time.

8. Deluxe high-rent apartment areas tend to be established near the business center in old residential areas.

9. Real estate promoters may bend the direction of high-grade residential growth.

Hoyt's sector theory presents an interesting approach to an understanding of the development of the city. The conception of the growth of a city being a function of the migration of the higher class residential

[4] *Ibid.*, pp. 117–119.

areas casts considerable light on the reason why so many cities are
checkered in their distribution of the population and why the various
groups reside in their respective sectors within the community.

The Multiple-Nuclei Theory

The multiple nuclei theory was developed by Chauncy D. Harris and
Edward L. Ullman and provides yet another perspective on land-use
patterns and the development of cities.[5] In this concept, original concentrations in an area establish a pattern or trend which sets the tone for
later development and expansion.

A number of various centers (nuclei) are formed early in the history
of the city. These centers are based on historical accident, topography,
or other considerations. For example, business districts have generally
been situated because of the availability of transportation—thus many
cities were established near ports or navigable rivers and others sprang
up with the advent of railroads. The capacity to ship and receive goods
provided the geographic basis for the establishment of a business area,
and as the area itself grew (including the population needed to service
the businesses), cities developed.

The retail area of a city is an example of a nucleus. Retail districts
profit from the grouping of similar establishments because of the resulting concentration of customers. In almost all large cities these nuclei are
apparent; even in smaller cities they tend to be conspicuous. For instance,
used car lots tend to be located close to one another, as do pawn shops,
warehouses, industrial sites, and commercial enterprises.

Each of the foregoing land use patterns explores the spatial distribution of urban space from a different perspective, yet each underscores
the basic fact that land use within a city, and the growth of cities, are
far from random events. A large number of complex, intertwining factors
operate to determine the social ecology of the city. This has become
especially evident in recent years in the changes which are occurring in
the inner cities.

Inner City Deterioration and the Formation of Crisis Ghettoes

As has been previously noted, recent decades have witnessed a massive
influx of lower socioeconomic blacks into the inner city areas of the large
cities. As these low income, non-upwardly mobile blacks entered the

[5] Chauncy D. Harris and Edward L. Ullman, "The Nature of Cities," *The Annals
of the American Academy of Political and Social Science*, Vol. 242 (November 1945),
pp. 14–15.

cities, large numbers of middle-class whites left the cities for the suburban fringes.

This produced a pattern of urban decline and an accompanying suburban growth. However, until the 1960's, nearly all urban blacks, regardless of their socioeconomic status, had relatively little in the way of residential choice. As a consequence, black urban areas were often highly heterogeneous with middle and working class blacks providing a degree of overall stability to the black neighborhoods. However, within the past decade and a half, minority incomes have risen and more opportunity in housing has become available. As a result, the middle and working class blacks have also moved to better areas, leaving behind the poorest and most distressed families and individuals to occupy the oldest and least adequate homes.

With the rapid change in the ethnic and racial status of these neighborhoods, and as the socioeconomic level of the areas decreased, the once high market value of the property itself began to fall drastically. The urban riots of the late 1960's also had a major impact on these areas. Property values, which had been declining, dropped sharply and the market mechanisms affecting the inner city all but ceased to function. Investments in inner city housing became a liability, and lending institutions became reluctant to provide money for the purchase or repair of buildings situated in distressed areas of the city. To make matters worse, mortgage money, when available, was predicated on the investor obtaining insurance which became either unavailable or prohibitively expensive.

At the same time, a lack of investor demand and escalating maintenance costs, coupled with the lack of capital for either repairs or renovation, brought about a greater diminution in the maintenance of the buildings. All of these factors, plus others, have brought about:

A concentration of low-income, non-upwardly mobile families; large families and a high percentage of young people; an old housing stock and a high percentage of substandard buildings; a preponderance of rental properties and multiunit buildings which are suffering from long periods of deferred maintenance; a declining rate of home ownership; strongly antisocial tenant attitudes; minimum public services; a high or increasing vacancy rate; and, despite the high vacancy rate, overcrowding within occupied units.[6]

The outcome of this situation has been highly volatile. It includes the abandonment of housing units by owners, at least in the sense that many of them have discontinued mortgage and tax payments and no longer

[6] *Abandoned Housing Research: A Compendium,* U.S. Department of Housing and Urban Development (Washington, D.C.: Government Printing Office, 1973), p. 81.

invest in any building maintenance. Many such units have been vacated, vandalized, and physically abandoned by both owners and tenants. In fact, the problem of abandonment has even become contagious in some areas with whole blocks being affected.

As the deterioration of the inner city continues, it becomes less fit for habitation and all who can do so attempt to leave it. The lack of economic viability in turn contributes to a decrease in tax revenues, while the demands for public services increase. Problems of crime, delinquency, vandalism, and social disorganization become endemic, and more demands are made on the financial resources of the city than it is able to meet.

These patterns vary from one city to the next, and at the present time tend to be the most pronounced in the large urban centers east of the Mississippi. One factor which seems to play a role is the proportion of inner city housing in the form of multiunit apartments. The close crowding of people in substandard housing seems to be closely related to the social dysfunction associated with such areas. At any rate, a new and somewhat gloomy picture is beginning to emerge with respect to many cities and their development.

Burgess' concentric zone theory portrayed the development of relatively dynamic cities. By the same token, Hoyt's concept of sectors within the city also reflected positive growth trends, as did the multiple nuclei theory of Harris and Ullman.

However, the concentration of distressed minority citizens in central cities, which are rapidly deteriorating, augers ill for the future. The crisis ghettoes, as they are now developing, are characterized by: [7]

1. Decreasing median family income.
2. Increasing unemployment.
3. Increasing number of female headed households.
4. Declining total population.
5. Increasing public assistance dependency.
6. Increasing rates of crime and vandalism.
7. No increase in the median years of school completed and in the percent of high school graduates.

These inner city areas are becoming places of despair, alienation, and apathy. They pose an economic drain on heavily burdened tax resources, and they also present a devastating loss of human potential. At the same time, the cities are rapidly being viewed as places which are not desirable because of the diminished quality of life, and because those who do reside within the city and who are economically productive are being asked to

[7] *Ibid.*, p. 40.

pay ever increasing taxes in order to provide social and public services to those who are poor and dependent. This in turn fosters an attitude of bitterness which frequently has racial overtones.

The Challenge and the Response

The President's Commission on Law Enforcement and the Administration of Justice reported in 1967 that the fear of crime in cities had eroded the basic quality of life for many Americans. The commission pointed out many of the consequences of crime, but at the same time it recognized that widespread crime also implies a widespread failure by society as a whole. They pointed out that warring on poverty, inadequate housing, and unemployment is tantamount to warring on crime itself—and that there is far more to controlling crime than that which is involved in the work of the police.

However, at the time the report of the President's Commission was issued, there had been considerable violence in American cities and on college campuses. In response to the public mood, the Congress passed the Omnibus Crime Control and Safe Streets Act of 1968. One consequence of that particular piece of legislation was the infusion of large sums of money into the criminal justice system (but primarily into the police). The same Act also created the Law Enforcement Assistance Administration (LEAA) within the Department of Justice.

The LEAA was established to (1) encourage states and units of general local government to prepare and adopt comprehensive plans based upon their evaluation of state and local problems of law enforcement; (2) authorize grants to States and units of local government in order to improve and strengthen law enforcement; and (3) encourage research and development of new methods for the prevention and reduction of crime and the detection and apprehension of criminals. From 1969 through 1973, the Congress appropriated $3,950,111,000 so that the objectives of the LEAA could be met.

Unfortunately, the appropriation of this large sum of money apparently did not result in the desired outcomes; the House Committee on Government Operations issued a report in 1972 which addressed itself to the block grant programs of the LEAA. One summary conclusion they reached was that:

The block grant programs of LEAA have too often been characterized by inefficiency, waste, maladministration, and in some cases, corruption. They have had no visible impact on the incidence of crime in the United States. Moreover, State and local governments have not received meaningful leadership or direction from LEAA to enable them to find new ways to reduce crime and improve the operations of the system of criminal justice.[8]

There can be little doubt that American police have long been in need of serious efforts to upgrade them. However, instead of new, innovative programs designed to reduce or prevent crime, massive amounts of federal money have been invested in operational hardware: riot gear, weapons, two-way radios, and other equipment. Such approaches are more interested in coping with police problems rather than at solving them. Although the basic challenge of disintegrating cities remains pretty much the same, responses continue to lag behind.

Because of the disparity between the challenge and the responses, the LEAA established a National Advisory Commission on Criminal Justice Standards and Goals in 1971. The report of this commission, which was issued in seven volumes in 1973, again recognized the broad social nature of the crime problem in what is an essentially urban society. The reading which accompanies this chapter is taken from their volume which deals with the development of a national strategy to reduce crime and shows how government responsiveness must include far more than an upgrading of police agencies.

[8] "Block Grant Programs of the Law Enforcement Assistance Administration," Committee on Government Operations, Chet Holifield, Chairman. House Report No. 548 (Washington, D.C.: Government Printing Office, 1972), p. 6.

Government Responsiveness *

Some of the problems faced by the criminal justice system can be alleviated to some degree by responsive action on the part of other segments of government.

Open, responsive governments can encourage citizen involvement in crime prevention. When citizens find government complex, confusing, and uninviting, a chasm can develop between city hall and the community. The burden of cutting through the red tape of an impersonal bureaucracy falls primarily on those most dependent on its services and least equipped to deal with its complexity—the elderly, the poor, the uneducated, those with language barriers, and minority and ethnic populations unfamiliar with governmental structures.

To maximize government responsiveness, the Commission recommends

* The following is taken from *A National Strategy to Reduce Crime,* National Advisory Commission on Criminal Justice Standards and Goals, Russell W. Peterson, Chairman. Washington, D.C.: U.S. Government Printing Office (1973), pp. 48–58. The National Advisory Commission on Criminal Justice Standards and Goals is the Commission referred to throughout the article.

that government units open neighborhood offices and that local governments develop complaint centers. These programs, together with a greater flow of information, can bring the community together.

City governments should establish neighborhood facilities, such as multiservice centers and "little city halls," to aid in dispensing government services and to improve communication between citizens and government agencies.

In this way citizens can receive effective services close to their homes with a minimum of bureaucratic red tape. A neighborhood center can help to convince citizens that government is concerned about their needs. The objectives of decentralization are a more citizen-oriented service delivery system and increased citizen participation in government.

The concept of decentralized municipal services is not new. Since the late 1920's, branch city halls that provide most city services have been operating in Los Angeles, Calif., to reach more conveniently more than 40 subcommunities in the city.

Before community involvement in governmental processes can become a reality, community members must be able to obtain information on which government decisions and programs are based. Informing citizens about the activities of the local government will help assure the public that the government is working in its best interest.

The Commission believes that local governments should provide access to such information by:

• Enacting "right to know" laws that provide citizens with open and easy access to agency regulations, audits, minutes, and other pertinent information.

• Permitting local radio and television stations to cover official and public meetings on a regular basis.

• Holding public hearings to acquire an understanding of the real concerns of the community.

An orderly and effective mechanism for general redress of citizen grievances will also bring local government closer to its citizens. Individual agencies often do not have the time or personnel to respond to complaints. In addition, citizens sometimes find bureaucracy so confusing they are unable to locate or identify the department that could help them. Citizens' attitudes toward government are adversely affected when local governments rely solely on haphazard procedures to respond to citizen complaints, and when there is no regular monitoring to insure the public is served adequately.

Municipal governments should establish a central office of complaint and information to improve government effectiveness and to permit

citizens to obtain information and direction on any problem with a minimum of "red tape."

The Commission also proposes the establishment of mass media action line programs that will assist government officials to respond to citizen requests and complaints. Direct exchange can allow the public to become familiar with city officials and to gain insight into the complexities of governmental processes. It also will help insure greater accountability to the public of elected and appointed officials.

The remoteness of government and a declining sense of community have been noted as two significant characteristics of urban America. They are undoubtedly linked, but they need not become permanent conditions. There are signs of a renewed interest among citizens in the problems—including crime—of their cities and towns. A responsive government can help sustain this interest.

Delivery of Public Services

The need to deliver all public services in a comprehensive fashion is becoming increasingly apparent in urban areas. Education, employment, health, sanitation, and criminal justice agencies frequently have found themselves addressing mere segments of larger problems. An illustration of the fact that social ills rarely occur in isolation comes from the Model Cities Program of the Department of Housing and Urban Development. What follows is a profile of a 1970 neighborhood typical of many depressed areas in cities and towns across the country.

Unemployment in the low-income model neighborhood (MN) is 6.2 percent, compared with 3.4 percent for the entire city. Ten of the 11 schools in the target area have mental maturity, reading, and arithmetic norms one and two grades below the national average. The high school dropout rate is 16 percent, compared with 9 percent for the school system as a whole. Only 4 percent of the model area housing is "standard." Existence of outside toilets attests to primitive conditions.

Overcrowding is characteristic in the model neighborhood. Since 1960, the population has increased but the number of housing units has decreased. The target area has only three supervised playgrounds with a combined area of 2.6 acres. Thus 5.9 percent of the total city-supervised playground area serves 15 percent of the city's population. There are 8 miles of unpaved streets and sidewalks in the MN, in sharp contrast to the historic section of the city, with its beautiful old buildings and well-kept parks and gardens.

Health conditions in the MN are below the city and county rates. In 1968, infant mortality rates per 100,000 persons were 42.5 in the county and 60 in the MN; tuberculosis rates were 42 in the county and 105 in the MN; infectious syphilis rates were 27.6 in the county and 115 in the MN.

Dependence on public welfare is heavy, yet few social service agencies are located within the MN or have outreach services there. Residents complain of inadequate coordination between the public and private agencies that provide social services.

Finally, life in the target area is threatened by a high incidence of crime. With only 15 percent of the population, the MN experiences 33 percent of the homicides and rapes and 27 percent of the felonious assaults. Juvenile delinquency, as represented by the number of arrests, is also high. The arrest rate of persons under 18 years of age in the target area is 48.2 per 1,000, compared with 33.8 per 1,000 for the whole city.

As the Model City example suggests, public services are not always adequate to meet the pressing needs of many individuals. Those in need of public services are likely to have multiple problems: youths involved in crime are often dropouts and unemployed; a drug-dependent person may require not only medical treatment, but employment counseling and skill training as well.

In some neighborhoods important services are simply not available or are severely deficient. Low income areas often suffer while middle- and upper-class neighborhoods receive a high level of service.

The Commission believes municipal services should be allocated to neighborhoods on the basis of need.

Achieving this end will require the expenditure of sufficient funds to maintain equally effective services in all areas of the city or jurisdiction. Also needed is a means of coordinating existing social, medical, and rehabilitative services so that persons may be treated comprehensively.

Social Service Delivery Mechanisms: Youth Services Bureaus

In addition to the equitable delivery of services, there is a need for coordinating existing social, medical, and rehabilitative services. Efforts must be made to develop comprehensive service delivery systems that avoid wasteful duplication, open lines of communication to the community, and better assist individual clients through a coordinated delivery of services to arrive at their best functioning level. One of the most important examples of comprehensive services delivery is the youth services bureau.

These bureaus in large part were the result of a recommendation by the 1967 President's Commission on Law Enforcement and Administration of Justice, which urged communities to establish them to serve both delinquent and nondelinquent youth referred by police, juvenile courts, schools, and other sources. The bureaus were to act as central coordinating units for all community services for young people.

A national census in 1972 identified 150 youth services bureaus in operation in many States and territories. In the absence of national standards, local youth services bureaus have developed according to the needs and pressures of each community.[1]

In most localities, however, the youth services bureau, at a minimum, is a link between available resources and youth in need. It first identifies services and resources in the community and then refers clients to an agency that can provide the required services. Social services made available might include employment, job training, education, housing, medical care, family counseling, psychiatric care, or welfare.

Once a young person has been directed to another agency, the youth services bureau follows up to assure that adequate services are being provided. The bureau acts as a services broker, matching the young person with the service he or she needs. When services are not available through governmental or volunteer sources, they may be purchased from private agencies or independent professionals.

In Worchester, Mass., for example, coordination of services for individual youths is taking place through case conferences. Representatives of all agencies involved with a young person meet to gain a complete view of the youth's problems and to develop a comprehensive plan to meet his needs. In some instances, the youth or the youth and his parent attend the case conference. In order to strengthen the youth's responsibility, he is encouraged to contribute to the decisions that will affect him. After the youth is referred to another agency, the bureau systematically follows up to assure that services are being provided.

Specialized services often are needed to help a child and to keep him out of trouble with the law. A child might need services that are not available in the community, such as an alternative educational experience, career training, drug treatment, a group residence, or psychiatric services. It is frequently the responsibility of the youth services bureau to identify these gaps in service and to promote the development of needed resources.

The Youth Development Service in Billings, Mont., as an example, provides little direct service to youth. Instead, it brings agencies together to develop community priorities, to eliminate service duplication, and to redirect resources when current projects are inappropriate. The Youth Advocacy Program in South Bend, Ind., attempts to influence youth-serving agencies to develop innovative programs. Field workers are assigned to five agencies —the recreation department, schools, a family and child agency, city government, and Model Cities—with the task of making them more responsive to youth.

Youth services bureaus sometimes provide specific services themselves

[1] William Underwood, *A National Study of Youth Service Bureaus,* U.S. Department of Health, Education, and Welfare, Youth Development and Delinquency Prevention Administration (December 1972).

when the services are not easily available through other public or private agencies. A number of bureaus, for example, provide temporary shelter for runaways. In Los Angeles County, Calif., the Basset Youth Service Bureau sponsors a free clinic in conjunction with other community groups, staffed primarily with volunteers. The clinic includes a counseling center in addition to an outpatient medical clinic. Venereal diseases, unwanted pregnancies, and drug use are the most frequently treated medical problems.

Clients come to youth services bureaus from a variety of sources. Individuals may be referred to bureaus by schools or other community agencies, or young people may come to the bureau on their own seeking help. The police and juvenile court can also be major sources of referrals. A nationwide sample of more than 400 cases from 28 youth services bureaus showed that 13 percent of the referrals were from law enforcement; 30 percent were referred by self, friend, or family; and the remainder were referred by schools and other public and private agencies.[2] (See Youth Services Bureau Chart.)

Enough information has now been gathered on existing youth services bureaus for the Commission to recommend that bureaus be established in communities experiencing serious youth problems. Each year a vast number of young people become involved in the justice system for acts that are not crimes for adults: incorrigibility, truancy, running away, and even stubbornness. In addition, many youths are processed through the juvenile justice system for minor offenses that are neither recurring nor a serious threat to the community. Such behavior is often an indication that a young person needs special attention, but not necessarily punitive treatment.

Many of what are now considered delinquency or predelinquency problems should be redefined as family, educational, or welfare problems and diverted from the juvenile justice system. Such diversions can relieve overburdened probation offices and courts and allow them to concentrate on offenders that need serious attention. In addition, diversion through youth services bureaus can avoid the unnecessary "delinquent" label that frequently accompanies involvement with the juvenile court.

Unfortunately, existing youth services bureaus have been underutilized as a diversionary resource by law enforcement. In many communities, police seldom refer young people to community agencies. In 31 interviews with juvenile officers in one large metropolitan area, fully one quarter of the officers could name no community resources and only two of the 31 used direct referral practices. Some police agencies have a policy of no diversion —all arrested juveniles are processed in the system.[3]

Youth services bureaus should make a particular effort to attract the diversionary referrals from the juvenile justice system. At the same time,

[2] Ibid.
[3] Malcolm W. Klein, "Issues in Police Diversion of Juvenile Offenders: A Guide for Discussion" (unpublished paper, University of Southern California), pp. 7, 16.

law enforcement agencies and courts should make policy changes that would allow for the diversion of every juvenile who is not an immediate threat to public safety and who voluntarily accepts referral to a youth services bureau.

The Youth Service Project in San Antonio, Tex., provides an example of how an administrative policy change is bringing about diversion in that city. The police chief has ordered his officers to deliver to one of the three neighborhood youth centers in the city juveniles picked up for such offenses as glue or paint sniffing, liquor violations, and running away.

Accessibility of the bureaus' offices to law enforcement is another asset in encouraging diversion. Until recently, the Youth Service Bureau of Greensboro, Inc., in Greensboro, N.C., was across the street from the police department. Not only did this enable bureau staff to pick up "paper referrals" each day from the police department, but it also increased understanding between the police department's juvenile officers and the bureau staff during the youth services bureau's developmental stages.

Legislation is another means of overcoming the reluctance of law enforcement and court personnel to utilize diversionary alternatives. Legislation accompanied by State funding also would increase awareness of the youth services bureau concept and could stimulate the creation of bureaus in the less affluent and less powerful communities of each State.

Each State should enact enabling legislation that encourages local establishment of youth services bureaus throughout the State and that provides partial funding for them. Legislation also should be enacted to mandate the use of youth services bureaus as a voluntary diversion resource by agencies of the juvenile justice system.

To avoid misunderstanding, criteria for referrals should be developed jointly and specified in writing by law enforcement, courts, and youth services bureau personnel.

Diversion can take place only if there is cooperation and communication between concerned parties.

In California, some of the criteria presently considered by juvenile justice agencies in diverting youth to youth services bureaus include: nonprobation status, first offense, age, minor offense that does not threaten the public safety, residence in the project area, cooperative attitude toward voluntary referral, and the need for additional services the bureau can provide.

In a few communities, what masquerades as a youth services bureau is actually a field office for probation surveillance. Where probation services are particularly limited, court referrals ordering youths to participate in the bureau's programs may seem to be an expeditious alternative. But such action negates the role of the bureau as a program in which young people participate by choice. The bureau becomes part of the traditional enforcement machinery by deciding, in effect, whether or not a youth must be returned to juvenile court. Thus, the stigma of a coercive officially mandated service remains, without the legal safeguards currently emerging in the justice system itself.

Referrals to the youth services bureau should be completed only if they are voluntarily accepted by the youth. Youths should not be forced to choose between bureau referral and further justice system processing.

In making this recommendation, the Commission departs from the original recommendation of the President's Crime Commission. In its report, that Commission said that the youth services bureau could be vested with the authority to refer back to court within 30 to 60 days "those with whom it cannot deal effectively."

Such a practice can result in an extension of control over the youth by community institutions, without providing the legal safeguards of the justice system. Sherwood Norman, writing in *The Youth Service Bureau: A Key to Delinquency Prevention,* stated that to refer to court upon a young person's failure to cooperate ". . . would be a clear indication to him that the youth services bureau was not a voluntary agency but rather part of the justice system and therefore coercive."

The essence of any social service delivery system is the marshaling of resources in a coordinated way to bring clients to the best functioning level. As stated earlier, the youth services bureau provides a useful model for delivery of service systems which should be applied to adults as well as young persons.

Employment

There is a definite association between unemployment or underemployment, and crime. Some individuals who cannot find satisfactory jobs or who are discriminated against in the labor market will turn to illegal activity as a source of income. The President's Commission on Crime in the District of Columbia in 1965 found that of adult offenders surveyed, 60 percent had no history of regular employment at the time of arrest and the majority, whether employed or not, were in unskilled occupations. Among the offenders about whom income information was available, 69 percent earned less than $3,000 annually and 90 percent earned less than $5,000.[4]

A 1972 study comparing national youth arrest rates, unemployment rates, and labor-force participation rates over 2 decades concluded that lack of

[4] *Report of the President's Commission on Crime in the District of Columbia* (1966), pp. 127, 130.

employment opportunities among white and black youths was a key factor in generating property crime.[5]

Assisting those with severe employment problems is, in the Commission's judgment, an important way to prevent crime. As in other areas, particular attention must be given to programs for young persons. Unemployment among young people became gradually more serious during the 1960's. In 1960, the unemployment rate for teenagers aged 16 to 19 was three and one-third times the adult rate; in 1971, it was more than four times the adult rate.[6] The problem is even more critical among minority youths in cities. In 1971 the unemployment rate among nonwhite teenagers aged 16 to 19 in low income urban areas was 38 percent compared with an overall unemployment rate for all teenagers of 16.9 percent.[7]

Ex-offenders are another group that has traditionally experienced difficulties in the labor market, particularly in periods of rising unemployment. Evidence from manpower programs suggests that in slack labor markets, training, placement, and job development tend to be less effective than when there are many unfilled jobs. In the Manhattan Court Employment Project, which has continued up to the present time, placements have dropped from 270 in the first year to 135 in the third, even though, judging by placements per referral, efforts have apparently improved. The problem is that fewer employers are willing to talk to or hire ex-offenders as long as qualified candidates without criminal records are available.

It is increasingly doubtful that the private sector alone can provide enough jobs to produce satisfactory changes in unemployment rates among urban youths and ex-offenders. Even in the best of times, meaningful public employment will be needed if the chronically unemployed are to be put to work.

The Commission urges expanded public employment programs in areas of high unemployment. Programs should offer full-time, part-time, and summer employment.

Most likely, these programs will require joint cooperation and funding from two or more levels of government. There are a number of different public employment strategies whose adoption depends upon community priorities: transitional jobs that would serve as stepping stones to permanent jobs in the public sector; permanent jobs that would provide a program of education, experience, and training needed for advancement; temporary job slots for offenders immediately after their release from confinement; and

---

[5] Llad Phillips, Harold L. Votey, Jr., and Darold Maxwell, "Crime, Youth and the Labor Market," *Journal of Political Economy* (May/June 1972), pp. 491–504.

[6] *Manpower Report of the President*, U. S. Department of Labor (March 1972), p. 79.

[7] *Manpower Report of the President*, U.S. Department of Labor (March 1972), Table 1, p. 78, and U.S. Department of Commerce, Bureau of the Census, *Statistical Abstract of the United States*, 93rd edition (1972), Table 356, p. 223.

jobs that would serve as an alternative to incarceration for misdemeanants.

In the private sector, the Commission urges employers and unions to institute or accelerate efforts to expand job or membership opportunities to the economically and educationally disadvantaged. Various employment approaches could include work-study programs, summer and after-school employment, and job training and development for out-of-school youths.

In its *Report on Community Crime Prevention,* the Commission notes outstanding examples of private initiative. One of the most successful summer programs was developed by the Philadelphia Urban Coalition's High School Academy in 1970 and repeated in the summer of 1971. This effort provided work for students under 17 who were too young to get regular summer jobs. Under the auspices of the Urban Coalition and with the assistance of Junior Achievement, the students formed their own company, the Edison Electric Shop. The youths earned $1.75 an hour, and functioned under their own management with the help of a teacher-director, whose salary was paid by the Coalition.

Youth for Service in San Francisco, Calif., developed jobs for inner city youth by contracting with urban development and community action programs to build, repair, and maintain mini-parks in the blighted areas of the city. A similar group in Chicago, Ill., is running a food store, a boutique, a paper recycling program, and a restaurant.

The success of public and private efforts to expand employment opportunities depends to a large extent on general economic conditions. The close relationship between poverty area unemployment and national economic conditions suggests that a high national employment rate is essential if inner city unemployment is to be reduced. From 1968 through 1971 unemployment rates in urban poverty areas dipped below 5.5 percent only twice,[8] a level that most economists and politicians decry as unacceptable. At both times the national unemployment rate was around 3.5 percent.[9] The increase from 3.5 percent total unemployment at the end of 1969 to 5.9 percent in 1971 was accompanied by a rise in urban poverty area unemployment from 5.5 to 9.7 percent.[10]

The Commission recommends that economic policy be concentrated on maintaining aggregate employment at a high level. The Commission believes that the ultimate goal of such policy should be to assure that the unemployment rate in poverty areas is no greater than the national rate.

[8] Bureau of Labor Statistics, U.S. Department of Labor, *Handbook of Labor Statistics—1971,* p. 104, and *Handbook of Labor Statistics—1972,* p. 113. The poverty neighborhood classification used is based on a ranking of census facts according to 1960 data on income, education, skills, housing, and a proportion of broken homes. The poorest one-fifth of these tracts are considered poverty neighborhoods.

[9] *Handbook of Labor Statistics—1970,* p. 125.

[10] *Handbook of Labor Statistics—1972,* pp. 113, 129.

Consideration must also be given to changing credit, taxation, and ex penditure policies that may have an impact on unemployment.

Criminal Records and Employment

Surveys estimate that approximately 25 percent of the national population may have nontraffic arrest records. The chances that a black male from an urban area will be arrested have been estimated at from 50 to 90 percent.[11]

There is little doubt that arrest records are a barrier to employment. In the private sector, few firms exclude former offenders as a blanket policy, but often selection criteria tend to have this effect in practice.

In a survey in New York City, 75 percent of the employment agencies contacted said they would not recommend an individual with an arrest record, regardless of the disposition of the charges against him.[12]

Barriers to employment are at least as forbidding in the public sector as they are in the private sector. Most States, counties, and cities ask questions about prior arrest records when hiring. Few of the applications state that a record does not automatically bar the applicant. Civil service statutes that govern hiring often use language that could be and apparently is grounds to exclude large numbers of individuals with mere arrest records.[13]

Responses from employers indicate that employees with criminal records are not different from other employees. Agencies in a national survey were asked whether employees with criminal records were better than, the same as, or worse than other employees in each of eight categories: punctuality, attendance, honesty, judgment, initiative, cooperativeness, accuracy, and industriousness. There was little difference between employees with criminal records and other employees. What little difference there was in the reports was favorable toward employees with records.[14]

The Commission's standards on information systems (see Chapter 3) prohibit the dissemination of criminal records to private employers, provide for the return of arrest records of individuals not convicted of a crime, and direct the purging of criminal records after certain periods of time.

To eliminate arbitrary barriers to employment, legislation should be enacted prohibiting employers from inquiring about an applicant's criminal history after records have been purged or returned.

Government civil service regulations, moreover, should specify that no person can be barred automatically from taking a civil service test because of a criminal record.

[11] Herbert S. Miller, *The Closed Door* (prepared for the U.S. Department of Labor, February 1972), p. 147.

[12] Albert G. Hess and F. Le Poole, "Abuse of the Record of Arrest Not Leading to Conviction," *Journal of Research on Crime and Delinquency* (1967).

[13] Miller, *The Closed Door*, pp. 4, 6, 7.

[14] *Ibid*, pp. 100–101

Education

Schools are the first public agencies that most children contact. For this reason, the schools inevitably have been proposed as vehicles for the solution of a host of public problems including the problem of crime. In making its recommendations, the Commission is well aware of crushing demands already placed upon local schoolteachers, principals, and school boards.

Nevertheless, individuals sometimes come to the attention of the criminal justice system because the educational system has not met their personal needs. The fact that the public schools have not helped a large portion of young people is reflected in high youth unemployment rates and high dropout rates. Twenty percent of those who now enter grade five leave before high school graduation, and only 28.7 percent of 1971 high school graduates went on to college. Yet 80 percent of the effort in schools is structured to meet college entry requirements.[15] Too often classroom instruction is not related to life outside. Undoubtedly many of the 850,000 students who left elementary and secondary schools in 1970 and 1971 did so because they felt their educational experiences were irrelevant.[16]

The Commission believes that the primary goal of American education should be to prepare and interest people in satisfying and useful careers.

Schools should plan programs that will guarantee that every child leaving school can obtain either a job or acceptance to an advanced program of studies, regardless of the time he leaves the formal school setting.

The San Mateo, Calif., school district, for example, formally accepts responsibility for insuring that students are employable whenever they choose to leave school—whether as dropouts from the 10th grade or with advanced degrees.

If schools are going to make guarantees of this kind there must be a shift to career education. In career education programs, instruction is related to the world of work and opportunities are provided to explore or receive training in a career. Career education may begin in first grade or earlier and continue beyond high school graduation. It should bring an awareness to students of the wide range of jobs in American society and the roles and requirements involved.

The Seattle, Wash., public school system has a prototype career education program that offers occupational information to students at all grade

[15] Statistical data abstracted from: (1) Kenneth B. Hoyt, R. Evans, Edward Mackin, and Garth Mangum, *Career Education: What It Is and How to Do It* (Olympus Publishing Co., 1972); (2) U.S. Department of Health, Education, and Welfare—Office of Education Materials; and (3) U.S. Bureau of Census, *Statistical Abstract of the United States—1972.*
[16] National School Public Relations Association, "Dropouts: Prevention and Rehabilitation" (Washington: NSPRA, 1972), p. 3.

levels, from kindergarten to grade 12, and integrates materials into every subject of the curriculum. Another program inverts the curriculum. Students choose preparatory trade areas as electives, staying in each long enough to become oriented to the occupation, explore it, or be trained in it. A core of general education courses—communications and humanities—accompanies the program.

A significant approach to career education is a cooperative education program, Project 70,001, operating since 1969 in Wilmington, Del. The program provides on-the-job work experience and related classroom instruction to students unable to participate in or benefit from regular programs of education and training. Similar programs have been started in Dover, Del.; Harrisburg, Pa.; Kansas City, Mo.; and Hartford, Conn. The Wilmington project combines the efforts and resources of a large shoe manufacturer, the Distributive Education Clubs of America, the Delaware Department of Public Instruction, and the Wilmington Public Schools.

In the Education chapter of the Commission's *Report on Community Crime Prevention,* additional approaches designed to make school systems more responsive to the individual student are recommended.

Varied alternative educational experiences should be provided to students who cannot benefit from classroom instruction. School counseling and other supportive services should be available. There should be bilingual programs for young people who are not fluent in English. There should be a guarantee of functional literacy to every student who does not have serious emotional, physical, or mental problems.

Aside from fulfilling the primary objective of preparing young people for adult life, school systems may also contribute to community crime prevention by serving as centers for community activities. The traditional school operating 5 days a week for 39 weeks a year is an unaffordable luxury. Schools can become total community opportunity centers for the young and the old, operating virtually around the clock, 365 days a year.

In Flint, Mich., schools are used for a wide variety of community services: adult education and retraining; recreation and counseling; civic meetings; health clinics; YMCA, YWCA, Boy and Girl Scouts, Big and Little Brother activities; job counseling and placement; senior citizen activities; and parent aid in developing curriculums. Members of the community are represented by a neighborhood council that advises the school and expresses the desires of the residents. There are 92,000 people per week using schools after hours; 80,000 adults enroll in classes each year. The accessibility of the school and the wide variety of programs offered there have greatly increased citizen involvement in the community. Special programs for men and women in trouble with the law have been tremendously successful in Flint schools.

Among the total population, there are indications of decreasing rates of juvenile crime, dropping out of high school, and parole recidivism.

The Flint experience and others like it provide positive examples of the multipurpose use of educational facilities. The Commission urges authorities to make schools available to all citizens as centers for community involvement and adult education.

Appendix A
The Logic of Metropolitan Growth*

Much of what has happened—as well as of what is happening—in the typical city or metropolitan area can be understood in terms of *three imperatives*. The first is *demographic:* if the population of a city increases, the city must expand in one direction or another—up, down, or from the center outward. The second is *technological:* if it is feasible to transport large numbers of people outward (by train, bus, and automobile) but not upward or downward (by elevator), the city must expand outward. The third is *economic:* if the distribution of wealth and income is such that some can afford new housing and the time and money to commute considerable distances to work while others cannot, the expanding periphery of the city must be occupied by the first group (the "well-off") while the older, inner parts of the city, where most of the jobs are, must be occupied by the second group (the "not well-off").

The word "imperatives" is used to emphasize the inexorable, constraining character of the three factors that together comprise the logic of metropolitan growth. Indeed, the principal purpose at this point is to show that, given a rate of population growth, a transportation technology, and a distribution of income, certain consequences must inevitably follow; that the city and its hinterland must develop *according to a predictable* pattern and that even an all-wise and all-powerful government could not change this pattern except by first changing the logic that gives rise to it. The argument is not that nothing can be done to improve matters. Rather, it is that only those things can be done which lie within the boundaries—rather narrow ones, to be sure—fixed by the logic of the growth process. Nor is it argued that the only factors influencing metropolitan development are those that relate to population, technology, and income. Countless others also influence it. Two of these other factors are of key importance, even though they are not part of the logic of the process.

The following scheme describes in a generalized way how most American cities, small as well as large, have developed and are still developing, but it does not describe completely (or perhaps even accurately) how any *particular* city has developed. The city under discussion here is a highly simplified model.

The logic of metropolitan growth began unfolding the moment the cities were founded and it has not changed since. More than a century ago, in 1857, a select committee of the state legislature described the forces that were shaping New York. These were, as the committee made clear, the same forces that had always been shaping it. And they were the same ones that are shaping it and other cities still:

* SOURCE: Edward C. Banfield, *The Unheavenly City*. Boston: Little, Brown and Co., 1968. Copyright © 1968, by Edward C. Banfield. By permission of Little, Brown and Co.

"As our wharves became crowded with warehouses, and encompassed with bustle and noise, the wealthier citizens, who peopled old 'Knickerbocker' mansions, near the bay, transferred their residence to streets beyond the din; compensating for remoteness from their counting houses, by the advantages of increased quiet and luxury. Their habitations then passed into the hands, on the one side, of boarding house keepers, on the other, of real estate agents; and here, in its beginning, the tenant house became a real blessing to that class of industrious poor whose small earnings limited their expenses and whose employment in workshops, stores, and about the wharves and thoroughfares, renderetd a near residence of much importance. At this period, rents were moderate, and a mechanic with family could hire two or more comfortable and even commodious apartments, in a house once occupied by wealthy people, for less than half what he is now obliged to pay for narrow and unhealthy quarters. This state of tenantry comfort did not, however, continue long; for the rapid march of improvement speedily enhanced the value of property in the lower wards of the city, and as this took place, rents rose, and accommodations decreased in the same proportion. At first the better class of tenants submitted to retain their single floors, or two and three rooms, at the onerous rates, but this rendered them poorer, and those who were able to do so, followed the example of former proprietors, and emigrated to the upper wards. The spacious dwelling houses then fell before improvements, or languished for a season, as tenant houses of the type which is now the prevailing evil of our city; that is to say, their large rooms were partitioned into several smaller ones (without regard to proper light or ventilation), the rates of rent being lower in proportion to space or height from the street; and they soon became filled, from cellar to garret, with a class of tenantry living from hand to mouth, loose in morals, improvident in habits, degraded or squalid as beggary itself." [1]

What was happening in New York (and elsewhere as well) was the expansion of the city outward under the pressure of growth at its center. Typically, land closest to the point of original settlement (always the point most accessible to waterborne transportation) became the site of the central business district. Great accessibility to wharves, markets, shops, and offices, and later to railheads, meant that commercial and industrial activities had to be located there; the closer a site was to the most accessible center, the more it tended to be worth. Accordingly, most people lived on the outskirts of the central business district, where land prices were not prohibitively high. Only the very rich, to whom the price of land did not matter, and the very poor, who occupied undesirable sites near factories and wharves and endured great overcrowding, lived in the very center of the city.

[1] "Report of the Select Committee Appointed to Examine into the Condition of Tenant Houses in New York and Brooklyn," transmitted to the Legislature March 9, 1857 (Albany, N.Y.), pp. 11–12.

5

As the central business district grew, it absorbed the residential neighborhoods adjacent to it. The people who lived in them were pushed outward into unsettled or sparsely settled districts where land prices were still low. To say that they were "pushed" makes it sound as if they went against their wills. Probably most were glad to go. Those who owned their homes profited from the rise in prices; they could sell an old house close to the business district for enough with which to build a new and bigger one at the periphery of the city.

Much of the housing taken over in this way was torn down to make room for factories, stores, and offices. Some, however, was converted to more intensive residential use. When the only transportation was by horse, almost everyone lived within walking distance of his job in the central business district. Even afterward, when one could take a trolley to work, factory workers and office and store clerks generally preferred to pay relatively high rents for crowded quarters from which they could walk to work rather than spend the time and money to commute from neighborhoods where rents were lower. The central business district was therefore ringed with rooming houses and tenements. These establishments could afford the expensive land because they used it intensively. At the end of the last century, for example, some lodging houses in Chicago accommodated (if that is the word) as many as a thousand lodgers a night.

As the populations and income of the city grew, so did the number and proportion of those (the "well-off") who could afford new homes. In the nature of the case, most new homes had to be built at the periphery of the expanding city, where there was vacant land. Until the end of the Civil War, transportation in all large cities was by horsecar;[2] therefore, new housing had to be fairly close in and consisted largely of "three-deckers" (upper-story porches decking the front and rear of four-story tenements). Soon, however, it became feasible to build farther out. The first elevated steam railroads were built in New York in the 1870's, and twenty years later every sizable city had an electric trolley system.[3] Railroads and trolleys enabled more people to commute and to commute longer distances; the farther out they went, the cheaper the land was and the larger the lot sizes they could afford. One- and two-family houses became common.

Wherever this outward movement of the well-off passed beyond the legal boundaries of the city, it created special problems. As early as 1823, Cincinnati officials complained that people living on the edge of town did not contribute their fair share of taxes, and a few years later the council of

---

[2] In the Boston area, however, more than 20,000 passengers a day were being carried in and out of the city, by ferry and otherwise, as early as 1847. Oscar Handlin, *Boston's Immigrants,* rev. ed. (Cambridge, Mass.: Harvard University Press, 1959), p. 18.

[3] Blake McKelvey, *The Urbanization of America* (New Brunswick, N.J.: Rutgers University Press, 1963), pp. 78–79. See also Glaab, *The American City,* p. 178; and Sam B. Warner, Jr., *Streetcar and Suburbs* (Cambridge, Mass.: Harvard University Press and M.I.T. Press, 1962).

St. Louis, which had the same problem, petitioned the state legislature to enlarge the city to include the settlers just beyond its borders who had "all the benifits [sic] of a City residence without any of its burdens."[4] Many cities were enlarged, thus postponing—in some instances almost to the present—the emergence of an acute problem of city-suburb relations. The motives that impelled people to move outward were essentially the same, however, whether the boundaries of the city were near in or far out, and the strength of the outward movement seems to have been roughly the same in every era and in every place. The "flight to the suburbs" is certainly nothing new.[5]

The movement of the well-off out of the inner city was always regarded (as it had been by the select committee in New York) as both portent and cause of the city's decline. The well-off were sure that without their steadying and elevating influence the city would drift from bad to worse and become "the prey of professional thieves, ruffians, and political jugglers."[6] As a committee of leading Bostonians explained in the 1840's:

"An individual's influence is exerted chiefly in the place where he resides. Take away from the city a hundred moral and religious families, and there will be taken away a hundred centers of moral and religious influence, though the constituted heads of those families spend the greatest part of their time in the city, and hold in the metropolis the greatest proportion of their property. Those who remove their residence from the city, remove also their places of attendance on public worship, and the children of those families are removed from our primary and higher schools, public and private. . . . They are not here to visit the poor and degraded, and by their example and conduct to assist in resisting the tide of iniquity that is rolling in on us."[7]

People said that they moved because the city was no longer habitable: they could not stand its dirt, noise, and disorder, not to mention the presence near them of "undesirable" people. (When they moved beyond the borders of the city, they added political corruption and high taxes to this list.) Actually, they would have moved anyway, although not in all cases quite so soon, even if the inner city had been as clean and fresh as a field of daisies. They would have moved sooner or later because, as the city grew, the land they occupied would have to be used more intensively. Or, to put it another way,

[4] Richard C. Wade, The Urban Frontier (Chicago: University of Chicago Press, Phoenix Books, 1964), p. 307.
[5] In Philadelphia the outward movement was proportionately greater between 1860 and 1910 than between 1900 and 1950 (Hans Blumenfeld, "The Modern Metropolis," Scientific American 213 (September 1965), p. 67. For an account of Philadelphia's early pattern of growth, which was not that of the ideal type described in the text, see Sam B. Warner, Jr., The Private City (Philadelphia: University of Pennsylvania Press, 1968), chapter 3.
[6] Edward Crapsey, The Nether Side of New York (New York: Sheldon and Company, 1872), p. 9.
[7] Quoted in J. Leslie Dunstan, A Light to the City (Boston: Beacon Press, 1966), p. 91.

they would have moved because only the very rich could afford to forego the advantage of much cheaper land on the outskirts.

As the well-off moved outward, the "not well-off" (meaning here those who could not afford new houses or the time and money to travel half an hour to work) moved into the relatively old and high-density housing left behind. Indeed, it was in part the pressure of their demand for this housing that caused the well-off to move as soon as they did. The result in many places was to thin out the most overcrowded districts ("rabbit-warrens," the reformers of the 1880's called them) adjacent to warehouses, factories, stores, and offices.

Had the supply of the not well-off not been continually replenished by migration from abroad and from the small towns and farms of this country, the high-density tenement districts would have emptied rapidly at the end of the last century as incomes rose and more people moved outward. As it happened, however, immigration continually brought new workers who, for at least a few years—until they, too, could move on—were glad to take refuge in the housing that the others had left behind.

Heavy as it was, migration to the city seldom fully offset the decentralizing effect of the commuter railroad and the trolley and of the expansion of commercial and industrial land uses near the city's center. In many cities the densest slums were either displaced by stores, offices, and factories or drained to reasonable densities by improvement of transportation, or both. The Basin tenement area of Cincinnati, for example, lost one-fourth of its population between 1910 and 1930, a period of rapid growth for the rest of the city. In Chicago, New York, and Philadelphia much the same thing happened.[8]

In the first half of the twentieth century the process of growth was accelerated by changes of technology, although its character was not changed in any essential way. Invention of the mechanical refrigerator, along with a vast increase in the variety of inexpensive canned foods, reduced the number of boardinghouses and restaurants. Dispersal of factories was brought about by the use of heavy-duty power transmission cables and, even more, of the assembly line (horizontal processes required more land). Probably of equal importance was the introduction of cheap and rapid highway transportation.[9] By 1915 nearly 2.5 million automobiles were in use; five years later there were 1.1 million trucks. The automobiles facilitated the creation of residential neighborhoods still farther out from the central business district, and the trucks cut factories loose from railheads (and thus from the center of the city also). Stupendous sums were spent for automobiles and for highways, in effect subsidizing the development of the hinterland.

[8] Mabel L. Walker, *Urban Blight and Slums* (Cambridge, Mass.: Harvard University Press, 1938), pp. 18–21.
[9] Constance McLaughlin Green, *The Rise of Urban America* (New York: Harper & Row, 1965), pp. 132–133.

The federal government gave outward expansion a further push when during the Depression it created the Federal Housing Administration. As was noted in the previous chapter, FHA's assistance (and later the Veterans Administration's as well) went mostly to those who bought new homes. For the most part these were in outlying neighborhoods of the central city or in the suburban ring, the only places where vacant land was plentiful. Had it been disposed to do so, FHA might have stimulated the renovation of existing housing and thus the refurbishing of the central cities. If it had done this, it would have assisted many of the not well-off, a category that included most Negroes as well as other minority group members. In fact, it did the opposite: it subsidized the well-off who wanted to leave the central city, while (by setting neighborhood and property standards that they could not meet) refusing to help the not well-off to renovate their central-city houses.[10]

The Depression slowed down but—thanks to the FHA—did not stop the outward movement of the well-off. It did, however, interrupt and even reverse the flow into the city of the not well-off. In the 1920's more than four million immigrants had come from abroad, the great majority of them settling in the larger cities. There also had been a considerable movement of Negroes from the rural South to the large cities of the North, especially New York. (The Negro population of New York more than doubled in this decade, rising from 152,467 to 327,706, and Harlem, which had only recently been occupied by outward-bound, second-generation Jews and Italians, was suddenly transformed.[11]) When the Depression struck, people not only stopped coming to the city but left it in large numbers to go "back to the land" and back to the old country. Now, partially drained and no longer being replenished, the inner city began to stagnate. Neighborhoods that had been packed a few years before were more or less depopulated; people who lived in them no longer expected to follow the "tenement trail" out of the city. They seemed to have been left permanently behind and it appeared to some people that a new and serious problem had arisen. As Edith Elmer Wood explained in a bulletin written for the Public Works Administration in 1935:

"The blighting effect of slums on human lives and human character was less acute during the period of immigration and rapid population growth than it is now. Newcomers sought the cheapest and therefore the worst housing, literally pushing out, and necessarily into something better, the last previous immigrant wave. They were able to afford the move because rapidly expanding population meant rapidly expanding jobs. . . . Living in the slums was a

[10] Davis McEntire, *Residence and Race* (Berkeley: University of California Press, 1960), pp. 300–301. FHA discriminated against Negroes until well into the Truman administration. Afterward it discriminated against them *in effect* by insisting on very low-risk loans.
[11] Gilbert Osofsky, *Harlem: The Making of a Ghetto* (New York: Harper & Row, 1963), p. 128.

temporary discomfort, cheerfully endured, because of an animating faith that prosperity and comfort were just ahead. . . .

"Since immigration stopped, all that has changed. The situation has become static. A superior family climbs out here and there, but it is the exception, not the rule, and for every one that goes up, another must come down. Discouragement or bitterness has taken the place of hope. It is only recently that we have seen a generation reach manhood and womanhood which was born and bred in our city slums, which has known no home but a dingy tenement, no playground but the city streets. And worst of all, it has little hope of attaining anything better except by the short-cuts of crime." [12]

The "defense boom" and then World War II quickly filled the inner city to overflowing once again. Now the well-off could not move away because of controls on residential construction; at the same time, large numbers of workers, most of them unskilled, came from small towns and farms until all the inner city housing that could possibly be used was occupied. A huge amount of new factory capacity was built in two or three years, most of it at the periphery of the city but within its borders. Had this expansion taken place under normal circumstances, most of the new factories would have been located in the suburban ring, beyond the borders of the city. The effect of the war, therefore, was to slow down somewhat the decentralization of the city.

As soon as wartime controls were lifted, the logic of growth reasserted itself. A huge pent-up demand on the part of the well-off, whose numbers had been swelled by formation of new families, wartime prosperity, and the home-loan provisions of the "G.I. Bill of Rights," burst forth in a mass exodus from the city to the suburbs: between 1940 and 1950 some 2.3 million persons moved out of the twelve largest central cities. Not all of these people went to the suburbs, of course, and 2.3 million was only 12 percent of the total population of these cities; nevertheless, the sudden outward surge was unprecedented in scale. As had happened before, when the well-off left, the not well-off moved into the housing left behind. The most nearly well-off of them took the best of it and left the housing that they vacated for others below them on the income ladder, who in turn passed their housing down to still others. Many of those in this housing queue—practically all those at the "far" end of it—were Negroes (in New York, Puerto Ricans also; in Los Angeles, Oakland, and some other cities, Mexicans also).

The heavy, rapid Negro migration to the city in the war and postwar years changed the situation markedly. In 1940 nearly three-quarters (72 percent) of the nation's Negroes lived in the South; twenty years later a little more than half (54 percent) lived there. The Negro had always been rural, but by

[12] Edith Elmer Wood, *Slums and Blighted Areas in the U.S.*, Administration of Public Works, Housing Division Bulletin Number 1 (Washington, D.C.: Government Printing Office, 1935), p. 19.

1960 he was urban: one-half of all Negroes lived in central cities; in the 1950 to 1960 decade in every one of the fifty largest central cities, the percentage of Negroes in the population rose.[13]

Massive as it was, this new migration into the large cities did not quite offset the movement of the well-off out of them. Consequently, by 1960 there was ample housing of a sort for most of those seeking it. Much of it was of a very good sort, built only thirty or forty years before and still structurally sound. All that was wrong with much of it was that it was out-of-date, aesthetically and otherwise, by the standards of the well-off—standards that had risen rapidly during the war and postwar prosperity. The not well-off very quickly occupied the better housing that came on the market. In the past, the least well-off had lived in compact, high-density districts. Now they spread out in all directions, leapfrogging neighborhoods here and there, covering miles and miles.[14]

By no means all of the well-off left the city. Some who could afford any rent lived in luxury apartments, a gold coast along the central business district. The number of such people was bound to grow, but not enough to change the inner city fundamentally. In the outlying neighborhoods, heads of families often remained even when they could afford to move; people getting along in years saw no point in moving from neighborhoods in which they had lived so long and to which they had become attached. It was their children and their boarders who moved away to the suburbs. On the lower East Side of New York in the early 1960's there were still some neighborhoods occupied mainly by remnants of the Jewish immigration of the early 1900's and the Puerto Rican immigration of the 1920's,[15] but the population of such neighborhoods was thinning out. The later migrants, mostly Negroes (and in New York, Puerto Ricans), had in most cases come to the city as young adults or children and were a remarkably fast-growing and fast-spreading population.

Looking at the neighborhoods they had left a decade or two before, suburbanites were often dismayed at what they saw—lawns and shrubbery trampled out, houses unpainted, porches sagging, vacant lots filled with broken bottles and junk. To them—and, of course, even more to the scattering of "old residents" who for one reason or another remained—these things constituted "blight" and "decay." To the people who were moving into these neighborhoods from old tenements and shanties, however, the situation appeared in a very different light. Many of them cared little or nothing for lawns and had no objections to broken bottles; they knew, too, that the more "fixed up" things were, the higher rents would be. What mattered most to them was having four or five rooms instead of one or two, plumbing that worked, an inside bathroom that did not have to be shared with strangers down the hall,

[13] Leo F. Schnore, *The Urban Scene* (New York: The Free Press, 1965), pp. 256–257.
[14] McEntire, *Residence and Race*, chapter 3.
[15] Raymond Vernon, *Metropolis 1985* (Cambridge, Mass.: Harvard University Press, 1960), p. 141.

and central heating. To the least well-off, "blight" was a blessing. They were able, for the first time in their lives, to occupy housing that was comfortable.

Although the appearance of neighborhoods declined as they were occupied by lower-income groups, the quality of housing in the central city as a whole improved dramatically. Housing was repaired and improved on a wholesale scale during the postwar years, some of it by government programs but more of it through the normal processes of consumer spending. Although differences in Census definition make precise comparisons impossible, more than half the housing in metropolitan areas that was substandard in 1949 was put in sound condition during the next ten years through structural repairs or by plumbing additions. At the end of the decade, some families still lived in housing that was appallingly bad, but their number was now small and getting smaller every year.[16]

The improvement resulting from the repair of substandard housing and the handing down of good housing by the well-off was widespread. This fact can be seen from the gains made by Negroes, the worst-housed group in the population, as shown in the table.

PERCENTAGE OF NEGRO FAMILIES OCCUPYING SUBSTANDARD HOUSING [17]

Metropolitan Area	1950	1960
New York	33.8	23.0
Chicago	59.3	25.4
Philadelphia	42.8	13.8
Los Angeles	19.0	6.2
Detroit	29.3	10.3
St. Louis	75.0	39.4
Washington, D.C.	33.9	13.6
San Francisco-Oakland	25.6	14.9

[16] On the comparability of 1950 and 1960 Census data, see Bernard J. Frieden, "Housing and National Urban Goals: Old Policies and New Realities," in James Q. Wilson, ed., *The Metropolitan Enigma* (Cambridge, Mass.: Harvard University Press, 1968), pp. 166–168.

Substandard housing is "dilapidated" or lacks one or more plumbing facilities. *Dilapidated* housing does not provide safe and adequate shelter and endangers the health, safety, and well-being of the occupants because it has one or more "critical defects," or a combination of lesser ones, or is of inadequate original construction. *Critical defects* are those that indicate continued neglect and serious damage to the structure.

Frieden divides the Census income categories into groups representing roughly the bottom third ($0–1,999 in 1950, $0–2,999 in 1960), middle third $2,000–3,999 in 1950, $3,000–5,999 in 1960), and upper third ($4,000 and above in 1950, $6,000 and above in 1960). The percentage of families in each third living in substandard housing was as follows:

	1950 (Percent)	1960 (Percent)
Upper Third	12	4
Middle Third	30	14
Lower Third	53	36

[17] The table is adapted from data presented by Bernard J. Frieden in *The Future of Old Neighborhoods* (Cambridge, Mass.: M.I.T. Press, 1964), p. 24.

By discarding housing that was still usable, the well-off conferred a great benefit upon the not well-off. Like many benefits, however, this one had hidden costs: in order to use the discarded housing, one had to live where it was; all too often this meant living where there were not enough jobs.

The central business district—and with it the central city as a whole—had long been losing its monopoly of accessibility. As the population at the periphery of the city grew, there was increasing support for large stores and other facilities that could compete with those of the central business district. People no longer had to go downtown for almost everything. At the same time, improvements in transportation, especially the building of expressways and of major airports that were some distance from the city, made it easier than before to get from one part of the metropolitan area to another without going downtown. Also, manufacturing always tended to move outward to cheaper land; beginning in the early 1930's, increases in plant size and improvements in materials-handling techniques hastened this movement. More and more manufacturers wanted single-story plants with horizontal material flows and aisles wide enough to permit mechanical handling of materials. This usually compelled them to move their operations to a less congested area close to a center of long-distance truck hauling.[16] After the Second World War, much manufacturing, and much retailing and wholesaling as well, moved out of the city.

The central business district retained its advantage of accessibility with respect to activities involving frequent face-to-face communication. Top executives had to be near to each other and to the bankers, lawyers, advertising men, government officials, and others with whom they dealt frequently; consequently, they kept their headquarters downtown. The rest of their operations—factories as well as record-keeping—they sent to the suburbs, where land was cheaper and clerical help easier to find, or to other areas altogether.

By far the biggest concentration of jobs for the unskilled was still in or near the central city. Service workers (for example, watchmen and elevator operators) were concentrated downtown, and "laborers" worked in the nearby industrial suburbs. There were not enough such jobs to go around, however, now that so high a proportion of the city's population consisted of the unskilled. Most of the *new* jobs for the unskilled, moreover, were in the suburban ring; that was where almost all the growth was taking place. Unskilled workers, most of whom lived near the downtown part of the central city, would have been happier had the jobs not moved outward. The outward movement of jobs did not leave them stranded, however; except in three or four of the largest metropolitan areas, a worker could travel from his inner city dwelling to a job anywhere on the outer perimeter of the metropolitan area in no more than half an hour. The radial pattern of high-

[16] See the chapter on technological change by Boris Yavitz in Eli Ginsburg, et al., *Manpower Strategy for the Metropolis* (New York: Columbia University Press, 1968), especially pp. 49–55.

way and rail transportation, although not planned for the purpose, was ideal from the standpoint of workers who were characteristically needed for a few days first in one suburb and then in another, the second being perhaps on the opposite rim of the metropolitan area from the first. "Reverse commuting"—that is, traveling from an inner city residence to a suburban job—became common among the unskilled workers of the central city. The advantage of living near the center of a radial transportation system may have been a major cause—conceivably as great a one as racial discrimination—of the failure of many workers to move to the suburbs.[19]

[19] It will be understood that the account that has been given of metropolitan development refers to an ideal type. Concretely, the older (Eastern and Midwestern) cities conform to the type much better than do the newer (Western and Southwestern) ones. Los Angeles, which had practically no history prior to the automobile and truck, conforms hardly at all. Chicago is fairly representative of most large metropolitan areas.

6

The Police in the Residential Area

Residential housing is one of the most important uses of land in the total make-up of any city. For one thing, much of the money expended in the provision of municipal services derives from taxes levied against residential property. Transportation systems, especially streets, are designed and regulated to facilitate the flow of persons to and from their residences and places of work. In addition, residential housing is big business in its own right: in real estate, rentals, investment properties, home repair businesses, and so on. Finally, housing patterns reflect other meaningful social and economic trends and patterns.

The police are often called into homes, and a considerable amount of their routine work activity takes place in residential neighborhoods. Most police officers are keenly aware that social and economic differences reflected in the make-up of the various neighborhoods provide important clues as to the types and frequency of police services which will be demanded by the people who live in those neighborhoods. In other words, it means different things to live in some parts of town than it does to live in others. James Q. Wilson recognized this in talking about the police when he said that:

> Various neighborhoods and subcultures have their own levels of tolerable disorder; what may appear to be weaker norms are only different norms. Nor are the members of such subcultures a threat to persons in other neighborhoods—police statistics show that almost all disorder, tolerable or intolerable, occurs among persons who are likely to share common norms because they are acquainted or related. Justice is not an absolute; it can be rationed, providing more or less of one kind rather than another to different neighborhoods.[1]

Types of Residences Found in Cities

When talking about housing, the unit which comes the quickest to mind is the single family dwelling, or perhaps the apartment house. There are, however, a number of other kinds of residential arrangements. These include (but are not restricted to) house trailers, condominiums, resident hotels, boats, nursing homes, hospitals, boarding houses, military barracks, and fraternity or sorority houses. Each type of living accommodation has its own particular characteristics and each caters to the

[1] James Q. Wilson, *Varieties of Police Behavior*. New York: Atheneum, 1971, pp. 286–7.

needs of its own type of resident. For purposes of analysis, living accommodations are broken down by the Bureau of the Census into two categories, housing units and group quarters.

Housing Units. The Bureau of the Census defines a housing unit as "a house, an apartment, a group of rooms, or a single room occupied or intended for occupancy as a separate living quarters." Separate living quarters are those in which the occupants do not live and eat with any other persons in the structure. Also, to be classified as a separate quarters it must have either (1) direct access from the outside of the building or through a common hall or (2) complete kitchen facilities for the exclusive use of the occupants. The occupants may consist of a single person living alone, more than one family living together, or any other group of related or unrelated individuals who share living arrangements.

Group Quarters. In general, group quarters are living arrangements for persons who reside in institutions or in other circumstances in which there reside groups containing five or more persons not related to the person in charge. The Census Bureau gathers information on both housing units and group quarters. The data covered by the Census encompasses a fairly wide range of items, and the interested reader will find a listing of them in Appendix A, chapter 4, p. 97.

The Distribution of Residences

In almost all cities of any size, there is a wide degree of variation in the distribution of residential property. As has already been noted, the belt which surrounds (or lies adjacent to) the Central Business District generally contains a high proportion of older buildings. These usually include large older homes which have been broken up into small apartment units, apartment houses built as such, publicly supported housing projects, and other types of multifamily structures. The neighborhoods in which these residences are located usually tend to be shabby in appearance and to cater to the needs of people in the lower socioeconomic category.

As one moves away from the central city, the quality of the residences improves (and the intensity of occupancy goes down). The relationship between social, economic and geographic distributions is clearly illustrated in Table 8–1. This table is a correlation matrix in which a number of "indicators" have been correlated on the basis of intensity of that indicator per census tract. The indicators were placed in a rank order by census tract and the correlations were based on differences in rank order. One

TABLE 8—1

A Correlation Matrix of Social and Economic
"Indicators" by Rank Order Among Census Tracts
(Little Rock, Arkansas)

	1	2	3	4	5	6	7	8	9	10	11	12
1	0	.42*	.50**	.38*	.49**	.40*	.57**	.02	.55**	.24	.25	.39*
2	.42*	0	.56**	.63**	.60**	.56**	.27	.39*	.60**	.61**	.60**	.35
3	.50**	.56**	0	.80**	.86**	.80**	.42*	.52**	.81**	.84**	.84**	.35
4	.38*	.63**	.80**	0	.80**	.79**	.64**	.73**	.80**	.89**	.89**	.63**
5	.49**	.60**	.86**	.80**	0	.65**	.30	.60**	.69**	.74**	.73**	.34
6	.40*	.56**	.80**	.79**	.65**	0	.44*	.55**	.81**	.78**	.79**	.41*
7	.57**	.27	.42*	.64**	.30	.44*	0	.21	.55**	.26	.26	.67**
8	.02	.39*	.52**	.73**	.60**	.55**	.21	0	.50**	.80**	.80**	.45*
9	.55**	.60**	.81**	.80**	.69**	.81**	.55**	.50**	0	.76**	.76**	.49**
10	.24	.61**	.84**	.89**	.74**	.78**	.26	.80**	.76**	0	1.00	.34
11	.25	.60**	.84**	.89**	.73**	.79**	.26	.80**	.76**	1.00	0	.40*
12	.39	.35	.35	.63**	.34	.34	.67**	.45*	.49**	.34	.40*	0

*P > .05 Correlations based on Spearman Rank Order Coefficients of
**P > .01 Correlation of Indicators by census tract (N = 30)

INDICATORS:

1. Dependency Ratio
2. Percent of Families with Female Head
3. Level of education (rank 1 = lowest)
4. Percent of families with incomes below the poverty level
5. Percent of adults (25 & over) without a high school diploma
6. Percent of unemployment
7. Infant deaths (rank 1 = highest)
8. Percent of homes renter occupied
9. Percent of households with more than 1.51 persons per room
10. Real Income (rank 1 = lowest)
11. Median Income (rank 1 = lowest)
12. Number of burglaries reported to the police (rank 1 = highest)

can see that the indicator of low education showed a positive correlation within census tracts with such things as income, infant mortality, percent of families with a female head of household and so on.

If census tracts are at least rough homogeneous groupings of the population, and this appears to be the case, then there should be differences among the groups of people who reside in the various census tracts and these differences should be reflected in lifestyles, including housing patterns. Although this is generally true, it should be borne in mind that there may still be considerable variation within any given census tract.

Housing Characteristics
Bureau of the Census

Tenure. A housing unit is "owner occupied" if the owner or co-owner lives in the unit, even if it is mortgaged or not fully paid for. A cooperative or condominium unit is "owner occupied" only if the owner or co-owner lives in it. All other occupied units are classified as "renter occupied," including units rented for cash rent and those occupied without payment of cash rent.

Persons. Persons occupying the housing unit include not only occupants related to the head of the household but also any lodgers, roomers, boarders, partners, wards, foster children and resident employees who share the living quarters of the household head. The data on "persons" show the number of housing units occupied by the specified number of persons.

Units with one or more roomers, boarders, or lodgers are shown as a separate category. Not included as "roomers, boarders, or lodgers" are foster children or wards, servants who live in, companions, and partners.

Year moved into unit. Data on year moved into unit are based on the information reported for the head of the household. The question refers to the year of latest move. Thus, if the head moved back into a unit he had previously occupied or if he moved from one apartment to another in the same building, the year he moved into his present unit was to be reported.

Complete kitchen facilities. A unit has complete kitchen facilities when it has all three of the following for the exclusive use of the occupants of the unit: (1) An installed sink with piped water; (2) a range or cookstove; and (3) a mechanical refrigerator. All kitchen facilities must be located in the structure, although they need not be in the same room. Quarters with only portable cooking equipment are not considered as having a range or cookstove. "Lacking complete kitchen facilities" means that the unit does not have all three specified kitchen facilities, or that they are also for the use of the occupants of other housing units.

Access. "Access only through other living quarters" means that the occupants of a housing unit must go through someone else's living quarters to enter their own; that is, they do not have a direct entrance from the outside or through a common or public hall.

Rooms. Rooms to be counted include whole rooms used for living purposes, such as living rooms, dining rooms, kitchens, bedrooms, finished recreation rooms, family rooms, etc. Not counted as rooms are bathrooms, porches, balconies, foyers, halls, halfrooms, kitchenettes, strip or pullman kitchens, utility rooms, unfinished attics, basements, or other space used for storage.

Persons per room. This is computed by dividing the number of persons in the unit by the number of rooms in the unit. The figures shown, therefore, refer to the number of housing units having the specified ratio of persons per room.

Year structure built. Year structure built refers to when the building was first constructed, not when it was remodeled, added to, or converted.

Units in structure. In the determination of the number of units in a structure, all housing units, both occupied and vacant, were counted. The statistics are presented in terms of the number of housing units in structures of specified size, not in terms of the number of residential structures.

A structure is a separate building that either has open space on all sides or is separated from other structures by dividing walls that extend from ground to roof.

Basement. Statistics on basements are presented in terms of the number of housing units located in structures built with a basement, and are separately tabulated for one-family houses with basements. A structure has a basement if there is enclosed space in which persons can walk upright under all or part of the building.

Plumbing facilities. The category "with all plumbing facilities" consists of units which have hot and cold piped water, as well as a flush toilet and a bathtub or shower inside the structure for the exclusive use of the occupants of the unit. "Lacking some or all plumbing" means that the unit does not have all three specified plumbing facilities (hot and cold piped water, as well as flush toilet and bathtub or shower inside the structure), or that the toilet or bathing facilities are also for the use of the occupants of other housing units.

Selected equipment. Statistics are presented for the number of housing units with the following selected equipment.

With more than one bathroom.—A complete bathroom is a room with flush toilet, bathtub or shower, and wash basin with piped water. A partial or half bathroom has at least a flush toilet or bathtub (or shower), but does not have all the facilities for a complete bathroom. A housing unit "with more than one bathroom" has, in addition to one complete bathroom, one or more partial or complete bathrooms.

With public water supply.—A public system refers to a common source supplying running water to six or more housing units. The water may be supplied by a city, county, water district, or private water company, or it may be obtained from a well which supplied six or more housing units.

With public sewer.—A "public sewer" is connected to a city, county, sanitary district, neighborhood, or subdivision sewer system. It may be operated by a government body or by a private organization. Small sewage treatment plants which in some localities are called neighborhood septic tanks are also classified as public sewers.

With air conditioning.—Air conditioning is the cooling of air by a refrigeration unit. A central system is a central installation which air-conditions the entire housing unit. A room unit is an individual air conditioner which is installed in a window or an outside wall and is generally intended to cool one room, although it may sometimes be used to cool more than one room.

Heating equipment. The list of heating equipment refers to the type of heating equipment and not to the fuel used. "Steam or hot water" refers to a central heating system in which heat from steam or hot water is delivered through radiators or other outlets. "Warm air furnace" refers to a central system which provides warm air through ducts leading to various rooms; central heat pumps are included in this category. "Built-in electric units" are permanently installed in the floors, walls or ceilings. A "floor, wall, or pipeless furnace" delivers warm air to the room right above the furnace or to the room(s) on one or both sides of the wall in which the furnace is installed. "Other means" includes room heaters with or without flue, fireplaces, stoves, and portable heaters of all types.

A housing unit "With central or built-in heating system" contains a steam or hot water system, a warm-air furnace, built-in electric units, or a floor, wall, or pipeless furnace.

Automobiles available. Statistics on automobiles available represent the number of passenger automobiles, including station wagons, which are owned or regularly used by any member of the household and which are ordinarily kept at home. Taxicabs, pickups, or larger trucks were not to be counted.

Value. Value is the respondent's estimate of how much the property (house or lot) would sell for if it were for sale. The term "specified owner-occupied units" means that the value data are limited to owner-occupied one-family houses on less than ten acres, without a commercial establishment or medical office on the property. Owner-occupied cooperatives, condominiums, mobile homes, and trailers are excluded from the value tabulations.

Mean value. Mean value is the sum of the individual values reported, divided by the number of owner-occupied units for which value is shown. For purposes of computation, the mid-points of the intervals were used, except that a mean value of $3,500 was assigned to housing units in the interval "less than $5,000" and a mean of $60,000 was assigned to units in the interval "$50,000 or more."

Contract rent. Contract rent is the monthly rent agreed to, or contracted for, even if the furnishings, utilities, or services are included. The term "specified renter-occupied units" means that the contract rent data exclude one-family houses on ten acres or more. Renter units occupied without payment of cash rent are shown separately as "no cash rent" in the rent tabulations.

Gross rent. Monthly gross rent is the summation of contract rent plus the estimated average monthly cost of utilities (water, electricity, gas) and fuels (oil, coal, kerosene, wood, etc.), if these items are paid for by the renter, in addition to rent. Thus, gross rent is intended to eliminate individual differences which result from varying practices with respect to the inclusion of heat and utilities as part of the rental payment.

Mean gross rent. Mean gross rent is the sum of the individual rental amounts divided by the number of renter-occupied units, excluding one-family houses on ten acres or more.

Gross rent as percentage of income. The yearly gross rent (monthly gross rent multiplied by 12) is expressed as a percentage of the total income in 1969 of the family or primary individual. The percentage was computed separately for each unit and was rounded to the nearest whole number. Units for which no cash is paid and units occupied by families or primary individuals who reported no income or a net loss comprise the category "not computed."

The Police in Residential Areas

As has been previously noted, the police spend a considerable amount of time in residential neighborhoods and in the homes of people who call for them. The remainder of this chapter will deal with three different perspectives of the police and their involvement with citizens at the neighborhood level. First, the family crisis will be discussed as an example of police response to *service* demands. Second, residential burglaries and the police will be examined; and, third, the emerging concept of "team policing" will be explored.

Family crisis intervention. When middle or upper class couples become involved in interpersonal stress and need outside help with their problems, they generally have ample resources at their disposal. They might turn to a clergyman or an attorney; or, they might consult with a marriage counselor or a psychologist.

Lower class couples also find themselves subjected to stresses and strains, and they also call upon outside help. They very often call the police. There are several reasons why they call for police assistance. In the first place, much of the lower class lifestyle is determined by finances (or the lack of them), and professional help can be expensive. Second, they are likely to call the police not only because they can't afford professional help but they might in fact not even be aware that it is available to them. Third, the lower class lifestyle does not place the premium on one's public reputation that is the case with middle class people (for many if not most middle class couples, having the police become involved in a domestic disturbance would be completely unthinkable). Finally, the police are available twenty four hours a day, and they will come if they are called.

What are the reasons the police are called for in a family crisis? [2] As was noted in chapter 3, one's class membership plays a very significant role in patterns of behavior and social perception. It was noted that those who fall within the lower class are more likely to have contact with the

[2] For an interesting treatment of one aspect of this problem, see Raymond I. Parnas, "The Police Response to the Domestic Disturbance," *Wisconsin Law Review*, Vol. 914, 1967, pp. 930–932, 937, 948.

police than middle or upper class citizens. Among the general concepts often found among lower class persons are those that one should be willing to stand up for one's self and that at least some violence may be appropriate in conflict situations.

A family disturbance among lower class couples is very likely to be a highly complex problem which involves financial stress and long-standing interpersonal difficulties (such as drinking, irresponsibility, etc.). Thus a lower class family disturbance although aggravated by economic hardship and might be a smoldering kind of fire between a couple which periodically flames up due to situational circumstances. In any event, when the crisis reaches serious proportions, it is likely to include pitched emotional feelings which can develop into shouting and shoving matches or even more serious physical violence ranging from a punch in the face to a homicidal assault. A housewife who has been insulted and slapped may believe that she has gone as far as she can and that she needs help; the police are available and are called. Or, neighbors may hear an altercation and call the police, either because the noise is disturbing them or because they fear that the affray will escalate into a genuinely serious phase in which one or the other of the participants might be injured or killed. Indeed, it is quite common for police officers to be dispatched to the scene of a family crisis with the warning that a weapon might be involved. Although members of the middle class are by no means totally unwilling to use violence in a family crisis, it is considerably less likely that they will. As has been said, their crisis is more likely to wind up in a lawyer's office or in the hands of some other professional.

Other specific factors also play a role. For one thing, the party calling the police may not be as much interested in having the offender arrested as in having the police "make him behave." Or, perhaps the complainant may simply wish to use the police to convince the offender that "she's not kidding." That is, although she may not wish to have him arrested, she might want to impress upon him the fact that she is willing to call the police and that she *might* just go ahead and have him arrested. One of the most common reasons the police are called into a family disturbance is simply to get them to make the offender leave the house, at least for a while.[3]

Although these reasons seem simple and straightforward enough, they do pose some difficult problems for the police. In the first place, the police do not have the authority to make people "be good"—especially according to the definitions irate wives are likely to put forth. If a man wishes to come home intoxicated and in a foul mood, it is not within the

[3] Wilson, p. 24.

purview of police authority to do anything about it or to tell him to do otherwise. Nor do the police usually have the right to make a man leave his own home.

If a serious enough offense has been committed within the home (such as an assault resulting in a personal injury), or if the disturbance can be considered to be a breach of peace, the police may arrest the offender. However, if a clear enough offense is not present or if the use of an arrest is not deemed to be the most advisable course of action, then the police must rely upon their powers of persuasion to calm the situation and to restore order.

Even in those cases where the police do attempt to make an arrest, the situation is not always easily resolved. In fact, it may even get worse. Many a policeman has attempted to arrest a drunk and disorderly husband at his wife's urging—only to be attacked by the wife when they are compelled to use force to subdue the husband when he resists arrest.

The police are aware that a man's home is his castle and that much of what goes on within a person's home is considered to be both personal and private. Under these circumstances the police are naturally often seen as unwelcome intruders when their involvement goes beyond acceptable limits, and exactly what limits are acceptable are individually defined in each case. This places the police in an extremely weak position because they are poorly prepared to accurately predict what will happen in any given situation.

In addition, the family crisis has a great potential for violence, both against the family members involved and for the police. Many of the family crises police respond to have been smoldering well before they arrive, and the mere arrival of the police may signal a crisis point. Although police generally dislike responding to a family crisis, they nevertheless know that such calls can involve serious criminal matters. They know, for example, that a homicide is more likely to take place among members of a family than between strangers. They are also aware that many police injuries (and fatalities) have grown out of a family disturbance and that many complaints of police brutality have likewise developed out of what started as a simple family disturbance. It is not difficult to see why many officers are ambivalent about intervening in domestic disturbances.

On the whole, the family crisis, although it is a common police experience, is a call which few officers enjoy responding to. They know that they must enter other people's homes—often uninvited by either party—and that they must deal with potentially violent participants who are emotionally charged and that they must do this with a minimum of resources.

Domestic disturbances impose another liability on many police officers.

Over a period of time officers enter into homes which are characterized by the extremes in distress and disorganization. Some of the scenes which policemen encounter would turn the stomach of even the most hardened veteran: incredible filth and disarray, neglected children, stench, and disorder. Officers who work those neighborhoods which contain the lowest social strata of society see such pathological scenes on a regular basis, and it is easy for many of them to conclude that their clientele are just animals who are incapable of living effectively in an ordered society. Such an attitude is sometimes difficult to avoid, yet the fact that the police are continuously subjected to the worst that society has to offer has a conditioning effect. When officers develop a contempt and disdain for their clientele, it becomes more difficult for them to maintain the objectivity which is so essential to their job.

Officers who develop negative or hostile attitudes toward their clientele find it difficult to keep such attitudes from creeping into their working personality. This leads, in the case of family crisis intervention, to advice which may seem pragmatic but which in reality is ill-advised. This writer has heard police officers offer the following advice in domestic disturbances:

—"If you can't get along, get a divorce."

—"If he attacks you again, just shoot him and then give us a call."

—"If you people can't get your stuff straight, I'll throw you both in jail."

—"This is a civil matter. Don't bother us with it."

—"If we have to come out here again tonight, you all go to jail."

In 1967 a new approach to the matter of family crises was developed. The New York City Police Department created an experimental family crisis unit specifically designed and trained to deal with family crises.[4] The New York experiment is the subject of the reading attached to this chapter and illustrates the complex nature of the police involvement in the family crisis.

The success of the specially trained family crisis intervention unit suggested that the police role might well include the need for paying more attention to manipulating the psychological environment of potential offenders in order to control behavior and prevent crime.[5] It has also

[4] Morton Bard and Bernard Berkowitz, "Training Police As Specialists in Family Crisis Intervention: A Community Psychology Action Program," *Community Mental Health Journal*, Vol. 3, No. 4 (Winter, 1967), pp. 315–317.

[5] John L. Grenough, "Crime Prevention: A New Approach—Environmental Psychology and Criminal Behavior," *Journal of Police Science and Administration*, Vol. 2, No. 3 (September 1974), pp. 339–343.

6

been suggested that the use of family crisis intervention techniques by specially trained police officers might also be an effective means for the improvement of police/minority relations.[6]

In any event, the family crisis will undoubtedly continue to be an area in which police will be called upon to intervene. For the most part, this will continue to involve the police in their service role. However, it is hoped that as the police develop better skills and greater competency through specialized training, they will not only be able to enhance their image within the community but will also be able to reduce the volume of violence and disruption which has been associated with family crises in the past.

Residential burglaries. A burglary is the breaking and entering of a structure with the intent to commit a crime inside. The most frequent offense committed inside a structure by a burglar is a theft. The breaking itself need not be an actual breaking of wood or glass; it may be "constructive." That is, a burglar who simply goes in an open door or who opens an unlocked window is considered to have broken into the structure. About half of all burglaries are of residences.[7]

The prospect of a burglary in one's home is particularly distressing, because the:

> . . . feeling that what is at stake is the continued availability and stability of those conditions that make life meaningful and satisfying for people who struggled for a place in the suburbs, namely the exclusive access to a private life space contained in the family home.[8]

Actually, it makes little difference if the offense takes place in the suburbs or the city itself; the violation of one's private and highly personal life-space within the home is a traumatic event. The loss in money or goods alone cannot measure the total damage done to a person who has had his home violated by a burglar.

Recent research on burglary has disclosed information on the various aspects of the problem.[9] With respect to the nature of the offense itself, it has been learned that residential burglaries occur more frequently than

[6] Myron Katz, "Family Crisis Training: Upgrading the Police While Building a Bridge to the Minority Community," *Journal of Police Science and Administration,* Vol. 1, No. 1 (March, 1973), pp. 30–35.

[7] *The Challenge of Crime in a Free Society,* A Report of the Presidents' Commission on Law Enforcement and the Administration of Justice. Washington: Government Printing Office, 1967, p. 19.

[8] John E. Conklin and Egon Bittner, "Burglary in a Suburb," *Criminology,* Vol. 11, No. 2 (August, 1973), pp. 206–233.

[9] Harry A. Scarr, Joan L. Pinsky, and Deborah S. Wyatt, *Patterns of Burglary,* 2d ed. U.S. Department of Justice, National Institute of Law Enforcement and Criminal Justice. Washington: Government Printing Office, 1973, pp. 104–110.

non-residential burglaries and that they are increasing in frequency. In terms of what is most frequently stolen in burglaries, it seems that easily movable and easily convertive-into-cash items predominate, with specific emphasis placed on home entertainment equipment and cash. Burglars tend to enter through doors and windows but urban burglaries apparently involve forced entries more often than do suburban burglaries. As might be expected, non-residential burglaries are more likely to occur at night and on weekends whereas residential burglaries are likely to occur during the day and on weekends.

It has also been noted that burglary rates and burglary frequencies are strongly correlated with a variety of social characteristics in urban areas. For instance, a high correlation was found in one study between burglary and:

—percent overcrowded housing units
—percent black overcrowded housing units
—percent lower-cost rental units
—percent lower-cost housing units

In addition, it has been demonstrated that the victims of burglaries also tend to be the victims of other crimes as well. Interestingly enough, both victims and non-victims perceive similar kinds of problems, including crime problems existing in their neighborhoods yet non-victims report fewer crimes occurring in their neighborhoods than do victims. Not unexpectedly, the victims of burglaries tend to want a greater increase in police activity than do comparable non-victims. Another interesting finding was that the amount of lighting and street traffic around sites does *not* differentiate between victims and non-victims of burglaries.

Research has further indicated that victims of burglaries tend to be very satisfied with police courtesy, promptness and even with the competence of the police; however, given this high absolute level of satisfaction, respondents are relatively most satisfied with police courteousness, next most satisfied with their promptness, and *least* satisfied with police competence.[10]

Responses to burglaries pose a difficult problem for the police. Burglaries are normally reported after they have been successfully carried out; that is, the burglar has entered the house, stolen what he wants, and has made good his escape. They normally leave very few if any usable clues behind (fingerprints are of value only if the police have a suspect to compare the prints with). Generally the objects which are stolen are by their very nature common: radios, stereo equipment, money, etc.

[10] *Ibid.*

6

Indeed, it is probably safe to say that most home owners do not keep records of the serial numbers of items which have them nor do they have any definitive means of positively identifying their property. All of this means that when the police are called, they arrive at a "cold trail" and often have almost nothing to work with. About all they know is that a burglary has taken place. In addition, police are often skeptical of the claimed loss, because it is not unheard of for a property owner to exaggerate his losses in order to secure a higher insurance return.

Although a burglary is a serious crime, and in spite of the fact that it calls for the police to act in their law enforcement capacity, as a matter of practical reality police responses become (at least in the eyes of the citizen) little more than a clerical duty. The officers arrive and fill out a report which sets forth the date of the offense, what was taken, who the victim was, and so on. However, since burglary is basically a crime of stealth, detection of the perpetrator is quite difficult. According to the *Uniform Crime Reports* for 1972, law enforcement officials were successful in clearing only 19 percent of the total burglary offenses.[11] However, to "clear" an offense does not necessarily mean that an offender is arrested or that if one is arrested that goods are recovered or that he is or will be convicted. Although it is difficult to say what percentage of active burglars are caught (or how many are convicted), it is safe to state that these figures are extremely low indeed.

What this means to the home-owner (or any other resident) is that the police can do very little to prevent burglaries and if one has been committed there is very little they can do about it. Exactly how this impacts on the public with respect to their attitudes toward the police is unknown, yet the popular cry among police executives for citizens to "support your local police" may reflect the existence of a problem.

[11] *Uniform Crime Reports for the United States, 1972.* U.S. Department of Justice, Federal Bureau of Investigation, Clarence M. Kelley, Director. Washington, D.C.: U.S. Government Printing Office, 1972, p. 21.

Team Policing *

In recent years, due in part to changes in the social climate and in part to changes in police patrol techniques (more patrol cars, less foot patrol), many police agencies have become increasingly isolated from the community. This isolation makes crime control more difficult. The need to increase police-citizen cooperation is self-evident.

Team policing is a modern police attempt to reduce isolation and involve

* The following text is taken from *Police,* a report of the National Advisory Commission on Criminal Justice Standards and Goals. Washington, D.C.: U.S. Government Printing Office, 1973, pp. 154–161.

include citizens as part of certain team policing units

community support. Team policing can be administered in small or large amounts. Syracuse, N.Y., the first U.S. city to try team policing, uses teams of 10 officers to patrol, investigate, and control crime. Team leaders have considerable discretion and authority. In Los Angeles, nine-member units have patrol responsibility; investigation remains separate, however. Dayton, Ohio, has an extremely advanced concept of team policing in operation.

What is team policing? Essentially it is assigning police responsibility for a certain area to a team of police officers. The more responsibility this team has, the greater the degree of team policing. For instance, team policing that has investigative authority is more complete than team policing that does not. Teams that have authority to tailor programs and procedures to the needs of their areas go even further.

The basic idea is that the team learns its neighborhood, its people, and its problems. It is an extension of the "cop on the beat" concept, brought up to date with more men and modern police services. It lessens the danger of corruption of a single officer in a single area.

The first experiment in team policing took place in Aberdeen, Scotland, in 1948. It ended in 1963. Several other attempts were tried but also abandoned. In 1966, a new modification known as "unit beat policing" appeared, also in Great Britain. This concept combined patrol and investigation personnel and stressed public cooperation. It is this form of team policing that made the trip across the Atlantic.

Police chief executives often lack information for determining the advisability of changes in police operations. Professional publications constantly report new ideas and programs, but they generally stress aspects flattering to the program's creator and avoid the problems of implementation. Most police administrators recognize the need for change in law enforcement in a changing society. Knowing what changes to make is difficult without objective reports from other cities.

Team policing has become one of the most popular forms of police reorganization. Practiced different ways in different agencies, it has received considerable publicity. No definitive study has yet been made that gives police chief executives a thorough understanding of what team policing actually is and what benefit an agency can expect from adopting the concept.

One of the most serious problems confronting police agencies today is isolation from the community. Several factors, including police organizational inflexibility and the attitudes of both the police and the public, have caused this isolation.

Team policing places the police officer in an environment that encourages cooperation with the public and thus reduces isolation. Team policing brings the police organization down to the community level. This enables individual officers to cultivate community support and build personal relationships essential to the goal of police-community partnership.

Effective police-community cooperation is critical to the success of a policing project. The public must be informed of the team policing concept, its objectives and goals; public assistance and participation must be solicited actively. Successful community involvement programs depend on direct participation of citizens in the planning stages. Ongoing public commitment is encouraged by continually seeking the opinions, ideas, and assistance of citizens in resolving problems of mutual concern.

The team policing concept has been viewed by some as a return to a bygone golden age of police work typified by the friendly, well-known corner cop who helped community residents manage the problems of urban life and learned a great deal about their lives in the process. In the late 1940's and early 1950's, however, reformers found this friendly officer on the foot beat to be corrupted by his familiarity with local residents and slow to respond to the scene of emergencies. To solve the latter problem they put him in a radio car. To solve the former they transferred him so frequently that he would not have a chance to know people well enough to become corrupt.

The impersonal police officer created new problems. The President's Crime Commission and the President's Riot Commission both emphasized lack of community contact between the police and the citizens as a serious weakness in patrol operations. The Crime Commission, in fact, urged that patrolmen should be thought of as foot officers who use vehicles for transportation from one point to another. Many patrolmen resist the idea of getting out of their patrol cars to talk to citizens; some even view this activity as a degrading form of appeasement. The idea also runs contrary to the tactical principle that the continual moving presence of motorized patrol on the street is required to provide adequate preventive patrol. Many police agencies embrace this principle to the extent that unnecessary or unofficial conversations with the public are discouraged by agency regulations. Recent research on the effectiveness of preventive patrol, however, indicates that any crimes prevented by passing patrol vehicles can be, and usually are, committed as soon as the police are out of sight. Police presence can only prevent street crime if the police are everywhere at once.

A more effective way to increase the risk involved in committing a crime is to raise the probability of apprehension after the crime has been committed. Without information supplied by the community, apprehension is quite difficult. The easiest way to obtain information about a crime is for the police to talk to community residents who may have knowledge of the crime or the offender.

Rapid response to serious or emergency calls for services, particularly those involving crimes in progress, is essential to crime control and criminal apprehension. Once a crime is committed, the police must switch their major tactical emphasis from prevention to interception. Again, police must depend to a great extent on information supplied by the public to increase their chances of intercepting a criminal while the crime is in progress or during his flight from the immediate scene.

Once prevention and interception have failed, the only tool left to the police is investigation. But like prevention and interception, investigation requires cooperation from the public in apprehending the suspect and providing testimony in any subsequent court proceeding.

Team policing in any of its various forms is an attempt to strengthen cooperation and mutual coordination of effort between the police and the public in preventing crime and maintaining order. The concept is rather simple but complex in its implementation. The degree of success of any agency's team policing program depends on the active participation of all agency personnel in cultivating the active and willing support of the public.

The lack of involvement of agency personnel in the planning and implementation of programs has been a basic defect in many team policing experiments.

Involvement begins with a personal and continuing commitment on the part of the police chief executive. This does not mean that the idea must originate with the chief, or that he must personally direct all planning and implementation. However, the chief executive must assume leadership by supporting the project and identifying himself with its implementation and long range operational aspects. The same is true of the agency's high ranking staff and command personnel. If support from all or some of these key personnel is withheld, the project's chances for success are reduced appreciably.

Middle management support has been missing from several team policing programs. The lack of this support, in many cases, can be traced to top management failure to communicate to middle management the value of the team policing concept and middle management's role in making the concept work. This problem can be avoided by providing sufficient planning and implementation time to allow full participation by middle management to develop.

Planning input and participation also are required from the officers and the supervisors who will carry out the program at the operational level. Horizontal and vertical team building can be supported by a participative planning process that reduces the traditional distance between ranks.

The Kansas City, Mo., Police Department developed a planning process that involved representatives from all ranks. Task forces were assembled in each division. The task force members communicated with all other divisional personnel to solicit ideas, obtain reactions to early plans, and build support for the proposed organizational change. This type of participative planning increases support of management and supervisory and field personnel, and greatly enhances the potential for success of any project.

The initiation of a team policing project offers an excellent opportunity to provide comprehensive training to police personnel at all ranks. With proper planning, there is great potential for obtaining widespread support for the project by acquainting all agency personnel with the project's objectives and goals, and with their roles in achieving those objectives and goals. Specific preparatory and inservice training should be provided to personnel according to their involvement in the team policing effort.

The training of team policing supervisors or team leaders should emphasize planning, managing, directing, and coordinating the activities of team members. Team leaders should also be taught the techniques for teaching and training team members on an ongoing basis. The role of the team leader requires knowledge for maintaining liaison between the team and all other involved agency entities and community organizations.

Placing the responsibility for decisionmaking at the lowest possible organizational level is an integral part of the team policing concept. In many agencies first line supervisors and patrolmen have never made decisions to the extent required in team policing. Adequate training in decisionmaking is essential for team leaders and, to a lesser extent, for other team members.

Patrol officers assigned to teams should be trained in the theory of team dynamics and provided with information to enable them to function effectively as team members. Communications, conference leadership, and interpersonal relations training will assist team officers in their work with the community. Traditional patrol, traffic, and investigative techniques and skills should also be emphasized.

The training of other agency personnel should emphasize the role of administrative, staff, and support personnel in attaining team policing objectives and goals.

Team policing has certain inherent difficulties. Combining patrol and investigation personnel into teams can cause friction. Investigation personnel are usually higher paid and think of themselves as farther up in the police hierarchy. This may cause friction among team members.

Team policing requires considerable individual initiative and responsibility. Many patrolmen are reluctant to exercise such authority. There are other situations that require quick, military orders and obedience. How can this be reconciled with team member equality?

These are the problems that are being worked out and answered in pilot programs now in progress. One definite benefit is that team policing concepts are rich in fresh thoughts; they stir police agencies to reexamine many assumptions about police procedures. Even when team policing is not adopted, examining other agency programs can prove beneficial to overall police thinking.

So far, even where team policing has proved most beneficial, programs are still in the experimental stage.

Larger agencies have the advantage of being able to try programs in certain precincts while carrying on routine police work in others. Smaller agencies have no such option. For the smaller agency, it is all or nothing.

The benefits of team policing, primarily greater police-public cooperation, are not automatic. Team policing only affords the opportunity for such benefits. It is up to the participants to go out into the community and foster the cooperation needed. The police agency must let the public know about its new program and what it hopes to achieve.

Just as importantly, in agencies where a team policing experiment is being prepared, all employees—not just those to take part—must understand and support the program.

Team Policing Systems

Total team policing can be defined as: (1) combining all line operations of patrol, traffic, and investigation into a single group under common supervision; (2) forming teams with a mixture of generalists and specialists; (3) permanently assigning the teams to geographic areas, and; (4) charging the teams with responsibility for all police services within their respective areas. Most team policing systems have not taken this total approach; they have limited operation to a small area within the agency or have concentrated on reorganizing only the patrol function without including investigative personnel or other specialists in the team.

Certain structures and goals are common to all team policing programs. Structurally, they all assemble officers who had previously functioned as individuals or two-man teams and assign them shared responsibility for policing a relatively small geographic area. The common goal is improved crime control through better community relations and more efficient organization of manpower.

Syracuse Crime Control Team

Syracuse, N.Y., was the first police agency to combine the patrol and investigative function into one unit with a geographic responsibility for crime control. The crime control team was implemented in July 1968, and consisted of a team leader, deputy leader, and eight policemen. The team was relieved of many routine, noncriminal duties and given responsibility for controlling serious crime, apprehending offenders, and conducting investigations in a small area of the city.

The team leader, a lieutenant, was given considerable discretion in directing the activities and operations of the team. The program was decentralized and operated independently of the rest of the agency. The crime control team concept was later extended to other agency operations after the project report on the experiment indicated considerable success in reducing crime and increasing crime clearance rates.

Los Angeles, Calif., Basic Car Plan

The stated objectives of the basic car plan were to help society prevent crime by improving community attitudes toward the police; to provide stability of assignment for the street policeman; and to instill in each team of officers a proprietary interest in their assigned area and a better knowledge of the police role in the community. Beginning in November 1969, the plan was tested in two divisions; it was expanded citywide in April 1970.

Each police division has geographic areas of varying size based on workload and crime occurrence data. A team of nine officers is assigned to each basic car plan area and given responsibility for providing police service on a 24-hour basis. Each team is headed by a senior lead officer. Supervisory responsibilities of the patrol watch commanders and field sergeants remained unchanged.

Formal meetings between the team and citizens in each area are held monthly; informal meetings occur frequently throughout the month. Investigative, traffic, and other specialized personnel in each division are not assigned directly as members of the basic car teams at this time. A comprehensive experiment in total team policing began in the agency's Venice Division in June 1972.

Detroit, Mich., Beat Commander System

The beat commander pilot program began in April 1970, in two scout car areas in Detroit's 10th precinct. The beat commander, a sergeant, was given command of approximately 20 men, including three detectives who investigated only those cases originating in the beat command area. Two additional sergeants were later assigned to provide around the clock supervision.

The principal element of the system was stability of assignment of the beat commander and the team to a specified neighborhood. The goals were to improve police-community understanding, cooperation in crime control, and police efficiency and job satisfaction.

New York, N.Y., Neighborhood Police Team

In January 1971, a neighborhood police team consisting of sergeant and 18 policemen began operations in one radio motor patrol sector. As a result of this experiment, the system was later expanded throughout the agency. The structure of the N.P.T. is similar to the Detroit system. N.P.T. patrolmen, however, take greater investigative initiative; detectives are not directly involved in the program.

Crime control and community relations are two principal goals of the project. Additionally, improved supervision and motivation have resulted in increased productivity and efficiency. Substantial reductions in response time to calls is also attributed to the team program.

Dayton, Ohio, Team Policing

Dayton designed its team policing project to test the generalist approach to police work, to produce a community-based police structure, and to change the police organization from its traditional military structure to a neighborhood-oriented professional model. All specialized assignments in the test area were eliminated. Discretion was allowed in the wearing of uniforms, modes of operations, and program development.

The experiment began in October 1970, in a district covering about one-sixth of the city area. The personnel consisted of 35 to 40 officers, 12 community service officers, a lieutenant in charge, and four sergeants who acted as leaders for teams of 10 to 12 men. The lieutenant was selected by the chief and approved by neighborhood groups. The officers selected by vote their team leaders from a slate of sergeants.

The Dayton team project is probably the most fundamental attempt to change police field operations. Most internal matters are settled democratically among team members. The project decentralized authority and function, and concentrated upon community participation in achieving its goals.

Numerous other police agencies have tested and implemented various forms of team policing. Among them are Cincinnati, Ohio; Holyoke, Mass.; Charlotte, N.C.; Tampa and St. Petersburg, Fla.; Albany, N.Y.; Tucson, Ariz.; and Culver City, Sacramento, Richmond, San Bruno, Palo Alto, and Simi Valley, Calif. The experience and knowledge gained by these cities make them a rich source of information for agencies contemplating a team policing system.

Testing a Team Policing System

Most agencies that have tried team policing have tested the concept on a limited basis. Many of the currently operating systems have not been expanded to include the entire agency but continue in a small area on a scale conducive to testing and evaluation.

Agencies that have attempted team policing innovations have usually approached the subject from the standpoint of demonstrating that the innovation will work rather than trying to prove or disprove team policing through extensive experimentation. A demonstration project attempts to prove that a particular idea is an improvement. An experiment tests alternative ways of solving a problem.

The overriding objective of most agencies—the avoidance of disruption of ongoing operations—precludes true experimentation. Police agencies should conduct extensive research and plan comprehensive testing prior to formal implementation of team policing agencywide.

For most medium size and large agencies, a limited test of a proposed team policing system can be accomplished by designating one geographic area as a test site. Smaller agencies with limited personnel may have to test the system agencywide. Agencies with less than 75 employees should insure that adequate planning and appropriate training is completed prior to agency-wide testing of a team policing project.

In all cases, the research and planning stage must include the establishment of program objectives and goals. It must provide for evaluation of the effectiveness of the program in reducing crime, increasing arrests, increasing the general level of service rendered to the community, and enhancing police-community cooperation. The police chief executive and the agency's staff, command, and supervisory personnel should understand and support the proposed plan. Personnel charged with making the concept work must be given appropriate training, support, and authority to achieve the project's goals and objectives.

Appendix A
Violence, Like Charity, Begins at Home[*]

*"An Experimental New York City Police Unit Is Learning
How To Break Up Family Fights Without Fighting"*

"All I've got for you is a little family trouble at Sixteen-Thirteen Madison." He'll tell you which floor and thank God it isn't the top, and so you'll climb, climb, climb, and all the while you'll be preparing to say, "Listen, what's the matter with you folks? Pipe down, can't you? Oh shet ep, sister. Look—people are complaining; you're waking up folks in the building. O.K.—so you can't get along. O.K.—so you're drunk too. Now, look, I want you out of here. And quit socking your wife, and if I see you around here again before morning—before you're sober and ready to behave—I'll break your head wide open!"

That's the little speech, the succession of disciplinary directions that you'll be composing as you trudge up the stairs; and then you hear the shuddering gasp, and somehow you're through the door before they've opened it for you, and he's standing there alone. The woman is on the floor with her skirt around her middle, and what beautiful red, rosy tights she wears—all slick and damp—and the tights are extending themselves into a big evil patch on the floor. But beyond her he is there. He's very large; he looks colossal to you now. He doesn't have anything on except a pair of striped underwear shorts, and his eyes are rolling. He keeps watching you. He has a bloody bread knife in his hand, and you keep saying "Put it down, put it down—let go that knife," as he comes toward you a step at a time, and as the woman grunts and shifts on the floor in her blood, and still he keeps coming in, you've got to decide, and all in the instant. Do you shoot or do you try to use your stick? Do you try to take the knife away from him? . . . You don't like to be alone, nobody would like to be alone.

—MacKinlay Kantor,
"Signal Thirty-Two"

The threatened cop in Kantor's novel, like policemen everywhere, had every reason to feel alone. The odds were against him because it seems that violence, like charity, begins at home. According to the Federal Bureau of In-

* Sullivan, Ronald: "Violence, Like Charity, Begins at Home," *The New York Times Magazine*, November 24, 1968, p. 59. © 1968 by the New York Times Company. Reprinted by special permission. (The Times, New Jersey correspondent, based in Trenton, and a veteran police reporter.)

vestigation, one of every five policemen killed in the line of duty dies trying to break up a family fight. The President's Commission on Law Enforcement and the Administration of Criminal Justice reported last year that family disputes "are probably the single greatest cause of homicides" in the United States. And if policemen don't get killed in a family fight, they still stand a good chance of being bloodied. "There is a strong impression in police circles that intervention in these disputes causes more assaults on policemen than any other encounter," the Commission reported in "The Challenge of Crime in a Free Society." In fact, the New York City Police Department estimates that 40 per cent of its men injured in the line of duty were hurt while responding to family disturbances. Moreover, the department estimates that such calls take as much time as any other single kind of police action. "Yet the capacity of the police to deal effectively with such a highly personal matter as conjugal disharmony is, to say the least, limited . . . an activity for which few policemen—or people in any profession—are qualified by temperament or by training" the Commission reported.

But that was before an experimental New York City Police unit began intervening in family quarrels in upper West Harlem. Despite the high statistical probability of being knifed, shot at, gang-jumped, or pushed down a flight of tenement stairs, none of the 18 volunteer patrolmen assigned to the Family Crisis Intervention Unit in the 30th Precinct has sustained a single injury, much less a fatality, in the unit's first 15 months of operation. Moreover, after intervening in more than 1,000 individual family crises—an average of a little more than two a night—the unit has not been involved in a single charge of police brutality, and this is an area in which such accusations are commonplace.

But perhaps just as important, none of the interventions resulted in either a homicide or a suicide. There are no conclusive records in the precinct to show how this deathless record compares with the outcome of family fights in the precinct in previous years. Nevertheless, Police Commissioner Howard R. Leary, the United States Department of Justice and the project's originator, Dr. Morton Bard, director of the Psychological Center at City College, are convinced that the new unit unquestionably has saved many lives.

There are no records connecting deaths with family fights because no police function is more misunderstood, more underrated, and more grudgingly performed than calls to break them up. Unlike other police activity, such as murder investigations or criminal surveillance, intervention in family fights is commonly regarded at all levels in the Police Department as a thankless job that poses the danger of grave personal risk and the distinct possibility of becoming embroiled in charges of police brutality, with very little, if any, promise of reward. A cop makes detective or becomes a sergeant by the big arrest or the daring rescue—not by breaking up a family fight. It is not surprising, then, that there are few references to the subject in police literature or at police training academies.

Now, however, it seems likely that the apparent success of the Family Crisis Intervention Unit will have an impact on the way policemen are motivated, trained and ultimately rewarded by their departments. In fact, this year's report by the National Advisory Commission on Civil Disorders recommended New York's pilot program as a "model for other departments." The report said, "The Commission believes the police cannot and should not resist becoming involved in community service matters. Such work can gain the police the respect and support of the community."

Its importance was pointed up by the Governor's Select Commission on Civil Disorder in New Jersey. After investigating the causes of the Negro rioting in Newark in July, 1967, the Commission reported that most complaints of police brutality originated from incidents that began as family disturbance calls—and that these complaints had been increasing before the rioting broke out.

According to Dr. Bard, outmoded police organization is the silent factor underlying the growing tension between police and community, particularly in the urban ghettos. And the violence of family conflict in these areas is matched only by the indifference of society outside to its existence. Professor Bard emphasizes that only the police, of all social institutions, are present 24 hours a day, every day of the year, to answer the call when family violence threatens.

Thus, with the full support of Commissioner Leary, and $94,736 from the Federal Government, Dr. Bard's Psychological Center began a two-year experiment last year in training police to intervene in family fights. The pilot program, which is scheduled to end next April, does not aim to turn cops into psychologists or social workers. "That's just exactly what we're attempting to avoid," says Dr. Bard, who was a cop himself for a short time in the late nineteen-forties before he became a group worker with street gangs and ultimately a professor of psychology. "We have no intention of creating a family cop, or a family division, or making family crisis intervention an esoteric police speciality. All we're trying to do is give the ordinary policeman a new skill, one that will help him do better what he now does most—and that is help people in trouble." If, at the same time, he can become a primary mental-health resource in the community, so much the better, of course.

The program also is part of a growing revolution involving the training of clinical psychologists and the development of community mental-health programs in the cities. There simply never will be enough psychologists to treat poor persons in the slums, where most of the aggressive behavior and mental disorder is. So the idea at the center is to train psychologists to train other persons to do it.

At the same time, the university is given the chance to break out from its pedagogical shell by turning the surrounding community into a teeming psychological laboratory rather than a hostile environment. What better place is there than Harlem to study marital breakdown, aggression, sado-masochism,

6

and the effect of violence on early childhood development? And who is better equipped to study it than the persons who face it every day, like Patrolman John E. Bodkin, a 32-year-old, cigar smoking, no-nonsense, seven-year veteran and member of the Family Crisis Intervention Unit?

"It was up on 145th Street," he said. "And the couple was from the South. We went in there and I could see right off that this guy was tight, very tight. He was a Negro fellow, about 21 or 22 years old, only up in New York six months. She had called the police because of a dispute—a minor thing. But there he was, a little guy, and he was really tense because when we walked in with our uniforms and sticks, you could see that his earlier associations with police officers must have been very rough.

"You could see the fear in his eyes, the hostility in his face. His fists were clenched, and he was ready to do combat with us. God knows what he would have done if he'd had a gun or a knife. I moved toward the kitchen table and opened my blouse and I told him in a nice quiet way that I wanted to talk to him, but he's still looking at my stick. Well, the stick is under my arm so I hung it up on a nearby chair, purposely, to show there's no intent here. 'Look, I don't need it,' I'm trying to say to this guy. 'I don't need it because you're a nice guy in my eyes. You don't threaten me, so I'm not going to threaten you.' I've got to show this guy that I'm not a bully, a brute, a Nazi or the Fascist he thinks all cops are.

"So he calms down a little. Then I took my hat off and I said, 'Do you mind if I smoke?' And he looks funny at me. And I say, 'I'm a cigar smoker and some people don't like the smell of a cigar in their house, so would you mind if I smoke?' And the guy says, 'Oh sure, sure,' and you could see he was shocked. I felt he saw a human side of us, that I had respect for him and his household.

"Then the guy sat down and he and his wife proceed to tell us what it was all about. When we explain to her why he's upset, she smiles. 'Yes, yes, yes.' You see, she thinks we're on her side. Then we tell him why he's mad and he smiles. 'Yes, yes, yes.' Now we're on his side. Well, they eventually shake our hands; they were happy and we never had another call from them."

Patrolman Bodkin and the 17 other policemen in the family crisis unit operate in biracial pairs out of the 96-year-old, four story 30th Precinct station house on the southwest corner of 152nd Street and Amsterdam Avenue. The 30th is one of New York's smaller and more insignificant precincts, running north from 141st to 165th Streets and east from Riverside Drive to Edgecombe Avenue. Most of the old apartment houses on Broadway have been taken over by Puerto Rican and Negro families. The remaining whites in the precinct, many of them apparently Jewish, are virtually barricaded in the big apartment houses overlooking the Hudson on Riverside Drive, Actually, the 30th is just what Dr. Bard was looking for: a poor, rat-infested neighborhood, but without the wretchedness of some of the other black precincts in Harlem, one free of big crime and big institutions and one that comes alive every week when the welfare checks roll in.

Like Bodkin, most of the cops in the family unit were already working in the 30th before the program began. None of them was picked because he evidenced a bleeding heart for minority problems. All of them, and this includes the nine Negroes were used to feeling hated, feared and envied in the ghetto. None of them has a college degree. They tend to be young, in their late 20's and early 30's, because it is very hard to teach old cops new tricks. What Dr. Bard, along with Dr. Bernard Berkowitz, a psychologist with 12 years as a policeman in his background, looked for in choosing from among 45 volunteers were experienced cops who expressed enthusiasm for the experiment and frustration with their present inability to deal effectively with family crises, and who showed every indication of being sensitive to the changing role the police must assume in cities.

The 18 men, who were released from duty, spent nearly a month with professional psychologists at the center in mutual exploration of the best methods of successful intervention. The psychologists knew all about such things as aggression, trauma, neurosis, alcoholism and all the other behavioral patterns associated with family violence. And that is what they taught the men during the first three weeks of intensive psychological classroom work. But the center's pedagogy and its proclivity for reflective analysis generally failed the psychologists when they departed from the laboratory or the textbook for the explosive, instant-action world of police confrontation with family violence. "No one has a textbook for that. This is where we had to learn from each other," says Dr. Bard.

During the third week the cops were subjected to three days of family-crisis psycho-skits staged by a group of professional actors. The short plays showed typical family crises and were written without conclusions; the endings were improvised by the patrolmen themselves, who intervened in pairs at the end. For example, in one play, a young Negro actress portrayed a wife who was cowering against the rear classroom wall, away from a tall, husky Negro, playing her wife-beating husband.

"He's going to hit me, he's going to hit me again," she screamed as the two cops burst on the scene and split, one of them going to the aid of the stricken woman, the other confronting the man.

"Whaddaya doing that for?" the patrolman snarled at the man as he pushed him toward a corner of the improvised stage. "That's no way to treat a woman, that's no way for a man to act. You're no man." With that, the Negro actor, even though he knew it was only a play, reacted angrily and moved toward the advancing patrolman, bellowing, "Who says I'm no man . . . ?"

At that point, the play was stopped and the cops and the actors analyzed their respective reactions. For one thing, the cop who confronted the husband was told this is how most cops get hurt—challenging a man's masculinity.

Moreover, the cops were told that the wife may very well be a masochist who has spent the day provoking the man into attacking her. He gets an outlet for his aggression; she has the simple pleasure of getting beaten up. The idea, the policemen were told, is to give the combatants alternatives and the help they need to understand why they fight.

But an unsophisticated cop can only go so far, and this is where their fourth week of training came in. They took field trips to various social, health and welfare agencies where experts explained the kinds of help available to poor families in trouble. Later, the men took part in human relations workshops where they were prompted to examine, in group sensitivity discussions, their individual prejudices and preconceptions of disrupted family life in the ghetto.

After this, the unit began operating out of the 30th station house in the precinct's special family car. Two members of the unit work each of the day's three eight-hour tours and are dispatched on all complaints involving family disturbances. They also continue their normal police duties—they give out parking tickets and speeding summonses; they patrol a given sector of the precinct; they are expected to respond to any emergency just like any other cop on the beat. At the start, they were subject to considerable jeering from other patrolmen, but their capacities to handle both missions effectively has turned the initial jibes at the station house into inquiries on how to deal with family crises.

Meantime, all of the 18 men continue their training, taking part in six-man discussion groups led by professional psychologists. In addition, each man has a weekly private consultation with a third-year graduate student in clinical psychology. The consultation cuts both ways. The officer reports the way he reacted to a particular family crisis and is given advice on ways he might have responded differently. Some of the students have become intrigued with the research opportunities afforded by these exchanges. One has formulated a research proposal in which he will attempt to measure differences in aggressive threshold stimuli among children of families in which day-to-day violence is a part of the environment. These children will be matched with children raised in nonviolent homes.

Adrian Halfhide, a 27-year-old Negro cop assigned to the family project, is convinced that 60 per cent of the people in every block in the precinct are aware of the new unit. "We're more aware of them, too," he says. "We go into a family dispute and we can pick up certain signs, statements, gestures, looks and facial expressions that enable us to get a basic idea of what's going on. For example, I notice whether a man is gritting his teeth, whether the veins in his temple are throbbing. Before, I only looked for whether he had a weapon, or whether he was bigger than me. Later, when they just want someone to yell at, I say, 'O.K., get mad at me.' Then everybody yells at me. But they're all together, yelling together but at me, and that's groovy."

Halfhide and the other family cops have some fundamental ground rules.

They always stay calm; they don't threaten and they don't take sides. They don't challenge a man's masculinity; they don't degrade a woman's femininity. They intentionally give people verbal escape routes to save face. And mother isn't always right—they know about Oedipus complexes. They notice that most family fights tend to break out on Sunday night after a festering weekend of drinking. They say the major causes of conflict are, predictably, money and sex. Families fight more in the summer because it's hot, and more in the winter because it's so cold outside they can't escape one another.

On the back seat of their patrol car the family cops keep two small wooden boxes with card files showing whom the unit has previously been sent to. The file is kept by street numbers so the men on duty can determine immediately whether any other team has called upon a family to which they are on their way. The cards show whether an earlier intervention involved any weapons so that the responding patrolmen can be on guard. The cards have 35 entries, including besides usual vital statistics: "What happened IMMEDIATELY before you arrived? What do you think led up to the immediate crisis? (Changes in family patterns?) (Environmental changes, etc.?) Impressions of the family: How long has this family been together? Who is dominant? What is the appearance of the house? Appearance of the individuals? Other impressions? What happened after your arrival? (How did each disputant respond?) How was the dispute resolved? Mediation ( ). Referral ( ). Aided ( ). Arrest ( ). Full details. Summarize the crisis situation and its resolution."

Every intervention is different and each of the nine teams react differently. Nevertheless, there are some standard procedures. The patrolmen go in together, then split, with one of them going toward the antagonists, the second toward the other. Guns are rarely drawn. In fact, the cops often leave their nightsticks in the car. They don't shout, they don't push and they don't threaten to lock up everyone in sight. All the while the two men are scooping up any knives, scissors or other weapons, putting them where no one can get at them. Windows are checked in case the crisis involves a potential suicide. Children are accounted for.

Generally, the cops attempt to mollify both sides, taking the combatants into separate rooms so they can be questioned without one of them challenging the other's version of the crisis. The cops try to draw out the underlying facts, compare differing versions and then, in a kind of group therapy, they attempt to explain to the family why it is fighting and recommend ways for it to stop. Normally the family will be referred to a health or social agency. The cops carry printed slips with the addresses, offer to make the appointment —and in some cases drive the family down in the patrol car.

Many times, interventions do not involve violence. There is, for instance, a five-story walk-up on Amsterdam Avenue, a squalid rooming house taken over by prostitutes and narcotic addicts. But on the top floor an old Negro couple—she in her late 70's, he in his 80's—were barely surviving in abandoned isolation in a tiny rear room. He was weak from advanced age and malnutrition and had fallen out of bed. She did not have the strength to lift him back. They had no children, no friends, no neighbors and no money. So she called the police and the family unit was dispatched. Instead of just putting him back in bed, which is what a lot of cops would have done, the unit called the Visiting Nurse Service. The V.N.S. told them that they should call a physician. So the cops went out and got one. And the couple are now visited regularly by V.N.S. nurses who make sure they are getting along the best they can.

Violence, though, or the forestalling of it, is the rule—especially as weekends draw to a close and the relief checks are gone, some of them spent on gin. This particular night, Patrolman Bodkin and his partner, Frank Madewell, get the call on the police radio: "Man with a gun at One-Six-Three Street and Amsterdam." They weave fast against traffic and screech up at the address behind three other patrol cars. Upstairs there are six cops in the third floor hall and a thin, hysterical woman in her nightgown shouting obscenities—alternately through a closed apartment door and at the cops for not breaking it down. "He's got my kids inside, and he's got a gun!" she screams.

From inside, the man roars, "You come in and I'll blow your —— head off." With that, a burly sergeant pushes by the woman and bangs on the door. "Let's go! Open up, or we'll kick it down!" he shouts. "Come right ahead, ——," the man bellows back.

Meantime, Madewell goes back to the car and checks the address in the card file. The couple has quite a file; he is marked as violent and possibly armed. Madewell goes back up and tells the sergeant, who jerks his thumb toward the closed door and replies: "O.K., you're the family cops. You go in." And slides out of the line of fire.

"First, we used his first name," Madewell recalls. "We tried to con him. I said, 'I can't scream through the door, and besides it's cold as hell out here and all your wife wants is her clothes.' But he just tells me to do you-know-what and I'm sweating. 'You can at least give her her clothes,' I say to him. 'We won't' say a word to you; we won't even look. C'mon, it's getting late and we can't stay here all night. Tell me what happened; you're a man. Did she try to put you down?'

"God, I'm talking to this guy, and the other cops are over by the stairs with their guns out. Finally—I can't say how long—I feel the lock give and the door open a crack and we go in and take him."

Later, detectives from the 30th squad determined that the man had attempted to fire a .32-caliber revolver at the sergeant through the closed door, but that the firing pin failed each time to strike the shell hard enough to shoot the bullet. The man said he had stopped trying to shoot when Madewell called him by his first name and started to talk to him.

Or spend the early morning hours of a recent Saturday on duty with Albert

Robertson, a 42-year-old family cop, a Negro with 11 years in the department, most of them in the 30th. He and his partner, William Robison, a nonunit patrolman who has been pressed into family-car duty on this tour, prowl through the precinct's garbage-strewn streets.

The first radio call sends them to St. Nicholas Avenue, where they climb, climb, climb to the sixth floor. At an open door, the young, buxom Negro woman who called the police lets them in and jerks her thumb toward a big man asleep in the bedroom. "Robbie," she says to Patrolman Robertson, whom everyone on his beat seems to know, "he's nothin' but a bum who's been whippin' me for eight years. I want him arrested before he kills me. He beat me somethin' awful before he drank hisself to sleep."

"But, sweetheart," Robertson replies, "you know he'll be out tomorrow. And are you going to give him the bail money?" (It turns out later that she simply wanted to get rid of him for the weekend so she could go to Atlantic City.)

There's another call. And at 150th Street and Amsterdam a woman shouts down from a second-floor tenement window: "Robbie! Robbie! He's got a gun. He's messin' with us with his pistol."

So Robertson and Robison draw their guns this time, and tell the woman to stand back. "Open the door!" yells Robbie. "For what?" the man inside growls. "That bitch is nuts." He finally opens up but he has no gun on him—and they have no search warrant.

Then it's quickly back to a big, run-down apartment house on St. Nicholas Avenue where a man and wife in a shabby basement apartment have been at each other all night. She says: "Look at what he done to me; he kicked me in the belly. I want him locked up officer." He says: "Hell, lock her up, too," and holds out his arm to show where his wife has cut him with a kitchen knife. "I'll go as long as she goes, too; otherwise, you got to fight me."

Carefully, with a look of weariness in his round, good-natured face, Robertson takes off his blouse and cap, lays his black notebook on the hall table, and sinks slowly into the only comfortable chair in the living room. "What's you folks been drinkin'?" he asks. "Scotch," the glowering, heavy-set man answers. "Sweetheart," Robertson says to the woman, "get me a small drink, will you?" Then he takes off his shoes and rubs his arches and wiggles his toes, and the man just sits and looks at him incredulously. The man gives Robertson the Scotch, but the drink has no ice, so Robertson asks the wife to bring him some.

"By this time," Robertson explains later, "they're so shook up with me sitting in *their* chair, sippin' *their* Scotch (he actually never drank it) that now we can find out what they're really fighting about. Before you know it, I'm part of the family."

Sometimes the intervention ultimately fails, as happened earlier this year when a woman, mumbling incoherently, her hands and legs covered with blood, staggered into the 30th station house and threw a bloody paring knife on the desk. Two unit patrolmen, Tony Donovan and Joseph Mahoney, happened to be there and they led her gently to a side room.

"O.K., sweetheart," one of them asked her quietly, "where are you hurt? What happened?" They gave her a cigarette and lit it for her. As she held it in her trembling hand, she moaned: "He kept nagging me. All day, kept after me. Couldn't stand it no more. Oh, God, go help him."

Six months earlier, the woman had called the police and the family unit had been sent to stop a fight between her and her husband. The unit determined then that both were alcoholics and tried to get them to go to Alcoholics Anonymous, but they refused. However, they did agree to separate, but he came back later. The drinking began again, and the inevitable happened. They began to fight. But instead of calling the cops this time, she had stabbed her husband, nearly killing him.

Or there's the night when Patrolman John Edmonds, a quiet, 41-year-old Negro, and John Mulitz, a tall, 35-year-old Pennsylvania Dutchman, get the call: "A man shot," and Mulitz, who's driving, turns on the flashing red light and uses the siren to get through traffic up Broadway to 163d Street. The address is not in the car's card file. The dying man, a middle-aged Puerto Rican, is on his back in the bedroom. Part of his intestine has bubbled through his abdomen where the steel-jacketed bullet came out. His wife mumbles incoherently to Edmonds: "We have ze argument. He goes in ze bedroom . . ."

"Maybe if she called us earlier . . . ," Edmonds says.

Then it's another call and Mulitz and Edmonds pull up in front of a sagging tenement on 149th Street where a young, scrawny Negro, his right hand swathed in bandages, comes rushing out screaming that one of his wife's sisters just threw acid on him. It seems that he and his wife had got drunk together earlier. They started to fight, and he put his hand through a bedroom mirror. When he tried to resume the fight after being treated at Harlem Hospital, one of his wife's three monumental sisters (they could have been a beef trust, Mulitz remarks later) heaved him out while another threw a panful of cleaning ammonia on him. In the scuffle, he stabbed his wife in the leg.

When Mulitz tells him that he must be arrested for this, the Negro takes out another knife hidden under his belt and snarls: "I ain't goin', and you can't make me." Mulitz orders him to drop the knife, but he continues to move up the front steps. Mulitz opens his holster and shouts: "Drop it!" but the man just looks at him.

Finally, Mulitz, who towers easily more than a foot over the man, crosses his arms and says: "Listen, you don't have to prove you're a man to me or to your wife and her sisters. I know you're a man; you already proved it to me. Now drop the knife like a good fellow." The man stops, waivers a few seconds, then bursts into tears—and drops the knife.

And one night, George Timmons, 33, and his partner, Ernest Bryant, a 33-year-old Negro who cuts his hair Afro style and wears love beads off-duty, pay their fifth visit to a Puerto Rican couple on 145th Street who are determined to destroy each other. This time, the husband has methodically dismantled the family bed and stacked the pieces neatly against the bedroom wall before leaving for his nighttime job. "She's no goin' to mess around in this bed while I gone," he says.

Normally, the man's wife would have tried to kill him for taking the bed apart. In the past 16 years she has opened him up across the chest with a carving knife, shot him on three separate occasions, and once has thrown lye on his sexual organs. She is an obvious sadist. He, on the other hand, doesn't seem to mind much and he proudly pulls up his workshirt to show the cops his battle scars. She only glares at him and turns to the cops. "You think he look bad now, ha," she says. "He keep this up, he's really goin' to get hurt."

Federal officials such as Louis A. Mayo, Jr., the 39-year-old program manager of the family-intervention project in the National Institute of Law Enforcement and Criminal Justice, a new agency within the Department of Justice, consider the experiment a success, even though its full results have yet to be evaluated. "We are very encouraged," Mayo said recently. "For a very limited financial investment, there's been a handsome payoff on a cost benefit basis alone—and that doesn't include the personal agony that goes with a homicide."

"Look," says Mrs. Carole Rothman, a petite and attractive 23-year-old graduate student in Dr. Bard's project. "I used to have the typical 'dumb cop' image. I simply couldn't believe a cop had the capacity to figure out the psychological nuances of family conduct. But you should see how fantastically sensitive they really are. They pick up on things that I would miss, and they challenge things I would let go by. Now I've become intolerant of people who have cops stereotyped. I see cops as faces, not uniforms."

"If you ask the average psychologist, 'Who becomes a cop?' " says Dr. Bard, "you know what quick, glib answer you get off the top of his head? You get: 'A sadist, a latent criminal, a paranoid.' I have yet to have someone answer: 'Somebody who wants to help.' I suspect very strongly that a significantly large percentage—not all—of the men who seek to become cops do so out of a wish to help. They're idealistically motivated."

"But the police establishment quickly disabuses any such notion. There's no mechanism for a guy to develop along these lines. He learns very quickly that the only way he can make it is to give up this helping aspiration. The system does not reward this kind of behavior and it does not encourage it because its guiding principles are repressive, restrictive and in keeping with the horse-and-buggy days when conflicts were resolved in the middle of Main Street by the man with the quickest draw.

6

"Some of these guys make a compromise; they go into youth work or rescue service. A significantly large number quit. The ones who stay make more compromises and become the most cynical transmitters of the same values which they themselves deplored when they first came in. Now, a wholly different organizational structure of the police must prevail in which the system addresses itself to the problems that society really has, rather than those which society once had. The way it is now is neurotic."

"Let's face it. The very nature of the cop is to preserve the status quo. And the reason for the confrontation between the police and the intellectual is that, if there is anything the intellectual is for, he is for change."

A former New York City police official said: "It is a fact that until very recently a patrolman who got in a gun battle was immediately rewarded with a promotion to detective. And it is unfortunately a fact that the tradition of rewarding the man who winds up in a violent confrontation is still a very real part of the New York City Police Department and most other departments, too."

Dr. Howard E. Mitchell, director of the human resources program at the University of Pennsylvania, and an expert on police, contends that the day of holding a once-a-year Brotherhood Week at the station house, on the one hand, while beefing up the Tactical Patrol Force on the other, is over. "It's a different ball game now," he says. "The police are going to have to make a lot of changes, and it doesn't take any great intelligence to know that a person trained for riot control is not the one to send out to stop a family fight in a tense community."

In a sense that is pretty much what the Family Crisis Intervention Unit is all about. Or, as Capt. Vincent T. Agoglia, the commanding officer of the 30th precinct and a 30-year veteran, remarked as he watched his men turn out the other morning: "You've got to have the people in the community on your side or else you can forget about police work. Look at the changes here in the way the community has reacted. We've got families now who come in here and ask for the family cops. Last year, they might have come in here looking, instead, for the civilian complaint review board. It's not what the police *say*, but what they *do*, that counts."

7

Cities, Commerce, and the Police

One of the main reasons people live in or near cities is because of their use as centers of business and commerce. In them, goods are produced and sold, services are offered and used, and various kinds of enterprises are administered. This activity, much of which is fundamentally commercial in nature, is the basis for a large proportion of the mosaic of urban employment. It is this employment in and near cities that in turn underscores residence patterns, as most people are obliged to live within a reasonable distance of the place where they work.

The commercial aspects of the city are far more complicated than they might appear to be at a first glance. The business and commercial activities of any city not only provide the economic wherewithal for much of the population, but they are also the basis for a considerable amount of the demand made upon the police for various services. This chapter will examine the commercial nature of cities and will relate it to the police function.

The Commercial Structure of the City

The commercial structure of a city involves considerably more than the over the counter sales of goods; it also includes a wide range of activities such as banking and finance, insurance and real estate, the provision of services, and the administration of private and public enterprise. These various activities are carried out in shops, stores, warehouses, and in office buildings and they take place in varying degrees in virtually every part of town. At the core of the commercial structure of the city is the Central Business District, about which more will be said later in the chapter. However, for purposes of analysis, certain elements of the commercial structure of the city will be discussed first.

Retail Commerce: Its Location and Function. In a nutshell, retail business enterprises are those which provide goods and services directly to the consumer. This category includes most of the businesses which are the most highly visible to people traveling city streets. It includes such things as restaurants, clothing stores, supermarkets, car dealerships, variety stores, and many others.

The greatest concentration of retail activity has traditionally been focused in the Central Business District, where the volume of business is greater than anywhere else in the city. However, the post World War II era has seen the emergence of new patterns of retail business locations. There has been a movement away from the congested downtown area in favor of locating shops and stores closer to the consumers who have themselves fled the central city in favor of the suburbs or outlying areas. This pattern first took the form of shopping centers which sought to capture the trade of the residents of neighborhoods or new developments. More recently there have developed larger shopping malls which attempt to reach much larger markets. Shopping centers typically contain branches of large department stores or discount houses, as well as supermarkets, clothing stores, shoe stores, and other convenience establishments. The shopping centers normally offer the shopper ample parking space, which is generally not available in the Central Business District, and they tend to be located at sites which make them convenient for many motorists. The shopping center originally sought to cater to the needs of people living in fairly specific residential areas. There has been a drift in recent years, however, toward the establishment of regional shopping centers which are much larger than the earlier neighborhood shopping center. These new regional shopping centers typically house a nearly full range of consumer requirements, including specialty shops. In addition to providing for ample parking facilities, many of these centers have taken the form of indoor malls which offer carefully engineered climate control and aesthetic decor. Customers for the regional shopping centers are attracted from the community as a whole, or at least a very substantial geographic part of it.

Retail establishments are also frequently found situated along major traffic arteries. These businesses derive a considerable proportion of their clientele from passers-by. They usually offer store front parking, and tend to be owner operated. These types of retail houses are normally rather small, and their owners count on a high volume of street and sidewalk traffic for the success of their business.

Another pattern of retail establishment is that which includes stores or shops located along a strip of roadway extending for several blocks within residential neighborhoods. The stores which are so situated generally tend to count on residents of the immediate area for their business. These neighborhood stores also tend to reflect the socioeconomic character of the areas in which they are situated. For example, in upper-middle class neighborhoods one would expect to find the usual grocery and drug stores along with such specialty outlets as beauty shops, book stores, gourmet food stores, and gift shops. On the other hand, in neighborhoods which are composed of lower class residents one would expect to find more used furniture stores, pawn shops, bars, and thrift shops.

Finally, commercial retail outlets may exist as single, isolated stores or as a small cluster of complementary businesses. It is convenient to look at retail establishments as falling into one of two general patterns. On the one hand, they may be part of a ribbon or string of businesses located along a traffic artery. Or, they may be part of a complex of retail establishments which exist in a cluster type of arrangement. These retail clusters, such as shopping centers, are often situated at the intersection of two major traffic arteries so as to take advantage of the high volume of traffic which at the same time makes them more convenient to customers who travel either by automobile or by public transportation.

Wholesale Commerce: Its Functions and Location. According to the *Standard Industrial Classification Manual* of the U.S. Bureau of the Budget, wholesale commercial activities are basically those which sell merchandise to retailers; to industrial, commercial, institutional, or professional users; or to other wholesalers.

Because of the fact that wholesalers are in the business of supplying retailers, it is to be expected that they generally deal in relatively large quantities of the goods which they wholesale. This implies that greater emphasis must be placed on warehousing. As a consequence, wholesale establishments are often located close to but outside of the Central Business District of the city. They also require ready access to railroad or truck transportation lines in order to facilitate the receiving and shipment of goods.

A good example of the recent trend in the development of wholesale business districts within cities is exemplified in Dallas, Texas. Dallas has a large and relatively new wholesale/industrial district located just outside of the Central Business District and away from the residential areas. This area is composed of warehouses and offices and is convenient not only to transportation facilities but is also adjacent to several wholesale merchandise and apparel marts.

Retail Business, Crime, and The Police. Retail establishments are frequent victims of criminal activity, although not all types of retail establishments share an equal likelihood of victimization. Although there are a number of ways in which retail business may be victimized, perhaps the three most common categories are through employee theft and shoplifting, fraud, and robbery.

Employee theft and shoplifting are major problems to retail merchants. It has been estimated that as much as 75 to 80 percent of all retail inventory shrinkage is the result of some kind of dishonesty.[1] The President's Crime Commission has estimated this loss at between 1 to

[1] President's Commission on Law Enforcement and the Administration of Justice, Nicholas deB. Katzenbach, Chairman. *Task Force Report: Crime and Its Impact—An Assessment.* Washington, D.C.: U.S. Government Printing Office, 1967, p. 48.

189

2 percent of the value of all retail sales. However, it is extremely difficult to tell exactly how much of this loss is attributable to employee theft and how much is due to shoplifting. Nevertheless, the few studies that exist are nearly unanimous in asserting that employee theft accounts for a far greater percentage of inventory loss than does shoplifting, with some sources indicating that the percentage might run as high as 75 to 80 percent of the total.[2] Employee theft is seldom reported to the police, and because of the complexity of some business records or inventory procedures it is likely that a considerable amount of employee theft goes undetected.

Shoplifting is likewise very difficult to estimate, although it is known to result in substantial losses to retail merchants. As with employee thefts, large amounts of shoplifting go undetected and perhaps a majority of the shoplifters who are caught are not turned over to the police. Most shoplifting is carried out by amateurs ("snitches") rather than by professionals ("boosters"). Shoplifters tend to represent all socioeconomic classes, and women shoplifters greatly outnumber men. Most shoplifters steal for their own use, and few of them see themselves as criminals. They often have elaborate rationalizations in justification of their stealing.

Most retail establishments tend to view employee theft and shoplifting as an unpleasant economic fact of life, and as long as it does not exceed a given margin, it generally does not receive much concern. Large retail houses frequently have their own security departments which are employed to deal with employee dishonesty and to cut down on losses through shoplifting. In some places employees are subject to polygraph examinations prior to employment (or after they have been employed), and in some types of stores technical equipment is installed to monitor goods or customers to cut down on shoplifting. Although some stores rigorously prosecute all shoplifters (or employees who steal), many are more interested in cutting down on loss than in the punishment of the offender. Most retail establishments do not expect municipal police to play an active role in problems of employee theft or shoplifting, except under unusual circumstances. The police likewise do not typically see themselves as being obliged to actively prevent this type of criminal activity. The most frequent (if not the only) police involvement in them is in the picking up of shoplifters who have been apprehended by store personnel for transportation to the police station for booking.

Retail businesses are also subjected to various types of frauds. Fraud is an offense which covers any method of obtaining money or goods by cheating or false pretenses, except through forgery or counterfeiting. Rates of criminal fraud are difficult to estimate because the line dividing it

[2] Ibid. See also Mary Owen Cameron, *The Booster and the Snitch*. New York: The Free Press of Glencoe, 1964.

from civil fraud is that of criminal intent, which is often very difficult to establish.

The type of fraud most commonly employed against retail establishments is that involving bad checks. Many retail outlets have sought to cut down on check frauds through such tactics as either not accepting checks or by accepting them only from customers who have special cards issued by the store. Some stores routinely photograph a person writing a check (along with the check). Other stores limit the amount of a check to that of the purchase and others may limit the total dollar amount of the check. When a bad check is returned to a store, only rarely are the police notified. As was mentioned above, part of the problem lies in proving criminal intent on the part of the person who wrote the check. One way this may be done is for the merchant to contact the writer and to advise him that his check did not clear; if within a certain period of time he has not made good on the check, this may serve as evidence of his intention to defraud. Also, checks given in payment of a pre-existing debt are not generally prosecutable as a fraud because that for which the check was written has already been obtained on credit. Therefore, checks given for payments on charge accounts or open accounts are not normally prosecutable as a fraud (although civil recovery is available). In addition, promises made by a customer to pay at some date in the future are not usually considered fraudulant even if the promises are broken at a later date. Therefore, if a post-dated check is given for payment, it is a promise to pay in the future and is not the proper subject of a criminal prosecution for fraud.

Because of the complexity of laws and procedures dealing with checks and other negotiable instruments, both police officers and merchants are reluctant to make a legal issue out of a bad check. Merchants are more interested in collecting the money they feel they are due, and policemen are adamantly against being used as a collection agency. Some merchants will call the police in an attempt to effect a recovery, and might in fact become quite angry at the police when they fail to jump right into the affair. However, merchants are much more likely to *threaten* to call the police in order to coerce the writer of a bad check into making it good. In some areas merchants will refer bad checks to the local prosecuting attorney who in turn will advise the writer of the check that no action will be taken if the check is made good. Basically, however, bad checks are generally viewed by the police as a business problem and not a police problem.

Of the many ways in which a retail house can be victimized, perhaps none is more traumatic than that of robbery, especially armed robbery. Robbery is the crime of theft by force. The force may be actual, or it may consist of an offer to use force together with an apparent ability to carry it out. It is the combination of force and theft which makes robbery a much feared crime. This is especially so since merchants know that some robberies do in fact include the use of violence, including death, and that all robberies have the potential for serious violence. Whereas most merchants are willing to cope with some loss due to employee theft, shoplifting, or bad checks, robberies are viewed in an entirely different light. Merchants normally call the police to report robberies and the police themselves place a very high priority on responding to them.[3]

The police realize that the probability of success in apprehending a robber is directly related to the promptness with which they respond to the call. Robbers are of course also aware of this, and therefore site selection and ease of escape are factors usually considered in deciding what kind of business to rob. As a result, some businesses have a higher risk of being robbed than do others. The types of stores which would be included in the high risk category would include liquor stores, service stations, motel offices, and convenience markets, especially those which are open late at night.

In some cities the police have actively sought to reduce robberies, especially armed robberies, through innovative offensive tactics. These include the use of tactical forces deployed in high risk areas at times when robberies are most likely to take place. In some cities the police have even concealed officers in stores which have been frequent targets of robberies. One southern city even has a policy of truthfully announcing at Christmas time when the robbery rate is high, that police officers armed with shotguns are concealed in some of the numerous mini-markets in that city—a program which is believed to have had a significant impact on the decrease in the number of armed robberies carried out against those stores!

Wholesale Business, Crime, and The Police. The most serious threat to wholesale establishments is that of burglary, as large concentrations of valuable goods are frequently housed at one location. Because of the potential loss which could accrue, and because of requirements made upon them by insurance companies, wholesale firms typically take advantage of industrial security services and technical security devices. Most commercial warehouses are secured by burglar alarms and may also utilize protective lighting and fences. In addition, industrial security firms provide armed guards and patrol service as well as night watchmen or sentry dogs. Because of the use of such devices and because of the very limited contact between wholesale operations and non-employee

[3] For an interesting and informative treatment of the problem of robbery see John E. Conklin, *Robbery*. Philadelphia: J. B. Lippincott Company, 1972.

personnel, these firms have less occasion to deal with the police than do their retail counterparts.

The Central Business District

It has already been pointed out that the Central Business District is the core of the commercial structure of the city. It is an area in which concentrated commercial activities take place and is characterized by a large number of multistory buildings used for commercial (including retail sales, offices, and administration) purposes.

The Central Business District is still the focus of commercial activity in most areas; however, it is increasingly beset with serious problems. Some of them stem from difficulties in transportation and include inadequate mass transit, lack of adequate parking facilities, and severe traffic congestion arising from access problems and inadequate thoroughfares. Other problems have arisen out of the competition to retail trade from shopping centers in residential areas. Even other problems are financial in nature and stem from the flight of the more affluent resident from the city and their replacement by people who are poor.

The Commercial Core. At the very heart of the Central Business District is the *commercial core,* which is the apex of the commercial portion of the Central Business District. It is at this point, which is an intersection of streets, that the front-foot values of land are the highest. The commercial core of the city is also characterized by very intense vehicle and pedestrian traffic. As one moves out from this point, land value begins to drop off, as does the intensity of land use.

Away from the commercial core and situated around the edge of the downtown area is usually a belt of land which appears to be run-down or deteriorated and which reflects a general quality of blight. This zone was referred to in Chapter 5 as the *zone in transition.* Although many cities have instituted model cities programs or urban renewal projects in this area, its fundamental character remains apparent in most instances. It is in this blighted zone that one finds the old, multistoried apartment houses intermingled with light industry and with commercial activities, a number of which are of a marginal nature, such as junk stores, used appliance stores ,bars, liquor stores, strip-joints, and other similar types of business.

The Central Business District and the Police

Social scientists have long agreed that on the whole, the highest crime rates are found in the Central Business District. In fact, on the basis of rates per 100,000 population, the risk of criminal victimization is greater in the central portion of the city than anywhere else. According to the President's Crime Commission,

> Of all types of offenses known to the police the central segment contributes the largest proportion of all types of fraud (65 percent) and all types of robbery (63 percent) including purse snatching and nonresidential robbery. Some of the offenses for which the central segment accounts for more than half of those known to the police are assaults (60 percent), felonious homicide (52 percent), miscellaneous forms of robbery (88 percent), and residential robbery (79 percent)....[4]

The reasons for the consistent and high rates of criminal misconduct in the central business district have been the topic of considerable interest among social scientists. One reason for this interest is that:

> Whenever the indicators of a social problem, such as crime, follow a regular pattern in their geographical distribution and their pattern persists from one time period to another, it suggests that a systematic set of underlying social, economic, or phychological pressures is operating to produce the pattern.[5]

The exact dynamics behind the patterns of high crime in the central city are complex and not fully understood. These dynamics are undoubtedly related to such forces as population change and mobility, fertility differentials, housing patterns, and such population characteristics as age, sex, race, ethnicity, income, employment, education, and class status. Each of these elements in turn is affected by such things as the delivery of social services, nutrition and health care, and such environmental factors as crowding, pollution, and even noise levels.

However, when considered from the perspective of the police, these factors, important though they are, are obviously beyond the scope of police authority, training, and organization. The police must deal with problems and people largely as they find them. The police have little control over the causes of most problems which confront them; theirs is basically a reactive role. As a result the police "do the best they can with what they have," but what they have is often woefully inadequate or inappropriate. When police efforts become obviously unproductive, people have the tendency to blame the police themselves for their lack of productivity, the police in turn are prone to believe that they are doing the right thing and doing it well, but that they simply don't have sufficient

[4] *Task Force Report: Crime and Its Impact,* p. 63.
[5] Ibid., p. 60.

manpower or equipment to get the job done the way it should be. Nowhere is this more painfully reflected than in police efforts in the central sector of the city.

The Central Business District and its surrounding belt of blight contain conditions highly conducive to crime. Yet the crime is basically the outcome of the social, economic, physical, and psychological forces which merge together in the central sector of the city. Traditional police responses to crime in this area may be *valid*, but they certainly have typically had little to do with eliminating the causes of that crime.

Zoning

There are a variety of kinds of businesses in any city, and these businesses naturally require different types of buildings and facilities. Obviously, it would be a source of considerable consternation if a developer were to erect a twenty story office building in the middle of a quiet, relatively isolated area composed exclusively of private residences. Problems of this type are avoided through the use of zoning ordinances.

Zoning is basically the division of the community into districts each of which limits land use to certain requirements dealing with how the land may be used. In other words, zoning is a means of controlling land use within the community; however, zoning has been far from an unqualified success. For one thing, the first zoning ordinance was passed in 1916 in New York City, and although the use of zoning ordinances subsequently spread very rapidly, considerable land use patterning had already been established by prior development.

Although the history of zoning contains numerous controversial episodes, one thing seems to remain clear: zoning has played a key role in maintaining the integrity of the better residential neighborhoods. By implication this has contributed to the concentration of business and industry in certain other portions of the community.

Zoning places particular restrictions on business, for it determines which kinds of businesses may exist in what areas. Further limitations are established with respect to such things as the ratio of floor area to the size of the total lot, building size and height, off-street parking requirements and so on.

Zoning maps and ordinances are available where they are in effect. Ideally, they should be reviewed by members of the police department so that officers might have a more accurate and informed idea of the nature of the districts in which they serve. Police officers who are familiar with zoning ordinances and with the distribution of the zoning districts will be more familiar with the land use patterns of immediate concern to those with whom they come into frequent contact.

Illegal Commercial Enterprises

A considerable volume of business is carried out in large cities which involves, in the words of the President's Crime Commission, "A net addition to the resources of the criminal sector and a diminution of the resources available for other purposes to the legitimate sector." This is the commerce in illegal businesses, willingly entered into by citizens who do not see themselves as either criminals or as supporters of criminal industries.

The chief activities in this category involve illicit commerce in gambling, narcotics, loansharking, and prostitution. Commerce in these activities runs into the billions of dollars annually on a national scale and represents a tremendous loss in unpaid taxes. In addition it supports organized crime and contributes in a number of ways to a reduction in the quality of life in American cities.

Not only do those who seek out these goods and services generally see themselves as respectable citizens, they typically resent the "interference" on the part of the police in such matters. As a result they do not report purveyors of these goods and services to the police, and they usually decline to assist the police in their investigations of them.

Because these activities are willingly entered into by their consumers, they have come to be called "victimless crimes." This is not to say that the consumers are not ultimately victimized, but simply that they are not victims in the more conventional sense. The issue of victimless crimes has raised considerable sociological controversy in recent years. Many people argue that these types of offenses ought not to be illegal, and that by "criminalizing" such conduct legislatures have introduced laws which are at best ineffective and at the worst counterproductive. It has been argued that people always have and always will indulge in vices or in immoral conduct and that the reach of the law ought not to extend into areas of morality.

It has also been pointed out that in order for the police to secure evidence in these types of cases, they cannot rely on the cooperation of either its merchants or users. They must therefore rely upon techniques which they develop themselves, such as informants and technical surveillance or undercover operations. It is in these sensitive areas that the Supreme Court has historically found evidence of considerable police conduct which was itself either illegal or unethical. In any event, when the police are required to enforce morality they are then confronted with a task which is both unpopular and nearly always impossible to carry out with any degree of effectiveness.[6]

[6] See for example Edwin M. Schur, *Our Criminal Society*. Englewood Cliffs, New Jersey: Prentice-Hall, Incorporated, 1969, pp. 191–228.

In addition, the enforcement of laws against victimless crimes places the police in the unfavorable position of being obliged to enforce laws which distribute in reality along socioeconomic lines. For example, the social disorganization characteristic of the racial ghettoes typically produces offenders in this category who are relatively easy for the police to catch because of their high visibility: streetwalkers, numbers runners, drug users and so on. To the extent that these things go on in more affluent areas, they tend to be far less visible and those who carry them out tend to have more resources available to them and are often able to avoid the reach of the law. This gives the impression of a double standard of justice which in turn generates resentment on the part of the poor or the disadvantaged. Perhaps the most serious argument against police intervention in these problems is that the police response has nothing to do with their etiological nature. Again, the police usually deal with the problem only at the symptomatic level, thus assuring their own ultimate failure in *preventing* the reoccurence of such offenses. To the extent that society insists on the criminal justice system being responsible for the "treatment" of this type of social problem, then other and perhaps more appropriate agencies will not have cause to develop other strategies. Ultimately, the police can only do an effective job if their tasks are realistic and if other social services are available and function as they are needed.

This problem area has been recognized by experts within the criminal justice system, as indicated in the report of the National Advisory Commission on Criminal Justice Standards and Goals:

Reevaluation of Laws*

The National Advisory Commission believes that the criminal code should reflect a more rational attitude toward current social practices and a more realistic appraisal of the capabilities of the criminal justice system.

Gambling, marijuana use and possession for use, pornography, prostitution, and sexual acts in private often are punished by incarceration. The National Advisory Commission questions whether incarceration serves as a deterrent to these types of behavior.

The existing criminal justice system was designed to deter potential offenders by the threat of punishment, to punish and rehabilitate offenders, and to protect society by incarcerating persons who pose a threat to others. This system has failed to some extent in almost every respect.

* Adapted from information presented in the report of the National Advisory Commission on Criminal Justice Standards and Goals *A National Strategy to Reduce Crime,* pp. 132–133.

The National Advisory Commission on Criminal Justice Standards and Goals thus recommend that states reevaluate their laws on gambling, marijuana use and possession for use, pornography, prostitution, and sexual acts between consenting adults in private. Such reevaluation should determine if current laws best serve the purpose of the State and the needs of the public.

The Commission further recommended that, as a minimum, each State remove incarceration as a penalty for these offenses, except in the case of persistent and repeated offenses by an individual, when incarceration for a limited period may be warranted. The recommendation insofar as it deals with removal of incarceration as a penalty does not apply to behavior in which a willful attempt is made to affect others in areas such as pandering, soliciting, public lewdness, and the sale or possession for sale of marijuana.

The Commission emphasized that it was not necessarily recommending decriminalization of these activities. It is up to each State to determine whether or not such behavior should be classified as criminal in nature. Some States may decide, upon reevaluation of existing laws, to retain the laws or to modify or repeal them.

The Commission was aware that prostitution and gambling might be associated with organized crime, and it urged States to take appropriate safeguards when enacting legislation and that there might also be some need to control pornography where children could be exposed to explicit sexual material.

The Commission, however, recommended that States that do not decriminalize these activities should at least reexamine the effectiveness of incarceration in enforcing the laws. The Commission itself made such an examination and concluded that incarceration is an ineffective method of enforcement. The Commission believed that incarceration should be abandoned and that probation, fines, commitment to community treatment programs, and other alternative forms of punishment and treatment be substituted.

The Commission also believed that the criminal justice system would benefit from the removal of drunkenness as a crime, as well as the repeal of vagrancy laws and the administrative disposition of minor traffic offences.

People and Commerce

Thus far this chapter has addressed itself to businesses rather than the people who are involved in them. Ultimately, however, commercial activities are the *personal* activities of individuals and must also be considered in that light.

In a society in which people are engaged in such a finite division of labor, and where the work ethic is so strong, people want an assurance that they will be free to go about their respective businesses without any unreasonable interference. Most people feel that it is very much a responsibility of the police to contribute to the security of their working environment. For this reason the police are frequently called upon to deal with disturbances and even with misunderstandings as they occur from time to time in the world of commerce.

But the police are also expected to provide for the security of business establishments, not only when they are closed but when they are open as well. Merchants see preventive patrol as the means whereby police monitor "what's going on." Police officers are expected to be present in the general area and to be prepared to respond to calls for assistance, if needed. The police are also expected to periodically check buildings at night and on weekends or holidays and to notify the proper persons if a business has either been inadvertently left unsecure or if it has been entered. Generally speaking, police officers accept these responsibilities, although "door-shaking" is not a favorite police activity.

However, in order to accurately understand the relationship between merchants and the police, it must be borne in mind that each group views the same subject from a different perspective. In the case of merchants, they are primarily interested in protecting their businesses. The police, on the other hand, are basically oriented toward apprehending offenders.[7] Although these two perspectives have the same general impact, the merchant is more interested in prevention while the policeman is more interested in apprehension (not that he is insensitive to the preventive aspects of police work). A policeman's professional reputation, for better or for worse, it not based so much on what he has been able to *prevent* as it is on his track record in making good arrests, clearing offenses, and recovering property.

Many merchants are fully aware of this, and since they frequently like to encourage police presence in or near their establishments, they may seek to encourage police officers through the use gratuities or reduced cost of goods or services. And police officers in many cities receive sufficiently low pay that such amenities are welcome. Sometimes nothing more is expected in return other than police presence; however, sometimes merchants come to expect policemen to extend reciprocal "courtesies": assistance with bad checks; more intensive patrol of the area during certain hours; or, "permission" to keep a prohibited weapon on their person or in their place of business, and so on.

[7] Albert J. Reiss, Jr. *The Police and the Public.* New Haven: Yale University Press, 1971, p. 70. See also chapter 3 ("A Sketch of the Policeman's 'Working Personality'") in Jerome Skolnick, *Justice Witout Trial.* New York: John Wiley & Sons, 1966, pp. 42–70.

It has become increasingly recognized that police cooperation through people who are overly friendly with them can have consequences which are as serious as the problem of poor relations between policemen and their clientele.[8] The matter of corruption and malfeasance will be discussed in greater detail in Chapter 10.

As a matter of practical reality, it is not the problems of the employed which concern the police so much as the problems involving those who are not employed or who are underemployed. People without a stable source of income, or those whose income is inadequate must still meet their needs and many do so by resorting to criminal conduct. This is not to say that the employed are not also represented among the ranks of criminal offenders or that unemployment itself is a direct cause of criminal misconduct. However, unemployment is only one piece of a complex pattern of interacting forces which collectively structure the basis for urban crime. The reading appended to this chapter, which is taken from the report of the National Advisory Commission on Criminal Justice Standards and Goals, spells out a number of these interrelationships.

The police must deal with people, typically under adverse circumstances. How these people will respond to the police will be a function of factors which directly involve those people. The police are not free to alter the environment in which they find their clientele, and as a result they have little control over a large part of the quality of their relationships with them. The businessman will have his set of expectations, as will the vagrant or the wino. These expectations will play a major role in the nature and the outcome of the contacts between citizen and policeman. To be sure, the policeman can always aggravate these contacts through inconsiderateness or insensitivity—or through plain ignorance—but he has little to do with the structure of the community he serves or the individual motivations of the people with whom he must deal.

Exploitation of Disadvantaged Consumers by Retail Merchants*

The relationship among merchants, citizens, and the police also includes problems which involve merchants who engage in illegal or exploitive retail practices. This is not to suggest that most merchants or even a majority of them are involved in such practices. However, if citizens see the police as supporters of the business community, and if

---

[8] See also William A. Westley, *Violence and the Police.* Cambridge, Massachusetts: The MIT Press, 1970, especially pp. 56–72.

* Portions of the information in this section have been taken from the *Report of the National Advisory Commission on Civil Disorders,* Otto Kerner, Chairman. Washington, D.C.: U.S. Government Printing Office, 1968. pp. 139–141.

they see the business community as being exploitive, then the situation arises where the police are themselves seen as hostile social agents. When this happens community support may be withdrawn from the police and their job made all the more difficult.

This problem was brought to the attention of the public in the Report of the National Advisory Commission on Civil Disorders in the aftermath of the urban riots of the mid-1960's. The commission found significant grievances concerning unfair commercial practices affecting black citizens in eleven of the twenty cities which they studied.

It is difficult to assess the precise degree and extent of exploitation. No systematic and reliable survey comparing consumer pricing and credit practices in all-Negro and other neighborhoods has ever been conducted on a nationwide basis. Differences in prices and credit practices between white middle-income areas and Negro low-income areas to some extent reflect differences in the real costs of serving these two markets (such as differential losses from pilferage in supermarkets), but the exact extent of these costs differences has never been estimated accurately. Finally, an examination of exploitative consumer practices must consider the particular structure and functions of the low-income consumer durables market.

Installment Buying

This complex situation can best be understood by first considering certain basic facts:

1. Various cultural factors generate constant pressure on low-income families to buy many relatively expensive durable goods and display them in their homes. This pressure comes in part from continuous exposure to commercial advertising, especially on television. In January, 1967, over 88 percent of all Negro households had TV sets. A 1961 study of 464 low-income families in New York City showed that 95 percent of these relatively poor families had TV sets.

2. Many poor families have extremely low incomes, bad previous credit records, unstable sources of income or other attributes which make it virtually impossible for them to buy merchandise from established large national or local retail firms. These families lack enough savings to pay cash, and they cannot meet the standard credit requirements of established general merchants because they are too likely to fall behind in their payments.

3. Poor families in urban areas are far less mobile than others. A 1967 Chicago study of low-income Negro households indicated their low automobile ownership compelled them to patronize neighborhood merchants. These merchants typically provided smaller selection, poorer services and higher prices than big national outlets. The 1961 New York study also indicated that families who shopped outside their own neighborhoods were far less likely to pay exorbitant prices.

4. Most low-income families are uneducated concerning the nature of credit purchase contracts, the legal rights and obligations of both buyers and sellers, sources of advice for consumers who are having difficulties with merchants and the operation of the courts concerned with thesse matters. In contrast, merchants engaged in selling goods to them are very well informed.

5. In most states, the laws governing relations between consumers and merchants in effect offer protection only to informed, sophisticated parties with understanding of each other's rights and obligations. Consequently, these laws are little suited to protect the rights of most low-income consumers.

In this situation, exploitative practices flourish. Ghetto residents who want to buy relatively expensive goods cannot do so from standard retail outlets and are thus restricted to local stores. Forced to use credit, they have little understanding of the pitfalls of credit buying. But because they have unstable incomes and frequently fail to make payments, the cost to the merchants of serving them is significantly above that of serving middle-income consumers. Consequently, a special kind of merchant appears to sell them goods on terms designed to cover the high cost of doing business in ghetto neighborhoods.

Whether they actually gain higher profits, these merchants charge higher prices than those in other parts of the city to cover the greater credit risks and other higher operating costs inherent in neighborhood outlets. A recent study conducted by the Federal Trade Commission in Washington, D.C., illustrates this conclusion dramatically. The FTC identified a number of stores specializing in selling furniture and appliances to low-income households. About 92 percent of the sales of these stores were credit sales involving installment purchases, as compared to 27 percent of the sales in general retail outlets handling the same merchandise.

The median income annually of a sample of 486 customers of these stores was about $4,100, but one-third had annual incomes below $3,600, about 6 percent were receiving welfare payments, and another 76 percent were employed in the lowest paying occupations (service workers, operatives, laborers and domestics), as compared to 36 percent of the total labor force in Washington in those occupations.

Definitely catering to a low-income group, these stores charged significantly higher prices than general merchandise outlets in the Washington area. According to testimony by Paul Rand Dixon, Chairman of the FTC, an item selling wholesale at $100 would retail on the average for $165 in a general merchandise store and for $250 in a low-income specialty store. Thus, the customers of these outlets were paying an average price premium of about 52 percent.

While higher prices are not necessarily exploitative in themselves, many merchants in ghetto neighborhoods take advantage of their superior knowledge of credit buying by engaging in various exploitative tactics— high-pressure salesmanship, "bait advertising," misrepresentation of prices, substitution of used goods for promised new ones, failure to notify consumers of legal actions against them, refusal to repair or replace substandard goods, exorbitant prices or credit charges, and use of shoddy merchandise. Such tactics affect a great many low-income consumers. In the New York study 60 percent of all households had suffered from consumer problems (some of which were purely their own fault). About 23 percent had experienced serious exploitation. Another 20 percent, many of whom were also exploited, had experienced repossession, garnishment, or threat of garnishment.

Garnishment

Garnishment practices in many states allow creditors to deprive individuals of their wages through court action, without hearing or trial. In about 20 states, the wages of an employee can be diverted to a creditor merely upon the latter's deposition, with no advance hearing where the employee can defend himself. He often receives no prior notice of such action and is usually unaware of the law's operation and too poor to hire legal defense. Moreover, consumers may find themselves still owing money on a sales contract even after the creditor has repossessed the goods. The New York study cited earlier in this chapter indicated that 20 percent of a sample of low-income families had been subjected to legal action regarding consumer purchases. And the Federal Trade Commission study in Washington, D.C., showed that, on the average, retailers specializing in credit sales of furniture and appliances to low-income consumers resorted to court action once for every $2,200 of sales. Since their average sale was for $207, this amounted to using the courts to collect from one of every 11 customers. In contrast, department stores in the same area used court action against approximately one of every 14,500 customers.

Variations in Food Prices

Residents of low-income Negro neighborhoods frequently claim that they pay higher prices for food in local markets than wealthier white suburbanites and receive inferior quality meat and produce. Statistically reliable information comparing prices and quality in these two kinds of areas is generally unavailable. The U.S. Bureau of Labor Statistics, studying food prices in six cities in 1966, compared prices of a standard list of 18 items in low-income areas and higher income areas in each city. In a total of 180 stores, including independent and chain stores, and for items of the same type sold in the same types of stores, there were no significant differences in prices between low-income and high-income areas. However, stores in low-income areas were more likely to be small independents (which had somewhat higher prices), to sell low-quality produce and meat at any given price, and to be patronized by people who typically bought smaller sized packages which are more expensive per unit of measure. In other words, many low-income consumers in fact pay higher prices, although the situation varies greatly from place to place.

Although these findings must be considered inconclusive, there are significant reasons to believe that poor households generally pay higher prices for the food they buy and receive lower quality food. Low-income consumers buy more food at local groceries because they are less mobile. Prices in these small stores are significantly higher than in major supermarkets because they cannot achieve economies of scale and because real operating costs are higher in low-income Negro areas than in outlying suburbs. For instance, inventory "shrinkage" from pilfering and other causes is normally under 2 percent of sales but can run twice as much in high-crime areas. Managers seek to make up for these added costs by charging higher prices for food or by substituting lower grades.

These practices do not necesarily involve exploitation, but they are often perceived as exploitative and unfair by those who are aware of the price and quality differences involved but unaware of operating costs. In addition, it is probable that genuinely exploitative pricing practices exist in some areas. In either case, differential food prices constitute another factor convincing urban Negroes in low-income neighborhoods that whites discriminate against them.

Appendix A
Economic Considerations, Employment Problems [1]

Economic Disadvantage and Crime

The Employment Problems of Offenders

Final statistics from the 1970 census were not available at this writing, but the testimony from earlier studies reveals that the average offender, particularly the offender who serves a term of imprisonment, is a loser in the world of work. Characteristics of enrolees in criminal treatment projects uniformly reveal high levels of unemployment and peripheral work patterns. Some of the best available data comes from a comprehensive 1964 survey of males released from Federal prisons. This survey shows that 11 percent of the group had never been employed and more than half had been employed a total of less than 2 years before incarceration, even though their median age was 29 years. [2]

Post-release experiences were equally dismal. As of une 30, 1964, less than three-fifths of the study's sample were employed full time and 16 percent were unemployed. Comparative figures for the national male civilian labor force showed that four-fifths were employed full time and only 5 percent were unemployed. More than half of those studied in the survey had worked in unskilled or service jobs prior to commitment; more than two-fifths returned to such jobs upon release. The median monthly income of those employed was only $256 in 1964, while average income in the private, nonagricultural sector was $394.

The Criminal Dimensions of Economic Problems

Offenders are not the only ones with economic problems. The 1964 data on Federal releases show that three out of five had completed less than a ninth grade education, and only a fifth had completed high school. Of all men 18 years of age and over in 1970, nearly 10 million had not completed ninth grade; 18 million had not completed high school. Only 80 percent of those who had not completed high school were in the labor force, compared with 90 percent of those with a diploma. Among those nongraduates who worked, 21 percent were laborers and farm or service workers, as compared with only 15 percent of all male high school graduates.

These data suggest that for every offender with employment problems there are many nonoffenders in equally serious trouble. Many nonoffenders

[1] From *Community Crime Prevention* National Advisory Commission on Criminal Justice Standards and Goals. Wash. DC., USGPO, 1973, 113–124.
[2] George A. Pownall. *Employment Problems of Released Prisoners* (University of Maryland mimeograph).

also have motivational problems, low skills, educational deficiencies, and limited opportunities.

The economically disadvantaged are a minority of the total work force but a majority of the offender population. Statistically, then, they are much more likely to commit crimes than those with greater success in the labor market. Just as the boundaries between legal and illicit activities have become obscured in the subcultures of crime, the distinction between the offender and the nonoffender has become blurred. The losers in the competition for jobs must be regarded as a pool of potential offenders requiring preventive help and attention.

In many core city areas, street life often leads to contact with the law as part of growing up. The late teens, when economic necessity is not usually a prime motivation, are a period of testing and search in the labor market. In poverty areas of the 100 largest Standard Metropolitan Statistical Areas (SMSA's), more than 25 percent of all nonwhite males from 18 to 19 years of age are not in the labor force. The reason for this is something other than health, housekeeping responsibilities, or school attendance. Even though more than 60 percent are labor force participants, their high rate of exit and reentry suggests that a majority of these youths experience life on the street at one time or another. When they are out of money, when hustling is not productive, or when the "heat" is on, they may be willing to take a low wage job they will leave after the first payday. With money in their pockets they can afford leisure and can wait around for the opportunities to earn good money for a short time, either through legitimate work or illicit activities.

The availability and attractiveness of employment opportunities are a major factor governing commitment to street life versus the straight life.

Increasing wages and employment opportunities will lure the disadvantaged potential offenders off the street and out of trouble. Many will continue the cycle of work and leisure, but with increasing time spent on the job and decreasing time on the street. Formerly discouraged workers will be drawn into the labor force on a part-time basis; peripheral workers will discover that they can get the full-time well paid jobs they wanted but could not formerly find.

Problems can arise when economic opportunities are limited. It has been estimated that between 50 and 90 percent of all inner city males have a serious encounter with the law before they reach age 25. Arrest records often rule out legitimate employment. A 1972 study prepared for the Department of Labor reported that an arrest record was an absolute bar to employment in nearly 20 percent of the jurisdictions and public agencies surveyed. More than 50 percent of jurisdictions barred employment on less specific grounds—e.g., poor moral character—in which arrest records often were taken into account.[3]

[3] Herbert S. Miller, *The Closed Door*, prepared for the Manpower Administration, U.S. Department of Labor (February 1972).

An arrest record, which seems almost inevitable for young males in the inner city, often increases the likelihood that these youths will turn to illegal activities. According to a study in Harlem, at least two out of five 18- to 24-year-olds there have some form of illegal income.[4] Too often inner city youth find the traditional ways of achieving meaningful work, status, and high income indirect or frustrating, and illegal activities seem to offer an easier road to recognition and economic success.

Concentration on the Highest Crime Risks

This Commission believes that if more numerous and attractive job opportunities were available many potential offenders would take them. Recent experience in cities shows long waiting lists of people seeking training or job placement assistance. There is abundant documentation of the relationship between the availability of jobs and the level of criminal activity. Glaser and Rice found that property crimes by adults vary directly with the level of unemployment.[5] Fleischer's complex statistical analysis estimated that for every 1 percent increase in unemployment there is an 0.5 percent increase in the rate of delinquency.[6]

A more recent study, "Crime, Youth, and the Labor Market," concluded that changing labor market conditions are sufficient to explain increasing crime rates for youth. Crime rates could be explained not only by the unemployment rates but by participation rates which represent the proportion of each age group in the labor force.[7] Other studies have demonstrated that property crimes are more likely to be committed by those in the lower socio-economic classes.[8] The cause-and-effect relationship cannot be proven beyond question nor quantified precisely, but it is clear that unemployment reduction will have a significant impact on criminal conduct.

One way to prevent crime is to assist those with severe employment problems. To maximize the impact, these efforts should concentrate on those most likely to commit crimes. Inner city, low income males between 16 and 24 are an obvious target group, especially those who have not completed high school. In 1967, 369 of 100,000 nonwhites were arrested for robbery, as against 23 of every 100,000 whites.[9] According to the Federal Bureau of Investigation's Uniform Crime Reports, males constituted more than 85 percent of all persons arrested in 1969, and persons under 25 made up more than half of the total. Overall crime rates are far higher in the low income urban core than anywhere else.

[4] *Manpower Report of the President, 1971,* pp. 98–99.

[5] Daniel Glaser and Kenneth Rice, "Crime, Age and Unemployment," *American Sociological Review,* Issue 24 (October 1959), pp. 679–686.

[6] Belton M. Fleischer, "The Effect of Unemployment on Delinquent Behavior," *Journal of Political Ecoomics,* Issue 61 (1963), pp. 543–555.

[7] Llad Phillips, Harold L. Votey, Jr., and Darold Maxwell, "Crime, Youth and the Labor Market," *Journal of Political Economy* (May/June 1972), pp. 502–503.

[8] E. H. Sutherland and Donald R Cressy, *Principles of Criminology,* J. B. Lippincott Company (1966), pp. 235-238.

[9] Fred P. Graham, "Black Crime: The Lawless Image," *Harper's* (September 1970), pp. 64–71.

7

To identify young inner city males as a target group in fighting crime through employment programs is not an act of discrimination; it is recognition of a fact. At the height of the economic boom in 1969, more than 25 percent of nonwhite 16- to 19-year-olds, and a smaller but still substantial portion of 20- to 24-year-olds in the central cities were unemployed—a rate more than seven times that for adults in the central city. Low income white youth and other minorities had similar problems, which undoubtedly contributed to high rates of crime.

Two other target groups in need of employment assistance are the more than five million individuals arrested annually, and those who have formerly been convicted of a crime. The FBI's Uniform Crime Report statistics indicate that a majority of those who are arrested are likely to be rearrested within 6 years. Many arrestees already have employment problems, and when they are released in the community again with a record, their employment problems are further complicated.

Drug Addiction and Economic Status

Current evidence and theory support the proposition that crime-producing personal deviancies frequently develop in otherwise normal individuals when they experience economic and social exclusion, and the frustration and despair that exclusion generates. Exclusion from the mainstream of community life, economic or otherwise, frequently presents individuals with their first stimulus for deviant behavior. Once even marginally involved in crime, the individual finds himself even further excluded from the community—a process sociologists have termed the "deviancy reinforcement cycle."

Such individuals, including drug abusers and addicts, are a logical target group for special economic attention. Efforts emphasizing integration or reintegration into the world of work are a necessary adjunct to treatment programs and social services designed to change the life pattern of the criminal. This is an approach that recognizes that the deviant is a person who has been gradually compelled to identify with and participate in a subculture which rejects mainstream community values.

As criminologist Donald Cressy has suggested, one of the best hopes for changing the habits of asocial criminals lies in the practical application of Sutherland's principle of differential association.[10] Asocial criminals must be encouraged and aided to participate in the world of work. There are many possible ways to meet and remove the criminal's immediate economic motivation to crime. Among these ways, increased employment opportunity offers these individuals the best chance to identify with the positive, anti-criminal values of the community from which they have become alienated.

[10] See R. Volkman and D. Cressy, "Differential Association and the Rehabilitation of Drug Addicts," 69 *American Journal of Sociology* 129 (1963).

Drug Addiction, Crime, and Unemployment

A high positive correlation between addiction, unemployment, and criminality is to be expected for certain groups, such as youthful addicts living in neighborhoods where drug use has reached epidemic proportions. For example, one recent study of a New York City neighborhood with high addict and crime rates found that less than 2 percent of the addicts there supported themselves by regular work.[11] For such persons, illegal acts such as selling heroin may be the most convenient way of financing their habits.

Research has uncovered heroin addicts who were able to function reasonably well as workers and provide for their families.[12] However, it is safe to say that drug addiction is often inconsistent with successful participation in the labor force.

In addition, the cost of maintaining a heroin habit is between two and 10 times what a typical street addict—probably with limited education and work experience—could hope to earn on an inevitably low paying job. Thus that addict is often driven to illegal acts to support his or her habit. These acts generally take the form of selling drugs, burglary, shoplifting, and prostitution.

The amount of property taken by addicts is large, though not so great as the public may think.[13] However, this does not negate the fact that drug addiction does produce significant increases in criminality of two kinds— stealing from innocent victims and selling heroin illegally.[14] But an important factor to keep in mind is that thus far drug-induced crime consists primarily (though not exclusively) of nonviolent acts against property rather than persons.[15]

Getting and using drugs lends goals and structure to the life of the addict; the cycle of self-administering drugs, hustling for cash, and purchasing more drugs is an invariable daily routine. Contrary to the popular image of the idle, self-indulgent life of the addict, the necessities of maintaining a habit generally dictate a demanding and time consuming round of activity. Furthermore, the hierarchical patterns of the drug subculture, based on such factors as the size of an individual's habit or his proficiency at avoiding arrest, reward "success" with status, much as economic and personal achievements are recognized in the context of legitimate work.

After their first few years of drug use, some narcotics addicts acquire an

[11] The results of this survey, conducted by the Community Council on Housing, are noted in "New Perspectives on Urban Crime," 32, American Bar Association Special Committee on Crime Prevention and Control (1972).
[12] L. Brill, "Drug Addiction." Encyclopedia of Social Work, National Association of Social Work (1971), pp. 24–38.
[13] James Q. Wilson and others, "The Myths of Heroin," *Washington Post* (December 31, 1972).
[14] *Ibid.*
[15] J. A. Inciardi, "The Poly-Drug User: A New Situational Offender (A Preliminary Overview)," (published in Proceedings of Annual Meeting, American Society of Criminology, November 3–7, 1971).

active desire to escape addiction. They commit themselves to hospitals, withdraw from drugs without medical assistance, and even seek incarceration in attempts to eliminate their dependence on narcotics. In typical treatment populations, almost every addict has undergone at least one "cure," and histories of 10 or more unsuccessful "cures" are not unusual.

Sincerity and motivation are not enough to counterbalance the attritions of drug use as an alternative to personal frustration. The lure of the addictive cure cannot substitute for legitimate, purposeful activity. If no assistance is offered to the former addict who desires to reenter the economic and social life of the larger community, he can only be expected to return to drug use and possible criminality. Since estimates of the Nation's population of criminal heroin addicts range as high as 250,000 or higher, every consideration must be given to employment programs that will assist addicts themselves to reduce the epidemic trend of growth in that population.

Systematic Economic Considerations and Crime

Economic and Social Characteristics of High Crime Areas

The earlier sections of this chapter have concentrated on the economic problems of particular groups in the community who pose high risks of criminal behavior. Just as present and potential offenders have problems that can be addressed by programs serving these individuals, so do neighborhoods display typical, endemic economic problems. To solve these problems at least two things are needed: (1) programs of systematic reform that will affect the levels of criminal activity of all residents, including those not singled out as members of any identified target group, and (2) more effective programs designed to reach the target groups by improving the environment in which program participants will make their venture into the world of work.

Street crimes, the kinds of crime that worry most citizens, are closely associated with a host of social and economic factors that define inner city poverty neighborhoods. Among those factors is the substantial gap between the average family income of whites and minorities in this country.

Factors contributing to delinquency rates include income, family stability, and population density in the residential area. Available data tend to support the idea that delinquency rates are highest in urban slum areas where these socioeconomic conditions are worst.[16] In Washington, D.C., for example, neighborhoods with the highest delinquency rates are those areas that have the highest rate of public welfare recipients, the largest percentage of births without prenatal care, and the greatest population density in the city.[17]

[16] Sutherland and Cressy, *op. cit.*, pp. 235–238.
[17] *Report of the President's Commission on Crime In The District of Columbia* (1966), pp. 1-141.

Police arrest records and crime reports show that the rate of street crime is highest in Washington's inner city neighborhoods.[18] Narcotics treatment officials report that drugs are most available in those areas and the greatest number of addicts are found there.

Even the casual reader of newspaper crime reports is struck by the disproportionate number of crimes that occur in the poorest urban neighborhoods. The incidence of unreported crime also is thought to be the highest in these areas, where residents are often more hostile to the police and where the quality of police service may be lower than in the rest of the city.

Attempts to isolate cause and effect in these associations between crime, income, race, and social factors are difficult because of circularity. For example, narcotics-related crime in the inner city is certainly affected by the aura of despair resulting from unemployment, low wages, decaying housing, and the dominance of white society. But widespread narcotics abuse aggravates all these problems and contributes to core city deterioration. Even without demonstrations of formal cause-and-effect relationship, this close correlation between crime rates and a complex of other factors suggests that one way to combat crime is to change the social and economic conditions related to it. Street crime is spawned, in part, by the factors that exist in many low income areas.

National Economic Conditions and Unemployment

The Bureau of Labor Statistics has estimated that the unemployment rate among inner city youth is as high as 35 percent. However, unemployment statistics only count people who are actively looking for work and have jobs for less than 15 hours during the week of the survey and do not take into account those who are underemployed. Underemployment is usually defined to include those who are working more than 15 but fewer than 35 hours per week, those who have wanted jobs in the past but have become too discouraged to continue to look for work, and those whose pay is so low that their jobs cannot represent satisfactory long-term employment. A moderate estimate of the underemployment rate is that it roughly equals the official unemployment rate, although formal statistics on underemployment do not exist.[19]

Unemployment in inner city neighborhoods is sensitive to conditions in the national economy. From 1968 through 1971, unemployment rates in poverty areas averaged 60 percent above the national unemployment rate. In only 4 of the 16 quarters in these 4 years was the difference below 50 percent or above 70 percent of the national rate. When the core city's underemployment is added to its unemployment, it seems obvious that slackness

---

[18] Graham, op. cit., pp. 64–71.
[19] Harrison, Bennett, Education, Training, and the Urban Ghetto (The Johns Hopkins Press, 1972), pp. 43–49.

in poverty area labor markets is roughly 3 to 3.5 times greater than in the entire national economy—assuming national underemployment is less extensive than underemployment in the inner city.

These data show that national economic conditions have an enormous impact on inner city employment. From 1968 through 1971, unemployment rates in urban poverty areas dipped below 5.5 percent only twice, a level that most economists and politicians decry as unacceptable. Both times the national unemployment rate was around 3.5 percent. The increase from 3.5 percent total unemployment at the end of 1969 was accompanied by a rise in urban-poverty-area unemployment from 5.5 percent to 9.7 percent. Unemployment in the inner city is sensitive not only to conditions in the national economy, but also to economic policy intended to stabilize national employment and combat inflation.

The implications of this sensitivity for the members of high risk target groups in low income areas are even more extreme. When the economy is expanding, poor youth find more opportunities for entry level work; conversely, they are the first victims of the economy's decline. The pattern is the same in Chinatown, San Francisco, Calif.; Spanish Harlem, New York, N.Y.; or Watts, Los Angeles, Calif. The long-term trend shows that their employment problems have been growing more severe relative to others in the labor force, but cyclical fluctuations around this trend—related to the rise and fall of overall unemployment—have had an even greater impact on their welfare. A comparison of the quarterly changes in average unemployment rates for nonwhite youths in the slum areas of the 100 largest cities with those for white youths throughout these cities demonstrates the impact of cyclical fluctuations.

Between 1967 and 1970, aggregate unemployment declined and then rose steeply. In the fourth quarter of 1967, unemployment stood at 3.9 percent; by the fourth quarter of 1968, it had fallen to a low of 3.4 percent; but with the subsequent recession it rose to 5.8 percent in the fourth quarter of 1970. Black inner city youths were at the tip of the whiplash of these changes. The 0.5 percentage point drop in aggregate unemployment between the fourth quarter of 1967 and the fourth quarter of 1968 was accompanied by a 9 percentage point decline in the rate, not seasonally adjusted, for black teenage males, and a smaller but still significant decline for those in their early twenties. Conversely, while the aggregate unemployment rate rose 2.4 percentage points between the fourth quarter of 1968 and the fourth quarter of 1970, the rate of black teenagers' unemployment increased 15 percentage points.

The health of the economy is not the only factor causing these changes. Between 1965 and 1968, the number of potential workers who were drawn out of the civilian labor force by military service increased rapidly; since 1968 it has declined. This undoubtedly accentuated the changes in unemployment, since fewer workers were available when jobs were plentiful in 1968, but there were more potential workers in 1970 when jobs were scarce.

Effective crime prevention demands more than macroeconomic policies that will have a positive effect on employment in high crime areas. It also demands careful scrutiny of other national policies—economic and social— that may have indirect, undesirable, and sometimes unexpected effects on poverty and unemployment.

The Dual Labor Market Hypothesis

Among the aggregate economic and social policies with the greatest apparent potential for affecting problems of unemployment and underemployment in poverty areas are Federal and State policies relating to racial discrimination in hiring and promotion. One of the reasons why inner city unemployment rates are much higher than national averages lies in the operation of labor markets. Discrimination against blacks and other minority groups by employers and by unions has been well documented. Its pervasiveness led to equal opportunity requirements in Federal contracts and Title VII of the Civil Rights Act of 1964. The latter has wide-ranging provisions calling for equal job opportunity. The dismal performance of these measures testifies to the dimensions and complexity of the problem that they were intended to solve.

Government policy has differentiated between equal employment opportunity for equally qualified candidates and programs to provide jobs and remedial training for the educationally disadvantaged. When the Civil Rights Act of 1964 was passed, it was believed that compensatory education programs would increase the skill levels of the disadvantaged to a par with the rest of the labor force, and that equal opportunity legislation would remove the racial barriers causing high minority unemployment rates. But many studies by economists since 1964 show that education has failed to increase minority employment rates to white levels. Today, for example, a black high school graduate has little more chance of finding a job than a black with only an eighth grade education, and a much lower probability of being employed than a white high school graduate. Among those who are employed, black high school graduates' incomes are far below whites, and not significantly higher than the incomes of blacks with less education. Among whites the value of a high school diploma is much greater, both in terms of finding a job and the wage rate that the job offers.

Some economists have proposed a dual labor market explanation of these persistent employment differentials. According to this explanation, certain jobs within a firm are reserved for whites, and others are reserved for blacks or other minority groups. These occupational patterns may reflect past discrimination or may result from the unionization of particular occupations. Alternatively, jobs higher on the promotion and pay scale may require greater educational background and skill, and an employer may choose to use race as a surrogate for these personal qualities. Standardized testing, widely used for screening job applicants, is now known to discriminate against blacks and other minority groups.[20]

Some of these considerations are used to justify the perpetuation of discrimination. Employers and unions may argue, for example, that minority group applicants are not as well qualified as white applicants and therefore are not entitled to equal pay or promotion under the Civil Rights Act. Requiring the promotion of a qualified black or other minority member may interfere with the employer's right to promote a more highly qualified white. Increasing the formal education of a minority group member still may not enable him to compete on an equal footing with whites if a firm's hiring channels do not extend into minority communities.

The dual labor market explanation is only one theory to explain why minorities have had such difficulty in reaching equality in labor markets. Evidence supporting this explanation is increasing. The studies described above show that education by itself does not increase the welfare of minorities or make them more competitive with whites in labor markets. In the slack economic conditions of the past few years, seniority rules and the scarcity of jobs have kept racial occupational patterns stable. High black unemployment rates at all educational levels are consistent with black access to dead-end jobs only. If racial discrimination is a persistent structural characteristic of the American economy, then new, more aggressive strategies will be required to eliminate this type of discrimination.

The Flight From the City

Another reason for high inner city unemployment rates can be found in the growing trend of industry to move from urban areas. Traditionally, industries have operated in cities because of the advantage derived from city locations: access to transportation facilities; residential proximity of the labor force; urban mass transit for workers; and in the case of consumer-oriented industries, proximity to a large market. These incentives for urban location persisted into the 1950's.

In the last 2 decades several factors have contributed to the disappearance of the locational advantages of central cities. The decline of railroads and the growth of trucks as a transportation medium has made suburban and rural locations competitive with cities. Since the late 1940's, residential patterns have been shifting out of central cities, causing dispersion of the labor force over a larger area. At the same time, the proliferation of automobiles and highway networks has increased the ease of travel throughout

[20] *Ibid.*, pp. 30–38.

the urban fringes while increasing congestion and the failure to expand mass transit facilities have made travel within the central cities difficult. Residential dispersion into the suburbs has also eliminated much of the advantage of cities as natural market areas.

These changes have imposed costs on firms located in cities. With employee reliance on automobiles for transportation, companies have had to incur parking costs either directly or in the form of higher wages to retain their employees. The population shift of higher income groups to the suburbs and lower income groups to the central cities has led to the deterioration of the urban property tax base and the increase in tax rates on remaining property. As tax rates have risen, maintenance costs on the older physical plants in the cities also have increased. Overall data on the extent of industrial shifts are not available, but even large corporations that may have the most to gain from locating in business and financial centers have now begun to leave central cities such as New York, N.Y., and Washington, D.C., for suburbs like Stamford, Conn., and Alexandria, Va.

The Dilemma of Minority Enterprise

Because of this movement of white-owned and white-operated business from the inner city, it is important to look at the characteristics of businesses that remain. Minorities comprise over 17 percent of the population, but own only about 4 percent of the business establishments in the United States. These businesses account for less than 1 percent of total national sales.[21] Minority-owned businesses are smaller than their white counterparts. Some of the difference is related to the nature of the business. The typical minority business has a much greater likelihood of being a small retail store or a small service establishment such as a beauty salon, barber shop, or laundry. Few minority-owned businesses are in manufacturing, construction, or finance.

Partly because of these industry differences, minority-owned firms are much less profitable than white businesses. In the economy as a whole, average yearly sales per retail establishment are around $200,000. Minority-owned businesses have average yearly sales of about $30,000, but the median income of minority firms is much lower because over two-thirds of all such businesses have no full-time employees, excluding the owner, and average annual sales of only $7,000. In the service industries, over 80 percent of all minority-owned firms have no full-time employees and average yearly incomes of only $6,000.[22]

These statistics are important because they describe the availability of jobs in inner city neighborhoods. New black-owned enterprises located in the inner city are statistically likely to be retail or service establishments that

---

[21] Sar A. Levitan, Garth A. Mangum, and Robert Taggert, *Economic Opportunity in the Ghetto: The Partnership of Government and Business* (The Johns Hopkins Press), p. 5.
[22] Office of Minority Business Enterprise Program (January 1972).

cannot expect high profits or rapid growth because inner city poverty limits the size of their markets. Many of the jobs available in minority-owned firms pay low wages and offer only part-time employment. One study of black and white inner city businesses found that only about 20 percent of full-time employees, but nearly half of part-time employees, were black. Ninety percent of the employees in white-owned businesses were full-time, but in black-owned firms only about 60 percent were full-time.[23]

The dual labor market theory, the changing focus of business activity from city to suburbs, and the limited availability of employment and income in inner city minority firms all are intimately related to the perpetuation and increase of inner city crime. Overall economic opportunity in urban core areas is very limited, and the prospects are only slowly improving. Under these circumstances, crime is not only a way of life in central cities, but for many of their residents it represents the only available way of life.

Overcoming the Employment Problems of High Risk Potential Offenders

Efforts to alleviate the employment problems of urban minority youth, arrestees or ex-offenders, and drug abusers are likely to show some measurable results in terms of crime reduction, since these groups are often considered high risk potential offenders. The strategies available to assist these target groups are essentially different, though they often overlap.

Helping Inner City Youth

No single, simple solution exists to help overcome the obstacles to employment that confront young people in the Nation's central cities. A systems approach, incorporating a multifaceted attack on the causal factors, is needed. There are a variety of alternative and complementing strategies that are being used or could be used, and each has a role to play. These fall into several major groups. Macroeconomic measures are the most indirect, since they affect the whole economy and are not focused only on minority youths; nevertheless, such measures are essential. Through monetary and fiscal policies the government can often regulate aggregate demand which, in turn, affects the level of unemployment. To the degree that nonwhite youths are the last hired and first fired, they benefit less from reductions in unemployment and suffer most from its increase.

Detailed consideration of specific economic measures will be reserved for the section of this discussion that deals with "Improving the General Economic Environment." Here, measures will be considered that have more specific effects on the individual problems of low income minority youth.

Among the most important of these efforts are those to end discrimination

[23] Alan R. Andreasen, *Inner City Business, A Case Study of Buffalo New York* (Praeger, 1971).

in hiring and to upgrade minority youths. A discussion of the school to work transition is more fully covered in the education chapter of this report. Available research on dropouts indicates that little is gained by forcing these students back to school as the school is presently structured.[24] Compulsory education laws created part of the problem. Dropouts frequently are delinquent, but their delinquency invariably begins when they are in school. Rather than force youngsters to endure school failure and frustration, the school should provide a more meaningful education in relation to the probable career objectives of the student, and, together with the community, should assist these youth in making the transition into the world of work.

For example, subsidies based on the real costs of employing initially less productive workers can be given for hiring and training the unskilled and semiskilled. Since black and other minority youths are often found in these groups, such a subsidy program can operate as a positive incentive to eliminate discriminatory practices, leaving the employer with no excuse to turn down a minority member because he is less educated or experienced.

Another program element is to improve the minority youth's preparation for the world of work. Great strides have been made in recent years to increase educational attainment, but minorities are still behind whites in their achievement levels. As long as this is the case, differentials in income and in employment levels are inevitable.

Training is a necessary part of the total approach. Manpower programs that emerged in the 1960's offer a variety of arrangements for income maintenance, basic and vocational education, health care, counseling, placement, and related assistance. "Training" thus describes a flexible package of services whose purpose is to increase the employability of the participant and his ability to compete for jobs in the private sector.

Another approach is to provide public employment opportunities. For many inner city youths, jobs are not available even after training. Some may need work experience before they can move into gainful private employment. Others may have limited abilities and will require a permanently sheltered, subsidized work situation.

Finally, there is the approach of special employment efforts directed toward the young, such as summer and work school programs.

Most of the strategies just outlined have been tried during the past decade. Experience yields some indication as to the role these approaches may play in alleviating employment problems among this high risk crime group.

Combating Discrimination

Widespread discrimination affects all aspects of the employment experience of blacks and other minorities. They are hired last, fired first, paid least, and given the most unattractive jobs. Young people are hurt perhaps more

[24] Jerald G. Bachman, Swayzer Green, Ilona D. Wirtanen, *Youth in Transition: Dropping Out—Problem or Symptom,* Volume III (Institute for Social Research, 1971).

than others. They have difficulty in finding even low-paying jobs. They are denied access to the occupations, the industries, and the opportunities within each firm that promise real advancement. The discrimination that channels minority youths into the secondary labor market is as detrimental as that which restricts the number of jobs available to them.

The Nation's record of fighting discrimination has not been impressive. There have been many Federal efforts, but they have had little impact. Efforts under State and local legislation have generally proved even less effective.

Of all the Federal efforts, the Equal Employment Opportunities Commission (EEOC), created by the Civil Rights Act of 1964, has had the broadest mandate and the feeblest tools. Under that Act the five-person Commission was empowered to investigate complaints of discrimination and, if it found a complaint just, to attempt a voluntary conciliation between employer and employee. When conciliation failed, the Commission had no further recourse in most cases. Under the Equal Employment Opportunity Act of 1972, the EEOC has new powers to bring enforcement actions where conciliation fails. The potential of this new power remains to be tested in practice.

Another agency charged with combating discrimination is the Office of Federal Contract Compliance (OFCC), which has the authority to delay or cancel any Federal contracts with employers who do not take affirmative action to provide equal employment opportunity. Those who are especially recalcitrant can be denied government contracts. If enforced, this power would have far-reaching significance. Executive Order 11246, which gives the OFCC its broad powers, is more inclusive in combating discrimination than the Civil Rights Act of 1964. The order not only precludes discrimination but requires contractors to take positive steps to overcome its effects. In some instances, especially areawide bargaining with builders, this has been interpreted to mean that equal entry is not sufficient, but that quotas or other numerical goals can be required to bring minority participation up to stated levels. However, contractors frequently ignore or postpone contract compliance recommendations because the OFCC is reluctant to use its powers.

Other tools are available to the Federal government for fighting discrimination. All grants-in-aid to States contain a prohibition against discrimination in employment. Since federally supported programs are vital to the States and localities, the antidiscrimination provisions could have a major impact if enforced. The Federal Civil Service could also take more vigorous steps to reduce employment discrimination within the Federal government itself.

To date, antidiscrimination efforts have had little impact on minority youths. The problems of teenage workers have gone all but unnoticed. Workers in their early twenties have been helped somewhat, but most emphasis has been directed to combating discrimination in skilled occupations that largely involve adult workers. A notable exception has been the effort to eliminate entry barriers to minorities, and especially minority youths, in the construction trades. This experience demonstrates both the promise and the problems of helping those entering the world of work.

The construction industry offers many attractive job opportunities, especially for unionized workers. But apprenticeship programs and the skilled trade unions often exclude minority youth. These young people are under-represented in the higher paying construction jobs and are being over-represented in the lower paying trades.

Some progress has been made over the past decade in correcting this situation. Many factors have been involved, and the experience is instructive. First, minority interests have continually pressured the unions, employers, and governments to take action. They have done this through repeated demonstrations, demanding quotas in many cities, and halting work on public construction. Second, the AFL-CIO leadership and its Building Trades Council have spoken out against discrimination and have supported efforts to move minorities into the trades. Third, the Federal Government has used its authority to demand affirmative action toward the elimination of discrimination. Fourth, federally and privately sponsored outreach programs have been initiated to persuade minorities to apply for job training positions that have been inaccessible in the past. Finally, many local unions operating in central cities have voluntarily abandoned their discriminatory practices. Although local union leaders may have resented the demands of militant minority leaders, they could not ignore militant power to halt or hinder construction.

This experience suggests that even the most entrenched discriminatory practices can be overcome to some degree when public pressure, minority group activism, governmental policy, and private leadership combine to carry out a social goal.

Educating Youth for Employment

The inadequate education of many inner city youths is also a major cause of their labor market problems. The white youth's high school diploma is generally accepted by employers as a legitimate credential, but that diploma is frequently disregarded if the youth is black or brown. This double standard is based on the employer's subjective attitude that the average white is much better educated than the average minority youth with as many years of schooling.

If the quality of education available to minority students could be improved, employers might give more credence to their diplomas, although the final outcome would depend on the elimination of ethnic discrimination. Some of the most controversial social issues of our day center on the means of improving education for youth. Busing, relevant curricula, school financing, and community control are subjects of angry debate.

These dilemmas must be resolved before education can be improved overall for low income youth. But there is reason to believe that work-related instruction can be improved separately and more easily than other aspects of education. The Federal Government has funded vocational education for over 50 years, and private interests have shown more concern with work preparation than with other facets of education. Because improvements in such training promise an immediate payoff through increased employability, they may be more acceptable to the community and to the youths themselves than other education reforms.

There are a variety of old and new approaches to improving the preparation for work provided by the school system. The oldest is the vocational or career education program. Available evidence indicates that, despite problems, this is effective in helping minority youths. Academic courses generally concentrate on preparation for college, although less than half of high school graduates will attend college. The large proportion of youth are in general studies programs that are typically without direction, providing little more than a weak exposure to academic subjects. Only in career education courses are students likely to acquire useful occupational skills and exposure to the demands they will encounter outside of school.

More experimental educational reforms may also be in order. For example, the private sector might become directly involved, with large corporations offering a wide range of assistance to schools in low income neighborhoods. Cooperative education, in which the student's curriculum is adapted to his vocational needs in a particular career, is another possibility. The Opportunities Industrialization Center (OIC) has had substantial success with this approach in many cities. Central to its program are periodic skill shortage surveys to determine the future manpower needs of an area. Vocational curricula are then devised in cooperation with local unions and employers to satisfy entry level requirements in a variety of trades. The OIC experience demonstrates that involving potential employers in program design frequently results in a higher rate of successful job placements and fewer trainees frustrated by job shortages.

Another notable example of a successful cooperative education program is Project 70,001, operating in Wilmington, Del., since 1969. The program combines the efforts and resources of a large shoe manufacturer, the Distributive Education Clubs of America, the Delaware Department of Public Instruction, and the Wilmington Public Schools to provide on-the-job work experience and related classroom instruction to students unable to participate in or benefit from regular programs of education and training. The success of the Wilmington pilot project has resulted in similar programs being located in Dover, Del., Harrisburg, Pa., Kansas City, Mo., and Hartford, Conn.

The Double E program in Chicago, Ill., is a similar program designed for high school dropouts. Participants go to class 3 days a week and work 3 days a week. Classroom instruction is related to actual work experience.

Businesses that hire the students pay regular wages and provide counseling services and other support.

Expansion of Job Opportunities for Youth

So long as minority youth are failing in, or being failed by, the educational system, they will not be able to overcome the economic gap separating them from the larger society. However, other forms of education and training may compensate to some degree for initial handicaps. This is the principle underlying the manpower programs initiated in the 1960's to provide compensatory services to the unskilled, including a large proportion of minority youths. Blacks under 22 years of age constitute a major segment of the total enrollment, with an estimated 460,000 served in fiscal 1970. Many of these are inner city residents. In fiscal 1969, there were esttimaed to be 175,000 16- to 21-year-olds in the civilian noninstitutional population of the six city slums surveyed by the Labor Department. Of these, 14,400 had completed manpower training outside school, the armed forces, or manual apprenticeship programs. An additional 26,500 were enrolled during that year, including 16,000 in the Neighborhood Youth Corps.

The Manpower Development and Training Act (MDTA) program is the oldest of the manpower efforts. It was initiated in 1962 to help workers who had been displaced by technological change. Gradually, it was altered to serve the less skilled, including many minority youths. At present, 33 percent of its enrollees are 16- to 21-year-old blacks. Since it is designed to serve those individuals who can benefit from training, participants are generally better qualified than the enrollees of other manpower programs.

The major purpose of MDTA is to provide vocational training in some skill for which there is a demonstrated demand. For those who are educationally handicapped, however, basic education may be provided preliminary to training. The seriously disadvantaged may be given concentrated assistance in special skill centers that combine counseling, education, and supportive services with multioccupational training.

As a rule, black youths benefit less from the program than do other participants. Institutional data show that black trainees in general are less successful in the program than whites, while those who are young have especially severe problems and usually find only very low paying jobs. Nevertheless, black youths are willing to participate in MDTA training programs because the experience offers them more chance to improve their absolute if not their relative position. According to surveys of participants, more blacks than whites feel the program offers them a real chance, even if the benefits of participation will be limited because of inequities in the marketplace.[25]

In Riverside, Calif., several companies formed a Job Opportunities Council,

[25] Gerald Gwin, *A National Attitude Study of Trainees in MDTA Institutional Programs* (Institute for Social Research, University of Michigan, 1970).

which acts as their agent in hiring, identifying, and recruiting the unemployed. The Council is financed by the Manpower Development and Training Act, through on-the-job-training payments to member employers. The Council insures that future employees receive the training they need to meet special standards set by member companies. These companies have agreed to fill a certain percentage of their new jobs with disadvantaged individuals referred by the Council.

Job Corps

The Job Corps concentrates on a clientele with even more needs, residential and nonresidential basic education and other intensive services to youths aged 16 to 21. In 1970, almost 66 percent of enrollees were black—61 percent male and 39 percent female. Among the blacks, only 4 percent of the boys and 25 percent of the girls had completed high school.

Working intensively with such a group, often providing room and board, the Job Corps is inevitably expensive. Annual costs still average about $6,500 per enrollee despite drastic cost cutting. Unfortunately, the results to date have not demonstrated that the investments are justified. Innovative educational techniques have not proved as effective as had been hoped. The enrollees who had trouble with conventional academic programs have had almost as much difficulty in the Job Corps. Followup studies suggest that the gains in earnings of former enrollees, both white and minority, were slight in comparison with a control group and that the incidence of unemployment among the minority youth was not noticeably affected by the Job Corps experience.

Several conclusions can be drawn from the experience of the MDTA-institutional and the Job Corps programs. First, minority youths are likely to benefit less from training than whites—an indicator of racial bias in the labor market. Second, remedial programs for severely disadvantaged inner city youths are expensive while consequent improvements in employability are not likely to be impressive. Third, minority individuals who can be trained without prior remedial education will usually find the programs offer access to better jobs, even when training is of less benefit to them than it is to whites. The overall conclusion is that where funding for manpower programs is limited, and where minority and other youth with fair academic records and abilities are destined for unemployment, underemployment, and perhaps crime, the first priority in the allocation of resources should be training in specific skills that will facilitate entry into better paying jobs.

Neighborhood Youth Corps

The out-of-school Neighborhood Youth Corps provides work for 16- and 17-year-old dropouts who come from poor families. Most of the jobs are in the public or nonprofit sectors at the entry level, and the program has had a checkered career. After it reached an average enrollment of 99,000 in fiscal 1966, a major reassessment of its usefulness led to a halving of enrollment by fiscal 1970. Almost all jobs provided were menial and unattractive, and little basic education was actually available to improve the employability of the participants. A comprehensive followup of enrollees leaving the program between January and September 1966 showed that nearly 25 percent of those who had been in the labor force were unemployed, a proportion about equal to that of comparable youths who had not enrolled in NYC.[26]

The program has just been revamped and the budgeted annual expenditure per enrollee has been increased to provide more intensive vocational training and education. Past experience, however, suggests that the difficulty of creating meaningful jobs for young participants will continue. Despite the claims of unmet manpower needs in urban areas, few cities have been able to place young dropouts in productive work.

The summer segment of NYC has a different focus, providing income and part-time work during the summer for 16- to 21-year-old students from poor families. The projects are sponsored by public or nonprofit agencies and usually hire youths for ten 26-hour weeks at a rate of $1.25 per hour. There is little emphasis on meaningful work experience.

Appropriations permitting, the enrollment in summer NYC grows larger each year. About 400,000 slots were funded in the summer of 1970 and about 50 percent more were provided the following year. It is estimated that more than 50 percent of the enrollees are inner city minority youth, with males slightly outnumbering females. The program is regarded by many as antiriot insurance. Each year, as summer approaches, cities panic and ask for increased funding.

The summer NYC experience demonstrates that the number of youths available for work in the summer on a part-time basis is many times greater than the program's capacity. Every city has applicants who are turned away due to lack of funds. There are many teenagers who want to work, even in menial tasks at low wages, but who cannot find jobs of any description. This is especially true in cities where general employment conditions are weak. Though many of these youths are potential offenders, they are far from being offenders by choice.

Other Programs

More than four out of five employed minority youths now work in the private sector, and even a doubling of public employment would still leave 70 percent dependent on private sector jobs. For this reason, partnership programs to hire and train low income youths are of primary importance. Such pro-

[26] Sar A. Levitan and Garth L. Mangum, *Federal Training and Work Programs in the Sixties* (Institute of Labor and Industrial Relations, University of Michigan, 1967), Part 2.

grams combine government subsidies and other assistance with private efforts of businessmen.

The largest partnership program is Job Opportunities in the Business Sector (JOBS). Initiated in 1968, JOBS offers Federal subsidies to private employers who agree to hire and train specifically designated workers. A number of firms have agreed to hire and train people without subsidy.

The target population of the JOBS program includes school dropouts from jobless or low income families, persons under 21 or over 45 years of age, and members of minority groups. The Labor Department estimated that in fiscal 1970 nearly 50 percent of those hired under the JOBS program were less than 22 years old, and most of the youths were black males. In terms of participation, the JOBS program is thus the most important manpower effort for needy youth, other than NYC.

JOBS was hurt by the economic slump of 1970. An increasing proportion of hiring has been subsidized rather than voluntary, and it has not been easy to find takers for these subsidies, despite loosened requirements and increased efforts to sell the program. This experience suggests that private sector programs are not very effective in a slack economy and that Federal subsidies lose their attractiveness when better qualified workers are actively seeking jobs.

Nevertheless, if overall unemployment can be reduced, intensified anti-discrimination measures could stimulate the demand for minority workers, and employers might then turn to JOBS and analagous programs to help them comply with equal opportunity requirements. Under such circumstances, the provision of government subsidies to private employers would be clearly warranted.

8

Transportation, Cities, and the Police

The development of transportation throughout the ages has closely paralleled the development of cities. In earlier times primitive societies had little contact from one community to the next. As a result, there was little incentive to produce more goods than the community itself could consume. These communities were limited in contact with one another because of an absense of facilities for transportation. Such self-contained communities are called *subsistence economies* because they produce no more than they require for their own sustenance.

With the advent of a transportation medium which could be used to ship goods, it became not only possible but advantageous to produce a surplus. Such a surplus could then either be traded for things needed by the community or could be sold, thus adding to the overall economic viability of the community. The availability of a means of transportation eventually gave rise to a class of merchants who made it their business to act as brokers for the surpluses produced along the routes of travel.

The first significant transportation was by water. Because of the commerce which developed out of shipping, cities tended to develop where there were harbors or natural ports. However, water transportation was severely limited because of a lack of navigational capability, the small size of the ships involved, and the dependence of ships upon currents and winds.

Perhaps the most significant milestone in the history of transportation was the harnessing of steam. Through the use of steam to power engines, larger and faster ships could be constructed and they could carry bigger loads over longer distances and they could do it more rapidly. Ships became free from the constraints of currents and winds and could travel upstream as well as downstream and could therefore avail themselves of new markets. Steam also made fixed rail transportation possible, thus producing land as well as water routes. Steam was simultaneously harnessed by industry resulting in the production of more goods at cheaper unit costs.

The age of steam was a very significant part of the industrial revolution because it provided cheap energy and made the factory system possible. Increased production of material goods was in turn reinforced by the availability of efficient transportation systems, and the two worked hand-in-hand to bring in the industrial age. One consequence of this new age was, as has been noted, the rapid development of cities.

Therefore it may be easily seen that American cities are themselves social units the productivity of which is based on the capacity for the transportation of men and material. As modes of transportation have become increasingly sophisticated, so have the cities. Cities are composed of people and objects which are on the move, and this movement provides for much of the demand for urban police. People abuse transportation systems and the police must act as regulators and expeditors; accidents occur and the police must deal in transportation crises which involve the loss of lives, injuries, and the disruption of the orderly flow of people and things; and finally, transportation systems provide criminal opportunities which have had a profound impact on American life.

The present chapter will discuss the several modes of urban transportation and will not only look at their methods and background, but will also examine the role played by the police.

Water Transportation

Road construction began in the United States in the late 1700's and although some excellent roads were built, there were considerable difficulties. Engineering problems, financing, and political disputes all hampered the construction and use of roads.

On the other hand, water transportation was much more convenient and practical, especially in the first half of the nineteenth century. For instance, the Mississippi river, with its many tributaries, was but one natural body of water which encouraged transportation. Of course its one main disadvantage was that until the age of steam, trips on the Mississippi were one-way: downstream! In 1807 Robert Fulton constructed his famous steamer, the *Clermont,* and by the 1830's steamboats were working the Mississippi in both directions from Pittsburgh to New Orleans. The water transportation system on the Mississippi played a major role in the growth of such cities as Cincinnati, Louisville, Memphis, and New Orleans.

During the first half of the 1800's there was also a boom in canal construction, led by the Erie canal which was completed in 1825. The Erie canal brought prosperity to Buffalo, Rochester, Syracuse, and to other towns and served as an impetus for other regions to develop their own canal systems. Thus it is clear that water transportation has been traditionally important in the development of many American cities.

Water transportation is still important in a number of large cities, although the primary focus today is for the most part on port facilities. Ports have become those nexus points where the water transportation system interfaces with the other transportation systems and are only one part of a broader overall transportation complex.

Although ports with good harbors are clear assets in a commercial sense, they are not without their problems. Port areas typically have large, unstable populations of people associated with shipping, with ship's crews constantly coming and going. Ports are often noted for vice problems and other criminal activities which cater to a highly mobile and impersonal clientele. In addition, ports present opportunities for smuggling and cargo theft. The police in any city with a large and active port encounter a number of problems which relate specifically to the water transportation system.

Fixed Rail Transportation

The second major American transportation boom was also a product of the age of steam: railroads. Railroad construction began in the early 1800's and grew at an accelerated pace for most of the nineteenth century. This growth in the nation's railroads was somewhat different from the growth pattern in water transportation. Railroads could be built where they were needed and did not have to follow an arbitrary course, as was the case of rivers and lakes. The railroads traversed the country and underwrote agricultural expansion by enabling farmers and ranchers to reach distant overland markets in short periods of time. New cities blossomed as a result of the railroads (such as Chicago) and older ones prospered. In time railroads virtually overpowered water transportation by providing quick, cheap, and reliable access to markets, thus stimulating the economy of the entire nation. The railroads actually reached their zenith between the end of the Civil War and the advent of the First World War. Although the majority of American cities were established before the coming of the railroad, their subsequent presence was responsible for a very considerable amount of urban growth. The railroads linked the port cities with inland markets (and vice versa), and it is far from coincidental that both the railroads and the cities underwent massive simultaneous growth during the second half of the nineteenth century.

Within cities themselves, railroads lie along lines or rights of way which have been long established. Passenger terminals tend to be located in the center of the city, while freight yards, repair shops, and switching areas generally lie outside of town. Today there is relatively little passenger traffic and a great many of the old downtown terminals have fallen into disuse. However, railroads continue to play a major role in the shipment of freight. Because of the noise and unaesthetic qualities of railroads (especially before the diesel engine came into use), the areas immediately abutting them tended to be less attractive and hence were occupied by lower income families. These areas have become part of the blight in many urban areas. Indeed, the old saying that one was from "the wrong side of the tracks" indicates the influence of the physical presence of the railroad on the socioeconomic structure of the community.

The police have relatively little to do with the railroads; the biggest problems tend to be those associated with vandalism of goods in transit or thefts from boxcars.

Somewhat related to the railroads are other fixed rail systems, such as streetcars, interurban railways, subways, and elevateds. Streetcars operating on fixed rails have largely passed from the urban scene, as have the interurbans. Elevateds and subways tend to be found only in certain of the larger cities and there are relatively few of them.

However, recent demands for rapid transit within cities have seen the re-awakening of interest in fixed rail transportation both within and between cities. The Rail Passenger Act of 1970 created Amtrak and represented a major governmental effort to preserve intercity rail passenger service and the new San Francisco Bay Area Rapid Transit (BART) was the first new rail transit undertaking in the United States since 1907. Other cities are actively considering implementing some type of rapid transit system which will employ a combination of fixed rail and bus (or other) service.

Road Transportation

Roads and streets have been a part of social organization from the earliest times. However, the importance of roads depends on how they are used. Although roads have always been important, their true prominence has been achieved only since the advent of the motor vehicle.

In most cities the existing roads and streets predate the coming of autos and trucks, and as a consequence the modern users of today's roads are actually using them for purposes other than those for which they were designed. Not only are a great many streets inadequate in terms of how they are used, but they are used by a variety of vehicles and each vehicle type has its own requirements and liabilities.

Trucks. A very considerable portion of intercity shipping is carried out by common carrier trucking firms which use large tractor semitrailer trucks to transport their wares. These large trucks offer significant economies in terms of the movement of goods; however, when they come into cities their size often imposes a number of problems. Because many city streets are narrow and congested, large trucks can create serious problems for the movement of other vehicles. Because of this, many cities have designated truck routes through (or around) cities in order to prevent unacceptable levels of traffic congestion. Another problem posed by large trucks is that of parking. Most cities were not designed to accommodate such large vehicles and have not been greatly modified to solve the problem. Some cities have encouraged the development of trucking terminals which have been built outside of the city proper, or at least away from the central business district. Other cities have sought to develop industrial parks or warehouse districts so that commercial activities may avail themselves of adequate trucking facilities and at the same time avoid the congestion of the central business district.

Yet another problem associated with the use of trucks is that of accidents. Accidents involving large trucks often make for super accidents, both in terms of casualties and property losses. Major truck accidents can result in enormous property loss or damages and can snarl traffic in all directions for hours at a time. However, because of strict insurance requements, federal interstate regulation, and special licensing and inspection procedures, common carrier trucks account for only a relatively small proportion of motor vehicle accidents.

Buses. Buses have taken the place of trolley cars and continue to serve as an effective means of transportation: two buses carrying 100 people can do the job of 66 cars which carry, on the average, only 1.5 people. Although buses have the potential for providing fast and inexpensive transportation for large numbers of people, they have been ignored by a considerable proportion of their potential users. In some cities buses are foul smelling and dilapidated, are expensive to their users, and have limited routes. Many privately owned bus companies have had difficulty in making a profit and have allowed their maintenance schedules to go unmet and have permitted the level of service to diminish until the bus company either went out of business or was sold to the city.

The federal government has given considerable encouragement to cities to upgrade their bus systems as a part of an urban mass transit program. Some cities, as a result, have developed very efficient and worthwhile bus systems.

City buses pose very few problems for the police. The biggest problem that police have had with buses has been that of robberies. Since buses often operate late at night and in somewhat isolated areas, they have been easy targets for robbers. The problem of bus robberies has been dealt with in several ways. In some cities the operator does not make change and riders are forced to have correct change when they get on the bus, and the operator does not have access to the device into which the money is placed. In other cities police officers have ridden the buses to either catch the robbers in the act or to act as a deterrent to them.

The Motor Vehicle: Urban Trends *

It was into the urban environment in which the automobile first made its appearance, and the first clumsy horseless carriages to bounce along cobbled city streets did not look like the harbingers of an urban revolution. There was little appreciation of the fact that this was a new transportation technology that permitted people to control their own movements rather than depend on the schedules of railroad or traction companies, although there had to be some realization that the automobile was not only a more individual but also a more flexible mode of transport. If a family wished to visit friends in a different section of the city, it could go directly by car, as far as the street layout permitted, while using public transportation almost invariably required a trip downtown, a time-consuming change, and a trip out again.

Essentially, however, the automobile had to function on street systems that had never been designed for it and were about as poorly adapted to it as it was possible to be. Some optimists in the early days hoped that fast-moving vehicles would relieve traffic congestion. They should have been right, and they might have been if the nature of automotive transportation had been recognized sooner and if prompter measures had been taken to adapt to it. Instead motor vehicles were expected to merge into existing traffic and transportation patterns and to share the same streets with trolley cars, carriages, wagons, bicycles, and pedestrians, with no discrimination between local and through traffic or between fast and slow vehicles. The automobile, moreover, quickly emerged as an attractive way of traveling to work, but since the predominant urban pattern had business and industry concentrated at the center, commuting by car resulted in increasing masses of vehicles converging on the central city area and inevitably in the massive rush-hour traffic congestion that plagues cities everywhere.

The response for the most part was—and regrettably too frequently still is —to improvise. If conditions at an intersection became sufficiently intolerable, a traffic light would be installed. Crowded narrow streets were made one-way, and parking in congested sections was restricted. An occasional bypass or circumferential route was marked through side streets, frequently over the opposition of retail merchants who were afraid of losing business if traffic was diverted from their doors—until they discovered that traffic jams and inadequate parking were far worse for business.

In time these techniques became more sophisticated. Traffic lights could be synchronized or activated by the flow of vehicles instead of having to change at arbitrary intervals. They even became a status symbol and were

* The following text is taken from John B. Rae, *The Road and The Car in American Life.* Cambridge, Mass.: The M.I.T. Press, 1971, pp. 206–222. © 1971. Reprinted with permission of the publisher.

installed at points where they served nothing but civic pride, unless it was to trap out-of-town motorists for the benefit of local revenues. But while there were improvements, none were a satisfactory substitute for systematic street design and location. These were expensive measures, and most municipalities felt unable to accept the cost, even though the alternative was to accept the higher but indirect costs of congestion.

In spite of the handicaps under which it had to function, the motor vehicle in a surprisingly short time became the dominant element in urban transportation and therefore in urban development. Its first conspicuous effect was on existing transit systems. Two forces were at work here. First, as automobile ownership increased, people used their own cars for trips that they would formerly have made on public transportation. Second, railborne transit, especially streetcar and interurban lines, found itself in a losing contest with the motor bus, which was cheaper to operate and also enjoyed a flexibility that no railborne system could have.

The interurbans went first, leaving behind nostalgic and generally inaccurate memories about the quality of their service. Central city streetcar lines followed; most were gone by the Second World War. A few survived in large cities into the 1960s, but for the United States as a whole the trolley car is now a museum piece. Rapid transit continued to function where it was already established, subject to chronic financial difficulties for which automobile competition was only partly responsible. Commuter rail service stood up well during the 1920's because the increase in suburban population was great enough to offset a steady decline in the proportion of suburbanites commuting by rail.[1] The depression years, however, brought a sharp drop in patronage, which has continued, except for the temporary stimulus given by the Second World War, to the point where rail commuter service has disappeared from all but a few major metropolitan areas. Even in those it has to be subsidized by public funds to keep it in existence.

The specific shifts in emphasis among transport media depended on the characteristics of each city. Professor George Hilton identifies two broad metropolitan patterns. One, with New York as the outstanding example, has a large financial community or some other business structure whose tendency is for firms to concentrate in the central business district, and natural barriers that inhibit dispersal and define travel corridors rather rigorously. Boston, Philadelphia, Chicago, and San Francisco share some of these characteristics with New York, and all have retained railborne transportation. San Francisco's initial network of commuter and interurban lines shriveled, but the city is now in the forefront of "the second generation of rapid transit projects—built, not in the expectation of profitability, but in the hope that their incidental consequences of reduction of traffic and stimulation of central business districts

[1] George W. Hilton, "The Decline of Railroad Commutation," *Business History Review*, Vol. 36, No. 2 (Summer 1962), p. 172.

will provide substantial social benefits.[2] At the opposite end of the spectrum is Los Angeles, with no major financial community, few industries congregating about the central business district, and ample room to spread out. It became so diffused that only highway transportation could serve its needs. Its extensive interurban electric system was not suited to a dispersed metropolis and disappeared; 95 percent of all trips between all points in greater Los Angeles came to be made by automobile. Similar conditions existed in large cities like Houston and Indianapolis, and in most small and medium-sized American cities, and these likewise became dependent on buses and automobiles.

Detroit is not a financial center, and neither its automobile factories nor their executive offices congregate in the downtown area. It does have both a water barrier and an international boundary on its east side, but neither has noticeably constrained Detroit's expansion, and Detroit relies entirely on the highway for urban transportation. Cleveland, where rapid transit has survived, is a special case. It has a sizable financial community and some channeling of growth by Lake Erie and the gorges of the Cuyahoga and Rocky rivers. However, its rapid transit began as a synthetic product stemming from a real estate operation in the 1920's and entering the downtown area on the right-of-way of the Nickel Plate Railroad, so it was poorly located to serve the shopping district. The subsequent development of the system is in San Francisco's "second generation" category.

For those who see only the streets and freeways choked with cars at the rush hours and who assume that getting rid of the cars would get rid of congestion, the shift from mass to individual transportation is to be deplored. Historically, this position confuses cause and effect. The automobile intensified urban congestion, but the congestion was there first, and it will remain as long as economic and other activities are concentrated in a limited central city area. There is also the undoubted fact that these masses of motor vehicles contribute to pollution of the atmosphere. In our present context the essential point is that automobile-generated pollution stems fundamentally from having too many cars in too small an area, so measures taken to reduce congestion will automatically reduce pollution also.

The second conspicuous impact of the automobile on urban development relates directly to the problem of congestion, namely, the decentralizing effect of automotive transportation. (See Figure 6.1.) The rail transit systems began the dispersal of urban residential areas; the automobile permitted the process to be carried much further because it greatly enlarged the area of choice. The expansion of cities followed the rail and transit lines until about 1935, when it began noticeably to spread to other areas.[3] The nature of the change is

[2] George W. Hilton; "Rail Transport and the Pattern of Modern Cities: The California Case," *Traffic Quarterly*, Vol. XXI, No. 3 (July 1967), pp. 379–380.
[3] Homer Hoyt, "The Influence of Highways and Transportation on the Structure and Growth of Cities and Urban Land Values," in Jean Labatut and W. J. Lane, eds., *Highways in Our National Life: A Symposium*. Princeton, N.J.: Princeton University Press, 1960, pp. 137–138.

Figure 6.1 Changing patterns in urban traffic flow

Washington, D.C.'s growth has been governed by traffic and living patterns as shown by these area maps developed by the National Capital Planning Commission. In the 1930s, downtown Washington drew heavy traffic, but by the mid-1950s cross-movement of traffic began to develop and the urban area had enlarged as a result. By 1980, traffic will still be heavy to the center of the city but cross-traffic will increase greatly, demanding a transportation system that serves both types of movements.

shown in the fact that urban residential building in the 1920s emphasized apartments and two-family houses just outside the central city and near mass transportation, while after the Second World War the bulk of residential construction was single-family homes farther out from the center, with availability of public transportation a secondary consideration.[4] Thus, like its predecessors, automobile transportation promoted both concentration and dispersal. By providing a cheap and flexible means of transportation, it enabled people to live a greater distance from work than had previously been feasible, but it also enabled them to pour into central business districts in unmanageable numbers. What was not understood was that the centralizing aspect was an unnecessary consequence of restricting the potentialities of highway transportation by confining them within an urban structure designed for past conditions.

We have developed a society in which four-fifths of all families own an automobile and use it by preference for their ordinary day-to-day journeying—and all over the world other people are doing exactly the same thing as fast as they are given the opportunity. It is also a society whose inhabitants have made it clear that for the most part they prefer single-family dwellings with at least a suggestion of open space to central city apartments (or tenements). This proposition may seem self-evident, but it need not be accepted on faith. It has been elaborately investigated, with results that show a definite linkage between housing preference and the availability of automotive transportation. The following are some of the conclusions that have been reached.

1. A large proportion of the people studied wanted to move away from the city center and were not deterred by considerations of distance or inconvenience.

2. More people wanted to move from apartments to single-family dwellings than vice versa.

3. The choice of mode for the journey to work was not especially sensitive to cost considerations. Many people do not attempt to estimate the cost of traveling to work by car, and those who do have widely differing results.

[4] Raymond Vernon, *Metropolis—1985.* Cambridge, Massachusetts: Harvard University Press, 1960, pp. 137–138.

4. People overwhelmingly preferred to go to work by car if the factors of cost and time were no greater than what was offered by public transportation.[5]

Urban Trends

The decentralizing tendencies of motor vehicle transportation and the outward thrust of residential preferences created powerful counter forces to the centripetal pull of the central business district. They have been, indeed, so powerful that the crux of our urban problem has been the decay of central cities because of the migration of both population and business to the suburbs. Since the advent of the automobile the forces of urban decentralization seem to have been in the ascendant. Perhaps they should be, but in the meantime the central cities are here, representing an enormous investment in human and material resources.

The decline of central cities can be and frequently is attributed to the rise of the motor vehicle, but this is at best only part of the story. Blighted areas, slums, and ghettos are not an invention of the twentieth century; they have been inherent in urban life since cities began. What the twentieth century really has to offer is the technological and economic capability of doing something about them, and modern highway transportation is an inherent part of this capability. Automobile transportation is not by any means incompatible with the existence of healthy urban core areas. It is unlikely that central business districts will recover the dominant position they once possessed, but it is equally unlikely in the foreseeable future that all the activities that make up the life of a city can be so completely decentralized as to make the CBD unnecessary.

The reason for whatever adverse effects the motor vehicle has had on the central city has been explained: a new transportation technology was forced into an old transportation network. It can be restated in the words of the great architect and city planner Constantine Doxiadis:

> In the growth trend we demolish, we choke the center of our cities. Why? Because we allow a city which was prepared to stand up to the pressures of half-a-million people to get 5 million people and later 20, and then 50 million. If I asked any business man here who has a generator of 50,000 kilowatts to enlarge this generator so that it will be a generator of 100,000 kilowatts, he would laugh at me. But this is what we try to do with our cities. We bring all of our machines, all of our pressures, all of our cars downtown, and we choke downtown to death.[6]

[5] J. B. Lansing and Eva Mueller, *Residential Location and Urban Mobility*. Ann Arbor, Michigan: University of Michigan, 1964, pp. iv–v; and J. B. Lansing, *Residential Location and Urban Mobility: The Second Wave of Interviews*. Ann Arbor, Michigan: University of Michigan, 1966, pp. 1–3.
[6] Constantine Doxiadis, "Toward the Ecumenopolis," *Rotarian,* Vol. 112, No. 2 (March 1968), p. 20.

Recognizing the problem is one thing; finding remedies is another. The improvisations of the past have manifestly not worked, and there is nothing to suggest that they will do any better in the future. Among possible long-range solutions, the revival of public transportation systems, and especially of rapid transit, attracts a good deal of support, and deservedly so. Good public transportation is an absolute necessity for any city, large or small, because many people must make trips who cannot drive a car or do not have one available. A survey made in Pittsburgh showed that 85 percent of the transit system's patrons either had no driver's license or no car, and a survey in Chicago showed that half the users of rapid transit and 65 percent of all public transportation patrons were in the same category.[7]

The largest share of attention is going to rapid transit systems, railborne on their own rights-of-way, as the most promising method of carrying large numbers of people without overloading the streets. Technical improvements, as demonstrated in Toronto and Montreal, can provide rapid transit that is smoother and faster than the subway and elevated lines built early in the century. The technical problems involved in building rapid transit systems are in fact the easiest to solve. The real difficulties are social and economic. Rail transit may be greatly improved qualitatively, but it remains subject to the limitations described by Professor Hilton; to be economically feasible it requires high-density traffic along fixed corridors, and only a few American cities can meet this condition. For most cities, public transportation needs can be adequately met by bus service. Besides, as the experience of Chicago and Pittsburgh testifies, people who are accustomed to driving their own cars are poor prospects as patrons of mass transit, and it will take a good deal of persuasion, perhaps even compulsion, to make them change their habits.

There are advocates of compulsion—not in the physical sense, but in terms of proposing in all seriousness that automobiles be excluded from "downtown." (Presumably the ban would not extend to trucks, since this would stop the movement of essential commodities in and out of every central business district in the country.) Such a policy might just work if only those people who had jobs in the CBD needed to be considered. They could come and go by public transportation, although for most cities a substantial expansion of public transportation facilities would be necessary—and expensive, since these facilities would be used only for two hours inbound in the morning and two hours outbound in the afternoon. But if the revival of the central city is what is desired, there also has to be an influx of people to do business there—to shop, dine out, seek entertainment—and few such people will take a long bus or rail trip downtown when they can do the same things elsewhere by car. The issue was expressed pungently by the Cleveland *Plain Dealer* when the mayor of that city was quoted as saying that cars would have to be kept out of the central city:

[7] A. S. Lang and R. H. Soberman, *Urban Rail Transit: Its Economics and Technology.* Cambridge, Massachusetts: The M.I.T. Press, 1964, p. 88.

While no one would deny that the mayor of Cleveland has a great many problems, he really ought to be told that keeping cars out of downtown is NOT one of them. Suburban shopping centers, with their department and discount stores, theaters, restaurants, health spas and recreation centers, along with free parking and other blandishments, are doing quite a job of keeping cars [people] out of the central city, and this is what ails downtown. . . .Take cars out of downtowns and you really have ghost cities.[8]

While the central city has nothing to gain by excluding cars indiscriminately, it can definitely be helped by keeping out of the downtown area the cars that do not belong there and do not even want to be there. Traffic surveys have repeatedly demonstrated that at least two-thirds of the cars in city centers are simply passing through. There is no need for them to be where they are, but the configuration of city street systems is such that they are forced to pass through the center, thereby adding quite unnecessarily to downtown congestion.

Thus the adjustment of the metropolitan core to the situation created by automotive transportation seems to fall into two broad categories. First, an adequate public transportation system is called for, capable of providing ready access between center and outskirts. The character of this system, whether railborne or highwayborne or a combination of the two, has to be determined by the nature and needs of the urban area to be served. Second, the central city needs a street network designed and located so that traffic in and out of the CBD can move with reasonable facility and a minimum of congestion and also so that traffic that is merely passing through is routed around the CBD, preferably outside the central city area altogether.

There have been two major inhibiting factors to taking steps of this kind. One is cost. Construction of both urban highways and rapid transit facilities in built-up areas is expensive, and cities lack the resources to undertake such work on their own on the scale that is really necessary, particularly in an era when demands for other municipal services have been mounting rapidly. Yet failure to act has put central cities in a damaging downward spiral. As inadequate transport facilities produce greater congestion, more people and more business concerns move out, leaving the central city with diminished resources and therefore less able to provide adequate services. Not until the passage of the Interstate Highways Act was really effective federal aid made available for urban highway development. Since that time additional federal programs have opened the possibility of a thorough approach to urban transportation and traffic problems.

The second handicap is more difficult to deal with. It is the chaotic and

[8] Quoted from The Ohio Motorist (March 1969).

largely archaic structure of municipal government. Without exception, the American metropolis is a conglomeration of conflicting and overlapping political jurisdictions. This situation seriously obstructs coherent and coordinated planning for present-day urban needs, including highway and transportation systems. There has of course been a fair amount of success in dealing with specific mutual interests through metropolitan commissions and authorities, established to administer joint functions such as public transportation, water supply, or parks. These bodies, however, have limited powers; they do not deal with the problems of the metropolitan complex as a whole. Yet a comprehensive view and some overall authority are desirable, indeed necessary, if the transportation facilities of Metropolis are really to serve the total community. Decisions have to be made regarding such matters as the design and location of freeways, the relationship between core area and suburbs, the integration of highway improvement with plans for urban renewal, and the type of mass transit to be adopted. The issues are complicated and frequently controversial.

Dealing with them intelligently requires keeping facts straight. There is a vociferous body of opinion which asserts that American cities have been detrimentally given over to the automobile and which supports its claim by citing figures on the amount of ground space allocated to freeways, streets, and parking facilities. Los Angeles, the most completely dependent on motor vehicle transportation of major metropolitan complexes in the United States, probably in the world for that matter, is usually cited as the prime example, with the assertion that two-thirds, or three-fifths, or more than half of the area of downtown Los Angeles (depending on how the calculation is made) is devoted to the automobile. The actual figures appear in Table 6.3, with comparative figures (street area only) for other cities in Table 6.4.

The Los Angeles CBD gives 59 percent of its ground area to streets and parking: 35.2 percent to roads, streets, alleys, and sidewalks, and 23.8 percent to parking lots and garages not incorporated in buildings with other functions. One important qualification is that sidewalks are included in the street area, and they constitute 10.5 percent of the total acreage. Since the sidewalks are for pedestrians, the area allegedly devoted to the motor vehicle has to be reduced by this amount, which makes the street area actually used for vehicular movement about a quarter of the whole CBD. And is this space really "devoted to the motor vehicle?" True, it is *used* by motor vehicles, but cities had streets for several millennia before the automobile was born, and they would continue to need streets even if the automobile had never existed. The purpose of streets is to permit movement about the city and to give access to property; the method of movement is secondary.

Analysis of the data reveals that motor vehicle transportation actually requires less street space than most cities had in the pre-automobile era, even including the substantial area taken by freeways. The reason is that when the

Table 6.3   Los Angeles Central Business District Area Ground and Floor Uses

The following figures, based upon the Los Angeles Central Business District (CBD) Parking Study of 1967, indicate the area taken by the various ground and floor uses in Los Angeles. The ground area for roadways and sidewalks (35%) compares favorably with that found for CBD land uses in other major cities, such as Chicago (31%), Detroit (38%), Pittsburgh (38%), and Minneapolis (35%). Ground area used for surface parking lots and single-use (freestanding) parking garages total 24%. This percentage is above that utilized in the cities previously noted, which range from 10% to 14%. The trend toward increasing the number of parking spaces in structures which is taking place in Los Angeles would tend to reduce this variance in the future.

Comparison of Study Area Ground and Floor Uses		
Type Area	Square Feet (1,000)	% of Total
Ground area		
Ground area occupied by buildings and grounds*	22,825.8	41.0
Ground area occupied by sidewalks (10.5%), roadways, and alleys†	19,542.0	35.2
Ground area occupied by single-use parking garages	359.3	0.6
Ground area occupied by parking lots	12,920.3	23.2
Total study ground area	55,647.4	100.0
Floor space and ground area§		
Building gross floor area‡	57,694.7	60.0
Ground area occupied by roadways, alleys, sidewalks, malls, plazas, etc.†	19,542.0	20.4
Parking garage floor area	5,829.6	6.1
Ground area occupied by parking lots	12,920.3	13.5
Total area inventory	95,986.6	100.0

* Includes internal parking, but excludes freestanding garages.
† Includes sidewalk area in street right-of-way, which is 10.5% of the land area.
§ Total area in use.
‡ Excludes parking facilities.
Source: Compiled by Vince Desimone, Transportation Planning Engineer, Automobile Club of Southern California, 1968.

fast-moving through traffic is put on built-for-the-purpose arterial roads, then the amount of ordinary street space needed for strictly local movement and for access to property drops sharply. Even the amount of land taken for urban freeways turns out to be surprisingly small in terms either of total urban acreage or of the volume of traffic they carry. No existing or contemplated urban freeway system requires as much as 3 percent of the land in the areas it serves, and this would be exceptionally high. The Los Angeles freeway system, *when complete,* will occupy only 2 percent of the available land; the same is true of the District of Columbia, where only 0.75 percent will be pavement, with the remaining 1.25 percent as open space.[9] California studies estimate that in a typical California urban community 1.6 to 2 percent of the

[9] The data that follows come from F. C. Turner, "The Highway Program Faces New Challenges," address to the Illinois Editors' Highway Safety Seminar, Rockton, Illinois, May 3, 1968.

Table 6.4 Proportion of CBD Land Devoted to Streets and Parking

Central Business District	Year	Total Acres	Percent of CBD Land Devoted to		
			Streets	Parking	Streets and Parking
Los Angeles	1960	400.7	35.0	24.0	59.0
Chicago	1956	677.6*	31.0	9.7	40.7
Detroit	1953	690.0	38.5	11.0	49.5
Pittsburgh	1958	321.3*	38.2	†	†
Minneapolis	1958	580.2	34.6	13.7	48.3
St. Paul	1958	482.0	33.2	11.4	44.6
Cincinnati	1955	330.0	†	†	40.0
Dallas	1961				
Core area		344.3	34.5	18.1	52.6
Central district		1,362.0	28.5	12.9	41.4
Sacramento	1960	350.0	34.9	6.6	41.5
Columbus	1955	502.6	40.0	7.9	47.9
Nashville	1959	370.5	30.8	8.2‡	39.0
Tucson	1960	128.9	35.2	†	†
Charlotte	1958	473.0	28.7	9.7	38.4
Chattanooga	1960	246.0	21.8	13.2	35.0
Winston-Salem	1961	334.0	25.1	15.0	40.1

* Excludes undevelopable land.
† Not itemized.
Source: Transportation and land-use studies in each urban area.
From: Wilbur Smith and Associates, *Transportation and Parking for Tomorrow's Cities*, p. 59.

area should be devoted to freeways, which will handle 50 to 60 percent of all traffic needs, and about ten times as much land to the ordinary roads and streets that carry the rest of the traffic. By comparison, when John A. Sutter laid out Sacramento in 1850, he provided 38 percent of the area for streets and sidewalks. L'Enfant proposed 59 percent of the area of the District of Columbia for roads and streets; urban renewal in Southwest Washington, incorporating a modern street network, reduced the acreage of street space in the renewal area from 48.2 to 41.5 percent of the total. If we are to have a reasoned consideration of the impact of highway transportation on contemporary urban development, it would be well to approach the subject in the spirit of this statement by the Executive Director of New York's Citizens' Housing and Planning Council:

Many components of a city are highly desirable, but only two are absolutely essential. One is people, and the other is transportation. Sometimes the critics need to be reminded that without transportation the people would be unable to build shelter, or feed themselves, or have water to drink, or power to light their homes. Without transportation, urban men would choke on some of their own waste products and find themselves buried in others. Transportation makes cities possible.

The assumption by critics that cities necessarily deteriorate has led them to write about technology, which grows constantly more vital to the cities, as though it were a distressing law that could be repealed, like Prohibition, or a state of affairs to be overcome with prayer and protest, like segregation in public accommodations. They refuse to understand that the problem is not how to ban technology and its products, such as the automobile, but how to use them to widen human chances in the city as a whole.[10]

Road Transportation and the Police

The average citizen is most likely to encounter the police in their efforts to enforce traffic laws. When people observe police officers, the officers are usually directing traffic, stopping a violator, or are themselves driving around in their squad cars (and to many people their driving around is virtually synonymous with looking for traffic violators). Indeed, it was the development of the automobile that for the first time brought large numbers of people into direct contact with the police.

However, the relationship between the police and traffic involves a great deal more than simply handing out citations. The police role in traffic management breaks down into three components: enforcement, education, and engineering. Each of these components are interrelated and collectively provide the rationale behind police involvement in road transportation.

Enforcement. The enforcement role is, unfortunately, the most conspicuous activity in participation of police in traffic management. Since voluntary compliance with traffic regulations is unrealistic, state and local legislative bodies have established laws to regulate the flow of traffic, to delineate who may operate motor vehicles, and how vehicles may or may not be operated. These laws provide penalties ranging from minor fines to confinement in state penitentiaries, depending upon the offense. As with the majority of other laws, the police are charged with their enforcement.

The chief means of traffic law enforcement is through the use of the citation—"tickets." A traffic ticket is not a conviction unilaterally imposed by a police officer, as some people think, but is a statement that a policeman has observed a motorist in violation of some traffic law. When the motorist signs the ticket he is not admitting guilt, but is promising to appear in a traffic court to answer to the charge. In almost all jurisdictions a violator may elect not to contest the charge, but may simply pay a fixed fine. In some cases where the officer has reason to believe that the violator will not appear to answer to the charge, he may arrest him and take him

[10] Roger Starr, *The Living End: The City and Its Critics.* New York: Coward-McCann, 1968, pp. 185–186.

into custody. The violator may then post a cash bond as a surety for his subsequent appearance; if he fails to appear, he accepts conviction and forfeits his cash bond.

The idea behind the use of citations and court imposed fines is that it is easier to drive within the boundaries of the law than to be continuously subjected to the punishments which come with violations. It therefore becomes the responsibility of police officers to cite the offenders.

The matter of traffic citations has some interesting side issues. For one thing, some departments use the traffic citation as a means of revenue. Other departments have used the volume of traffic citations as an index of officer efficiency, with informal "norms" (the term "quota" is unpopular) for acceptable levels of officer productivity. For example, one department feels that an officer who is doing his job should write at least one traffic ticket per hour. Unfortunately, such practices are known to take place in various jurisdictions, although they are contrary to the purpose of the traffic citation.

Another problem is that involved in traffic tickets which go unpaid. The offender who receives a ticket and who declines to act on it runs the risk of having a warrant issued for his arrest. In some jurisdictions these traffic warrants are actively served on offenders, while in other areas they are simply kept on file. If a motorist is then stopped by the police and the warrant file is checked and an outstanding warrant is being held, then the offender is arrested and taken into custody. Part of the problem lies in the fact that those who are poor are more likely to take their chances on not getting caught again. However, when they do get caught, what originally started out as a simple traffic matter may become an expensive, time consuming process for the offender. Verbal warnings and warning tickets are used in some cases where the officer feels it will have the most desirable impact on the offender, whereas other cities have strict enforcement policies and do not issue warning citations.

Police also employ selective enforcement tactics which may include driver's license checks or special details which are targeted against specific types of offenders, such as intoxicated drivers or speeders. The purpose of selective traffic enforcement is to zero in on specific problem areas. The purpose of traffic law enforcement is to compel drivers to use their vehicles and the public roads in such a manner as to prevent unnecessary loss of life, injuries, and property damage. The goal is not to see how many motorists they can hassle or how much revenue can be generated. Few citizens ever take the time to reflect on the fact that police officers very frequently see the consequences of poor (or illegal) driving and that the enforcement of traffic laws has a very real meaning to those who must periodically assist in the removal of bodies from wrecks or to administer aid to those who have been injured.

Education. Ideally, the police officer who stops a violator hopes that his actions will have a beneficial impact on the person he stops. If a violator can be made to understand the seriousness of his offense, then perhaps he will avoid doing the same thing in the future. Police also involve themselves in traffic safety education in a great many cities, conducting workshops and driver education programs. By being aware of the consequences of non-compliance with traffic law, the police can warn errant motorists and perhaps convince them to drive with greater care. Unfortunately, many citizens resent being chastised by police officers. Most veteran officers have heard the bored offender who has said, "Just skip the lecture and give me my ticket." Nevertheless, traffic law enforcement is designed to educate as well as to punish.

Engineering. Transportation accidents involve three elements: the road, the vehicle, and the driver. Defective vehicles and faulty roads may contribute to accidents every bit as much as driver error. Roads become modified under varying weather conditions, and unless they are well maintained, may tend to deteriorate rapidly. Automobiles may also vary in efficiency depending upon age, condition, and climate. Good drivers, carefully operating safe vehicles on good roads, have a high probability of not being involved in accidents. Poor drivers operating defective vehicles on dangerous roads have a much higher chance of being involved in an accident.

Police investigate traffic accidents to see the extent to which the vehicle, the driver, or the road contributed to the accident. In those cases where defective road conditions exist, the police can make recommendations to the city's public works director or traffic engineer to make the needed modifications. Perhaps all that might be required is a stop sign, a traffic light, a warning device, or an alteration in the speed limit. By the same token, large numbers of accidents which involve defective autos might suggest inspection requirements designed to reduce the number of cars operating on the roads with such defects as bad tires, faulty exhaust systems, or worn brakes.

Defective drivers may also display trends which might act as guides for police officers. For instance, if large numbers of older persons are at fault in traffic accidents, this might suggest the need for improved or revamped licensing requirements. Or if there is an increase in the volume of accidents involving DWI's, then this might suggest the need for selective enforcement against drinking drivers.

The human element of transportation also requires that police officers be both intelligent and that they have a degree of sensitivity. The police have considerable discretionary latitude, as some circumstances may justify the violation of traffic laws by drivers (as when necessary to avoid an accident, or in the case of a medical emergency). Finally, traffic officers must have a good sense of humor. This author was told by a highway patrolman that he had once stopped a woman who had been driving on an interstate highway at speeds well over a hundred miles per hour. He asked her why she was speeding, to which she indignantly replied that she had *not* been speeding: she saw a mouse underneath her accelerator pedal, and she was trying to squash it!

There has been some argument that the traffic function is not an appropriate role for policemen, and that accident investigations are not used to improve the transportation system but rather to benefit insurance companies. This latter argument has some merit, because a great many police departments do not effectively use the data they collect, and they do make the reports available to insurance companies.

With respect to the first charge, recent studies have indicated that police officers per se may *not* be necessary in traffic law enforcement. For example, the city of Fort Lauderdale, Florida is now using police para-professionals called "Traffic Safety Aides" to handle traffic problems. These aides must undergo 200 hours of training in accident investigation, courtroom presentation, traffic law, first aid, and other subjects. They operate Traffic Accident Investigation Vans and have responsibility for handling traffic accidents, pedestrian accidents, traffic direction, and the enforcement of traffic laws. They do not carry weapons and do not respond to non-traffic calls. "Traffic wardens" have also been used in the United Kingdom with success, and available information indicates that programs of this type have sufficient merit to warrant further exploration.

Auto Theft. The theft of automobiles has become an increasingly severe problem in recent years. The auto theft rate as reported in the 1972 *Uniform Crime Reports* was 423 offenses per 100,000 inhabitants.[1] People in cities with over one million inhabitants were victimized by auto thefts at a greater rate than any other population group, thus making the offense primarily a large city problem.[2]

The F.B.I. has reported that on a national basis, one out of every 109 automobiles was stolen.[3] Although the police have been successful in recovering the vast majority of stolen automobiles, the clearance rate for this offense stands at around 17 percent.[4] Of course a clearance is not

[1] *Crime in the United States: Uniform Crime Reports, 1972*, United States Department of Justice, Federal Bureau of Investigation. Washington, D.C.: U.S. Government Printing Office, 1973, p. 25.
[2] *Ibid.*
[3] *Ibid.*, p. 28
[4] *Ibid.*

an arrest, nor is an arrest a conviction. Hence the number (or percent) of persons who steal cars and who are subsequently convicted is quite small.

Not only is auto theft primarily a large city problem, it is also a problem involving youthful offenders. The F.B.I. has reported that:

> Persons arrested for auto theft come primarily from the young age group population. In 1972, 54 percent of all persons arrested for this crime were under 18 years of age. When persons under 21 are included in the computations, the proportion of arrests rises to 72 percent.[5]

The response to auto thefts has generally been somewhat limited. In the past, police departments often issued officers "hot sheets" which listed the license numbers of cars which had been reported to the police as being stolen and officers would check suspected vehicles against the hot sheet list. This presented several difficulties. In the first place only local auto thefts were usually listed. Second, every once in a while a stolen auto would be recovered and returned to its owner who would then be stopped by police officers who had not received a cancellation of the number! Police have been able to greatly increase their effectiveness in this area through the use of computerized data banks, such as the National Crime Information Center, operated by the F.B.I. Police agencies all across the country enter stolen auto data into the NCIC, and any police department having a terminal on the system can check a suspected vehicle. Thus a police officer in Denton, Texas can get a "hit" on a stolen car which had been stolen in Paramus, New Jersey but which had Connecticut license plates!

In spite of recent technological advancements, there is still relatively little that the police can do to prevent the theft of autos. One might suspect that the best preventive measures would involve programs which sought to reach young males in large cities or which removed the opportunity for the easy theft of an auto.

Mobility of Offenders

One very significant aspect of the rapid development of the transportation technology has been the greatly increased mobility of offenders. It is now quite easy for a person to go from one city (or from another state) to another for the purpose of committing a criminal offense and then returning to his "home town." Indeed, the interstate nature of a

[5] *Ibid.*

great deal of criminal activity has involved the federal government in law enforcement activities at a rate undreamed of just a few decades ago.

Although police departments in cities are "fixed" by their geographic boundaries, the importance of police cooperation among cities and other jurisdictions has become highly evident. Increased cooperation together with the sharing of technological resources and information has greatly increased the sophistication of many police departments, especially those located in urban areas. This overall increased sophistication has also manifested itself through the demand for officers with high educations and greater versatility, thus bringing into the police service (at the community level) young officers with better educations and a higher degree of social awareness. This in turn has moved in the direction of shortening the gap between citizen and policeman and it may well be suspected has greatly enhanced the public image of the police. At the same time the police are clearly becoming more professional in their training and education and they are developing better technologies, thus fulfilling the cycle.

Appendix A
Traffic Operations*

Commentary

The role of the police in motor vehicle transportation systems has undergone significant changes through the years. The traditional police function has centered around traffic law enforcement, accident investigation, and traffic direction and control processes. In today's highly complex and mobile society, the police officer's responsibilities have been expanded beyond the restrictive area of traffic supervision and have evolved into a more comprehensive service that includes motorist service, public information, motor theft prevention, and other activities vital to the safe and efficient movement of traffic.

This increase in the level, scope, and quality of police traffic services is tied in with a general and persuasive demand by the public for increased services by all agencies at every level of government. The wide range of activities performed by the police in the highway transportation system can be classified under the broad general title of highway traffic management.

An important factor in the expansion of police traffic services in the United States was the enactment of the Highway Safety Act of 1966 and the promulgation of highway safety performance standards by the U.S. Department of Transportation. A principal feature of the Highway Safety Act is the provision of Federal financial assistance to State and local governments for the improvement and expansion of their highway safety programs in accordance with uniform performance standards. The Omnibus Crime Control Bill was enacted in 1968. Together these far-reaching pieces of Federal legislation have served as a catalyst for the improvement of police policy, performance, and effectiveness in this country. . . .

Officers arriving at the scene of a traffic accident have many duties to perform. They must be alert for spilled gasoline or other dangerous substances. They must locate victims, protect them from further harm, and summon other emergency service as needed. They must protect personal property from theft or destruction. At the same time, they must ascertain whether hit-and-run or another crime is involved, take immediate steps to apprehend the offenders, locate witnesses, secure physical evidence, maintain order, and keep traffic moving as though no accident had occurred.

In the midst of the activity, an investigation must be conducted, and later, accurately and completely reported. Report writing is considered the lifeline of a good traffic program. The finest possible investigation is useless if not accurately and completely reported. Reports must be accurate, clear, and as brief as possible.

The Fort Lauderdale, Fla., Police Department has been operating remark-

* National Advisory Commission on Criminal Justice Standards and Goals, *Police.* Washington, D.C.: U.S. Government Printing Office, 1973, pp. 226–232.

ably well with its innovative Field Office/Traffic Laboratory on Wheels, established in 1965. The Accident Investigation Unit has converted standard mobile vans into rolling offices, complete with typewriter, drawing board, desk, drawers, and investigative tools. Zone patrol cars and motorcycles, regularly assigned to all areas of the city, usually arrive at the scene of the accident first and perform initial procedural actions pending the arrival of the accident investigation laboratory. Upon arrival, the accident investigation crew quickly relieves units already at the scene, making them available for other police duties. Such a system permits maximum time in the field for accident analysis and minimum time at the station for writing reports.

To complement reporting, an efficient traffic accident records system, emphasizing quality control, must be implemented to evaluate cost effectiveness of highway safety measures.

Followup units are necessary to act on the results of preliminary investigations of accidents where a traffic crime has been committed. One of their primary functions is to seek criminal complaints for the prosecuting agency. These units also should maintain liaison with the coroner's office to determine causes of death to accident victims. It should be a further responsibility of these units to receive and obtain statements from additional witnesses to serious accidents.

Investigations should be conducted of all accidents involving fatalities, injuries, or when one or more vehicles must be towed from the scene. However, traffic accidents not requiring official written reports by officers should not prevent the officers from taking other appropriate action such as keeping the peace, alleviating traffic congestion, and assisting all concerned persons.

Traffic Control and Direction

A number of recommendations have been made for dividing the various police traffic service functions among other existing governmental agencies or to place all or part of them in some newly created quasi-police agency. Reasons for this proposed redistribution have ranged from pure economics to an effort to improve police public relations.

Even in countries such as New Zealand where traffic control and enforcement are vested in a nonpolice agency, it has become a problem to draw the line between crime on one hand and traffic offenses on the other. A compromise has been employed in New Zealand wherein nonpolice traffic wardens handle minor accidents and most traffic offenses, while the State police retain the power to deal with personal injury accidents and drunken driving.

The relationship between the use of motor vehicles and the commission of serious crimes is of sufficient magnitude that police crime suppression activities could be impeded significantly if the traffic control function were vested in a separate nonpolice agency. This is not to say that every effort should not be expended to use of civilian personnel to the maximum, under the direct supervision of the police, to perform certain routine nonhazardous or clerical police traffic service subfunctions.

Several police agencies have utilized nonsworn civilian personnel successfully in a variety of police traffic service capacities. The use of individuals who need not meet the stringent entry requirements of regular police officers should be expanded in routine police traffic service functions that do not require a sworn officer.

The two chief functions of personnel assigned to traffic control and direction are direction of vehicular and pedestrian traffic, and the enforcement of laws regulating parking. Deployment of personnel should be guided by peak traffic periods and posted parking restrictions. Regular beats should be established to conform with parking meter locations, business districts, posted time zones, and complaints of parking abuses. Where available, electronic traffic surveillance devices should be used to assist personnel engaged in intersection traffic control, or to relieve those personnel for other duties.

Officers assigned to this function also should be responsible for impounding vehicles and directing traffic at special events.

Planning and Policy

Planning, policy, and procedure are vital to the successful operation of a police traffic services program. Without proper planning, and the development of policies and procedures to put those plans into effect, any program is doomed to failure.

Policy should be written and should become a part of duty manuals, general orders, and instructional material.

To insure impartial enforcement, procedures for issuing citations and warnings should be carefully delineated.

Policy also should comply with jurisdictional agreements within the State, clarifying which agency has primary responsibility and authority for traffic supervision in specific areas. For example, should a State traffic agency maintain jurisdiction over a State highway running through a municipality under the control of another local police agency? Such distinctions should be clearly delineated, and the officers of each agency should be aware of their traffic duties and responsibilities.

Ancillary traffic services are those police activities that have an indirect effect on traffic flow. Comprehensive guidelines on aiding disabled motorists, removing hazards, controlling auto theft, disposing of abandoned cars, and safeguarding property, should be conveyed to all personnel.

State Licensing Responsibility

The major factors in a traffic accident are, of course, the driver, the vehicle, the highway, the weather, and traffic density.

Improving driver performance can significantly reduce accidents. The most important purpose of driver licensing is to establish minimum driver performance levels through initial screening.

To insure uniform and optimum statewide driver licensing standards, every State should assume complete responsibility for licensing all drivers. State officials responsible for driver examination, licensing, and record keeping functions should not be police officials. In addition to driver examination and licensing, State agencies should assume the responsibility for annual vehicle registration and vehicle inspection. The regulation of commercial vehicle operator license issuance, and commercial vehicle inspection and control criteria, should be an added function of State non-police agencies.

Accurate and efficient records systems must be maintained to facilitate the prompt reporting of any individual's or organization's failure to comply with State motor vehicle code regulations. To minimize problems in accuracy, it is imperative that the State licensing agency maintain complete jurisdiction over personnel in charge of initial data collection.

Carefully defined license suspension and revocation policies should be strictly enforced against violators. License suspension is a strong deterrent against unsafe driving practices. License revocation should result when a driver has been convicted of manslaughter, of using a vehicle in the commission of a felony, of perjury under motor vehicle laws, or for leaving the scene of an accident.

Specialized Equipment

In an effort to implement effective traffic programs, every police agency should acquire, or share with larger agencies, specialized equipment, such as radar and breathalyzers, operated by specially trained police officers or civilian technicians.

Conviction rates increase when jurors can see and hear how a drunk driving defendant behaved. Both the New York City Police Department and the California Highway Patrol have recently initiated pilot projects employing sophisticated electronic devices aimed at the drunk driver problem and highway-freeway congestion. The New York Police Department's Accident Investigation Division decided in September 1969, to experiment with videotape as a means of enhancing court presentations in drunk driving cases. Twenty trained chemical technician-photographers received 80 hours of training in chemical testing using the Harger Drunkometer, and 120 hours of training in the operation of the videotape camera. The results of their experiment revealed that sound movies are probably the best method of corroborating an officer's testimony on the actions and condition of an arrestee at the time of intoxication.

On a broader scale, but still within the realm of traffic safety operations, the California Division of Highways' Freeway Operations Department is developing electronic hardware that will provide safer and more efficient use of freeways. Incidents such as car accidents, truck turnovers, stalled vehicles, fires, and other "random events" account for about 50 percent of the present total congestion, equalling the congestion at predicted known sites during peak traffic hours. A pilot project has been completed on a 42-mile loop of the three major Los Angeles freeways. The pilot surveillance system includes 6-foot squares of wire buried in the roadbed to provide instant data on volume and density of traffic. Telemetering equipment relays that information to the control center, where a computer analyzes the input and transfers the data to an information message displayed on huge signs visible to motorists.

The first phase of the project began with on-ramp control that is instantly responsive to freeway traffic flow. On-ramps beyond the site will be metered automatically to restrict vehicle entrance until the troubled area is clear. The second phase incorporates the dispatching of a California Highway Patrol helicopter to the scene as advised by the computer and signal system, and subsequent transmission of the incident over closed circuit television to the control center. The California Highway Patrol will then determine and dispatch the necessary emergency equipment. The system developers say the electronic surveillance project is the first step toward a fully automated traffic control system.

Specialized Investigation and Enforcement

The decision to specialize is extremely important to the police administrator because of its pervasive effect on all aspects of the department's operation. The concept of specialization involves the question of whether to divide the department into separate units based upon tasks to be performed, and to what degree this should be done.

With respect to traffic law enforcement and accident investigation, the determination involved is whether these functions and responsibilities should be in a separate division or within the purview of the patrol division. This determination is not entirely an either/or decision; it may involve varying degrees of specialization. Pertinent considerations include, but are not limited to, the size and sophistication of the department training capabilities; the size of the geographical area to be served; the necessity for ready availability of certain services; and the dissimilarity of tasks to other duties. In addition to those broad categories, consideration should be given to traffic services, traffic volume, and congestion. Included within these categories should be questions involving accident frequency and the volume of such specific offenses as drunk driving.

In 1970, the International Association of Chiefs of Police adopted a policy toward specialization in police traffic operations. This policy recommends the following guidelines:

1. Every agency, regardless of size, should have someone either in a staff capacity or in the line function, trained in highway safety management and in a position to stimulate and evaluate effective action.

2. In the event that a specialized traffic unit is determined to be necessary, careful evaluation should be made in terms of public protection, cost, and benefits, to determine what duties should be performed by the functional units (patrol, traffic, and investigative).

3. Regardless of the degree of specialization within the department, most street traffic duties should be performed by the motorized patrol division.

4. Specialization should be dictated by need. Some specialization is necessary, but police manpower is limited and increased specialization usually results in diminished patrol. Public protection and cost benefits should be considered.

Deployment

It is essential that manpower be fully and properly deployed at those locations and times identified as having high potential for the occurrence of traffic accidents.

The concept of selective enforcement has long been recognized by those in the police and highway safety field as a valuable tool in reducing traffic accidents and the overwhelming loss of life and property they entail. Its central feature embodies the concentration of a force of men, indoctrinated in traffic enforcement, in those areas with heavy traffic volume, high accident rate, violation frequency, and congestion.

One of the most successful selective enforcement programs developed thus far is in operation in Flint, Mich. The Flint program employs the selective enforcement concept in an effort to reduce all traffic accidents, particularly serious accidents involving physical injury or death, and to improve implementation of accident investigation data. The program became operational on July 1, 1969. At that time, according to statistics compiled by the National Safety Council (NSC), Flint ranked 10th in cities of its size, with a death rate of 14.2 per 100,000 population. In 1970, the fatality rate was reduced to 6.7 per 100,000. This reduction was achieved by enhancing the enforcement emphasis on hazardous moving violations such as speeding, running traffic signals, and driving under the influence of alcohol and drugs. Emphasis on these violations was determined by analyzing statistical data that reflected the accident picture.

The reduction of traffic accidents was accomplished by inducing the public to comply voluntarily with traffic laws and safety standards. This was accomplished by a quantitative and qualitative increase of public contacts of a formal nature, such as issuance of citations, and verbal and written warnings, and of an informal nature, such as aiding disabled motorists.

Finally, information obtained from accident investigations provided a base for the analysis of the violations involved, calculated to the type and quantity of enforcement used. As a result, a practical program was devised in which enforcement was implemented at the optimum time in the most critical locations to obtain the highest possible traffic safety return on enforcement activity.

The National Highway Traffic Safety Administration initiated the Selective Traffic Enforcement Program (STEP) in February 1971. The project's purpose was to evaluate the efficacy of sustained projects utilizing the concepts of selective enforcement from different perspectives. The program was implemented in the cities of Chattanooga, Tenn.; El Paso, Tex.; Sacramento, Calif.; Fort Lauderdale, Fla.; Tacoma, Wash.; and the States of North Dakota and West Virginia. The program's effectiveness has not yet been fully evaluated, but preliminary reports are favorable.

California, Connecticut, Indiana, and many other State and local police agencies have conducted studies which demonstrated a marked decrease in accidents as a result of intensified enforcement activity on a special section of roadway.

Every agency should have one person with administrative responsibility who is trained in highway safety management. The operational functions of police traffic services should be performed by the patrol unit. Certain tasks requiring specialized skill or knowledge, such as accident investigation, could be performed by officers assigned primarily to those tasks. Thus, the traffic division would consist, in most cases, of an administrative officer with overall management responsibility, and a number of traffic specialists. Most police traffic services would be performed by the patrol unit under the supervision and control of the traffic division commander.

Administrative Functions

Supervisory and administrative police personnel play a vital role in an effective traffic management program. Police administrators have the responsibility for planning, supervising, training, analyzing traffic records, and securing necessary cooperation and liaison with other related groups such as the courts, engineers, and State licensing agencies.

Middle management or supervisory personnel also play an extremely important role in the total traffic law enforcement process. Their understanding, enthusiasm, and interest in the goals and objectives of a traffic law enforcement program often spell the difference between success and failure. Too often, well-conceived programs fail due to a breakdown in this critical link. Planning is essential to the successful conclusion of any serious undertaking. Planning must be done at all supervisory levels. Each supervisor must determine how to accomplish tasks and ascertain needed resources and procedures.

Other supportive functions such as property control and equipment supply operations should be accorded proper emphasis. Laboratory services providing scientific assistance in accident investigation are an indispensable asset to resolving previously "unsolvable" cases.

Inservice training and research programs are vital functions that need to be implemented in all police agencies. The Highway Safety Act of 1966 provided the impetus to encourage all States and their political subdivisions to develop comprehensive training programs in traffic management.

Public information services, using mass media communication, provide the means for department safety campaigns. Such a service should be used by all municipal police agencies servicing large communities.

As management tasks become increasingly demanding, highway traffic administrators seek more effective tools. One of these is an invigorated traffic records system designed to yield facts on which to base decisions, and data to guide the agency in formulating programs and procedures relating to the safe movement of vehicular and pedestrian traffic.

A traffic records system should call attention to activities which need special attention. Precise standards against which present conditions can be measured should be developed as they have been for quality control in manufacturing. It is not enough that a records system produce monthly and annual summaries of traffic accidents, citations, and convictions; the system should highlight deviations from the norm and changes in trends.

A traffic records analyst should make full use of a modern system. He should analyze routine reports and records to detect patterns and should compare them to identify trends. Traffic record analysts can multiply the effectiveness of a records system as a tool for management, increasing the effectiveness of administrative decisions and saving valuable time.

Public Traffic Safety Programs

Vehicle traffic accidents inflict enormous social and economic loss each year. The National Safety Council estimates this loss for 1970 at $13.6 billion. This figure represents only direct costs resulting from motor vehicle accidents and not the burden on public service activities such as police, fire, and courts, or the cost to employers, etc. This loss, coupled with the unquantifiable personal suffering and disruption of family life created by permanent physical disability and death, points out a condition that has been described as a social and economic malignancy.

Therefore, police agencies should focus more attention on traffic education. They should cooperate as much as possible with educational institutions throughout their jurisdiction in the preparation and presentation of traffic safety education programs.

The results of a National Safety Council questionnaire distributed at the 1970 national conventions of the American Association of School Administrators, National School Boards Association, and National Education Association, indicate that more than 90 percent of administrators expressed support for driver education in high schools. A need exists for traffic safety education for the general public as well. Police agencies should develop procedures for the periodic release of police traffic safety information to the public.

Based on the success of numerous traffic education programs initiated throughout the United States, it was found that the 5- through 8-year old age group was the most receptive and impressionable. It has been found that youth does not generally require any dispelling of preconceived ideas about the police. Therefore, a conceptual framework of traffic safety consciousness should be instilled at as early an age as possible.

The Tacoma, Wash., Police Department's Talking Motorcycle Program, initiated in February 1971, concentrated on elementary schools. It relied upon the premise that the closer the child could identify with the traffic officer, the more impact a message would have. By animating the motorcycle with a tape recorder device mounted in the saddle bag, the officer and motorcycle carry on a conversation stressing bicycle and pedestrian safety while explaining the role of the police in general, and the traffic officer in particular. The response was outstanding from children, teachers, and parents.

Peoria, Ill., is the site of Safety Town, a model street network with traffic signs, traffic signals, and street markings installed to represent an actual street system. It is used to teach children proper traffic procedure.

Some local police agencies, such as the West Covina, Calif., Police Department, have developed portable Safety Town facilities that can be taken to schools, parks, and shopping centers. Through the 6-month period following the program's inception in May 1972, traffic officers have contacted over 10,000 youngsters.

Similar pedestrian safety projects have been initiated in New York City, where education for mentally retarded children is provided, and in the State of Alabama, where rural nighttime safety is taught.

Education oriented activities designed to improve traffic safety have largely been limited to schools and students. It is equally important to educate those not presently attending school. Driver education programs must be made available throughout the community.

9

The Media, Police and Public Opinion

The twentieth century has witnessed an explosion of technologies as knowledge has multiplied itself several times over. Added knowledge has enhanced technological capacities, and the advancing technologies have then contributed to the expanded existence of knowledge. This has been an ever quickening cycle which has led man into entirely new dimensions of existence. These new technologies have had both positive and negative consequences, and for many of them, it has not yet even been possible to assess their consequences.

On the positive side one may note that man has a far greater understanding of his universe than has ever been the case in the past. Lifespans have been significantly lengthened through medical advances; the rapid development of the transportation technologies has radically altered the economic nature of cities and nations; computer technology has almost completely transformed traditional concepts of data storage and retrieval —and in the process has also altered a number of other technologies as well. The list could go on for pages, yet the point is clear: the modern technologies have changed the quality of life.

Not all of the change, however, has been for the better. For the first time in the history of man, the means of almost instant annihilation at the push of a button is a reality. Wars have already taken millions of lives through the use of technologies which have been developed during the current century. The prospects remain great that yet more lives will be lost in international conflicts employing the last word in weaponry.

The new technologies have also changed the role of man in the overall scheme of things, and this has produced in many people feelings of alienation, disaffection, apathy, and displacement. Indeed, the modern technologies have moved so rapidly that there is good reason to question whether man has moved fast enough to keep pace with them.[1] Change comes so fast that people don't seem to have the time to adapt to one before the next crosses the threshold.

One technology which has escalated by leaps and bounds in complexity and scope is that which deals with communications. The advances in communications technology have likewise had a major impact on the remainder of society—including the police.

[1] See for example Alvin Toffler, *Future Shock.* (New York: Bantam Books, 1971).

9

Communications

Just what exactly have the great advances in communications wrought? One writer suggests that:

The communications revolution has had implications far beyond those that arose from the physical application of steam to transportation and production. The social and economic consequences of the Industrial Revolution in the nineteenth century were so far reaching that their impact is only now being recognized, a hundred years after the event. The ultimate results of the communications revolution are still conjectural, largely because the headlong rush of events has made any real perspective an impossible task.[2]

Not only is it impossible to keep up with all that is being communicated, it is almost as difficult to even select from among the media used for communicating. It should come as no surprise that the consequences of the communications revolution are as of yet far from being fully understood.

In its simplest sense, communication involves the transmittal of information. It may be by word of mouth, through the use of symbols, or through the use of electronic media, to name but a few. Some communications systems are two-way; that is, they allow for feedback. Others are one way. Perhaps the bulk of modern communications techniques are of the one-way variety. One might add that they are very often targeted at large audiences. Because of their large audiences these communications media have come to be called the *mass media*. Foremost among them are radio and television, newspapers and magazines, and the movies.

The Mass Media

The mass media communicate essentially on a one-way basis with large audiences for two primary reasons. The first is to provide information, and the second is to provide entertainment. Of course it should be borne in mind that "information" may be entertaining, and entertainment may also be informative. However, the perspective to work from is not that of the receiver but that of the sender. For purposes of the present discussion the term "news" will be used to denote communications designed to inform.

The Mass Media and the News. Practically all people are acquainted with a multitude of concepts and events through their own experiences,

[2] Charles S. Steinberg, ed., *Mass Media and Communication.* (New York: Hastings House, Publishers, 1969), p. xii.

yet their range of interests may extend to areas in which they have had little or no personal experience. Thus people may learn not only through their own experiences, but they may also learn from the experiences of others, as they are presented by the media. Millions of persons have seen the battlefields of Vietnam, the civil war in Bangladesh, and the carnage of the flood in Honduras in September of 1974—all from the comforts of their living room chair. Many people are interested in what's happening to other people in other places. The transmission of this information by the media is the *news*.

The news may be a simple announcement (such as the first reports of the assassination of President Kennedy), or it may be a lengthy and detailed examination of an event of current interest (such as the protracted Watergate hearings during the Nixon administration). However, given the multiplicity of events which take place at any given time, what winds up becoming reported by the media? One answer is that "It is not the intrinsic importance of an event that makes it newsworthy. It is rather the fact that the event is so unusual that if published it will either startle, amuse, or otherwise excite the reader...." [3] The kinds of things most likely to startle, amuse, or excite people tend to be "... the accidents and incidents that the public is prepared for; the victories and defeats on the ballfield or on the battlefield; the things one fears and the things one hopes for...." [4] Therefore, according to Walter Lippmann, newspapers do not try to keep an eye on all mankind. "They have watchers stationed at certain places, like police headquarters, the coroner's office, the County Clerk's office, city hall, the White House, the Senate, the House of Representatives, and so forth." [5]

The police have traditionally been a source of news because they are involved in a variety of unusual and "interesting" events, such as robberies, murders, major accidents and disasters, kidnappings, and so on. They are often the first to arrive at the scene (and also to take charge) and it is through them that much information concerning an incident will be released. The police, as it were, have an inside track on what's going on—and they are often participants in the newsworthy event itself. A good example occurred on January 7, 1973 when Mark Essex, a disturbed black extremist, murdered the proprietor of a New Orleans grocery store and then fled to the downtown Howard Johnson's motel. After entering the motel he killed seven people and wounded eight others. After a siege by hundreds of police officers, Essex was finally killed by automatic weapons fired at him from a helicopter. This was a sensational event and was given media coverage from coast to coast.

[3] Robert E. Park, "News As A Form of Knowledge: A Chapter in the Sociology of Knowledge," from Steinberg, *op. cit.*, pp. 134–135.
[4] *Ibid.*, p. 136.
[5] Walter Lippmann, "The Nature of News," in Steinberg, *op. cit.*, p. 142.

Sensational news items such as the Essex tragedy have long appealed to the public interest; as a result, the news media have given relatively thorough coverage of police activities, especially in the case of a sensational event or an unusual crime.

The Mass Media and Entertainment. The news, as portrayed by the media, deals with events which exist in objective reality. Entertainment, as provided by the mass media, may be based in whole or in part on factual events or they may involve the dramatization of entirely fictitious events.

Whereas the news media must wait for events to take place and must then cover them, the entertainment media operate under no such constraints. In fact, the entertainment media actively create what it believes the public would like to have. Again, the police have been used as a source of themes by the entertainment media. This is easily seen in police movies and television stories, detective magazines, and so on. Not only does the entertainment media create much of what it believes the public wants, they are able to control content and to provide special effects thus achieving a strong appearance of reality in many cases. The line between fiction and non-fiction often becomes blurred.

The mass media are big business and they reach large "receiver" populations. The entertainment they transmit is therefore received by very large audiences. For instance, the number of people who watch the *lowest* rated TV show has been estimated to be greater than the number of people it would take to fill (to a full house) a Broadway theater every night for twenty years.[6] Apparently Americans spend a considerable amount of time being entertained by the television: the average TV set is on five hours and forty-five minutes each day.[7] Movies also draw patrons in large numbers and magazines reach extremely large audiences.

The Media and the Formation of Public Opinion

It has been said that the mass media have simply catered to the demands of the public; however, it has also been noted that:

American public opinion has been radically transformed in a decade. ... the changes were neither the inevitable workings of history nor totally an informed people's logical response to events. The changes

[6] Joan Valdes and Jeane Crow, *The Media Works.* (Dayton: Pflaum/Standard, 1973), p. 100.

[7] *Ibid.,* p. 99.

were largely the cumulative consequences of thousands of newspaper, television and magazine stories.[8]

The moderating influence of the personal contacts people have with one another and of special interest groups notwithstanding, "The mass media still play a major role in the creation and the formation of public opinion."[9] How does this actually come about? One suggestion is that the public has become "homogenized" through constant exposure: "We are given the same things to think about, the same people to admire or ridicule, the same words and phrases with which to communicate, the same rhythms and sounds to groove with, the same fantasies to escape reality with, and the same goals to strive for."[10]

Mass media have national audiences and by constantly repeating selected themes via television, movies, newspapers and magazines, public opinion may gradually be molded and shaped by the media through exposure and reinforcement. As Sharkansky has pointed out, this can also affect the role of public policy makers:

The mass media—including newspapers, popular journals, radio, television—function as transmission belts between people and administrative units. The media also have their own influence on administrations—they help shape the agenda of public debate by emphasizing some issues and making them seem more important than others.[11]

Thus the mass media may not only direct the attention of the general public along certain lines but they may also play a major role in the formation of public policy as well. Such public policy may in turn have a great deal to do with what the police are expected to do and the means by which they are expected to carry out their responsibilities.

The shaping of public opinion by the media has undoubtedly had some major beneficial outcomes, such as the current widespread concern with problems of ecology (which had gone almost totally unnoticed until it became a favorite theme of the media). Astute reporting and the presentation of public debate on the ecology issue have probably gone a long ways towards enhancing the physical quality of our environment. Another example would be the media portrayal of political events. The

[8] Peter B. Clark, "The Opinion Machine: Intellectuals, The Mass Media, and American Government," in Harry M. Clor, ed., *The Mass Media and Modern Democracy*. (Chicago: Rand McNally College Publishing Co., 1974), pp. 37–84.

[9] Ralph H. Turner and Lewis M. Killian, *Collective Behavior*, 2d Ed. (Englewood Cliffs, New Jersey: Prentice-Hall, Inc., 1972), p. 214.

[10] Valdes and Crow, *op. cit.*, pp. 107–108.

[11] Ira Sharkansky, *Public Administration: Policy Making in Government Agencies*. (Chicago: Markham Publishing Company, 1970), p. 177.

media have underwritten political awareness through their journalistic efforts and there can be little doubt that the efforts of the media have contributed to the strengthening of our democratic ideals.

On the other hand, the molding of public opinion by the media has also created problems in some areas and may well have led public thinking astray in a number of important respects. This appears to be at least partially the case with the police.

The Mass Media and the Police Image

Have the mass media portrayed an accurate image of the police? If not, what have the consequences been of the image which they have projected? These are difficult questions to answer, as there is a lack of empirical evidence. However, the questions are sufficiently important that they merit serious consideration.

One of the issues that has been raised from time to time is whether or not the media portrayal of crime and violence has itself contributed to increases in crime and violence. The mass media have been accused of placing undue emphasis on crime, making it appear to be more common than it actually is, thus causing crime to loose its ugliness through familiarity.[12] The thesis that the media display more crime than really exists appears to have merit, for as one researcher has concluded:

> A sober look at the problem shows there is probably less crime today in the United States than existed a hundred, or fifty, or even twenty-five years ago, and that today the United States is a more lawful and safe country than popular opinion imagines.[13]

With respect to the question of whether or not the media actually *cause* crime, one would be hard pressed to find conclusive evidence establishing media content as a crime causing factor in and of itself. Yet, as one social scientist has said, "if media content does not lead directly to the commission of criminal acts, it may nonetheless be a major factor in shaping the public's view of crime problems."[14] This feeling that the media have shaped the public's opinions and understanding of crime has been reinforced by a number of writers.[15] These feelings are

[12] Virginia Lee Cole, *The Newspaper and Crime* (Columbia: University of Missouri Journalism Series No. 44, Masters Thesis, 1927), p. 60; cited in Elmer H. Johnson, *Crime, Correction and Society*. (Homewood, Illinois: The Dorsey Press, 1968), p. 112.

[13] Daniel Bell, "The Myth of Crime Waves," in *The End of Ideology*. (Glencoe, Ill.: The Free Press, 1960), Chapter 8, pp. 137–158.

[14] Edwin M. Schur, *Our Criminal Society*. (Englewood Cliffs, New Jersey: Prentice-Hall, Inc., 1969), p. 79.

[15] See for example Walter C. Reckless, *The Crime Problem*, 5th Ed. (New York: Appleton-Century-Crofts, 1973), pp. 400–401; see also Schur, *op. cit.*, p. 81.

based in part on media content analyses. For instance, one study conducted in 1967/68 analyzed the content of the shows aired during prime viewing hours by the three major television networks. They found that:

1. Violence occurred in eight out of ten programs;
2. Violence occurred in 93.5 percent of all cartoons directed at children;
3. More than half of the major characters were violent;
4. The "good guys" committed as much violence as the "bad guys";
5. The pain and suffering accompanying violence is rarely shown;
6. For every bystander who attempted to prevent violence there was another who assisted or encouraged it;
7. Nearly half of the killers suffered no consequences from their acts;
8. The majority of Americans interviewed believe that there is too much violence on television.[16]

Such massive emphasis on violence is believed by many to have had an impact on people's perception of violence.

This same process has probably also had an impact on public opinion of the police. One might well hypothesize that through the use of selective content in the news and entertainment media a distorted picture of the police has emerged. The presentation of crime and the police by the media, although they are analytically distinct, must nonetheless be considered as interrelated. That is, through the pairing of crime and the police by the media in specific situational contexts, they must be considered in conjunction with one another.

But just exactly what has happened? In the case of crime, the media has tended to show villains who are clearly bad—and who are bad pretty much because that's the way they want to be. By the same token, the police are usually shown as being very good (if not on strictly legal grounds then at least morally so)—and in the end, the police always win. In most police entertainment scenarios the plots are simple; in fact:

Experience with program ratings . . . has shown that the TV viewer doesn't want to ponder over a person or a situation, so people and their problems are reduced to their most obvious properties, and solutions are simple and final.[17]

The news media also tend to fall into the same trap, although most likely in an unsuspecting manner. The news they report tends to reflect what appear on the surface to be simple situations: homicides, robberies,

[16] Roger N. Johnson, *Aggression in Man and Animals*. (Philadelphia: W. B. Saunders Co., 1972), p. 155.
[17] Valdes and Crow, *op. cit.*, p. 122.

rapes and so on. However, the matter-of-fact reporting of the surface elements of these events in itself tends to oversimplify what are really complex situations and may in fact result in a distorted picture. For instance, the evening news on TV might carry the story of a homicide and an arrest. On the basis of both what is presented and what is not presented the viewer might be led to believe that the victim was "good," the offender "bad," and the police efficient. In reality, it could have been the case that the homicide was victim-precipitated and brought to the attention of the police by the offender.[18] The news media, however, have limitations on time and column inches so they must present a brief yet technically correct report, although in the process they may be distorting reality.

The entertainment media are prone to showing crimes as being exciting and crooks as being bad, and the police as being clever and heroic. That this may be in conflict with reality was pointed out by Menninger when he said that:

> Most criminal cases ... are dull. The dreary details of how some adolescents ... made off with somebody's automobile form a pattern of socio-legal difficulty that is repeated over and over with different names. Hundreds of bogus checks are tendered daily by improvident and immature boys and women to hundreds of careless or greedy shopkeepers, and some of these cases come to trial. All very dull.
>
> One cannot blame newspaper reporters for picking up the occasionally sensational or dramatic case and playing it up disproportionately.[19]

As was noted in Chapter 2, the President's Crime Commission even pointed out that partially as a result of the news and entertainment media "... the police have come to be viewed as a body of men continually engaged in the exciting, dangerous, and competitive enterprize of apprehending and prosecuting criminals." [20] And this image of both crime and the police is much like the mythical elephants' bone yard: much discussed but seldom encountered in reality.

How can such distorted images come to be so widely held? There are several possible explanations. In the first place, the plausible and the

[18] For a discussion of victim-precipitated homicide, see Marvin E. Wolfgang, "Victim-Precipitated Criminal Homicide," in Wolfgang, ed., *Studies in Homicide* (New York: Harper & Row, Publishers, 1967), pp. 72–87.

[19] Karl Menninger, *The Crime of Punishment* (New York: Viking Press, 1968), p. 97.

[20] Report of the President's Commission on Law Enforcement and the Administration of Justice, *Task Force Report: The Police.* (Washington, D.C.: Government Printing Office, 1967), p. 13.

implausible may be presented simultaneously with the hope that the former will validate the latter; for example:

> Reasonably true-to-life stories that are well within the realm of possibility suddenly present fight sequences that defy credence, where individuals inflict punishment on each other that no one could conceivably survive for more than a few seconds. In rapid order chairs that are bashed over heads will be ignored, punches that would fell elephants will be casually shrugged aside, and kicks ferocious enough to finish off any mortal will be greeted with no more than a momentary grunt from the hero. The pummeling will proceed resolutely for perhaps a minute or more until the villain succumbs.[21]

Another factor is that the entertainment media show something which the viewer can independently verify along with something which he cannot. For instance, the viewing audience is familiar with police officers and police cars: they often see them during the course of their daily activities. From time to time they see a police car running "emergency" with warning lights and siren (although usually without really knowing where the police are going or why). Television cops look like real cops, and so do their cars. Indeed, some TV police are exact duplicates of those found in actual cities (e.g., Los Angeles police, as in the TV show "Adam 12"). However, since the average viewer has only a limited experience with the police, he is not really in a position to question what the TV police are doing. If they *look* right and if what they do seems plausible enough, it must reflect reality—or so the faulty logic goes.

In chapter 3 it was pointed out that the programming of television content tends to be directed to the lower middle class. Yet both police and offenders portrayed on television seem to be largely middle-middle class or higher. One sees senior officers, such as police commissioners, captains, lieutenants, and at least one F.B.I. Inspector routinely involving themselves in investigative affairs (one might conclude their secretaries administer the departments). Even the crooks tend to be good looking, well spoken, and above average in intelligence. One might well suspect that this composite image serves several purposes. The first might be to lend credibility to the characters, for after all, doesn't a good appearance add to credibility? Perhaps a second reason would be that such a portrayal would serve to neutralize the police for purposes of entertainment. Lower middle class citizens may find contacts with the police to be mildly anxiety-provoking, yet the police they see on the television are so

[21] Herbert A. Bloch and Gilbert Geis, *Man, Crime, and Society*, 2d ed. (New York: Random House, 1970), p. 220.

presented as to not be a stimulus to anxiety. They are, after all, dealing at a social level beyond the scope of the average viewer and thus are nonthreatening. Perhaps it is easier for the solidly middle class viewer to identify with the cast of characters if they are shown as embodying middle class standards and values. At any rate, since the average person has only a limited concept of what the police do, the media are relatively free to present them in a somewhat unrealistic light and to do so without being challenged. This is not to imply that viewers actually believe the plots which are portrayed; however, they may well believe the procedures and methods they see the television or movie police using to solve their crimes.

How have the foregoing processes contributed to the actual function and structure of police departments? Manning has suggested that:

> In an effort to gain the public's confidence in their ability, and to insure thereby the solidity of their mandate, the police have encouraged the public to continue thinking of them and their work in idealized terms, terms, that is, which grossly exaggerate the actual work done by the police.[22]

He goes on to say that the public has responded by "demanding even more dramatic crook-catching" and that the public demand for arrests "has been converted into an index for measuring how well the police accomplish their mandate."[23] As a consequence, police efficiency has come in general to be measured by arrests, both in quantity and quality. The prestige of a policeman within his department is often a function of his ability to engage in what is considered to be the most significant of police activities: arrests.

Good arrests are unquestionably important; however, good police work should also involve other considerations as well. A good policeman is not merely a good law enforcement agent—he is also sensitive, understanding, and compassionate, in spite of the fact that such traits are not usually associated with the tough image idealized by the media (and adopted by many officers).

The emphasis on efficient police work (as measured by good arrests) has produced two problems. The first is that policemen must somehow adapt to what police work is *really* like most of the time: dull, monotonous, and clerical. The second problem is that the strong emphasis on arrests as a remedy for criminal conduct overlooks the dynamics behind

---

[22] Peter K. Manning, "The Policeman as Hero," cited in Isidore Silver, ed., *The Crime Control Establishment.* (Englewood Cliffs, New Jersey: Prentice-Hall, Inc., 1974), p. 100.
[23] *Ibid.*

many offenses. This results in the police repeatedly dealing with what are actually social problems but at a rather superficial level which fairly well assures their ultimate failure—at least on a long-term basis.

Also, by constantly stressing their law enforcement role, the media (and the police themselves) may well be avoiding recognition of the service role they also perform. By ignoring this role the police may in the process fail to develop the sophistication which the effective performance of the service role demands. This has become somewhat evident in the several years following the major urban riots of the mid and late 1960's. During this period of time large amounts of money have been spent on riot equipment, communications gear and other operational hardware while at the same time little recognition has been made of the social and economic bases of the disorders by police planners.

The Police, the Public and the Media

As a traditionally quasi-military agency, the police in most cities have been prone to performing their operations in relative secrecy. This has been done to assure the security of officers, informants, victims and others. In addition, restraints on the release of information are guided by the need to avoid prejudicial pretrial publicity by police officers which could jeopardize an upcoming case.

The controlled release of information to the media may also directly serve the interests of the police department and can have an effect on the image which the police presents to the public. For all of these reasons the police have traditionally sought to control the manner in which news is released about the department and its activities. Perhaps an additional factor in the regulation of the information released by the police is that although they gather very large amounts of data, many police departments find themselves in the position of not really knowing what they have or what to do with it. The non-release of information may thus serve the function of permitting the police department to look better organized than in reality it is.

Police secrecy is a problem which in some cities has resulted in a confusion of goals with the means by which they are to be accomplished. The use of secrecy to enhance police operations may thus be subverted to the use of secrecy as a goal in itself. A case in point is the Milwaukee Police Department.[24] In a report concerning that department, it was stated that:

[24] See *Police Isolation and Community Needs*, Report of the Wisconsin State Commission on Civil Rights, Percy L. Julian, Jr., Chairman, December, 1972.

The Milwaukee Police Department is not accessible to the people it serves. Most observers attributed this to Chief Brier's narrow definition of police work, in which he views himself as the official expert who needs no outside views.

The non-access pervades all aspects of police duty. According to a former community leader on the near south side, a group of police officers asked the Spanish Center for help in learning Spanish. A program was set up, but the officers suddenly withdrew because of pressure from the administration. An official of the Commission on Community Relations reports that in 1968 two police officers attended a meeting dealing with racial problems in a north side school. The principal black spokesmen at that meeting indicated their approval of this first expression of concern by the police. It was also the last, for the chief castigated the blacks for their rudeness and prohibited further participation by his officers.

... Suggestions from the lower ranks reportedly are routinely turned down; a proposed patrolman's handbook of functional Spanish phrases was one such victim.

Recitation of anecdotes depicting departmental unconcern could continue indefinitely. The list of those who have attempted in vain to meet with the department include, in addition to most community organizations in the city:

  —The Kerner Commission
  —Committees of the State Legislature
  —Kenneth Bowen, Community Relations Specialist of the Fire
    and Police Commission
  —The Social Development Commission
  —The American Civil Liberties Union
  —Milwaukee Aldermen
  —The State Attorney General
  —The State Crime Laboratory
  —The Professional Policemen's Protective Association
  —The Police Education Study Committee [25]

It was further noted that "In Milwaukee, no person or agency in a position of authority over law enforcement has demonstrated a willingness to discuss police policy with citizens." [26] Finally, the report disclosed that:

It was our judgment, having talked to the community groups in Milwaukee, that there was a great deal of frustration among people,

[25] *Ibid.*, pp. 85–86.
[26] *Ibid.*, p. 11.

the black community certainly, but not only the black community, with the fact that if there were issues, there was no one in the political structure in Milwaukee willing to talk about the problem. But the position taken by the Police Department was that there was nothing to talk about. That either they had no responsibility for developing law enforcement policy or if they did, it was not a matter which they were willing to discuss with the citizens.[27]

The police are in effect a sub-system within a broader municipal system. As a subsystem they have functional responsibilities within their areas of competency. However, at the same time the police are interrelated with all of the other subsystems in the city. In order for the police to perform their roles at an optimal level of effectiveness they must remain in firm contact with their constituency, which includes in one form or another nearly every one else in the city. The media provide the vehicle whereby the police can do this.

It is therefore important for the media to fairly and accurately report the activities of the police. By the same token, the police must themselves be open, honest, and accessible. Matters of security need not be compromised in order for the police to be candid with the public.

Finally, police executives should carefully consider the impact of the distorted image of the police which is so often presented by the media and should encourage the media to provide a clear and honest portrayal of the police, both as an agency and in the activities of its individual officers.

The need for an open interchange of communications between the police and the residents of the city has been the basis for the development of community relations programs in a number of cities. However, even in this area there has been some confusion between goals and means. Some community relations divisions within police agencies have been used as propaganda agencies to extoll the virtues of the police and to condemn the faults of citizens who fail to "support your local police." For a community relations activity to be legitimate, it should be based upon an honest desire to inform the public and in turn to be informed by them. One very significant goal of police-community relations programs should be to bring the public an increased awareness of the many tasks performed by the police. Such programs should appeal to a variety of audiences, each according to its unique needs. This would include efforts directed at the young or the old, ethnic or racial minorities, the business community, and others. The reading which accompanies this chapter is taken from the report of the Task Force on Police of the President's Crime Commission and discusses such programs.

[27] *Ibid.*

Appendix A
Special Police—Community Relations Programs*

Besides citizen advisory committees, existing community relations activities normally are of three types: programs to educate the public concerning some aspects of police work, programs to prevent crimes, and programs to provide services other than law enforcement to the community. These programs may be run by community relations units, advisory committees, public information officers, juvenile squads, or line officers. Each activity must be analyzed on the basis of the target population, the expectations as to what will be accomplished with that group, and a judgment whether the return is worth the expenditure of effort.

Public Education Programs

Citizens who distrust the police will not easily be converted by information programs they consider to come from a tainted source. However, even for these groups, long-term education based upon honest and free dialogue between the police and the public can have an effect. Indeed, this is one of the basic goals of the citizen advisory committees.

On the other hand, citizens who are neutral or supportive can benefit from increased understanding of the complicated problems and tasks of the police. Informational programs can also generate support for more personnel, salary increases, sufficient equipment, and other resources to improve the efficiency of police work. It can help the cooperative citizen to avoid becoming a victim of crime and show him how to work more effectively with the police. And, to the extent that the police department is genuinely working at improved community relations, dissemination of this information to the press and other media does have a positive effect on community relations.

Contacts with Civic Organizations and Individuals

Most police departments (95 percent in the Michigan State survey) readily accept speaking invitations to appear before civic organizations. Many run a speaker's bureau with a list of officers who can speak on specialized subjects such as narcotics, the canine corps, or traffic control. The San Diego bureau, for example, offers a choice of 35 speakers and is supervised by the community relations unit; the St. Louis speakers bureau makes an average of 50 speeches monthly; and St. Louis, Chicago, Philadelphia, and Oakland have pamphlets available on police topics.

The Michigan State survey found, however, that the speakers are not always chosen to fit the level of sophistication of the group; different or-

* From *Task Force Report: The Police*, President's Commission on Law Enforcement and The Administration of Justice, Nicholas deB Katzenbach, Chairman. Washington, D.C.: GPO, 1967, pp. 159–163.

ganizations may require a precinct commander, a patrolman, a community relations expert, or a college-trained administrator. Too often the topics offered are noncontroversial, and, if important, constitute merely a recitation of a department's outstanding programs. The survey found that many of the speakers were hesistant to engage in debate on police policies or to acknowledge possible departmental error. The groups with which the police had most contact were business or civic organizations. As a Philadelphia police inspector told the University of California survey:

[A]ny time I've ever attended a community meeting, I don't care what you try to get across, * * * they're not the people you want to get it across to, because they're not the problem.

Police departments, through community relations units and precinct community relations personnel, should attempt to maintain close liaison with, not merely make occasional speeches to, organizations of most importance to community relations. Active efforts should be made to reach out to low-income groups. The topics which interest these people may be the ones closest to their everyday experience, i.e., police protection in the area, arrest policies, and others. For the same reason, close contact should be maintained with militant civil rights organizations, civil liberties unions, and the like. The mere presence of a police officer in front of such a group, willing to listen and to explain, can have a positive effect by dispelling stereotypes of the police probably accepted by many in the audience.

For example, in San Diego, the lieutenant in charge of the community relations unit is personally involved in the Citizens Interracial Committees, the National Conference of Christians and Jews, and the citywide and neighborhood committees of the local antipoverty agency. His assistant works with the Student Non-Violent Coordinating Committee, other Negro civil rights groups, and the American Civil Liberties Union.

In addition to maintaining contact with community organizations, personnel should be in contact on the street with persons who do not belong to civic organizations. As a police captain in a Washington, D.C., slum neighborhood has said:

I feel their attitude could be changed—especially the younger ones. We've got to reach the people who don't go to meetings, or to church. * * * At one time, the man on the beat was the best source. But now we just don't have enough men for regular beats.

The people who do not belong to organizations—including, no doubt, the young men who cause the police the most difficulty—are probably in the majority in high-crime neighborhoods.

Tours, Cruises, and Demonstrations

In many cities, the public is offered tours of headquarters, demonstrations of police equipment, and rides in police cars on patrol. In St. Louis, there is an annual invitation for school children and citizen groups to come to police headquarters; and police cadets conduct tours for 1,000 persons a month. An annual open house with special demonstrations of police equipment, canine corps, and defense tactics is staged in each district. High school and college students ride in police cars on patrol. New York City has experimented with a police-citizen art show at the precinct to show the people that "they are welcome and * * * can have friendships [there]."

It is difficult to evaluate the effect of such attempts to broaden civilian understanding of the police. Although such programs can help the public understand the problems encountered daily by a policeman, it must be acknowledged that the public who responds to such programs is probably not the public involved in police-community tensions. In short, such efforts can be of some assistance but should never be allowed to become the core of a community relations program.

Police-Community Relations Institutes

Police departments, often under the sponsorship of private organizations, participate in institutes with the public on the subject of community relations. The St. Louis department participated in an institute sponsored by the NAACP in 1966 with police representation from every district. The Dayton department in 1965 participated in such an institute organized by the Human Relations Commission for 40 of its command personnel and 83 community leaders; and Texas A. & M. University holds such an institute for police and community leaders from 4 neighboring States. These institutes give the police and community representatives a concentrated block of time together to explore their problems in depth.

On the other hand, institutes lack the continuity and followup of an advisory committee that meets regularly. A combination of the two techniques involving many of the same participants holds promise. The institutes can help make the participation of community leaders and police officers in neighborhood or citywide advisory committees more effective. For maximum value, the institutes, like the committees, should include representatives of the poor from high-crime areas, as well as high and lesser ranking police personnel, and the discussion must be candid and nondefensive.

Institutes held on a neighborhood basis are valuable in reaching persons not affiliated with organizations. For example, with the cooperation of local ministers, the Philadelphia community relations unit has initiated a series of neighborhood meetings in high-tension areas. The audience is broken into small discussion groups led by a district police officer to discuss neighborhood police problems.

With the assistance of a financial grant from the Department of Justice, the Newark Police Department is bringing together 150 of its men of the rank of sergeant and below with 150 residents of the poverty districts, mainly young men between 20 and 30, to discuss problems between the police and community. The participants consider high-tension situations by playing out the roles natural to them in such encounters and accompany each other on police patrol and community activities. Expert lecturers address the group on the effects of poverty, the causes of criminal behavior, and intergroup reactions. The program, to cover 25 hours over a 10-week period, will be evaluated through analyses of the participants' attitudes before and after the sessions.

With financing from the Office of Juvenile Delinquency in the Department of Health, Education, and Welfare, Boston has already completed a program of 12 weekly informal discussions in the Roxbury area between 18 residents (representing a cross-section of the neighborhood, including 2 juveniles and a mother on welfare) and 10 policemen (including a captain and 4 sergeants). Detailed interviews showed that while only a few participants changed their points of view, all seemed able to discuss police-community problems on a basis of friendship and honesty by the end of the program and most learned about the problems of the other group.

School Programs

Over 80 percent of the departments in the Michigan State survey ran special school programs to tell pupils about police work or to explain special laws or problems which affect young citizens. The aim of such efforts is to portray the policeman as a community helper, rather than as an antagonist.

The St. Louis school program is one of the most complete. It begins in Headstart preschool classes when a patrolman comes to talk to the children about crossing streets safely; continues in grades one through four with more advanced talks and films on pedestrian conduct; and in grades five through eight provides further instruction on the role and duties of a police officer, and a special tour of police headquarters. A "Say Hi" program gives membership cards to school children who wave or yell "hi" to policemen they see. In high school, a Negro professional football player from the St. Louis Cardinals acts as a community relations consultant and, accompanied by an officer who is usually the district commander, narrates a film on police work. Social science classes are assisted by the district citizens committees to organize small-group field projects which may involve working with the police in such tasks as assisting juvenile officers in delinquency prevention programs. District and citywide prizes are offered for the best reports on these projects. A youth council composed of five representatives from each high school meets with police officials five times a year to plan the school programs. Selected high school and college students also ride in unmarked police cars with officers chosen at random and instructed to answer all questions.

The New York City police have experimented with comic books on police work, training courses for elementary school teachers, and composition and drawing assignments for the children on the role of the policeman as their friend. Programs in other departments include: intensive 4-day courses, with field trips, on police work in all six grades of high-crime area schools in one precinct (Washington, D.C.); provision of officers to answer the questions of teenage panels at open meetings (Washington, D.C.), integrated two-man teams visit schools on an informal basis to discuss students' conceptions of the police (Kansas City, Mo.); participation in a month-long law enforcement unit for grades five through eight featuring posters, student interviews with policemen, essay contests, panel discussions, and precinct tours (Gilroy, Calif.); and junior and senior high school programs taught by qualified police instructors on specific police topics such as curfew regulations, arrest laws, and use of force (San Diego, Calif.).

How much and for how long the appearance of a friendly policeman in the classroom affects pupil attitudes will vary. Those who already see the police as friends will receive confirmation in the schools. Those who have had hostile or threatening encounters on the street, or whose family or friends have had direct conflicts with the police, will often be skeptical.

In the upper grades, the police lecturer may perform an educational function if he informs juveniles of the laws which affect their conduct, the police criteria for stopping or taking juveniles into custody, and the kind of processing a juvenile goes through as well as its effects in later life. His account must, however, square with the facts of street life as the ghetto or slum teenager knows them, and the policeman must be willing to discuss frankly the complaints of the students. If the police officers try to convince students of ideas inconsistent with their experience, the result may be to make them more distrustful and cynical than before. For example, in Philadelphia, a settlement house had to discontinue a program that taught juveniles about due process of law because what they were taught did not conform to their own experiences.

The participation of nonpolice experts in designing courses is indispensable if they are to justify either the school's or the police department's time. For example, the University of Cincinnati under a Law Enforcement Assistance Act grant is developing a model curriculum on law enforcement for permanent use in Cincinnati schools. Scheduled for trial in 1967, the unit's success in molding constructive attitudes toward the police will be evaluated by student and teacher interviews. While more modest in scope, the same kind of intensive curriculum development is needed as has been occurring in the science field under the leadership of the National Science Foundation.

Crime Prevention Programs

It suffices here to recognize that programs can be useful to build support with citizens already favorably disposed toward the police. For either as individuals or in organizations like civic groups and neighborhood advisory committees, citizens can be involved in aiding the police.

In addition, the University of California study found a police reserve program in San Diego useful for community relations. Two hundred reserves, of whom 25 are Negroes, aid the regular force by working at special events and by accompanying 1-man patrols. The result is that members of minority groups and police officers have developed greater respect for each other.

Community Service Programs

Routine police duty involves many kinds of assistance to the public which has nothing to do with crime. Help in getting emergency aid for injured or sick persons, animal and human rescue missions, suicide prevention, redirecting confused or lost travelers, finding missing persons—all these are community relations activities in the truest sense of the word and are rendered on an ad hoc basis. For example, a New York City policeman who had been recently accused of brutality was cheered by a Negro crowd after he successfully saved a newborn infant's life.

It is sometimes suggested that at least some of the service functions can be more efficiently handled by one or more specialized government agencies which would allow the police to concentrate more fully on activities more directly related to combatting crime. However, "[p]olice time spent in furthering good relations may be justified even if it does not contribute directly to law enforcement." As an English author has written in answer to the argument that the rendering of services is not part of the duties and functions of the police:

> The answer is that the friendliness, confidence, respect, trust and affection that they receive from the people are almost the sole basis of the power and efficiency of the police of Britain.

Recreation Programs

Several police departments or citizen advisory committees sponsor Boy Scout Explorer troops, specializing in police-related subjects. In Washington, D.C., and New York City, officers escort boys and girls from minority neighborhoods on tours to local showplaces and ballgames, and give Christmas parties and dinners for them.

Police athletic leagues and boys clubs are common. In many cases, the funds for these activities must be solicited on a volunteer basis by the policemen themselves. The Police Boys Club in Washington, D.C., for example, has 8,300 members and includes baseball, football, basketball, and track teams; it operates on a $400,000 budget, has a full-time officer from each precinct assigned to it, and has both police and civilian volunteers. These kinds of programs have broad support from the police; a recent survey found that 75 percent of police officers believed that police agencies should operate such recreational programs.

Police-sponsored recreational programs have been criticized on the grounds that they overlap recreation department efforts; police solicitation of funds is said to raise question of propriety; and the boys who participate are not the kind who would get into trouble anyway. Such problems, however, if they exist can be overcome.

Police recreational programs offer opportunities to improve relations with children and their parents. They can change the negative image of the police in slum neighborhoods. As one Negro teenager in Washington said after a visit to the Police Boys Club:

> [S]ometimes, when you go down there you see polices there boxing. * * * I didn't even know it was a police til somebody told me. He looked just like a teenager to me. * * * I didn't even know police take up activity like that. I didn't think they care for nothing like that. I just think they care for getting drunks and beating them in the head and all that kind of stuff.

The effort should be concentrated with the poorest children, minority groups, and when possible, youngsters with past records of delinquency or misconduct. For example, in Washington, D.C., a baseball league in each precinct consisted of half precinct officers and half hard-core delinquents. The programs should be financed by means other than police fund solicitation. And they should be manned, whenever possible, with police officers, not paid staff or civilian volunteers, even if extra time or pay allowances are necessary.

Social Services to the Poor, Exoffenders, and Other Citizens

Many people think of the police first when they are in any kind of trouble; as a result, police departments frequently must relay complaints and refer persons to other government agencies. Information and complaint bureaus are set up in some police departments to guide the confused citizen through the bureaucratic maze of municipal government. This kind of public service should be expanded so that police who observe conditions on patrol that require attention from other agencies—uncollected garbage, locked playgrounds, housing code violations, consumer frauds—would take the initiative in reporting them to the appropriate agency. Although police personnel are already overextended in most communities, this valuable service could be performed for the most part by the community service officers discussed in chapter 5.

A few departments have become deeply involved in remedial work with the social and economic problems of residents. In San Francisco, the community relations unit has assigned six full-time community relations officers to the Economic Opportunity Council and to the Youth Opportunities Center of the U.S. Employment Service to help boys with police records to secure jobs. It has also taken on cases like the following:

1. A mother came to the office of the police-community relations unit with her daughter who had recently failed a civil service examination for clerk-typist. The mother informed the officers that she had attended several public meetings of the unit and wondered if they could help her. The officers conducted an investigation into the educational deficiencies of the young woman and made the necessary arrangements for enrolling her in an adult training center to correct these deficiencies.

2. Several complaints were received by the police-community relations unit that recreation facilities were inadequate for many youths, especially in minority group neighborhoods. It was felt that this lack of recreation caused many youths to commit crimes, particularly on weekends. The unit contacted recreation officials in the city and arranged to have the recreation centers remain open for part of the weekend and provided police volunteers to staff and supervise the activities.

The Atlanta Police Department also has assigned policemen to antipoverty centers as youth counselors to help juveniles obtain available services. "Operation Help" in Honolulu has a social worker on police call to help with the problems of juveniles brought to the station.

Active police involvement in what may be labeled "social work" programs raises profound questions about the role of the police. The traditional view espoused by most departments surveyed by Michigan State was that the police should stick to the role of preventing crime and enforcing the law; few regarded the "causes" of crime as their concern. Many police officials feel that they do not have resources to spare for any new functions and other persons criticize the lack of expertise of police officers to do social work.

On the other hand, new roles might well be welcomed by police officers. A survey of police officers found that over 65 percent believed that juvenile officers should try to find jobs for older juveniles who come to their attention. A Commission survey of police officers in eight precincts in three large cities found that the thing most liked about police work was the "feeling that comes from helping people." Forty-three percent of the officers considered this the thing that they liked best and 70 percent made it one of their first three choices.

In fact, police officers now spend much of their time in "social work" roles. They attempt to settle disputes between spouses and between neighbors, counsel children about attending school and obeying their parents, and decide when to make arrests for nonserious offenses, partially on the basis of whether the criminal process will be likely to help the individual or society.

Plainly, police service programs cannot be of sufficient size to solve the "causes" underlying criminality. But an expanded police role must be judged not only by whether it alleviates social conditions, but also whether it assists the police in improving community relations. Significantly, the Michigan State survey has found that the San Francisco program has probably been more successful in reaching the hard-core poor and members of minority groups, and changing their image of the police from an adversary to a friendly one, than any other community relations program.

These programs point the way toward a reevaluation of the basic police role which may have a more significant long-term effect than merely improvement of the police image. The possibility has been suggested that eventually the police may become part of a broader social service team which will include social workers, psychiatrists, and doctors acting as an intake screening unit for all kinds of antisocial or disturbing conduct. Individual decisions would then be made on what should be done with each case—whether the man should be processed through court, treated at a hospital or mental health clinic, or given social counseling and help in finding a job or in going back to school. Besides its other merits, the effect would be to improve police-community relations by reducing the adversary role of the police and by making them part of a broader process than merely arrest and conviction. Consequently, increased experimentation with new helping roles for the policemen, especially with youths and exoffenders, is promising.

At the same time, precinct stations might well be a part of community service centers. Meeting halls and athletic facilities could be opened to the public; other services, such as employment assistance or family counseling, could be in adjoining offices. While the consolidation of precincts is reducing the number of police buildings, small police centers—manned by sworn police officers and community service officers—might be part of other public and private service facilities. The result of such programs would be to reduce the separation of the police from the community.

Because of their insight into crime-breeding conditions, police officers and their organizations should be in the forefront of groups seeking legislation and other means to provide housing, employment, and recreational facilities, improve the schools, and otherwise overcome poverty and discrimination. Occasionally, police officials have taken such leadership. For example, the executive committee of the Michigan Association of Chiefs of Police recommended:

That the people of Michigan must oppose segregation in housing and education, because it creates distress for all who are entitled to the responsible exercise of their freedom, and creates tension which reduces the ability of the police to serve all people;

That the people of Michigan must protect their liberty by providing equal opportunities for employment, limited only by fitness and ability, so that every race and persuasion may enjoy the fruits of our prosperity, and so that one of the causes of poverty and crime may be reduced * * *.

Such police support, besides serving other beneficial purposes, is in the self-interest of police officers themselves since poverty and discrimination are basic causes of much of the hostility toward the police. As Vice President Humphrey told the 1966 annual convention of the International Association of Chiefs of Police: "[Y]ou're the ones that have to deal with the results of the social problems on the streets. You men are the ones who must stand there and be pelted with rocks." The Vice President's suggestion that the police support proposals to overcome these problems offers the opportunity for the police and civil rights and poverty groups, which have often been in tragic conflict, to join in a program of common interest.

10

Police Corruption and Police
Reform in the City

One of the most pressing concerns in contemporary law enforcement is the growing evidence of widespread corruption in the police departments of America's large central cities. The problem is not at all new, but has in recent years become increasingly visible to social scientists, political leaders, and the general public. For example, since 1960 at least a dozen departments in major urban areas have been tainted by the discovery of organized burglary rings among their own officers.[1] A defense commonly offered by departments in such circumstances has been that a few "bad apples" were allowed into the departmental barrel, and could easily be thrown out.[2] The great *extent* to which graft and other forms of corruption could exist and be routinely accepted by members of a big city police department was brought home with stunning impact by the report of the Knapp Commission in New York City.

During the Lindsey administration in New York, two policemen complained first to the Mayor's office and then to the press that they had been repeatedly exposed to corruption and invited to participate in illegal activities. In 1970, the Mayor appointed a civilian commission, headed by Whitman Knapp, to investigate charges of police corruption in the city department. The commission spent two and a half years conducting its inquiry.[3] Its report indicated a pattern of "widespread corruption" in the New York department. Investigators found evidence that bribery and kickbacks were accepted on a massive scale, that illegal activities in the city were protected by the police, that organized burglary rings operated in the department, and that illegal tactics were commonly used to clear cases—e.g., planted weapons and planted narcotics. To be sure, the corrupt activities were not evenly distributed in the department. The

[1] The departments have included Denver, Colorado; Chicago, Illinois; Nassau County, New York; Des Moines, Iowa; Nashville and Memphis, Tennessee; Birmingham, Alabama; Cleveland, Ohio; Bristol, Connecticut; Burlington, Vermont; and Miami, Florida. See Thomas Barker and Julian Roebuck, *An Empirical Typology of Police Corruption* (Springfield, Illinois: Charles C. Thomas, 1973), p. 36n. The report of the Knapp Commission also indicates burglary activities in the New York department. See *The Knapp Commission Report on Police Corruption* (New York: George Braziller, 1972), pp. 45–46 & 185. See also Lawrence W. Sherman, Ed., *Police Corruption: A Sociological Perspective* (Garden City: Anchor Press/Doubleday, 1974).

[2] See Barker and Roebuck, pp. 35–36 & 36n. Also see *Knapp Commission Report*, pp. 6–7.

[3] *Knapp Commission Report*, pp. 35–41.

commission found that the great majority of the officers involved within the department accepted corrupt benefits on only a small scale. Those who accepted graft in large amounts ("meateaters" in the jargon of the department) were a minority. Yet the "meateaters" were sheltered from exposure by the silence and acquiescence of virtually the entire department.[4]

An Analytical Approach to Corruption

The pattern of police corruption revealed in New York has also been exposed in other major urban departments as well, and the study of corruption is increasingly becoming a topic of empirical research by social scientists. In an effort to draw together a framework for empirical analysis, Thomas Barker and Julian Roebuck have catalogued the forms that police corruption may take.[5] For each type of corruption, their model identified the most likely agents of corruption and the degree to which the corrupt activity was likely to be condoned by members of a department. In all, they identified eight types of corruption:

(1) *Corruption of Authority*—by accepting gratuities such as free meals, rooms, sex, liquor, etc.; also, by acceptance of "finders fees" from burglary victims and bounties from bondsmen. The corruptor in such instances is usually the "honest" businessman or citizen, and the acceptance of such gratuities or payments is probably very widely practiced and condoned among members of urban police departments.

(2) *Kickbacks*—from towing companies, taxicabs, service stations, moving companies, trucking firms, etc. Again, the benefits are taken from "honest" sectors of the public who stand to benefit from a good working relationship with the police and from access to police information.

(3) *Opportunistic Theft*—of unprotected or confiscated property, for instance from accident scenes or from burglary sites.

(4) *Shakedowns*—acceptance of bribes in return for not making an arrest or issuing a citation.

(5) *Protection of Illegal Activities*—both criminal and legitimate businesses may pay for freedom to operate illegally. Examples of legitimate businesses operating illegally include stores violating blue laws and trucking firms running overweight trucks or using illegal routes. Illegal busi-

[4] *Ibid.*, pp. 4–5 & 65.
[5] See Barker and Roebuck, pp. 21–42.

nesses which seek protection include those dealing in narcotics, gambling, and prostitution.

(6) *The Fix*—in which the policeman accepts a bribe for helping to quash prosecution, for giving inadequate testimony, or for "taking up" citations such as traffic tickets.

(7) *Direct Criminal Activities*—such as organized burglary, extortion, or sale of narcotics.

(8) *Internal Payoffs*—in which one police officer purchases illegal favors from another. Examples include bribes paid to superior officers in return for assignment to lucrative posts, and the purchase of evidence to be used in setting up a shakedown. Barker and Roebuck suggest that internal payoffs are the symptom of very advanced corruption in a department, an indication that graft has become very pervasive and is accepted as a legitimate medium of exchange among the members of the department.

The paradigm developed by Barker and Roebuck focuses particularly upon activities through which the policeman may obtain illicit material benefits. In this sense, their definition of "corrupt" gain may be too narrow. The police officer who plants evidence on suspects in order to better his record for clearing cases also gains from illegal activities. When patrolmen fail to enforce traffic violations against those downtown businessmen who *expect* favored treatment, the officers benefit in the sense that they avoid conflict and curry favor with a politically influential segment of the public. One may even regard the sadistic pleasure which some officers obtain from beating up helpless victims as a sort of personal gain. For the present, attention will be concentrated on the problem of graft—corruption for *financial* gain.

From another perspective, acceptance of gratuities from businessmen might not appropriately be considered corruption unless an officer somehow uses his position to extract favors that would not be given if he did not take the initiative in seeking them. After all, numerous other occupational groups also receive special considerations from business firms.

What has become increasingly apparent during recent years is that "corrupt" activities among the police are largely controlled by social norms within the police departments themselves, and are not systematically checked by any formal authority or regulations based on democratic legal norms. It is the police themselves who will draw a distinction between "clean" and "dirty" money obtained through graft, and who will impose upon their colleagues whatever sanctions are to be imposed. For example, Barker and Roebuck suggest that most departments would condone the acceptance of gratuities and kickbacks from "honest" sectors of the public, and would not take opportunistic theft in small amounts very seriously. They suggest that rank-and-file officers in most departments would consider graft obtained from direct criminal activities or from narcotics operations to be "dirty money." However, the Knapp Commission warned that the theft and sale of narcotics by officers in the New York department, and the acceptance of bribes for protecting narcotics operations, were becoming increasingly widespread and legitimate among the rank-and-file of that department. The change in orientation was attributed to "more relaxed attitudes toward drugs, particularly among young people, and the enormous profits to be derived from drug traffic." [6]

It is impossible to know how widespread police corruption is in each of its various forms. Reliable information concerning corrupt activities of policemen is simply not available on a large scale. However, the findings of the Knapp Commission, the continuing operation of large vice rings in major urban areas, and the repeated exposures of criminal rings within large municipal departments all suggest that the more serious forms of corruption are fairly common.

Obviously, big city police departments have not been very successful at correcting internal corruption on their own initiative.[7] The informal norms of the departments usually include a strict rule of silence where the misbehavior of their own members is concerned. Internal security divisions have generally failed to check corrupt activities, either because their members are drawn from the department at large and share the prevailing defensive norms, or because they are attacked and harassed when they are too active. When scandals have broken, department chiefs have usually taken the lead in blaming a few "bad apples" for the trouble, and in arguing that the misguided few are in no way symptomatic of major internal problems. Even honest police administrators seem reluctant to expose the inner workings of their departments to public scrutiny, perhaps out of fear that they would themselves be punished for the malfeasance of their men.

The Impact of the City

The continuing pattern of corruption in urban departments poses a nauseating dilemma for the American democratic polity. The conven-

[6] *Knapp Commission Report*, pp. 92–93.

[7] For example, see Alan Edward Bent's description of an investigation of malpractice in the Memphis department in *The Politics of Law Enforcement* (Lexington, Mass.: D.C. Heath and Company), pp. 127–140. Also see the *Knapp Commission Report*, pp. 10–11.

tional wisdom of American politics holds that the decentralization of authority leads to democratic control of government operations by local communities, but the facts of administration and management in many urban police departments suggest that police corruption is to a large extent a *product of* urban political systems. That is, the deviational behavior of policemen represents a response to a confluence of social and political forces which arise from within the urban milieu. Typically, the urban police officer works in an organization characterized by such a heavy insulation against external political and social forces that it might well serve to shape his opinions toward law enforcement. He is confronted by immense frustrations in his attempts to enforce the law, and by equally immense opportunities for illegal or dishonest personal gain.

The opportunities which the city presents to the policeman for graft and self-aggrandizement are staggering in both variety and scope. It is in the large city that the police officer will find the major market for syndicated gambling, drug consumption, and prostitution, for illegal business operations, for organized burglary rings, for tow-truck and traffic kickbacks, etc. It is therefore also in the large city that he will find the hordes of frightened or opportunistic businessmen who will offer him substantial gratuities in return for favored treatment. Of course, the opportunities for graft are not equally available to all members of a department. The most lucrative opportunities will usually be found in the area of vice operations and drugs, and the detectives assigned responsibility for these areas have generally shown the greatest tendency toward corruption.[8] However, every member of a department will realize sooner or later that he can develop the opportunities if he can only achieve the needed rank or functional assignment.

The frustrations for the urban policeman, equally imposing in scope, include at least the following:

(1) *Involuntary Nonfeasance*—He cannot possibly pursue every violation of which he is aware, and he often must protect known criminals who serve as informers.

(2) *Inability to Compensate for Other Agents of Social Control*—He cannot correct the errors which schools, families, or churches may have made in their efforts to socialize young people. He cannot overcome the consequences of corrupt or ineffective courts or correctional institutions. He cannot through his own efforts compensate for ineffective social service agencies which are charged with alleviating poverty, drug addiction, alcoholism, or family trauma.

(3) *Political Manipulation*—He is often the victim of political exploitation. Patronage may still be a major criterion for employment and promotion, and the use of police departments as political "footballs" still offers

[8] Bent, p. 9, and *Knapp Commission Report*, pp. 1–2.

a strongly emotional topic to ambitious political candidates. Also, political leaders may sporadically intervene in the management of a department in an effort to change its enforcement priorities.

(4) *Low Status*—Both salaries and prestige for most urban police departments are still low. The policeman is still regarded by most Americans as a blue collar worker who cannot be very bright, and who is frightening because he possesses the legitimate authority to use coercive force.

Should he engage in corrupt activities, the policeman usually finds himself insulated from control and supervision by authorities outside of the department. The insulation of the department from external controls will include at least three major components: (1) the closed social system within the department itself; (2) an absence of constructive supervision from other legitimate agents of public policy; and (3) a public which is not oriented to professional police service.

The Police Department as a Closed System. The tremendous solidarity of the large urban police department reflects the impact of both formal and informal norms. Intense social interaction may be facilitated through a widely shared orientation to "machismo," a "locker room" attitude toward sexual matters, or a shared jargon.[9] The resulting peer group loyalties are reinforced by formal rules of recruitment, training, and promotion. Career systems in the urban departments are usually rigidly closed. Community residence requirements for entry and localized retirement systems discourage lateral mobility at any level. As a result, most supervisory personnel are recruited from within, even though they may have the same marginal educations they had when they entered the departments as recruits. The young recruits, who are the main source of new personnel, are given minimal formal training and are expected to "learn the ropes" mainly through interaction with more seasoned officers. Of course, the senior personnel are then in a position to socialize the recruit, teaching him the prevailing norms of secrecy, defensive solidarity, and indulgence toward the misbehavior of fellow officers. Those recruits who fail to respond may be readily identified by the senior men and may be socially isolated. Given the "silent treatment" by fellow officers, the uncooperative recruit will probably bring his career to an end very quickly or remain an isolate within the department. In addition to feeling the psychological pressure of ostracism, he will quickly discover that successful police work requires the free availability of information from other policemen, and that his life may depend on the support of fellow officers.[10]

[9] See Bent, especially pp. 15–16, and see Arthur Niederhoffer, *Behind the Shield* (Garden City, N.Y.: Doubleday & Co., 1969), pp. 58–60, 126.
[10] See Niederhoffer, especially pp. 51–54 and 70–72; and see Bent, pp. 36–39.

The Failure of External Controls. Police administrators commonly complain about the ill effects of "politics" on police work, but in fact political leaders in large cities rarely intervene in the management of their police departments in any systematic or sustained way. More precisely, municipal officials have tended to seek sustained involvement in departmental management for exploitative purposes while constructive efforts to improve standards and goals in police operations have occurred only sporadically, and even exploitative intervention in police management has probably declined in the years since World War II. The use of police departments as sources of political patronage and favoritism was pursued most thoroughly by the large urban "machines," which began to decline in the years prior to the war. Today, the machines have largely disappeared. If anything, the present trend is for municipal officials to leave day-to-day departmental management entirely in the hands of the chief. Even professional city managers seem to delegate virtually total responsibility for law enforcement to the department chief.[11]

Institutionalized civilian supervision of the police will tend to be found mainly in cities having commission governments, in which each elected commissioner heads one of the municipal departments. Commission governments probably exist in less than a fifth of America's large cities (those having populations over 25,000), and are even less prevalent in the large central cities (those of more than 200,000 residents).[12]

Other power centers in the cities do not fill the supervisory gap left by municipal political leadership. Courts, prosecutors, and the press generally do not attempt to impose standards of performance on municipal police departments, perhaps in large part because they depend upon cooperative relations with the police to accomplish their own purposes. Civilian review boards seem to serve primarily to energize departmental defenses against outside interference.[13]

For the most part, a protracted intervention in police department management by other urban power centers will occur only when a problem is called to the attention of several power centers simultaneously and insistently, and when the leadership in at least one power center is unusually responsible. Such appears to have been the case in New York City.

Police and the Public. Public attitudes concerning law enforcement are generally not conducive to greater police responsibility. When "crime

[11] For a general discussion of the absence of civilian supervision, see Bent, pp. 63–66.
[12] The figures are taken from Robert R. Alford and Harry M. Scoble, "Political and Socioeconomic Characteristics of American Cities," in International City Managers' Association, *Municipal Yearbook 1965*, pp. 82–98.
[13] Bent, p. 71.

waves" and riots do drag large numbers of citizens out of their customary
political apathy, the remedial measures which receive the firmest support
are usually simple, relatively cheap, short-term, and somewhat blood-
thirsty. The most typical response seems to be a demand for more manpower, more weapons, and reduced obligations to the rights of defendants.
These, at least, are the measures which political leaders feel they can offer
with the best chance of gaining support. The undercurrent of hostility
toward police authority and the low esteem for police personnel do not
abate, and widespread lawbreaking for personal pleasure continues apace
among "normal" people.[14]

Why Corruption?

Given the lack of sustained public support, the absence of civilian supervision, the opportunities for graft and the frustrations in accomplishing
their legitimate purpose, it is not surprising that many policemen become
cynical toward their own work.[15] However, it is still not entirely clear why
their frustrations might find an outlet in corrupt practices. One frequently
offered explanation is that the "old hands" in a department teach new
recruits to accept corruption as a fact of life. Acceptance then is often
followed by exploitation because the elements of police corruption are
intertwined—to accept gratuities from an honest businessman may lead
smoothly to the acceptance of bribes from the operators of illegal businesses, given a reasonable period for psychological conditioning and
adjustment.[16]

However, to account for police deviance in terms of post-recruitment
socialization, one must be prepared to answer other questions:

(1) Why should active corruption ever have started in the first place?

(2) Why have so many rookies been so routinely pliable and soft-
headed?

The answers to these questions must be largely speculative, for little
empirical research has been directed to them. Explanations may be
couched in terms of historical factors, personality traits, or occupational
values.

From a historical perspective, one might attribute current cynicism

[14] On police social status, see Charles B. Saunders, Jr., *Upgrading the American
Police* (Washington, D.C.: The Brookings Institution, 1970), especially pp. 1–15 &
117. Also see Bent, pp. 73–74.

[15] For a particularly penetrating discussion of police cynicism, see Niederhoffer, pp.
95–108.

[16] *Ibid.*, pp. 70–75. For an earlier, journalistic discussion of the gradual road to
hardened corruption, see David C. Wittels, "Why Cops Turn Crooked," *Saturday
Evening Post*, April 23, 1949, pp. 26–27, 104–107, 111, 114–122.

among police officers to the lasting effects of nineteenth century political machines in the cities. Thus the strong civilian control which was exercised over urban departments in the nineteenth and early twentieth centuries tended to support norms of favoritism and unequal enforcement of the law.[17] However, the machines have been gone a long time in most cities, and corruption in urban police departments antedates them anyway. Perhaps the first organized urban police force in the history of the Western world were the Bow Street Runners of London. Organized in the late eighteenth century to control highwaymen on the roads leading into the city, they quickly became corrupt and one of them left an estate of $30,000! [18]

The development of cynicism might also contribute to corruption based strictly on economic need. Salaries for patrolmen in most cities are still low enough that economic hardship is probably not unusual. The small degree of corruption practiced by most police personnel may simply reflect a realistic and reasonable adjustment to the economic environment. The experienced officer should have no illusions about eradicating crime, and he may feel that he can serve best by sustaining himself and attacking those problems he can reasonably hope to correct. As the Knapp Commission discovered, an officer may be very successful in clearing cases and very successfully corrupt as well.[19]

Psychological explanations for police corruption have been couched in terms of the interaction between personality traits and occupational choice. One viewpoint frequently adopted by psychologists and the general public alike is that police work attracts a disproportionate number of working-class men with authoritarian personalities.[20] Such men would supposedly value the symbolic power of the police and seek the deference they feel it merits, but they would place little priority on democratic legal norms. Thus they would be highly susceptible to corruption.

Arthur Niederhoffer, a policeman trained in sociology, makes a strong attack on the thesis of working-class authoritarianism among the police. He presents research findings which indicate that candidates entering the New York force tend to be somewhat lower in authoritarianism than the American working class in general, and also tend to be somewhat lower in anomia. He also presents evidence that the majority of young men entering police work are *not* attracted to it by a desire for power or by a missionary zeal for public service, but are drawn instead by a desire for

[17] Wittels portrays the influence of the machine in a particularly colorful way. See "Why Cops Turn Crooked."

[18] John Deane Potter, *The Art of Hanging: The Fatal Gallows Tree in English History* (New York: A. S. Barnes & Co., 1969), p. 49.

[19] *Knapp Commission Report*, pp. 50–56.

[20] For a discussion of police authoritarianism and directions to literature, see Niederhoffer, pp. 109–111.

10

job *security*—there are few layoffs on a police force! Niederhoffer's own explanation for the emergence of authority orientations among the police is the powerful socialization applied to the recruit.[21]

If a strong orientation to job security could in fact be demonstrated among all working class candidates for police work, the beginnings of a psychological explanation for police corruptibility might be at hand. Subsequent research might determine whether the security needs of men entering police work are of the sort that make them particularly susceptible to the temptations of corruption in its various forms, or to the socializing influence of corrupt peer groups. An exaggerated desire for job security might be associated with the desire to wield power or obtain deference.

Proposals for Reform

Whatever the causes of police corruption may be, its presence in urban departments is symptomatic of a discrepancy between the operating norms of predominantly working-class police forces and the values of democratic humanitarianism and bureaucratic efficiency which tend to be served primarily by intellectuals and community leaders. Proposals for generally upgrading law enforcement in the United States have tended to include measures which would reduce this discrepancy, and thereby reduce corruption in one or another of its forms. Some proposals involve a relatively direct attack upon some specific aspect of corrupt behavior while others are focused on the goal of infusing police organizations with democratic legal norms. Among the proposals that involve a specific attack on corruption itself are measures that would remove temptations to corruption, provide for policing of urban departments by other agencies, or reform the internal procedures of municipal departments. The more general approach to upgrading police norms and performance includes proposals for increased professionalization of the police, civilianization of departmental leadership and auxiliary functions, and a broad redefinition of the functional relationship between the police and the public.

Removing Temptations. The most frequently suggested means of reducing temptation for police officers is the legalization of vice. The proposal stems from the realization that such activities as gambling, prostitution, consumption of mild drugs, and violation of blue laws are widely practiced among the public and are therefore one of the most lucrative sources of bribes and kickbacks for those charged with law enforcement. Moreover, the effort expended to regulate vice consumes large amounts of police manpower that could be profitably used to combat other types of

[21] *Ibid.*, pp. 109–160, also pp. 69–75.

crime.[22] The principal shortcoming of the proposal is that it may run counter to the public will. There is no concrete evidence that a majority of the public violates the vice laws, and some who do violate these laws apparently believe that their activities should continue to be against the law! Thus the proposal would prove difficult to enact comprehensively, and if it were enacted the control of police behavior by public officials might be enhanced at the expense of popular control over the law itself.

Policing the Police. Another potential means for directly regulating corruption in municipal police departments would be to create some central authority, perhaps at the Federal level, to investigate and police local police forces. Such a central agency could certainly enforce external standards upon local departments, given sufficient legal mandate, but it would be strongly opposed. In the first place, it would be inconsistent with the continuing reverence for localism in American politics—it smacks of a national police force and the subversion of "home rule" for local governments. Moreover, creation of such an agency might accomplish little more than the substitution of Federal for local discretion in law enforcement. Local departments would be no more able to prosecute all violations of the law, and the priorities for investigation could be set at the Federal level. This might have seemed an attractive alternative in an earlier day, when Federal agencies seemed generally free of corruption in any form. Confidence in Federal law enforcement today may have been badly shaken by the revelations of the Watergate scandal. The prospect of a Federal agency which might set political priorities for investigation and prosecution, destroy evidence against corrupt but supportive politicians, and control as well the priorities of local police departments is simply terrifying. Nonetheless, some external and independent check on the practices of local departments may be essential if the abuses protected by the "rule of silence" are to be detected and remedied. Over the long run, the Federal agencies appear to have been relatively free of corruption and political bias, and a federal authority may prove the most reasonable check to impose.

Internal Reforms. A broad variety of improved controls within municipal departments have also been suggested as a means of reducing corruption. Certain recommendations of the Knapp Commission illustrate both the opportunities and the problems in efforts at internal reform. Note the following recommendations:

(1) A departmental doctrine "that every commander is responsible for rooting out corruption in his command" should be developed and enforced.

[22] See Bent, p. 165, and the *Knapp Commission Report*, pp. 18–20.

(2) The Inspectional Services Bureau (the internal security division) should be reorganized along the lines of the Inspections Office of the Internal Revenue Service by making it responsible directly to the chief and by making its members *permanently* responsible for investigating corruption. Thus the members of the division would never be faced with the prospect of moving into other divisions to work alongside men they had investigated and perhaps accused.

(3) Complete personnel records should be maintained to facilitate internal investigations.

(4) Reporting procedures should be strictly enforced—e.g., the provision that association with gamblers, criminals, or other persons engaged in illegal activities be formally reported. The objective would be to discipline officers engaged in corrupt activities even when evidence is not sufficient to bring a criminal case.

(5) Penalties in disciplinary action should be expanded.

(6) A rule should be enforced that informants be "registered" to all officers they deal with, and the rule that informants cannot be paid should be removed. These rules changes would reduce the likelihood of illegal transactions between officers and unregistered informants.

A department which attempted to implement these recommendations piecemeal could encounter serious problems:

(A) The proposals outlined above involve a frontal assault on the code of silence. Tremendous conflict could be expected between the reorganized Inspectional Services Bureau and the rest of the department. Division commanders charged with "rooting out" an endemic pattern of corruption would be juxtaposed against a chief with new and demanding standards of performance.

(B) The recommendations also seem to involve substantial additional paperwork for somebody. The burden would probably fall on uniformed officers in most urban departments, and even on patrol personnel, since they already do much of the clerical work of a department. Any addition to the clerical duties of uniformed personnel would seem a dubious practice.

(C) Finally, the enforcement of rules is punitive in orientation. Regulation of conduct by threat is usually a poor substitute for internally motivated performance.

In all fairness to the Knapp Commission, the recommendations considered above are drawn from a much larger list of proposals.[23] While their adoption on a piecemeal basis might lead to the problems men-

[23] From the *Knapp Commission Report*, pp. 21–23.

tioned, the Commission obviously had a more comprehensive approach in mind. Thus their recommendations included some of the measures that would more generally upgrade the quality of personnel and practices in American municipal law enforcement. The success of internal procedural reforms will probably hinge on the success of the more general efforts to upgrade quality.

Professionalization. A broad range of reform proposals have been made which, taken together, would raise police work in America to the status of a profession. Measures which have been proposed to this end include the following:

(1) *More Rigorous Standards of Recruitment.*[24] In particular, higher education levels are advocated for police officers, with an ultimate view to requiring the baccalaureate of entering recruits. Other measures for weeding out the "unfit" include psychological screening tests and more rigorous background investigations than are now conducted in most departments. To facilitate these measures, a program of active recruiting, especially on college campuses, is needed. Municipal departments must abandon recruitment procedures based on the assumption that there are hordes of qualified applicants waiting for every position that is made available.

(2) *More and Better Formal Training Both During and After Entry.*[25] Preliminary training for recruits lasts no more than a few weeks in even the largest American municipal police departments. Eighteen per cent of cities over 10,000 provide no training at all! By contrast, many European nations normally require training that lasts from several months to as much as two years.

The quality of the training given has also been at issue. Alan Bent has suggested that most training is conducted by senior officers who display racism, contempt for supreme court decisions, and a taste for "rough and ready" justice.[26] The content of the training is usually oriented to crime control, but the policeman will in fact spend the majority of his time dealing with problems in human relations. The President's Commission on Law Enforcement, obviously moved by a similar concern, has suggested that training should be oriented more toward human relations techniques, and should be carried out to a larger extent by professional educators and civilian experts.[27]

Finally, post-entry training has been rare in American depart-

[24] For a discussion, see Bent, p. 162, and see Saunders, pp. 40–44 & 79–116.
[25] See especially Saunders, pp. 117–151.
[26] Bent, p. 20.
[27] Cited in Saunders, pp. 129 & 131.

ments. Until a program of educational loans was established under the Law Enforcement Assistance Act, an officer who sought to upgrade skills while in service was pretty much on his own. This situation has been only partially alleviated by the LEAA loans, and it represents a stark violation of one of the fundamental tenets of good personnel administration—i.e., that training and development of skills are a never ending process.

(3) *Measures to Increase Lateral Mobility.*[28] Some analysts have suggested that personnel regulations which restrict lateral mobility be removed in order to increase the flow of "new blood" into police departments, particularly at the managerial levels. Specific suggestions include the formation of state retirement plans and the removal of residence requirements for entry. Of course, such measures may not have much effect unless the strength of insulary attitudes in the urban departments are also reduced.

(4) *Development of Professional Identity.*[29] Finally, if the police are to be truly professionalized, they must develop technical norms of performance which are congruent with the principles of elective government, and which are enforced through peer group association. The development of such norms has not been widely apparent in the recent unionization movements among urban police forces. Rather, the unions seem to be created prmarily as defense mechanisms, reflecting the insular solidarity of the municipal departments in which they appear.

Perhaps the broadest and most immediate obstacle to professionalization of American police forces is the lack of resources. Faced with problems in transportation, poverty, housing, and education, political leaders in the cities are not likely to provide the funds necessary to attract and keep a college educated police force. Nor are they likely to support the provision of additional Federal funds for the same purpose if those funds might be taken from other urban-oriented Federal programs. Simplistic public attitudes toward law enforcement provide little incentive for innovations by political leaders anyway.

Civilianization.[30] Another major proposal for changing the prevailing norms in municipal departments is to breach paramilitary command and career structures by infusing them with civilians in large numbers. Trained administrators would be assigned to managerial positions, and profes-

[28] For discussions, see Bent, pp. 157–158, and the *Knapp Commission Report*, p. 32.
[29] For discussion, see Saunders, pp. 31–34, and Bent, pp. 22–23.
[30] See Bent, pp. 155–159 & 163–164.

sionals such as lawyers would be recruited as investigators. Routine clerical and auxiliary functions could also be handled by civilians, freeing more uniformed officers for the streets. Such extensive utilization of civilian personnel has been practiced for years in European nations with no evident ill effects. The obvious objective in such a reform is to replace command personnel of working class backgrounds with those of middle class backgrounds. Indeed, civilianization of leadership may be necessary before other reforms can be carried out. Old-line police chiefs have been noted for their resistance to external interference in departmental management, their contempt for college education and professional norms in police work, and their "stonewall" denial of departmental problems in the face of scandalous evidence to the contrary.

Redefinition of Functional Role. Finally, a number of urban departments are experimenting with new concepts of the functional relationship between the police and the public, placing increased emphasis on positive public service and on the maintenance of rapport between the policeman and the community he serves. The experimental technique usually involves some variant of the community-based police team. Alan Bent describes an especially successful effort, the New Orleans Urban Squad.[31] The team was formed in February of 1971 to police the Desire Project, an area with the highest crime rate in the city. Members of the squad were screened by their commander for "an even temperament and an awareness of social problems." They patrol in civilian clothes, wearing only badge, gun, and handcuffs. Most importantly, they orient their investigations to the social causes of crime and they seek to meet social needs of the community beyond those of simple law enforcement. For example, they have taken an active interest in keeping wayward teenagers in school and in acquiring improved public services—such as rat control—for the Project. Bent reports that the Desire Project now has the lowest crime rate in the city, and the residents of another project have apparently requested the same type of police protection for their own neighborhood.

While the main thrust of such efforts is to improve community relations, such experiments may have far-reaching implications for police corruption. In the first place, the team concept promotes a closer *mutual* identity and contact between police officers and the community in which they live and work. The resulting decrease in social distance may produce as great a change in attitudes among the police as among the public! Social isolation may be reduced, and a sense of identity may develop with the ordinary citizens who are often victimized by corrupt practices. More-

[31] *Ibid.,* pp. 55–59.

over, when team efforts are as successful as the New Orleans Urban Squad, there is some reason to hope that police departments can substantially reduce levels of frustration and cynicism among their members by taking appropriate internal action.

None of the proposed remedies for police corruption carries a guarantee of success. Professionalization may seem an innately desirable goal, yet there is no evidence that the legal, medical, or teaching professions have been spectacularly successful at purging themselves of corrupt or incompetent members. Similarly, civilianization of leadership conforms to the highest democratic ideals, but the improvements worked under one civilian administration may be casually obliterated under an ensuing administration, either because it is politically expedient to attack the reformers or because the new administration is itself incompetent or ill informed.[32] The proposed reforms probably represent about the best remedial action that can be conceived within the framework of present technology.

Prospects for the Future

Despite the variety of measures which might be taken to combat corruption in urban police departments, the chances that any sharp progress will be made in the near future are probably modest. The most successful means of combatting corruption will probably be those which are integrated with a general effort to upgrade police performance in general. This effort requires the sort of resources that will not be made available in the short run without a substantial change in attitudes toward law enforcement among the general public and their elected leadership. In the American polity, such a pronounced reorientation tends to occur only when inspired and innovative leadership capitalizes upon a national disaster. At this time, there is no reason to believe that political leaders will abandon their traditional reliance on equipment and manpower as a solution to problems of law enforcement.

Certainly a major effort is needed if any permanent improvement in police performance is to be achieved. The *ad hoc* efforts of temporary agencies such as the Knapp Commission simply are not sufficient to produce a permanent change in performance. The Knapp Commission itself succeeded in generating an unprecedented body of information concerning operational practices in a big city department. However, their efforts to control corruption consisted of indictments and dismissals numbered in the dozens. In a department of 32,000, characterized by "widespread cor-

[32] For an example, see Bent's discussion of political events surrounding the Memphis department, pp. 109–126.

ruption," the direct benefit to be gained from exposing a very small fraction of the total work force is probably negligible. Now the Knapp Commission has ceased to exist, but the pattern of opportunities, frustrations, and operating norms in the department is probably very little changed from what it was before the commission was formed.

The improvement of law enforcement in America will necessarily be gradual. The infusion of college educated, "socially sensitive" personnel will be a protracted process, which will be accompanied by increased intergenerational conflict between the old hands and the better educated young recruits. Of course, such intergenerational conflicts represent in themselves a major obstacle to progress, for the recruits and therefore for their departments. For the recruit, conflict with the senior men can become a major source of frustration and cynicism. He will be pressured to accept the status quo, not only by the older men but probably also by those interests in the community which have benefitted from a corruptible police force. If the recruit yields to the pressure, his superior qualifications become worthless to the department and he will probably lose an amount of self-respect which is proportional to the amount he had to begin with. If he decides not to yield to the pressure, he must somehow survive in an environment quite different from the one he would probably like to have. His ethics will have to be sufficiently pragmatic to endure years of compromise.

For many, the frustration will become intolerable. Some will reduce the frustration by moving into routine administrative work, and municipal departments should benefit to some extent from this trend. Many others will drop out. One current and somewhat disconcerting trend is for people with graduate training in law enforcement to look first for opportunities to teach it. While good instructors are certainly needed in the classroom, the ultimate purpose of schools of law enforcement must be to put their people in the field.

Given the frustrations that younger personnel will face, departments which attempt to upgrade the force will probably experience a high level of turnover among the younger officers. This turnover creates a dual problem: First, improved mid-level leadership may be very difficult to develop unless some of the highly educated young men can be kept long enough to "move them up." Moreover, the real impact of innovative efforts will be felt when police officers of improved quality are working the streets in large numbers. That is where they are needed, even if it is not very apparent to them when they are out there.

To sustain younger personnel, the municipal departments will require dynamic leadership. Departments blessed with progressive career chiefs will have an innate advantage, while those with reactionary top management will require some sort of intervention from the outside if much improvement is to be accomplished on a permanent basis. Perhaps the most effective remedy for these departments will be civilianization of departmental management. It requires relatively little in the way of additional resources, and can therefore be accomplished in any city where the political leadership is willing to take the time and trouble to achieve it.

Appendix A
History of the Commission*

On April 25, 1970, *The New York Times* printed a story presenting lengthy and detailed accusations of widespread corruption in the Police Department. The story charged that police officers received systematic payoffs from gamblers, narcotics peddlers, and other law violators, and that the police hierarchy as well as officials of the City administration had been informed of specific charges of serious corruption and failed to take any action.

Mayor John V. Lindsay responded to the allegations by appointing a committee to investigate them.[1] The committee met several times and reported by letter [2] to the Mayor that a full-time citizens' commission was needed to investigate the problem. The committee said that it had received 375 complaints in response to a public plea by the Mayor for information and that the regular duties of the committee members prevented their devoting sufficient time to an independent investigation. Moreover, the committee noted the reaction among some segments of the public that an investigation of allegations of police corruption should not be conducted by those who conceivably might be responsible for the conditions they were supposed to examine.

In response to the Rankin Committee's recommendation, the Mayor, on May 21, 1970, issued an executive order [3] appointing this Commission and charging it with the tasks of determining the extent and nature of police corruption in the City, examining existing procedures for dealing with corruption, recommending changes and improvements in these procedures, and holding whatever hearings were deemed appropriate.

The City Council passed a bill [4] giving the Commission power to issue subpoenas and authorized $325,000 in funds to last through December 31, 1970. On July 25, the Board of Estimate ratified the authorization of funds. On the same date a legal challenge to the Commission's legitimacy was rejected by the courts.

. . .

Commissioner Leary resigned in August, 1970 and was replaced in October by Commissioner Patrick V. Murphy. Almost immediately, Commissioner Murphy announced—and began to carry into effect—an intention to make sweeping changes in departmental procedures for dealing with corrup-

---

* SOURCE: The *Knapp Commission Report on Police Corruption*. New York: George Braziller, 1973.
[1] The committee was headed by Corporation Counsel J. Lee Rankin and its members were Frank S. Hogan and Burton B. Roberts, District Attorneys of New York and Bronx Counties, respectively; Commissioner of Investigation Robert K. Ruskin and Police Commissioner Howard R. Leary.
[2] Appendix, Exhibit 1.
[3] Appendix, Exhibit 2.
[4] Appendix, Exhibit 3.

tion. This development had an important effect on the nature of our task. The extent and nature of corruption still had to be determined, but suggesting changes in procedures for dealing with corruption was reduced in importance. It became more important to make our findings on patterns of corruption clear to the public, so that the public would encourage the new Commissioner in his announced intentions of reform, and would support him in putting them into effect.

The ability to carry out our mandate was enhanced by the nature of our appointment. Our authority was derived from the Mayor who, as the City's chief executive officer, is ultimately responsible for the conduct of the Department we were called upon to investigate. This was the first time—in this or perhaps any other city—that the official ultimately responsible for a police department's conduct had authorized public investigation of allegations of police corruption.

The fact that the Mayor appointed us encouraged cooperation between the Department and us. This did not mean that serious differences did not arise between our Commission and the Department but, as the investigation progressed, cooperation became increasingly real and fruitful. While it is too early to say to what extent our investigation will help to bring about permanent changes in the Department, it may well turn out that any such change will result in part from the cooperation that has existed between us.

. . .

Summary

The Extent of Police Corruption

We found corruption to be widespread. It took various forms depending upon the activity involved, appearing at its most sophisticated among plainclothesmen assigned to enforcing gambling laws. In the five plainclothes divisions where our investigations were concentrated we found a strikingly standardized pattern of corruption. Plainclothesmen, participating in what is known in police parlance as a "pad," collected regular bi-weekly or monthly payments amounting to as much as $3,500 from each of the gambling establishments in the area under their jurisdiction, and divided the take in equal shares. The monthly share per man (called the "nut") ranged from $300 and $400 in midtown Manhattan to $1,500 in Harlem. When supervisors were involved they received a share and a half. A newly assigned plainclothesman was not entitled to his share for about two months, while he was checked out for reliability, but the earnings lost by the delay were made up to him in the form of two months' severance pay when he left the division.

Evidence before us led us to the conclusion that the same pattern existed

in the remaining divisions which we did not investigate in depth. This conclusion was confirmed by events occurring before and after the period of our
investigation. Prior to the Commission's existence, exposures by former
plainclothesman Frank Serpico had led to indictments or departmental
charges against nineteen plainclothesmen in a Bronx division for involvement in a pad where the nut was $800. After our public hearings had been
completed, an investigation conducted by the Kings County District Attorney
and the Department's Internal Affairs Division—which investigation neither
the Commission nor its staff had even known about—resulted in indictments
and charges against thirty-seven Brooklyn plainclothesmen who had participated in a pad with a nut of $1,200. The manner of operation of the pad
involved in each of these situations was in every detail identical to that
described at the Commission hearings, and in each almost every plainclothesman in the division, including supervisory lieutenants, was implicated.

Corruption in narcotics enforcement lacked the organization of the gambling pads, but individual payments—known as "scores"—were commonly
received and could be staggering in amount. Our investigation, a concurrent
probe by the State Investigation Commission and prosecutions by Federal
and local authorities all revealed a pattern whereby corrupt officers cus-
tomarily collected scores in substantial amounts from narcotics violators.
These scores were either kept by the individual officer or shared with a
partner and, perhaps, a superior officer. They ranged from minor shakedowns
to payments of many thousands of dollars, the largest narcotics payoff uncovered in our investigation having been $80,000. According to information
developed by the S.I.C. and in recent Federal investigations, the size of this
score was by no means unique.

Corruption among detectives assigned to general investigative duties also
took the form of shakedowns of individual targets of opportunity. Although
these scores were not in the huge amounts found in narcotics, they not
infrequently came to several thousand dollars.

Uniformed patrolmen assigned to street duties were not found to receive
money on nearly so grand or organized a scale, but the large number of
small payments they received present an equally serious if less dramatic
problem. Uniformed patrolmen, particularly those assigned to radio patrol
cars, participated in gambling pads more modest in size than those received
by plainclothes units and received regular payments from construction sites,
bars, grocery stores and other business establishments. These payments
were usually made on a regular basis to sector car patrolmen and on a haphazard basis to others. While individual payments to uniformed men were
small, mostly under $20, they were often so numerous as to add substantially
to a patrolman's income. Other less regular payments to uniformed patrolmen included those made by after-hours bars, bottle clubs, tow trucks,
motorists, cab drivers, parking lots, prostitutes and defendants wanting to

fix their cases in court. Another practice found to be widespread was the payment of gratuities by policemen to other policemen to expedite normal police procedures or to gain favorable assignments.

Sergeants and lieutenants who were so inclined participated in the same kind of corruption as the men they supervised. In addition, some sergeants had their own pads from which patrolmen were excluded.

Although the Commission was unable to develop hard evidence establishing that officers above the rank of lieutenant received payoffs, considerable circumstantial evidence and some testimony so indicated. Most often when a superior officer is corrupt, he uses a patrolman as his "bagman" who collects for him and keeps a percentage of the take. Because the bagman may keep the money for himself, although he claims to be collecting for his superior, it is extremely difficult to determine with any accuracy when the superior actually is involved.

Of course, not all policemen are corrupt. If we are to exclude such petty infractions as free meals, an appreciable number do not engage in any corrupt activities. Yet, with extremely rare exceptions, even those who themselves engage in no corrupt activities are involved in corruption in the sense that they take no steps to prevent what they know or suspect to be going on about them.

It must be made clear that—in a little over a year with a staff having as few as two and never more than twelve field investigators—we did not examine every precinct in the Department. Our conclusion that corruption is widespread throughout the Department is based on the fact that information supplied to us by hundreds of sources within and without the Department was consistently borne out by specific observations made in areas we were able to investigate in detail.

The Nature and Significance of Police Corruption

Corruption, although widespread, is by no means uniform in degree. Corrupt policemen have been described as falling into two basic categories: "meat-eaters" and "grass-eaters." As the names might suggest, the meat-eaters are those policemen who, like Patrolman William Phillips who testified at our hearings, aggressively misuse their police powers for personal gain. The grass-eaters simply accept the payoffs that the happenstances of police work throw their way. Although the meat-eaters get the huge payoffs that make the headlines, they represent a small percentage of all corrupt policemen. The truth is, the vast majority of policemen on the take don't deal in huge amounts of graft.

And yet, grass-eaters are the heart of the problem. Their great numbers tend to make corruption "respectable." They also tend to encourage the code of silence that brands anyone who exposes corruption a traitor. At the time our investigation began, any policeman violating the code did so at his peril. The result was described in our interim report: "The rookie who comes into the Department is faced with the situation where it is easier for him to become corrupt than to remain honest."

More importantly, although meat-eaters can and have been individually induced to make their peace with society, the grass-eaters may be more easily reformed. We believe that, given proper leadership and support, many police who have slipped into corruption would exchange their illicit income for the satisfaction of belonging to a corruption-free Department in which they could take genuine pride.

The problem of corruption is neither new, nor confined to the police. Reports of prior investigations into police corruption, testimony taken by the Commission, and opinions of informed persons both within and without the Department make it abundantly clear that police corruption has been a problem for many years. Investigations have occurred on the average of once in twenty years since before the turn of the century, and yet conditions exposed by one investigation seem substantially unchanged when the next one makes its report. This doesn't mean that the police have a monopoly on corruption. On the contrary, in every area where police corruption exists it is paralleled by corruption in other agencies of government, in industry and labor, and in the professions.

Our own mandate was limited solely to the police. There are sound reasons for such a special concern with police corruption. The police have a unique place in our society. The policeman is expected to "uphold the law" and "keep the peace." He is charged with everything from traffic control to riot control. He is expected to protect our lives and our property. As a result, society gives him special powers and prerogatives, which include the right and obligation to bear arms, along with the authority to take away our liberty by arresting us.

Symbolically, his role is even greater. For most people, the policeman is the law. To them, the law is administered by the patrolman on the beat and the captain in the station house. Little wonder that the public becomes aroused and alarmed when the police are charged with corruption or are shown to be corrupt.

Departmental Attitudes Towards Police Corruption

Although this special concern is justified, public preoccupation with police corruption as opposed to corruption in other agencies of government inevitably seems unfair to the policeman. He believes that he is unjustly blamed for the results of corruption in other parts of the criminal justice system. This sense of unfairness intensifies the sense of isolation and hostility to which the nature of police work inevitably gives rise.

10

Feelings of isolation and hostility are experienced by policemen not just in New York, but everywhere. To understand these feelings one must appreciate an important characteristic of any metropolitan police department, namely an extremely intense group loyalty. When properly understood, this group loyalty can be used in the fight against corruption. If misunderstood or ignored, it can undermine anti-corruption activities.

Pressures that give rise to this group loyalty include the danger to which policemen are constantly exposed and the hostility they encounter from society at large. Everyone agrees that a policeman's life is a dangerous one, and that his safety, not to mention his life, can depend on his ability to rely on a fellow officer in a moment of crisis. It is less generally realized that the policeman works in a sea of hostility. This is true, not only in high crime areas, but throughout the City. Nobody, whether a burglar or a Sunday motorist, likes to have his activities interfered with. As a result, most citizens, at one time or another, regard the police with varying degrees of hostility. The policeman feels, and naturally often returns, this hostility.

Two principal characteristics emerge from this group loyalty: suspicion and hostility directed at any outside interference with the Department, and an intense desire to be proud of the Department. This mixture of hostility and pride has created what the Commission has found to be the most serious roadblock to a rational attack upon police corruption: a stubborn refusal at all levels of the Department to acknowledge that a serious problem exists.

The interaction of stubbornness, hostility and pride has given rise to the so-called "rotten-apple" theory. According to this theory, which bordered on official Department doctrine, any policeman found to be corrupt must promptly be denounced as a rotten apple in an otherwise clean barrel. It must never be admitted that his individual corruption may be symptomatic of underlying disease.

This doctrine was bottomed on two basic premises: First, the morale of the Department requires that there be no official recognition of corruption, even though practically all members of the Department know it is in truth extensive; second, the Department's public image and effectiveness require official denial of this truth.

The rotten-apple doctrine has in many ways been a basic obstacle to meaningful reform. To begin with, it reinforced and gave respectability to the code of silence. The official view that the Department's image and morale forbade public disclosure of the extent of corruption inhibited any officer who wished to disclose corruption and justified any who preferred to remain silent. The doctrine also made difficult, if not impossible, any meaningful attempt at managerial reform. A high command unwilling to acknowledge that the problem of corruption is extensive cannot very well argue that drastic changes are necessary to deal with that problem. Thus neither the Mayor's Office nor the Police Department took adequate steps to see that such changes were made when the need for them was indicated by the charges made by Officers Frank Serpico and David Durk in 1968. This was demonstrated in the Commission's second set of public hearings in December 1971.

Finally, the doctrine made impossible the use of one of the most effective techniques for dealing with any entrenched criminal activity, namely persuading a participant to help provide evidence against his partners in crime. If a corrupt policeman is merely an isolated rotten apple, no reason can be given for not exposing him the minute he is discovered. If, on the other hand, it is acknowledged that a corrupt officer is only one part of an apparatus of corruption, common sense dictates that every effort should be made to enlist the offender's aid in providing the evidence to destroy the apparatus.

The Commission's Actions

The Commission examined and rejected the premises upon which the rotten-apple doctrine rested. We concluded that there was no justification for fearing that public acknowledgment of the extent of corruption would damage the image and effectiveness of the Department. We are convinced that instead of damaging its image a realistic attitude toward corruption could only enhance the Department's credibility. The conditions described in the Commission's public hearings came as no surprise to the large numbers of City residents who had experienced them for years. If, then, the Department makes it a point to acknowledge corrupt conditions the public already knows to exist, it can hardly damage its image. On the contrary, it can only promote confidence in the Department's good-faith desire to deal with those conditions.

The Commission looked at the question of morale in much the same way. We did not—and do not—believe that the morale of the average policeman is enhanced by a commanding officer who insists on denying facts that the policeman knows to be true. We believed—and continue to believe—that such false denials can only undercut the policeman's confidence in his commander. If a policeman listens to his commander solemnly deny the existence of an obvious corrupt situation, the policeman can draw only one of two conclusions: Either the commander is hopelessly naive or he is content to let the corruption continue.

Once we had rejected the premises of the rotten-apple doctrine, the Commission determined to employ one of the techniques that adherence to the doctrine had made impossible, namely to persuade formerly corrupt police officers to work with us in providing evidence of continuing corruption.

The mere decision to use the technique did not automatically produce a body of officers able and eager to assist us in this manner. Indeed, knowledgeable persons assured us that the code of silence was so strong that

10

we would never find a corrupt officer who could be persuaded to assist in exposing corruption. We ultimately did persuade four officers, including Detective Robert L. Leuci and Patrolmen William Phillips, Edward Droge and Alfonso Jannotta to undertake undercover work. Of these, all but Detective Leuci did so under the compulsion of having been caught by Commission investigators. Patrolmen Phillips and Droge testified at public hearings held in October 1971. Patrolman Jannotta was unavailable due to illness at the time of the hearings. The information disclosed by Detective Leuci was so vital that we did not, since our time was limited, feel justified in keeping it to ourselves. Leuci and the Commission staff members who had debriefed him and worked with him on his initial undercover operations were turned over to the Federal Government for the long-term investigation which was required. Leuci's work as a Federal undercover agent is now resulting in the series of important narcotics-related indictments being obtained by United States Attorney Whitney North Seymour, Jr.

Success in persuading these officers to assist in the investigation was a first step in demonstrating that the rotten-apple doctrine was invalid. Patrolman Phillips' three days of testimony about systematic corruption in various parts of the Department, corroborated by tape-recorded conversations with many police officers and others, was in itself enough to make the doctrine seem untenable. Patrolman Droge described how departmental pressures gradually converted an idealistic rookie into an increasingly bold finder of bribes and payoffs. Former Patrolman Waverly Logan, who volunteered to testify about corruption in which he had been involved, corroborated Droge's testimony and went on to tell about policemen in Harlem who received monthly as much as $3,000 each in narcotics graft. Patrolman Logan also introduced the Commission to two addicts who were willing to work with us in obtaining evidence to corroborate these assertions. The Commission's work with these addicts produced movies and recorded conversations of policemen selling narcotics. Some of the narcotics were paid for with merchandise the policemen believed to be stolen. Captain Daniel McGowan, a police officer of unquestioned integrity and experienced in anti-corruption work, testified that the picture of corruption presented by Patrolmen Phillips, Droge and Logan was an accurate one. In addition, there was testimony from, among others, a Harlem gambler, Commission agents describing their investigations, and witnesses in the business community revealing corrupt police dealings with the hotel and construction industries. Recorded conversations and movies documented instances of police corruption, including gambling and narcotics payoffs, fixing court cases and shaking down a tow-truck operator. The cumulative effect of these two weeks of testimony made it not only unrealistic but absurd for anyone thereafter to adhere to the rotten-apple doctrine, either publicly or privately.

The doctrine did not die easily. Institutional pressures within the Department seemed to force the high command to continue giving lip service to the doctrine even when speaking out against corruption. Commissioner Murphy in his early statements about corruption regularly included a pointed statement indicating that the corruption in the Department was limited to a few officers. On one occasion he went so far as to imply that there were no more than about 300 corrupt police officers in the entire Department. After Patrolman Phillips had completed two of his three days of testimony at our public hearings, Commissioner Murphy found it necessary to discount his testimony of widespread corruption, referring to him as a "rogue cop."

However, one week later, after Phillips had completed his testimony and had been followed by Patrolmen Logan and Droge and others, the Department, speaking through First Deputy Commissioner William H. T. Smith, forthrightly rejected the rotten-apple doctrine by name. Smith defined it as standing for the proposition that "police departments are essentially free of corruption except for the presence of a few corrupt officers who have managed to slip into police service and also into key assignments such as gambling investigations, despite rigorously applied screening procedures designed to keep them out." He said that traditional police strategy had been to react defensively whenever a scandal arose by "promising to crack down on graft, to go after the 'rogue cops,' to get rid of 'rotten apples.' " Smith said the Department now rejected this approach "not just on principle, but because as a way of controlling corruption it had utterly failed." He acknowledged that the result of adherence to the theory had been a breakdown in public confidence: ". . . they [the public] are sick of 'bobbing for rotten apples' in the police barrel. They want an entirely new barrel that will never again become contaminated."

Changing Departmental Attitudes

The public hearings, in addition to helping bring about official abandonment of the rotten-apple doctrine, have had dramatic effect on the way members of the Department discuss corruption. This change was graphically described shortly after our hearings by former Assistant Chief Inspector Sidney C. Cooper in colorful language: "Not very long ago we talked about corruption with all the enthusiasm of a group of little old ladies talking about venereal disease. Now there is a little more open discussion about combatting graft as if it were a public health problem." In short, the first barrier to a realistic look at corruption has been overcome: The problem has been officially, and unofficially, acknowledged.

Some time after the public hearings were over, it was revealed that Detective Leuci had been doing undercover work for the Federal Government for over a year and a half, and that he had been doing it with both the knowledge and protection of the Department's high command. News also began to spread throughout the Department that other formerly corrupt policemen were doing undercover work for the Department's Internal Affairs Division and for at least one District Attorney's office. These revelations had considerable impact, both direct and indirect, upon attitudes toward corruption within the Department.

To put the direct impact in proper perspective, it should be pointed out that any criminal activity, within a police department or elsewhere, cannot thrive unless all of its participants are able to maintain confidence in each other. Patrolman Phillips' testimony made this very clear. In testifying about his own corrupt activities, he described how he could, by making a few telephone calls within five or ten minutes, "check out" the reliability of any other officer whose assistance he might require in a corrupt enterprise. By way of illustration, he described instances where he had been similarly checked out while doing undercover work for the Commission. This ability to check out, and rely upon, an officer with whom one has had no previous contact rested on the assumption—unchallenged before the advent of our Commission—that no police officer who had once become involved in corruption could ever be persuaded to disclose the corruption of others. The actions of Detective Leuci and Patrolmen Phillips and Droge and of others as yet unnamed who are presently working undercover have undermined this assumption.

Even more important was the indirect effect produced by general knowledge that the undercover activities of these formerly corrupt policemen had been known to—and protected by—the Department's high command. Traditionally, the rank and file have shown a deep cynicism, well justified by history, concerning pronouncements of new police commissioners. They carefully examine the new commissioner's every word and action, searching for "messages": Does he mean business? Can he stand up against institutional pressures?

The initial lack of clarity in Commissioner Murphy's statements on the rotten-apple theory and his "rogue cop" reaction to the first widely publicized defiance of the code of silence were interpreted by some as suggesting a lack of commitment to total war on corruption. However, the Department's final repudiation of the doctrine, and the general knowledge that the Department was using and protecting policemen who had agreed to do undercover work, gave reassurance to the doubters.

In short, we believe that the Department's recent reactions to the Commission's activities have promoted realistic self-criticism within the Department. This spirit of self-criticism is an encouraging sign. For one thing, it is becoming less unusual for police officers to report evidence of police corruption. If this tendency continues, the day may be approaching when the rookie coming into the Department will not be pressured toward corruption, but can count on finding support for his desire to remain honest.

The present situation is quite like that existing at the close of previous investigations. A considerable momentum for reform has been generated, but not enough time has elapsed to reverse attitudes that have been solidifying for many years in the minds of both the public and the police.

After previous investigations, the mometum was allowed to evaporate.

The question now is: Will history repeat itself? Or does society finally realize that police corruption is a problem that must be dealt with and not just talked about once every twenty years?

Both immediate and long-term actions are mandatory. The reforms already initiated within the Department must be completed and expanded; there must be changes, both legislative and administrative, to curb pressures toward police corruption and to facilitate its control; and the momentum generated by the events before and during the life of this Commission must be maintained.

. . .

Police Witnesses

Throughout its investigation the Commission staff sought to find police officers actually engaged in corrupt activities who could be induced to describe openly and for the record their activities and their knowledge of the patterns of corruption observed during their careers. We were informed by people experienced in police work that no police officer had ever given such information and that none ever would, even if he himself were caught in a corrupt act and were offered immunity in exchange for his testimony. The tradition of the policeman's code of silence was so strong, we were advised, that it was futile to expect such testimony from any police officer. The most that could be expected was anonymous information or, if we were extremely lucky, testimony given under oath on an anonymous basis. All of the experienced people with whom we spoke agreed that if even one police officer could be induced to give inside information based upon personal experience, the testimony would be of inestimably greater value than any other evidence the Commission might uncover.

The search for a corrupt officer who would speak frankly and openly uncovered not one but five. However, the first and potentially most productive of these proved to be too valuable to keep to ourselves. Robert Leuci was a detective who had spent eleven years on the force and who had been assigned to the elite Special Investigation Unit (SIU) of the Narcotics Division. He had met police officers Durk and Serpico in 1970 and led them to believe that he would back up their charges that SIU had not adequately pursued certain narcotics cases. In the fall of 1970 Durk arranged for meetings between Leuci and various assistant district attorneys, the State Commission of Investigation, and the staff of this Commission. In these meetings Leuci's statements were inconclusive and not susceptible to investigation. He subsequently indicated that his purpose in submitting to questioning had been to discover how much information the Commission and other agencies possessed.

In February, 1971, Leuci was again interviewed by the Commission staff, and this time he was convinced to tell all he knew about corruption in SIU and to help the Commission expose it.

Leuci told of a Narcotics Division infested with corruption. Drawing on personal experiences as well as those he observed and discussed with fellow officers, he described enormous payoffs by narcotics violators, illegal wiretaps used to facilitate shakedowns, involvement of supervisory personnel in narcotics graft, and arrangements between police officers and organized crime members which gave the latter protection from arrest and advance knowledge of legitimate investigations involving them.

Leuci worked with Commission agents for about one month and obtained a number of incriminating tape-recorded conversations with police officers. It quickly became apparent that he had incalculable value as an undercover agent. His work, if allowed to continue for as long as it was productive, could result in criminal prosecutions which might well expose a network of narcotics related corruption involving many police officers and stretching outside the Department.

However, an investigation calculated to accomplish this end would, if successful, last for many months, even years, and would require concentrating on obtaining evidence in specific cases rather than on gathering information for the purpose of identifying patterns of corruption. Because the Commission's investigation was due to end in a few months, we decided that Leuci should be turned over to law enforcement authorities with the time and manpower necessary for such an investigation.

In March, 1971, Assistant United States Attorney General Wilson and Whitney North Seymour, Jr., United States Attorney for the Southern District of New York, were apprised of Leuci's activities to date and advised that the Commission was willing to forego any use of Leuci or the information he had provided in favor of an investigation directed at criminal prosecutions. The Commission also offered to refrain from revealing or further pursuing certain investigations into narcotics and related corruption which might draw attention to Leuci, and to allow the attorney and the two agents who had been working with Leuci to devote their full time to the proposed investigation. The Commission's offer was accepted.

The following month Commissioner Murphy and First Deputy Commissioner William H. T. Smith were informed of the investigation and arrangements were made to transfer Leuci back into SIU where he could work most effectively. The Commissioner agreed to keep his knowledge of the investigation entirely confidential and to give his full assistance whenever requested to do so.

The investigation was pursued with great success by the original investigative team aided by personnel from Mr. Seymour's office and, as the scope of the investigation broadened, by agents of the Federal Bureau of Narcotics and Dangerous Drugs, and a few carefully selected police officers. By the spring of 1972 federal authorities were confident that the investigation would result in far-ranging indictments involving organized crime members, police officers, and others in the criminal justice system including even judges.

However, Detective Leuci's participation in the investigation came to an end in June, 1972, when a story printed in *The New York Times* precipitated a general disclosure of his activities. Six indictments have so far been returned alleging corruption on the part of four police officers, an assistant district attorney, three lawyers, a bail bondsman and a private investigator. Other indictments are anticipated, but some of the most important cases have undoubtedly been aborted by the premature disclosure of the investigation.

The Commission could not, of course, call Leuci as a witness in its public hearings since at that time he was still working as a federal undercover agent. Moreover, findings in other Commissions investigations were withheld during the hearings so as to avoid areas where the focusing of attention might threaten his undercover activities.[5] With his exposure some of the information disclosed by Leuci and certain of the results of his undercover work can now be discussed and have been included, where relevant, in this report.

A second police officer who agreed, under significantly different circumstances, to cooperate with the Commission was Patrolman William Phillips. Phillips was a decorated police officer with fourteen years' service who had made arrests in every precinct in Manhattan. He had served as a foot patrolman and in a radio patrol car in the Nineteenth Precinct in mid-Manhattan, as a plainclothesman in the Sixth Division in Central Harlem, as a member of the Youth Squad assigned to southern Manhattan, as a detective in the Seventeenth Precinct squad in midtown and, finally, as a patrolman in the Twenty-fifth Precinct in East Harlem, which was the headquarters for organized crime figures running illegal gambling operations throughout Harlem. According to his own admission, he had been thoroughly corrupt throughout his career.

Despite the fact that he had had only one brush with disciplinary authority —resulting in his demotion from detective—Phillips' entire career had been

---

[5] Paul Curran, chairman of the State Commission of Investigation, also agreed to limit certain of his investigations into narcotics corruption when informed of Leuci's work by the Commission and Mr. Seymour.

one of virtually unrelieved corruption. He had, in his own words, been a "super thief." He told of having participated in comparatively petty graft involving construction sites, bars, restaurants, garages, bowling alleys, and other establishments making regular payments to officers on patrol. He had participated in organized shakedowns of gamblers which in one six-month period had netted him $6,000 to $8,000. He had dealt with organized crime figures who ran widespread gambling operations and paid for the ability to do so unmolested. He had engineered innumerable "scores" of gamblers, pimps, loan sharks, illegal liquor dealers, and other violators who had paid him as much as several thousand dollars for their freedom following arrest. He had arranged for the alteration of testimony in criminal trials. He had also collected all the traditional emoluments considered by policemen to be their due, from free hotel rooms—or, in Phillips' case, suites—to the traditional free meals—which again in his case had often consisted of dinner at Le Pavillon rather than a free hot dog. He knew all the illegal operations within his area of responsibility and was intimately familiar with the technical regulatory rules which could be used to shake down businesses subject to such rules.

Phillips' knowledge of corruption in the Department was not limited to his own experience. In fourteen years on the force, he had made innumerable friends who had, in the course of their own careers, scattered throughout the Department. He maintained contacts with many such officers and, through them, was quite well aware of conditions in other commands and areas. His use of the Department grapevine was revealing. He demonstrated on several occasions his ability to check on the reliability of any police officer. Invariably, he could find out if an officer could safely be approached with a corrupt proposal simply by placing a phone call to an acquaintance in the officer's command.

Phillips asserted that he drew a firm line reflecting the traditional notion in the Department of "clean" and "dirty" money, and the Commission found no evidence to contradict him. He said that he had never taken money in connection with narcotics or illegal guns because he found narcotics traffic abhorrent and an illegal gun could someday be used against him or another police officer. In addition, on grounds of self-protection rather than morality, he claimed to have followed a general rule of avoiding prostitutes because of their notorious unreliability. He proved the wisdom of this rule when he finally was caught because he ignored it.

Phillips was induced to testify not through appeals to his better nature but rather as a direct result of his being caught by Commission agents in the course of his involvement in the payment of some $11,000 in bribes by a midtown madam. Under this pressure, Phillips agreed to tell what he knew about corruption in the Police Department and to work as an undercover agent for the Commission.

From the outset, it was made absolutely clear to him that his chances of ultimately obtaining immunity from prosecutors with authority to grant it depended upon his veracity. He knew that he would be called upon to testify both before the Commission and in criminal trials resulting from his work, and that defense counsel in those criminal trials would cross-examine him in detail. He was, therefore, made acutely aware of the fact that if he strayed from the truth in an attempt to cover up his activities or to curry favor with the Commission it was virtually inevitable that any such misstatement would be uncovered.

The Commission staff selected certain situations from those described by Phillips which it felt were appropriate for investigation, and he began five months of undercover work. Having agreed to cooperate, Phillips displayed the same ingenuity—and courage—in exposing corruption that he previously had shown in practicing it.

In the two days following his first interview with Commission personnel, Phillips, wearing a transmitter and under surveillance by Commission investigators, contacted seven gamblers operating in East Harlem who were central figures in the Harlem bookmaking and numbers rackets. For several months he collected payments from these and other similar individuals on a regular basis. Several of these individuals, seven of whom have now been indicted by the federal government, were important members of organized crime who had for years been sought by federal law enforcement agencies. Recorded conversations with them demonstrated that payoffs to police were a regular part of their business.

After this start, Phillips continued his undercover work in a variety of situations.

He participated in meetings where an East Harlem organized crime figure, in order to protect a high stakes dice game, paid a lieutenant and, through Phillips, the patrolmen manning patrol cars in the mobster's area. That lieutenant, eight patrolmen and two civilians are now under federal indictment.

After spreading a rumor that he knew an underworld figure anxious to set up a large dice game in midtown Manhattan, Phillips was contacted by members of two plainclothes divisions who set up with him a monthly protection scheme and discussed, in lengthy tape-recorded conversations, the workings of organized graft among plainclothesmen. The operation was terminated after a few preliminary payments, since the Commission was not in a position to go into the gambling business. As a result of this investigation, four police officers and one civilian middleman have been indicted by a New York County Grand Jury.

A police officer had previously told Phillips about accepting $2,000 to cover up two mobsters' connections with a murder. Phillips engaged the officer in a conversation in which the story was recorded by Commission agents. The recording was turned over to the New York County District Attorney and gave rise to an investigation which resulted in five indictments and the reopening of the murder case. Those indicted included three police officers, two retired detectives, and the two men who had paid the bribe—one of whom was also charged with the murder.

Phillips also exploited his acquaintances in organized crime. He was arranging, in cooperation with federal narcotics agents, to participate in illegal shipments of quinine into the country for purposes of cutting narcotics when the operation was aborted because Phillips' underworld contact became the victim of a gangland-style slaying.

A plainclothesman in Queens who was purported to be the bagman for his division took money from Phillips, ostensibly on behalf of fellow officers, to allow a card game to be established in his area. In one tape-recorded conversation during these negotiations, the plainclothesman also told Phillips how he had taken part in an $80,000 payoff in a narcotics case. The case is under investigation by the United States Attorney for the Eastern District of New York.

Phillips accepted money, under Commission surveillance, from two notorious underworld loansharks and cooperated with federal authorities in an investigation of their activities.

Phillips engaged a number of police officers, including a captain, a lieutenant, a PBA delegate, a former narcotics detective, and the chauffeur of an assistant chief inspector, in conversations which further corroborated his descriptions of corrupt activities within the Department.

When Phillips had exploited most of the investigative opportunities available to him as a patrolman, the Commission decided to enlist the aid of Commissioner Murphy in transferring him to a plainclothes division. He attended plainclothes classes at the Police Academy with thirty-four other experienced officers who were part of a program intended to place in plainclothes divisions men of long service who presumably would have a stabilizing and anti-corruptive effect. Phillips reported that the attitudes of these thirty-four officers reflected, in about equal parts, a determination to "hide" so as to avoid being implicated in corruption and eager anticipation of the profits to be derived from it.

Phillips was assigned to the First Division in southern Manhattan and continued his work for the Commission. However, shortly after his transfer, and shortly before the Commission's public hearings, his role was discovered and his undercover activities came to an end.

Phillips' work provided the Commission with invaluable information on the patterns of corruption in the Department. He participated in a total of sixty-nine operations in which tape-recorded conversations involving corruption were obtained. In these recorded conversations it was clear that the participants assumed that police officers were almost uniformly tolerant of, if not involved in, the kinds of corrupt practices in which they themselves were involved. They talked openly not only about their own activities but about conditions in various commands and provided solid corroboration of descriptions by Phillips and other police officers who had talked to investigators on an anonymous basis about the widespread nature of corruption in the Department and the forms it takes.

Phillips' career gave the Commission insights into matters beyond facts indicating the nature and extent of police corruption. It demonstrated, for example, that a corrupt police officer does not necessarily have to be an ineffective one. Phillips possessed qualities of aggressiveness, courage, imagination, intelligence, and a highly developed knowledge of street conditions and the law. These qualities served him well in all his activities in the Police Department—both legitimate and corrupt. Among his fellow officers Phillips stood to gain approval, or at least grudging admiration, both for tough, aggressive police action and for skillful extracurricular money making. He was adept at both.

Phillips himself asserted that few of his comrades embraced corruption with his enthusiasm—and it is clear that the shock expressed by many police officers at the disclosures made in Phillips' public testimony was quite genuine. However, he reported that it was common for fellow patrolmen to pay the officer in charge of assignments for the privilege of being assigned temporarily as his partner. According to Phillips, those whose scruples, timidity or lack of expertise prevented them from attempting to match him in his corrupt endeavors were often quite willing to share the benefits of those endeavors on an occasional basis. One thing is certain—no fellow police officer with whom Phillips served ever turned him in.

Although Phillips' work for the Commission was not directed at making criminal cases, his efforts have, nevertheless, resulted to date in indictments of thirty-one individuals. Six federal and six New York County indictments have named a total of seventeen police officers; and fourteen other persons, most of whom are organized crime members, have also been indicted as a result of his undercover work for the Commission. More indictments flowing from his investigations are anticipated.*

A third cooperative police witness was Waverly Logan. Logan was a police officer of two-and-a-half years' experience who had served for eleven months on the Preventive Enforcement Patrol (PEP) Squad, an elite group

* The first criminal trial resulting from Phillips' work ended in the conviction of an underworld figure in the United States District Court for the Southern District of New York. Then, on March 20, 1972, Phillips was himself indicted for murder by a New York County grand jury. The crime of which he was accused was the double murder of a pimp and a prostitute which had remained unsolved since its commission in 1968. Phillips had attracted attention to himself in this regard by his public testimony before the Commission and subsequent detailed statements to police investigators to the effect that he had shaken down the pimp in 1965. The charge against Phillips was brought to trial in New York County Supreme Court in August of 1972 and resulted in a hung jury, with ten jurors voting for acquittal. A second trial is presently scheduled to begin in early January, 1973.

of twenty officers set up to deal with ghetto problems, particularly in narcotics. In June, 1971, he had been dismissed from the Department for corruption. Logan had consented to take part in an interview on WNEW-TV in which he described in general terms his experiences on the PEP Squad involving corruption in narcotics. Afterwards, Commission staff members interviewed Logan and persuaded him to testify in specific terms about corruption he had participated in and witnessed.

Logan described patterns of corruption he experienced in his early days as a patrolman which echoed those already familiar to Commission personnel —payoffs from gamblers and businessmen, thefts by policemen from burglarized premises, acceptance of gratuities, and the like.

Logan's testimony about the PEP Squad described a deepening involvement in corruption which culminated in the acceptance of narcotics payoffs by the whole squad in amounts of as much as $3,000 per month per man. Logan had been dismissed from the police force and, after his television appearance, was obviously in no position to work in an undercover capacity against police officers. However, he worked in several situations to obtain tape recordings and films of open narcotics and illegal liquor transactions and introduced the Commission's staff to two narcotics addicts who had worked with him as police informants. These informants worked for the Commission and obtained tape recordings of transactions with police officers who sold them narcotics in exchange for what the policemen obviously assumed to be stolen merchandise. Ten such meetings with ten police officers took place over a three-week period. An attempt was made at this point to broaden the activities of the informants by having them work with agents of the Federal Bureau of Narcotics and Dangerous Drugs but the informants' undercover roles became known and subsequent operations proved largely fruitless. Two of the police officers who engaged in transactions with the two informants were indicted in federal court in the Southern District of New York. Three others have been suspended and charged with departmental violations. Departmental charges are pending against two officers, and two others have resigned, one without permission, before charges could be filed against them.

Patrolman Edward Droge was the fourth police officer who agreed to testify. Droge was a young police officer assigned to patrol duty in Brooklyn when he became involved in accepting a $300 bribe from a narcotics defendant in a minor case. The defendant's lawyer contacted the Commission, and investigators conducted a tape-recorded surveillance implicating Droge. Not knowing that his illegal action had been discovered, Droge took a leave of absence from the Department and enrolled in a California university where he was contacted, informed of his predicament, and persuaded to cooperate.

Droge agreed to testify regarding his experiences with corruption during his four years in the Department. Again, the patterns were the same as those described by other police officers, involving illegal payments from gamblers, narcotics dealers, businessmen, and others, as well as instances of police theft and acceptance of various gratuities. Droge was neither as experienced nor as aggressive as Phillips, but his testimony was more typical of the involvement of the average police officer. He agreed to operate in an undercover capacity insofar as he was able. Droge's use as an undercover agent was limited because he was now a newly assigned and consequently untested member of a plainclothes unit and the Commission's public hearings were only a few weeks off. On one occasion Droge attempted to engage two police officers with quite notorious reputations in a transaction involving protection payments for an imaginary gambler. The officers apparently became suspicious and reported the matter to their superiors. The result was a meeting observed and recorded by agents both of the Commission and the Department, with each group unaware of the other's involvement until they met and recognized each other.

A fifth police officer, Patrolman Alfonso Jannotta, gave information and worked undercover but was unable to testify because of ill health. Jannotta, who had been in the Department for five years, was assigned to a radio patrol car in the Nineteenth Precinct in mid-Manhattan. He and his partner took a $30 payoff from a tow truck operator who was working as a Commission operative. The transaction was tape-recorded by Commission agents and filmed by a local television station which had made its equipment and personnel available to the Commission. Jannotta and his partner noticed the cameras, became suspicious, and Jannotta telephoned the tow truck operator to arrange a concocted story to be used in the event of an investigation. The telephone conversation was recorded by Commission agents. Jannotta was confronted with the evidence against him and agreed to tell what he knew about corruption. He told of sporadic participation in low level corruption involving construction sites, bars, tow trucks, and the like. He said that his yearly illegal take was less than $1,000. Jannotta, working with Commission agents, obtained a tape-recorded conversation with the police officer who had been involved with him in the payoff from the tow truck operator. Jannotta proved unwilling or unable to provide further cooperation with the police or the district attorney's office in making criminal cases and both he and his partner were indicted by a New York County Grand Jury.

Other police officers, including plainclothesmen and detectives, who had themselves been involved in corrupt activities, spoke to the Commission staff on a strictly confidential basis. They described patterns of corruption which lent added credibility to the testimony of police witnesses who spoke openly. One of these officers testified anonymously in public hearings held by the State Commission of Investigation and described patterns of corruption in narcotics enforcement which were similar to those described by Detective Leuci, Patrolman Logan and other Commission sources.

Honest police officers also provided the Commission with information about patterns of corruption in the Department. Captain Daniel McGowan has been a member of the Department for twenty-five years and had spent most of his distinguished career assigned to various anti-corruption units. Early in 1971 he provided information to the Commission regarding the handling—or mishandling—of corruption investigations particularly those involving allegations of corruption on the part of police officers which had been referred by federal law enforcement agencies. Although Captain McGowan testified at the Commission's public hearings, some of his most important information could not be presented because it would have focused attention upon conditions in SIU and jeopardized the federal investigation then under way involving the undercover work of Detective Leuci. Captain McGowan testified about his knowledge of conditions in the Department and confirmed the accuracy of the testimony of Officers Phillips, Logan and Droge. Other police officers, experienced in anti-corruption work privately confirmed the patterns testified to at the public hearings.

Another police officer who testified about his own experiences with corruption was Frank Serpico, whose charges of police mishandling of corruption had been presented in *The New York Times* story in April, 1970, which ultimately led to the creation of this Commission. Officer Serpico had refused to participate in corrupt activities but testified to patterns of corruption, particularly among plainclothesmen, which he had observed and which exactly paralleled the patterns described by the other Commission informants and witnesses.

11

Alienation, Cities, and the Police

On March 14, 1964 the *New York Times* ran a brief article on page 26; the article was entitled "Queens Woman is Stabbed to Death in Front of House."[1] The article simply reported that a 28 year-old woman was murdered in the early morning hours, and that her screams had awakened her neighbors. Apparently, the story was just barely newsworthy by New York City standards.

However, as additional information emerged the story began to take on a chilling quality; finally, on March 27, 1964 it again appeared in the *New York Times*: this time on the front page, under the title, "37 Who Saw Murder Didn't Call the Police."[2] The article stated that:

> For more than half an hour 38 respectable, law-abiding citizens in Queens watched a killer stalk and stab a woman in three separate attacks in Kew Gardens. Twice the sound of their voices and the sudden glow of their bedroom lights interrupted him and frightened him off. Each time he returned, sought her out and stabbed her again. Not one person telephoned the police during the assault; one witness called after the woman was dead.[3]

During the course of the police investigation witnesses were asked why they had not called the police. One man said "I was too tired. I went back to bed." Another said "I didn't want to get involved." Although the attack started at 3:15 a.m., the call to the police was not placed until 3:50 a.m. The police arrived at the scene within two minutes of receiving the call. Whether or not they could have prevented the murder of Kitty Genovese is a moot point; they never had the chance to find out.

The tragic case of Kitty Genovese stands as mute testimony to the effects of alienation and apathy. Indeed, alienation has become a matter of increasing concern to social scientists, to the police, and to those who live in the urban centers of the nation. Although alienation is not unique to present-day conditions, it does seem to have a contemporary flair. Perhaps this is because:

> The objectification of social relationships coupled with the paramilitary work ethic has borne fruit in this country over the last few

[1] "Queens Woman is Stabbed to Death in Front of House," *New York Times*, March 14, 1964, p. 26.
[2] "37 Who Saw Murder Didn't Call the Police," *New York Times*, March 27, 1964, p. 1.
[3] *Ibid.*

decades in the form of technological advancement, material abundance, and almost limitless opportunity to acquire. And the result approaches social disaster. Relative influence has become a poor surrogate for the solution of problems—such as alienation, whether it be generational, spiritual, or racial—whereas traditional theory assumed that problems would be solved by material well-being.[4]

The link between materialism and alienation was noted by Karl Marx, who was one of the pioneering theorists of alienation. Marx considered work as man's most important activity, and he felt that through his work man actually created himself.[5] In more contemporary terms he might have said that man achieves self-actualization through his work. However, when work became enforced and was no longer a spontaneous activity, Marx saw it as becoming "alien" to man's nature. In the modern industrial setting he felt that the specialization of labor separated the "manual" and the "intellectual" components of man's working world and in the process precluded the worker from being able to use all of his skills.[6] Finally, Marx noted that as a consequence the worker no longer had his own abilities at his disposal: "It is the machine which determines how fast he should work."[7] In summary, Marx saw the mechanization of labor at the peak of the industrial revolution as detracting from the human qualities which he believed had characterized earlier commercial enterprise. In fact, it was out of his beliefs on the nature of the relationship between the role of the worker and the nature of the distributive system that he formulated his "Communist Manifesto."

Kinds of Alienation

Alienation is not merely a diffuse and undifferentiated state, but rather appears to take several specific forms, each of which seems to have its own meaning and consequences.[8] Although several components to alienation may be identified, it might also be presumed that they interrelate with one another and are mutually supportive. A brief discussion of the several components should illustrate this point.

[4] Frank McGee, "Comment: Phenomenological Administration—A New Reality," p. 165, in Frank Marini, ed., *Toward a New Public Administration: The Minnowbrook Perspective.* (Scranton: Chandler Publishing Co., 1971), pp. 164–171.
[5] Joachim Israel, *Alienation from Marx to Modern Sociology.* (Boston: Allyn & Bacon, 1971), p. 37.
[6] *Ibid.*, p. 47.
[7] *Ibid.*, p. 48.
[8] See for example Melvin Seeman, "On the Meaning of Alienation," *American Sociological Review,* 24 (December 1959), pp. 783–791.

Powerlessness. This type of alienation comes closest to Marx's meaning of alienation. He saw the worker as being increasingly powerless to find expression of himself in his work, as the means of production became dominated by entrepreneurs. In more recent times, this definition of alienation has come to encompass "The expectancy or probability held by the individual that his own behavior cannot determine the occurrence of the outcomes, or reinforcements, he seeks." [9] As Seeman has noted, this is "A distinctly social-psychological view." [10] That is, alienation from this perspective is not indicative of conditions within society but rather relates to the subjective state of the individual within the society. The person *feels* powerless.

The issue of powerlessness is quite complex, and positions taken by many of its investigators tend to be more theoretical than empirical and more descriptive than analytical. [11] However, one very interesting viewpoint on powerlessness is that advanced by Coleman. [12] He defined "natural persons" (human beings) as opposed to "juristic persons" (corporate beings of various kinds). He stated that people (natural persons) tend to yield up direct control over their resources to juristic persons by either actually joining them or by investing resources in them. [13] In this sense people give up power in order to belong to collective bodies which in turn provide benefits which the individual alone could not obtain.

However, in the more traditional sociological sense, this dimension of alienation draws a picture of a person who feels he does not have the power to significantly control his own destiny and who accordingly feels lost and alone. Perhaps this is what Thoreau had in mind when he said that "The mass of men lead lives of quiet desperation." To be sure, there are many people in today's cities who feel they are the pawns of a capricious fate. Their feeling of inability to control their lives, according to this view, leaves them alienated from the society of which they are nominally a part.

Niederhoffer alleges that police officers themselves are often victims of alienation, and that "In the police system the typical adaptation . . . is cynicism." [14] He continues that in "the police world, cynicism is dis-

[9] *Ibid.*, p. 784.
[10] *Ibid.*
[11] See for example Bill Tudor, "A Specification of Relationship Between Job Complexity and Powerlessness." *American Sociological Review,* 37 (October 1972), pp. 596–604 and Claude S. Fischer, "On Urban Alienations and Anomie: Powerlessness and Social Isolation," *American Sociological Review,* 38 (June 1973), pp. 311–326.
[12] James S. Coleman, "Loss of Power," *American Sociological Review,* 38 (February 1973), pp. 1–17.
[13] *Ibid.*, p. 2.
[14] Arthur Niederhoffer, *Behind the Shield: The Police in Urban Society.* (Garden City, New York: Doubleday/Anchor Books, 1967), p. 98.

cernible at all levels, in every branch of law enforcement." [15] Nieder-hoffer sees this cynicism as being of two kinds, "one is directed against life, the world, and people in general; the other is aimed at the police system itself." [16] There are many factors in a police officer's life-space which can contribute to his feeling of alienation, including a feeling of powerlessness. Although policemen are generally viewed as "being in command," this perspective overlooks the fact that the policeman is in reality often cast in an extremely powerless role. For example, he knows the identities of numerous offenders whom he is powerless to arrest (be-cause the legal requirements for an arrest cannot be met); he handles many offenders on a repeated basis, many of whom are able to avoid prosecution or imprisonment; and finally, the police officer frequently finds the nature of his work dictated by social forces over which he is unable to exercise any control. To many urban policemen, their work seems like a treadmill, a task which is on-going but which has no realistic stopping point. For many it becomes a job with which its incumbents must learn to cope, and this process tends to foster cynicism. This was poignantly expressed by a police officer who was working a foot-patrol beat on a major tourist street in a large city. When questioned about the number of panhandlers, prostitutes, and bums the policeman told the author: "What are you going to do? Last week we arrested two hun-dred of 'em. Look around you. They're crawling out of the woodwork all over the place. It's the same old crap every day."

If police suffer from a feeling of powerlessness, what of their clientele? The most extreme and best documented examples of powerlessness have been found in the urban ghettos. As the Kerner Commission pointed out:

> ...there is a widening gulf in communications between local gov-ernment and the residents of the erupting ghettos of the city. As a result, many Negro citizens develop a profound sense of isolation and alienation from the processes and programs of government.[17]

It is interesting to note that the inability of the police to rely on the cooperation of citizens in controlling crime is especially acute in the slums and ghettos where the crime rates are high; "It is in these areas that alienation from the society is the greatest, and it is here that the loss of legitimacy of the law and the police is at its highest." [18] However the feeling of powerlessness felt by ghetto and slum residents is felt by

[15] *Ibid.*, p. 99.
[16] *Ibid.*, p. 100.
[17] Report of the National Advisory Commission on Civil Disorders, Otto Kerner, Chairman. (Washington, D.C.: Government Printing Office, 1968), p. 148.
[18] William J. Chambliss and Robert B. Seidman, *Law, Order and Power.* (Reading, Mass: Addison—Wesley Publishing Co., 1971), p. 361.

others within the community as well—such as people on fixed incomes, pensioners, and those of limited means who have seen inflation and rapid social change make their lives seem to be ever more precarious.

Alienation bred from a feeling of powerlessness could well be the reason why some of the witnesses to the Genovese murder (mentioned at the beginning of the chapter) failed to notify the police. Perhaps their failure to call the police gave the officers who finally responded even more reason to be cynical—and to feel powerless to effectively serve their community. This type of alienation seems to feed on itself and to have a contagious effect which makes it all the more difficult to combat.

One of the key features of a police-community relations effort should be to attack this feeling of powerlessness; to restore to the citizen the feeling that he can in fact exercise some measure of control over his environment. If citizens can be brought to the point where they believe that they can play a determining role in the maintenance of peace and order within the community then perhaps their feeling of powerlessness would be reduced. They might in turn then be more willing to cooperate with the police in controlling crime, which should (hopefully) reduce the feelings of powerlessness held by the police. This is, however, an extremely delicate issue, for if such programs are attempted and fail (for whatever reason), that failure can contribute to *increased* police cynicism and public alienation. Perhaps the key to success in such programs is to avoid confusing *inputs* with *outputs*. That is, a community relations program should have as one of its goals the development in citizens of a feeling of being in control of their personal environment (including making it free from crime). This might be brought about by a variety of means, but the means which are employed should not be allowed to become the goals themselves. Thus the use of beat committees composed of police officers assigned to a neighborhood and the residents of that neighborhood might be a good method of reaching the public and fostering the attitudes sought; however, the goal should remain one of reaching the public—not of establishing beat committees. The same can be said about other techniques, such as store-front operations, ride-along programs, and others. If the police fail to distinguish between the goals sought and the means by which they hope to achieve them, they will wind up playing to a selective audience: those whose cooperation and support they already have.

Meaninglessness. In the first type of alienation, the individual was characterized as feeling an inability to *control outcomes.* Alienation as a state of meaninglessness, on the other hand, refers essentially to a sensed *inability to predict the consequences of one's actions.* In the first instance, the person is alienated because he does not feel he has the ability to exercise control, whereas in this instance, he is alienated because he is unable to attach future meanings to his actions: "The individual is unclear as to what he ought to believe—when the individual's minimal standards for clarity in decision-making are not met." [19]

This type of alienation may be the basis for some of the recent radical social movements (such as the Black Panthers, for instance). These movements may well have grown out of a general attitude of social alienation based upon a feeling of meaninglessness. These types of movements in effect provide meaning by creating new social definitions for their members. Through group consensus, a measure of predictability and "meaning" is created for the participants. In a nutshell, these types of movements may give their supporters things in which to believe and norms or standards against which they may measure conduct, thus infusing meaning where there had previously been only confusion.

Alienation based on meaninglessness has been a serious impediment to the effective delivery of police services in the community. If the residents of the community (or a neighborhood) do not feel that they have the ability to accurately predict the performance of the police, it is only reasonable to presume that they will "reject" the police by either failing to call on them or by declining to cooperate with them if they are called by others. The citizen must see the police and their functions as being meaningfully related to them and they must also feel secure in their anticipation of how the police will respond to their calls for service.

The Kansas City, Missouri Police Department has initiated an "interactive patrol project" in their central patrol district, which encompasses Kansas City's central business district and low income residential areas (including a substantial portion of the city's minority population).[20] The police department noted that in this division, as in so many other cities, the relationships between the police and the citizens has "not always been a good one," and that "citizens are apprehensive about dealing with the police even through they live in constant fear of crime." [21] They note that "Reluctance to deal with police diminishes both a citizen's willingness to report suspicious events and to follow-up criminal occurrences with testimony or complaints." [22] A task force was formed within the central patrol division's area in order to study problems the police had been having. The task force attempted to find out what citizen attitudes were through random interviews of the residents of the area, and:

[19] Seeman, *op. cit.*, p. 786.
[20] Bill Oliver, ed., *Kansas City Patrol Projects, 1973.* (Kansas City, Missouri: Kansas City, Missouri Police Department, 1973), pp. 19–21.
[21] *Ibid.*, p. 19.
[22] *Ibid.*

The responses they got startled the task force members. A significant majority of the citizens reported a high regard for the Kansas City Police Department. The majority believed they were living in a relatively safe area. ... the survey results, the review of social help agencies, and the experience of task force members in the ghetto led the task force to draw two conclusions. First, there is little congruence between what police see in a neighborhood and what its residents see, i.e., in the way of problems and possible solutions. *This divergence of perspectives is the greatest single obstacle to better police-community relations.* Second, the mood of the black community is such that it is likely to reject any police program it has not had a hand in planning, regardless of the program's "rightness." [23] (emphasis added)

Both points raised by the Kansas City Police Department's task force are critically important to police-community relations' thinking. With respect to the first point, if residents of an area and the police who patrol it have different perceptions of the neighborhood and its needs, then each will respond to differents sets of cues or stimuli. This will produce a situation in which each group will appear to the other to be erratic, arbitrary, and indifferent. This in turn may be predicted to produce a feeling of alienation arising from a sensation of meaninglessness.

The second point (community participation) is also vitally important, because norms must be consensually held for them to be effective. If the residents of a community share in the planning for police services within the community, then they will in effect be creating common norms with the police department; that is, they will have a vested interest in the things the police are interested in and vice versa. This will also give predictability to police work, which so many residents of the city do not presently have. If the police and their clientele can view their area from the same (or at least a similar) perspective, and if the police will solicit and use feedback from the community then a strong basis will be established for the elimination of at least some of the meaninglessness which alienates both citizen and policeman.

Normlessness. Yet another dimension of alienation is that of "normlessness." This concept derives from the work of the French sociologist Emile Durkheim, who introduced the concept under the term *anomie*.[24] This has been described as a state of normlessness characterized by an absence of standards which is accompanied by apathy and despair. In general,

[23] *Ibid.*, p. 20.
[24] Robert K. Merton, *Social Theory and Social Structure*, rev. ed. (New York: Free Press, 1957).

anomie refers to the situation one finds when the social norms regulating individual conduct have broken down or in which they are no longer effective guides to behavior. Very rapid social change can create a state of normlessness, as can major demographic shifts. Such a rapid change —and population shift—and its accompanying alienation via normlessness may well have taken place in the cities as a consequence of the massive migration of rural blacks into the urban sprawls (of course other groups, such as Mexican-Americans, rural whites, and Indians have experienced the same phenomenon). Many of these people have become, in essence, displaced persons. Placed in a new and often hostile environment, many have found that their cultural templates were not suited to their new environment. The old norms and expectations simply did not fit the new circumstances; and for many, out of this situation has come lassitude, apathy, despair, and finally hostility. These conditions have produced highly volatile urban ghettos with extensive social dysfunction and high crime rates. The attitude of alienation coming out of such a setting is clearly reflected in James Baldwin's discussion of the ghetto policeman:

... The only way to police a ghetto is to be oppressive. None of the Police Commissioner's men, even with the best will in the world, have any way of understanding the lives led by the people they swagger about in twos and threes controlling. Their very presence is an insult, and it would be, even if they spent their entire day feeding gumdrops to children. They represent the force of the white world, and that world's criminal profit and ease, to keep the black man corraled up here, in his place. The badge, the gun in the holster, and the swinging club make vivid what will happen should his rebellion become overt ...

It is hard, on the other hand, to blame the policeman, blank, good-natured, thoughtless, and insuperably innocent, for being such a perfect representative of the people he serves. He, too, believes in good intentions and is astounded and offended when they are not taken for the deed. He has never, himself, done anything for which to be hated—which of us has? and yet he is facing, daily and nightly, people who would gladly see him dead, and he knows it. There is no way for him not to know it: there are few things under heaven more unnerving than the silent, accumulating contempt and hatred of a people. He moves through Harlem, therefore, like an occupying soldier in a bitterly hostile country; which is precisely what, and where he is, and is the reason he walks in twos and threes.[25]

[25] James Baldwin, *Nobody Knows My Name.* (New York: Dell Publishing Co., 1962), pp. 65–67.

Police officers may also suffer from varying degrees of alienation based on normlessness. This might be difficult to grasp at first, especially in light of the highly structured, quasi-military organization of the police service. The basis of this normlessness was presented by Campbell, *et al.*, who stated that:

> Perhaps the most important source of police frustration, and the most severe limitation under which they operate, is the conflicting roles and demands involved in the order-maintenance, community-service, and crime-fighting responsibilities of the police. Here both the individual police officer and the police community as a whole find not only inconsistent public expectations and public reactions, but also inner conflict growing out of the interaction of the police-man's values, customs, and traditions with his intimate experience with the criminal element of the population. The policeman lives on the grinding edge of social conflict, without a well-defined, well-understood notion of what he is supposed to be doing there.[26]

Rubin has pointed out that "Police are occupied with peacekeeping —but preoccupied with crime fighting." [27] Unfortunately, as Rubin noted, there are no built in rewards for good performance as a peace keeper.[28] He also stated that "Equally frustrating to the police in their roles as peacekeepers and community service agents is the insecurity which community service calls generate." [29] He goes on to say that because of their lack of training in medical matters, family crisis intervention techniques, and due to a lack of linkage with other community service agencies, the policeman often feels unable to even do a proper job as a community service agent.[30] The result is "Frustration with the peace-keeping and community-service roles" which leads the policeman "to become angry with the community he serves—particularly with the black community that calls on him for much of this service." [31]

If there are many and conflicting role demands placed on police officers, then by what set of norms do they abide? If the policeman must use "situational" norms, then one might suspect that official police conduct is guided as much by the exigencies of a given situation as by any set of

[26] James S. Campbell, *et al.*, *Law and Order Reconsidered: Report of the Task Force on Law and Law Enforcement to the National Commission on the Causes and Prevention of Violence.* (New York: Bantam Books, 1970), p. 291.

[27] Jesse Rubin, "Police Identity and the Police Role," in Robert F. Steadman, ed., *The Police and the Community.* (Baltimore: Johns Hopkins University Press, 1972), p. 25.

[28] *Ibid.*, p. 26.

[29] *Ibid.*, p. 27.

[30] *Ibid.*

[31] *Ibid.*, p. 28.

norms. Added to this are the informal occupational norms of the police profession, not all of which are entirely consistent with what members of the general public might expect from police officers. All of this may act in concert to produce periodic feelings of normlessness along with its attendant alienation. If the attendant conditions of normlessness include subjective states of apathy and despair, then those who are alienated are likely to be unable or unwilling to do much of anything about it. This may account, at least in part, for the often encountered dislike among police officers of police-community relations programs.

Isolation. Another category of alienation is that of *isolation.* According to Seeman, "The alienated in the isolation sense are those who . . . assign low reward value to goals or beliefs that are typically highly valued in the given society." [32] In more prosaic terms, such people march to the music of a different drummer. And certainly among the more isolated occupational groups in the United States, according to many writers, are the police.[33] Their isolation is both self-imposed and demanded by the larger society. Yet regardless of the basis for police isolation, the *consequences* are the important consideration. In order for the police to serve their community, they must see themselves as being a part of that community—not as being isolated from it. This is because the police:

> . . . draw their authority from the will and consent of the people, and they recruit their officers from them. The police are the instrument of the people to achieve and maintain order; their efforts are founded on principles of public service and ultimate responsibility to the public.[34]

Police isolation, however, is only part of the larger problem. One of the basic issues in many cities has become that of citizen fear; in fact, there is some indication that the fear of crime is more widespread than crime itself.[35] This fear of crime may play a major role in creating an environment "as dangerous as crime itself, for it distorts the facts and diverts resources." [36] In addition, this unreasonable fear of crime tends

[32] Seeman, *op. cit.*, p. 789.

[33] See for example Jerome H. Skolnick, *Justice Without Trial: Law Enforcement in Democratic Society.* (New York: John Wiley & Sons, Inc., 1966), especially chapter 3, pp. 42–70.

[34] National Advisory Commission on Criminal Justice Standards and Goals, Russell W. Peterson, Chairman, *Police.* (Washington, D.C.: Government Printing Office, 1973), p. 9.

[35] National Advisory Commission on Criminal Justice Standards and Goals, Russell W. Peterson, Chairman, *Community Crime Prevention.* (Washington, D.C.: Government Printing Office, 1973), p. 184.

[36] *Ibid.*

to focus on physical violence, especially street crime. The outcome has been that "this fear has manifested itself in a fortress or siege mentality —a retreat behind multiple locks, elaborate alarm systems, and guest screening devices." [37] And finally:

Fear may cause people to do the wrong thing; apathy insists that nothing can be done, or that someone else should do it. The voice of fear furnishes simple answers to difficult questions; the voice of apathy says that there are no answers or, more particularly, 'I personally can do nothing.'

Many apathetic persons do not want to know about the crime problem or they want to refer it immediately to someone else. Others come to accept crime as a normal condition in society. This passive acceptance of crime as an inevitable and unavoidable fact of American life results in social immobility and lethargy. Citizens in this state of mind may deny their ability to be effective, or may refuse to acknowledge their responsibility for taking action.

In some cases, apathy may have resulted from an individual's past failures in attempting to find solutions to problems. Whatever its source, the present degree of apathy regarding crime has exempted large segments of the population from direct participation in responsible crime prevention efforts. [38]

Clearly, a feeling of isolation breeds a sensation of alienation. This alienation can in turn reinforce feelings of isolation, thus forming a cycle which is especially difficult to break. This particular problem is difficult because first police officers themselves must avoid feeling isolated and must then help those within the community to avoid or overcome the same feeling. This suggests that police-community relations efforts which are designed to deal with isolation must start within the police departments themselves—and there may be considerable resistance to this. One very noteworthy effort in this direction has been made by the Kansas City, Missouri Police Department:

In October 1971, the Department established four task forces in its patrol divisions. Each task force was given the authority to identify the critical problems facing its division and to present to the Chief of Police a program to attack those problems.

The choice of task forces as a planning vehicle rested on two premises. First, that the ability to make competent planning de-

---

[37] *Ibid.*
[38] *Ibid.*, p. 185.

cisions exists at all levels of the Department. Indeed, Chief Kelley believed there was greater understanding of neighborhood problems among patrolmen than in higher ranks.... The second premise for the task forces was that for changes in patrol to win acceptance, those persons affected by the changes should have a voice in planning them.

For these reasons, the task force membership was comprised primarily of patrol personnel, normally the commanding officer of the division, a sergeant or captain and five or six patrolmen.... To make sure the chief heard what the patrolmen in the street thought his problems were and what he proposed to do about them, task force proposals were forwarded to him without change or veto.[39]

The efforts of the Kansas City Police Department address many problem areas, and initial reports indicate that their task forces may in fact produce some of the most far-reaching and important findings for police practices in the United States. A more quiet, but very important consequence of the task force approach has been that "Several task force members have turned down assignments to non-patrol divisions like Investigations and Staff Planning . . . to stay in patrol. More recently, requests to return to patrol from specialized units have become fairly commonplace." [40] The efforts in Kansas City seem to reflect a strong movement away from police alienation. The more difficult problem will then become that of encouraging the same within the various sectors of the community—although the prospects (at least in Kansas City) show very real promise.

Self-Estrangement. "To be self-alienated," according to Seeman, "in the final analysis means to be something less than one might ideally be if the circumstances of society were otherwise—to be insecure, given to appearances, conformist." [41] Seeman sees self-estrangement as being essentially characterized by activities from which the individual derives no personal satisfaction: "The worker who works merely for his salary, the housewife who cooks simply to get it over with . . ." [42] It is not hard to see how this can come about, when "Today our lives are increasingly regulated by machines which set standards of performance and product, telling us when to start working, when to stop, what to do, and how to

39 Bill Oliver, *op. cit.*, pp. 5–6.
40 *Ibid.*
41 Seeman, *op. cit.*, p. 790.
42 *Ibid.*

do it." [43] The consequences of working in a bureaucratic setting are much the same as for persons directly involved in the machine process.[44]

It is important to recognize that the police are not necessarily a prime cause of self-estrangement (or for that matter of any other form of alienation) and it is therefore unrealistic to presume that the police can be a primary cure for alienation. The police are but one component of the urban mosaic, and what they are in relation to other components of the city is determined as much by factors external to the police as to internal factors. Viewed another way, the traffic officer has little control over automotive technology, yet the nature of his work derives from that technology. Alienation is caused not by any unitary phenomenon, but by many factors operating together. The police may be affected by alienation and they may also play a role in reversing it; however, it will take far more than the police to overcome the effects of alienation or to remove it from the cities.

Alienation and the Cities

Fischer has pointed out that the literature on urban sociology tends to indicate that:

> ... the aggregation of great numbers of diverse people creates both the reality and the perception of individual impotence. At the same time, the protective withdrawal this environment forces the individual into and the destruction it causes to social bonds renders man isolated from, fearful of, hostile to, and manipulative of his fellow man.[45]

This summary mirrors the attitude of many people concerning life in the city: that the individual is powerless and that he is forced into a style of living which makes him afraid of his neighbors. From this viewpoint the city is seen as a harsh, unsympathetic, and cold place in which to live. There are of course numerous individual instances (such as the Genovese murder) which support this hypothesis; however, is this an accurate characterization of the city? Does the size of the city relate to its residents' feeling of powerlessness and social isolation? Fischer's studies have indicated that:

[43] Walter M. Gerson, "Alienation in Mass Society: Some Causes and Responses," in Clifton D. Bryant, *Social Problems Today.* (Philadelphia: J. B. Lippincott Company, 1971), pp. 24–31.

[44] *Ibid.,* p. 27.

[45] Claude S. Fischer, *op. cit.,* p. 311.

11

—Community size and powerlessness were *not* associated.

—There was a very small association between community size and the sensation of social isolation.

—With respect to involvement, presumably both cause and effect of social-psychological isolation, the findings were contradictory: attendance at social meetings was unrelated, but knowing one's neighbors was strongly related to urbanism—as was having relatives among those neighbors. The more metropolitan, the fewer know neighbors and the fewer have relatives nearby.[46]

Apparently, although there may be a rural-urban difference in the degree of association with neighbors, there is little difference in total real and felt social isolation.[47] People who live in cities are not necessarily more socially isolated than those who live in rural areas—it may be that they simply associate with people *other than their immediate neighbors.* However, people who live in large cities do seem to be more wary and distrusting; however, it is hard to tell how much of this is based on legitimate factors and how much of it is the result of the siege mentality mentioned earlier. The key for the police, however, is that they not be misled into believing that simply because an urban area is large and heterogeneous that it would be pointless to develop strategies aimed at dealing with citizen alienation. Indeed, perhaps the absence of such programs is a contributing factor to the perception of alienation.

The reading which accompanies this chapter discloses how one element of the criminal justice system, when abused, can operate to the detriment of the system as a whole and the people it is intended to serve. In addition, it demonstrates how a system (or a component of a system) can operate so that feelings of alienation—in all of its manifestations—will result.

[46] *Ibid.,* p. 322.
[47] *Ibid.*

330

Appendix A
An Investigation of a Magisterial System*

Brief Historical Resume

Philadelphia's magisterial system had its genesis in the office of the alderman created by William Penn's Charter of 1691. While numerous constitutional and statutory laws have modified the structure of the minor judiciary, the essential character of the magistrate's office has remained the same to the present date. In 1872, Judge Finletter traced the history of the minor judiciary in a single sentence:

"Complaints of the rapacity of the local magistrates have come down to us, continuously, from the earliest periods." [1]

Widespread public criticism led the Constitutional Convention of 1872–73 to abolish the aldermen's courts and install the magistrates without significantly altering the operation of those courts.

In each of the past five decades, major efforts have been made to reform the magistrates' courts. A survey of the administration of criminal justice was conducted from 1921 through 1926 exposing serious and notorious weaknesses. The Magistrates' Act of 1927 followed without correcting the deficiencies enumerated by the preceding inquiry.

After a preliminary four-month investigation by the District Attorney of Philadelphia and the Attorney General of Pennsylvania in 1935, a grand jury was specially charged to inquire into the practices in the magistrates' courts. Ten months later, an extensive presentment was returned condemning numerous practices. *While 27 of the 28 magistrates were indicted as a result of the findings of the 1935 Grand Jury, only four were brought to trial and all were acquitted.* The 1937 Magistrates' Court Act was designed to correct the deficiencies illustrated by the 1935 investigation, but the Ruth Commission in 1938 reported the basic deficiencies persisted.

There followed an investigation in 1948 which resulted in amendments of the prior legislation and indictments against five magistrates. The one magistrate who was brought to trial was acquitted, and the charges against the others were abandoned. During the 1950's, the prosecutions of three magistrates disclosed the continuation of practices which had been condemned by prior investigations. Only one conviction resulted from the three prosecutions in the 1950's and the numerous indictments arising out of the 1935 and 1948 investigations.

* SOURCE: *Pennsylvania Department of Justice, Report of the Attorney General on the Investigation of the Magisterial System, Harrisburg, 1965, pp. 1–26, 266–267. Reprinted by permission of The Pennsylvania Department of Justice.*
[1] *Commonwealth v. Alderman Hagan,* 9 Philadelphia Reports 574 (1872).

Against a background of 274 years of operation of Philadelphia's en-trenched minor judiciary and repeated inquiries which have paraphrased and repeated the conclusions of their predecessors, this Investigation of the magisterial system was instituted. Without the subpoena power, Justice Investigators were compelled to secure information through voluntary co-operation of those who had contacts with the magisterial system. By request-ing the appearance of many thousands of people, a portion appeared and a relatively small fraction gave candid answers. More than 7,500 individuals were asked to submit to questioning, in excess of 2,200 appeared and about 3 percent provided useful information.

Although the records were incomplete, the chief magistrate and the solicitor for the board of magistrates cooperated by providing the available documents. All but one of the magistrates gave unsworn testimony to Justice Investigators on general procedures. *When some of the magistrates were later asked to submit to questioning about specific complaints, all except one declined.* In addition, an estimated 50,000 documents in the magistrates' courts were examined and notes of testimony were analyzed in hundreds of cases. The Investigation was fashioned to conduct an intensive inquiry in sufficient depth to draw valid conclusions on the magistrates' courts in the minimum possible time.

The Magistrates' Problems

The magistrate in 1965 faces a tradition of criticism from the past and complex problems on the administration of justice in the present. He has inherited the mantle which was characterized by the Citizens Municipal Association of Philadelphia in 1873:

> All the worse arts of the professional politician are exerted to secure the position of alderman for those who are unfitted for it by training, by habits and by character. . . .[2]

Because of his political background, the magistrate is subjected to the gamut of community pressures from all sides. The legislation of 1927 and 1937 did not attain the goal of removing the magistrates from political involve-ment. *The position continues to be awarded to those who have risen through the ranks of their political parties after years of service which ordinarily culminates with being a ward leader. Once he assumes office, the magistrate is immediataely faced with demands for political favors.* When the deposition of one magistrate was taken, he candidly answered the question as to whether he receives requests for consideration on cases pending before him:

[2] Debates of the Convention to Amend the Constitution of Pennsylvania IV, 214 (1873).

"Who would call me in the divisional police court? A local politician. Who would call me in Traffic Court? A committeeman."

Efforts to influence the magistrate's decisions come from numerous sources in the community, in addition to requests from people active in politics. Consideration is sought by individuals in many other categories, as expressed in comments by two magistrates:

"... we get all kinds of requests from all types of people, doctors, attorneys, men and women in all walks of life."

"I have received requests from priests, members of the clergy, businessmen in the neighborhood, ..."

According to one magistrate, such requests even come from high-ranking city officials who seek to influence the magistrate to hold certain defendants. A high city official reached one magistrate by telephone at central police court in advance of a hearing and, after identifying himself, stated:

"I want you to hold some people you have in front of you this morning for high bail."

Magistrates are further subjected to requests from responsible officials to act in ways which tempt and induce the minor judicial official to exceed his jurisdiction. The substantial backlog in the court of quarter sessions inspired the district attorney, the police commissioner and the criminal trial commissioner in 1958 to request the magistrates to dispose summarily of minor cases. That request was widely misunderstood and resulted in the magistrates assuming summary jurisdiction in a wide variety of cases expressly prohibited by The Magistrates' Act of 1937. Similarly, as a matter of common practice, assistant district attorneys at preliminary hearings are still implementing the *1958 policy by urging magistrates to impose summary convictions where the defendants are charged with indictable crimes. The law limits the magistrate's power to either discharging the defendant or holding him for court on the indictable offense.* Such requests lead the magistrate to expand his authority and discretion in ways not contemplated by the law.

Such pressures serve to complicate the magistrate's already difficult job of deciding whether there is a prima facie case to hold the defendant for the action of the grand jury or whether a summary crime has been proved, where the defendant is so charged. The magistrate must also rule on difficult evidentiary questions as to what is inadmissible hearsay or incompetent for a variety of technical reasons. Such decisions are complex for judges learned in the law. It is virtually impossible for men of even great intelligence, who are untrained in the law to grasp and decide such issues properly.

In addition, enormous changes in criminal procedure have thrust upon the magistrate numerous new problems. The past quarter century has witnessed broad changes in the criminal law as a result of decisions by the Supreme Court of the United States expanding the meaning of the Due Process Clause of the Fourteenth Amendment as it relates to criminal practice in state courts. *The magistrate must decide what constitutes probable cause before issuing a search and seizure warrant.* While the issue of what is a constitutional search and seizure is left to the court of quarter sessions under the Pennsylvania Rules of Criminal Procedure, as a practical matter the magistrate is frequently drawn into decisions on these complicated questions. The recent decisions on right to counsel and the application of that rule to the preliminary hearing or the summary proceeding pose new problems. Such complex questions complicate the magistrate's daily decisions.

Against this background of legal problems and community pressures, the magistrate must apply his abilities which are, in practice, extremely limited in accordance with the minimal requirements on qualification established by the law for his office. *The Magistrates' Acts require only that the minor judicial official must be 35 years old, a citizen, a voter and a resident of Philadelphia.* While further inquiries are being made, it appears that one magistrate does not possess those qualifications. *The law imposed such limited qualifications contemplating that the magistrate would have limited powers and responsibilities.* This investigation has disclosed that the development of the law and practice in the magistrates' courts have called upon the magistrates to render judgments in areas far beyond their capabilities.

The Magistrates' Technical Performance

1. Copy of the Charge

One of the first magisterial acts in the chronology of a criminal case involves the signing of the copy of the charge, which authorizes the release of an accused between the arrest and the initial hearing. Under the Magistrates' Act of 1937, the magistrate must secure bail before releasing defendants charged with certain enumerated offenses such as narcotic violations, larceny and illegal lottery activities. *Investigation has shown that it has been the general practice among magistrates not to require the posting of bail in such cases even though the law makes it mandatory.* Interviews with hundreds of applicants for copies of the charge show that they obtained the release of defendants without posting any bail in cases where the law required that bail be posted. When questioned on this subject, magistrates admitted, without apparent concern, that they did not adhere to those requirements of the law.

2. The Further Hearing

The next immediate step in a criminal case is the hearing before a magistrate where a request is made for a further or continued hearing. Because of the historic abuse of the further hearing as a device to put pressure on the defendants or extract tribute, the Magistrates' Act of 1937 has imposed strict requirements on the subject. *No continuance of a hearing in a criminal case may be granted unless the person requesting the continuance states under oath the reason, which must be noted, together with the name of the requesting party, in the magistrate's docket and returned as part of the transcript in the case.* Even with the relatively recent history of criminal prosecutions in 1948 against magistrates for failure to note the reasons for continuances in their criminal dockets and transcripts, *this Investigation indicates that the clear requirements of law on this subject are generally disregarded.*

An analysis of cases involving assault and battery, gambling, liquor and morals charges disclosed more than 1,000 further hearings during the one year period from September 1, 1963 through August 31, 1964. The traditional opportunity for pressure exists in such types of cases. The magistrates have continued to ignore the definitive statutory requirements designed to curtail that opportunity for abuse.

3. Summary Convictions on Indictable Crimes

A review of the Magistrates' Hearing Lists showed that the magistrates entered in excess of 4,000 summary convictions for the two year period 1963 and 1964 on cases where the defendants were charged with indictable crimes. The Magistrates' Act contains an explicit prohibition against that practice. Such dispositions were noted in serious factual situations where defendants were charged with crimes such as attempted robbery, assault with intent to kill and aggravated assault and battery on a police officer; yet they were convicted merely of disorderly conduct. While the magistrates conceded their general practice of reducing indictable charges, they tried to defend their conduct on the grounds that the district attorney's office requested them to dispose of such cases at the magistrate's level.

4. Re-arrest and Ignored Cases

A study of re-arrest cases disclosed widespread practices of discharging defendants where strong cases had been presented with more than enough evidence to constitute a prima facie case. While there was a discernible pattern of discharges in cases on lottery and gambling offenses, the magistrates also failed to hold for court serious felonies where strong cases were presented. By contrast with the numerous cases which required re-arrest proceedings, the magistrates held more than 2,000 people during the year 1963 and 1964 on cases which were ignored by the grand jury. An examination of those cases disclosed that magistrates held substantial numbers of defendants where insufficient evidence was presented.

Subterfuges in Record Keeping

Like the failure to note reasons for continued hearings on dockets and transcripts, the magistrates' records were found to be deficient in numerous respects. Such a finding was not unanticipated in view of the limited qualifications for keeping records possessed by the magistrates and their clerks. In addition to errors and omissions, however, *a comprehensive pattern of false entries was detected which was made in the magistrates' efforts to give the appearance of technical compliance with the law where it had not been observed.*

Many magistrates had applicants for a copy of the charge execute a bond without the entry of good bail, such as cash, a recognized surety bond or real estate. Behind these bonds, a series of fictitious cash receipts were employed by some magistrates to present the facade that the applicant had posted cash. Their records contained a "cash bail receipt" which was purportedly given by the magistrate to the person posting cash, reciting that the magistrate had received a certain sum of money as set forth in the bond. Attached to those records was a "return of cash bail receipt" which was signed by the party who had executed the bond. That document bearing his signature purports to show that the cash bail had been returned to him. Investigation disclosed that those documents were fictitious with no exchanges of cash ever having occurred. Those receipts were designed as a subterfuge.

One clerk stated the magistrate did not require applicants for a copy of the charge to execute a bond when the copy was signed. On the following day, after the hearing had been held, the clerk would then make out all the bonds in a uniform sum which used to be $50 and since was raised to $100. The person whose name appeared on the bond was anyone who happened to be in the office on that day. The clerk added that the reason some of the signatures on the bonds varied was probably because she expected a particular person in that morning and filled out the bond with his name; then, when someone else came to the office, she would ask that person to sign the bond. Seeing that the bond was made out in the name of someone else, the person would simply sign the name which appeared on the bond. After the bond was signed, the clerk would give it to the magistrate who would execute the acknowledgment that the bond was signed in his presence.

Many bail bonds were found among the magistrates' records which were supposed to have been signed by the same individual; but, according to analysis by an examiner of questioned documents, it was concluded that different people had signed that name. For example, a bail bond would be purportedly signed by a person in the presence of the magistrate. Then the magistrate was obliged to certify that the bond was signed in his presence. In many situations two bonds, which were supposed to have been signed in the presence of the magistrate by the same person, were found to have been signed by different people.

Magistrates also made false representations on the original-white copy of the charge that bail had been required in a space designated "Amount of bail demanded on the above charge $_____." While many magistrates inserted a cash figure on those copies of the charge, numerous applicants in those cases advised that no cash or other good bail was, in fact, posted.

Evidence was also uncovered indicating doctoring of dockets to present the appearance of prior compliance with the requirement that the reason for the further hearing be noted. On a specific complaint, a magistrate's dockets were examined to determine whether there was compliance with the act requiring the notations of reasons for continuances. The docket showed a first hearing on a specific date in 1962 and a further hearing on a specified date in 1964. The magistrate sought to explain the inconsistency by stating that the year 1964 should have been 1962. The appearance of the dockets with different color ink and the erroneous entry of the year "1964" for the year "1962" indicated, on its face, that additions had been made to the dockets in an effort to comply with the requirements of the law after the magistrate learned of the complaint on that specific case.

Corruption

The Atmosphere

An aura of corruption has long permeated the magisterial system even though the prior investigations and prosecutions did not establish facts showing the existence of corruption. The magistrates themselves have expressed concern that the discharged defendants may pay someone, thinking the case has been fixed. This concern is illustrated by a magistrate's comment at the conclusion of a preliminary hearing held on May 6, 1964:

> "THE COURT: Due to the fact there is no case I am going to discharge you. Don't give anybody any money and don't let anybody say the Magistrate wanted so much money or you couldn't be discharged. The only reason you are being discharged is for lack of evidence. . . . Don't pay anybody money on the case. The case was not fixed."

In a similar vein, a magistrate's clerk testified that bystanders in the magistrate's court will approach the magistrate or the assistant district attorney and engage them in conversation. Later after a defendant has been discharged because of insufficient evidence, that person will prevail on the defendant for money on the representation that a pay off is necessary because the case was fixed.

Absence of Proof in the Past on Corruption

Even though this atmosphere has prevailed, the prior inquiries have not produced evidence to establish corruption. Except for the Costello case where the court ruled the evidence was legally insufficient, the criminal actions of the past 30 years have been based on bookkeeping violations or other charges which did not show a demand or acceptance of money to influence the disposition of a case. The prosecutions against the 27 magistrates arising out of the 1935 Grand Jury investigation were based on failure to enter proceedings in the criminal dockets. The charges against Chief Magistrate O'Malley in 1948 involved the imposition of the summary convictions on indictable offenses, a demand that a police officer stay out of South Philadelphia, failure to note reasons for continuances and changes in the dispositions of cases. The four other magistrates, who were arrested as a result of the 1948 investigation, were charged only with granting continued hearings without entering the reasons in their dockets.

Magistrate Molinari was tried for subornation of perjury in a factual situation which was not directly related to the conduct of his official duties. The only case involving a charge of a payment involved Magistrate Costello; and his acquittal was directed by the court on the ground that the evidence was tainted and legally insufficient. The only successful prosecution in the entire group, which was returned against Magistrate Knox, involved the acceptance of bail in violation of the Magistrates' Act.

The exhaustive study of the 1935 Grand Jury disclosed no evidence of corruption as reported in its 495 page presentment:

> "One of the inquiries to which the Grand Jury devoted earnest and thorough efforts was to ascertain whether or not any magistrate had accepted, directly or indirectly, any money or other valuable thing from any source whatever in return for any favor or disposition of any matter before him at any time as a magistrate. The Grand Jury constantly had in mind this possibility, and its inquiry on the point was thorough. It made specific inquiry of thousands of police witnesses and hundreds of prosecutors and defendants, and in no single instance did any witness directly or even by inference testify that such was the case.[3]

An Iceberg of Current Corruption

This Investigation has detected widespread corruption at every level of operation of the magisterial system. More than 40 cases have been discovered

[3] 1935 Grand Jury Report 449.

where pay offs have been demanded on the representation that they were necessary in order to influence the disposition of criminal cases in the magistrates' courts. Such demands have been made by magistrates, their clerks, attorneys, bondsmen, politicians and bystanders.

After reviewing documents in thousands of cases and interviewing hundreds of witnesses, Justice Investigators concluded that the detectable cases of corruption are like the small portion of the iceberg which is visible above the water with over 90 percent never appearing. Only a relatively small percentage of witnesses sought by Justice Investigators were willing to be interviewed. Among those who were questioned, many had already discussed their cases with others involved and were obviously not providing all the facts.

In addition, it was common for witnesses who were somewhat cooperative to avoid telling the crucial facts on corruption because it would involve them as well as others. There is probably no more difficult area to investigate than bribery and corruption since the telling of the tale ordinarily implicates the witness in the impropriety. Such transactions are conducted secretly with only two participants: the briber or corruptor and the party accepting the bribe or being corrupted. Because of these considerations, *Justice Investigators concluded that the significant quantity of detectable corruption indicated the presence of a very large underlying cesspool.*

In only a few cases did witnesses provide evidence which carried the demand for the pay off directly to the magistrate. Most of the direct evidence disclosed a chain of events which led up to individuals who were close to the magistrate, but ordinarily stopped short of the magistrate. There were many missing links because the insiders refused to talk to Justice Investigators. *Due to the lack of subpoena power, information could be gathered only from those who were willing to cooperate on a voluntary basis.* By seeking such potential witnesses in large enough numbers, sufficient volunteers came forward to provide substantial insight into the underlying operation of the magisterial system. In the absence of direct evidence, conclusions on any involvement of the magistrates in cases with missing links could only be inferred from circumstantial evidence including the magistrate's conduct in deciding the cases and his comments recorded in the notes of testimony. For illustrative purposes in this summary, only a few cases are described in general categories which overlap with limited cross references where a single case is particularly significant.

Magistrates

Where the direct evidence did implicate the magistrates in provable participation in the corruption, the defendants in the cases before them were charged with relatively minor crimes. Thus, suspicion would not be aroused by a discharge. In one such case, a defendant was charged with illegal lottery activity where the evidence showed one slip of paper containing 34 number plays. The magistrate threatened to hold the defendant under $1,000 bail for court which would have cost the defendant $100 for a bail bond premium, unless $100 was paid to the magistrate. After arrangements were made for the pay off, that defendant was discharged with little attendant concern because of the minimum evidence involved.

In another situation, the magistrate attempted to extort money from defendants who were charged with violating the Pennsylvania Liquor Control Act. There, a person who was temporarily in charge of a taproom had been arrested on a charge of allowing a minor to frequent the bar. The magistrate demanded a bribe stating in such situations "big people pay $500 and little people pay $200." When the magistrate was unsuccessful in extorting the money from that defendant, he utilized the device of ordering a further hearing and then issued a warrant of arrest for the owner of the taproom. When the magistrate's efforts to collect from the owner failed, he held him under $500 bail for action of the grand jury even though the evidence was insufficient. The grand jury ultimately returned an ignored bill of indictment, because of the lack of evidence, which resulted in final dismissal of the charges.

The Magistrates' Clerk

In several situations, the clerk to the magistrate was implicated in the demands for pay offs. One case involved a defendant who had been charged with writing 60 lottery bets and having one page of numbers impressions in a book which was used to keep accounts in a small grocery store. The magistrate's clerk talked to the defendant when he was in custody before being released on a copy of the charge; and at that time, the clerk demanded $100 to have the case discharged. The payment was not made. On the presentation of relatively little evidence, the magistrate held the defendant under $500 bail for court at the preliminary hearing on the following day.

In a complex arrangement involving a number of categories of people in the magisterial system, a magistrate's clerk was charged with being an intermediary in a case where a defendant made a payment to influence the disposition of a criminal case. After a committeeman arranged to secure the defendant's release on a copy of the charge, he contacted a relative, who was later to become a magistrate, and another committeeman. The second committeeman said "$100 should take care of it." The defendant then obtained $100 from a contact, which was verified by the cancelled check issued the day before the final hearing.

The second committeeman then advised the defendant that the connection had been made with the clerk. Before the hearing, the first committeeman, who was paid the money, was observed talking to and shaking hands with the clerk at the divisional police court. Shortly thereafter the case was discharged.

Both committeemen stated they were not involved in any effort to fix that case, and the first committeeman denied making any payment to the clerk. Similarly, the clerk denied knowledge of any wrongdoing in this case. Thus, this case illustrates a situation where the direct evidence stops one step before the clerk. Aside from the handshake at the divisional police court, which does not by itself prove impropriety on the part of the clerk, there is nothing to implicate the clerk. In this case, it is possible that the money did not get beyond the reputed fixer who may have shaken clerk's hand to give the defendant the impression that the clerk was reached on the morning of the hearing. Based on the defendant's affidavit, the committeeman was paid on the representation that the case would be fixed, but the evidence does not solidly extend to the clerk or the magistrate.

Bondsmen

One bondsman was implicated in two cases by complainants who executed affidavits charging that payments were made in efforts to influence the disposition of criminal cases. He was identified as being the recipient of $175 from a woman charged with writing numbers. She was discharged at the preliminary hearing. In a second case, the same bondsman told a defendant that he "could stop it right here" and the magistrate would impose a fine on her providing $75 was paid "undercover." That defendant with a record of eight prior convictions for similar offenses, was fined $10 and costs on a summary offense although she had been charged with an indictable crime. Since this bondsman refused to respond to a request by the Justice Investigators to answer questions, the full facts on any involvement by the magistrate are not known.

Two experiences with the same bondsman convinced one defendant that a payment to the bondsman influenced the magistrate's disposition of the case. On the first occasion, a bartender was arrested on charges of serving intoxicated persons. A bondsman approached the owner of the taproom and said it would cost $150 to have the bartender discharged. The $150 was paid to the bondsman; the bartender was discharged.

Approximately four months later the same bar owner and the bartender were both arrested on charges that visibly intoxicated customers had been served. At 3.30 on the morning following the arrest, the bar owner was visited in the police station cell room by the bondsman who said "... that's an expensive magistrate; he wants $250." How he had learned of the arrest or where the defendants were being held were facts unknown to the owner. This time she refused to pay.

At the preliminary hearing the following day, there were three other cases presented which were virtually identical with the facts on this owner and bartender. The defendants in all three of those cases were discharged; but the bartender and the owner who refused to pay were held for court. The same bondsman, who had propositioned the taproom owner, obtained the release on copies of the charge of two of the other defendants who were discharged.

A study of the notes of testimony in the four cases shows no justification for the difference in treatment based on the facts. The disparity in dispositions is explainable only in terms of factors outside the record. The fact that the bondsman was linked to two of the other defendants by obtaining their copies supports the conclusion that the bondsman had the ability to obtain the discharge, as he claimed, upon payment of the cash. Since the bondsman refused to talk to Justice Investigators, there is no direct evidence on the magistrate's involvement in these cases.

Bondsmen and attorneys were involved in corruption in a series of cases which were heard at one divisional police court arising from arrests on morals charges during a single month. From ten cases a pattern emerged showing that the defendants who were able to raise a substantial sum of money, ranging from $300 to $2,500, were discharged while those who could not were held under bail for court. While these cases differ in detail, the scheme is illustrated by one of the cases where the defendant was arrested on charges of immoral practices and assault and battery.

The arresting officer testified that the defendant sat next to him in a theater, pressed his leg against the officer, repeated that act and then reached over and squeezed the officer's private parts. Similar testimony was presented in many of those cases. After the defendant was placed in a cell at the police station, an officer advised him that he was wanted on the telephone. The caller said that he witnessed the arrest and could get the defendant out of jail for $20. Shortly after the defendant agreed to that price, a man appeared with a signed copy of the charge authorizing the defendant's release. The defendant was then taken to the bondsman who advised that he would take care of this matter for $1,000. When the defendant asked if it could be done less expensively, the bondsman replied, "No, you pay the $1,000 and everything is over. You won't have to worry about anything. I have to pay three or four people to take care of this. I can fix the case and you won't have to go to court."

Following the bondsman's instructions, the defendant met him the next morning near the police station where the bondsman introduced the defendant to an attorney. The bondsman told the defendant that the attorney was to represent him stating, "Everything is taken care of, you don't have to worry about a thing." *When the case was called by the magistrate, the attorney argued that the defendant was under psychiatric care and had been in a concentration camp in Germany. According to the defendant, neither statement was true and the defendant had not told the attorney any such thing.*

The magistrate then discharged the case. Following the discharge, the bondsman accompanied the defendant to his bank where the defendant withdrew $1,000 in cash and gave it to the bondsman. The defendant's version of that transaction is confirmed by the bank records which show that the defendant withdrew $1,000 on the same date that he was discharged by the magistrate. *When parting, the bondsman warned the defendant not to try anything funny or the police would get him.* There were no arrangements or discussion between the attorney and defendant as to fee.

The difference in the disposition of the ten cases cannot be explained by distinctions in the evidence against the defendants. An analysis of the testimony presented by the arresting officer shows that it is virtually identical in some cases where the defendants were held and in other cases where the defendants were discharged. Two examples of the arresting officers' testimony follow:

Case One

"Shortly after I was seated there, the defendant was sitting in the seat to my right, and with his left leg he pressed it against my right leg numerous times, and after about 15 minutes I left my seat and returned to the rear of the movies and purchased a soft drink. After finishing the drink I returned to my seat and the defendant was still seated in the next seat. At this time he repeated the same thing, and then he ran his left hand up my right leg and let it slide up till he placed his hand on my penis, at which time I pushed his hand away, and he immediately put his hand back on my penis and began to rub same. At this time I asked the defendant would he mind joining me for a smoke in the rear."

Case Two

"About 15 minutes later the defendant took a seat to the right of me and began to press his leg next to my leg. This was repeated a second time and I moved my leg. The defendant then, after 10 minutes, reached over with his right hand and grabbed my private parts and began to squeeze. I got up and I identified myself to the defendant. When the defendant stated where can we go, I said that I had my car outside, and when we started to walk back to go out, my partner came over and we identified ourselves as police officers and placed him under arrest."

The defendant in Case One was able to pay a substantial sum of money. He was discharged. The defendant in Case Two could not make a substantial payment; he was held for action of the grand jury.

In all ten cases there was a direct correlation between the defendant's abil-

ity to pay and his ability to obtain a discharge. The distinction was striking when one of the lawyers conferred with two defendants on the same morning at the police station. This attorney, who was called into other such cases by bondsmen, undertook to represent one man, but not the other. For the payment of a cash fee of $500 to $600, the attorney succeeded in securing one man's discharge with a single sentence, "I ask that the defendant be discharged" after the arresting officer had set forth a prima facie case. When conferring with that client, the attorney was asked to represent a second man who faced the same charge. When the second man told him he could pay only $20 a month, the attorney shrugged his shoulders and appeared disinterested. On the same morning, the second man was held in $500 bail for court upon the presentation of very similar testimony.

Since none of the bondsmen or attorneys, who participated in any case where any defendant was discharged, was willing to answer questions for Justice Investigators, no direct evidence was available on the involvement of any magistrate. The detailed facts provide circumstantial evidence on the underlying transactions.

Attorneys

In addition to attorneys' involvement with bondsmen in morals cases, this Investigation disclosed other allegations of corrupt practices by lawyers. One attorney was implicated in two cases where he advised his clients, the defendants in particular cases, that a pay off was necessary in order to obtain a discharge. In one such case, the lawyer advised the defendant that his fee was $175 and it would cost an additional $200 for the magistrate. According to the client's affidavit, he paid $375 to the attorney as requested. At the magistrate's hearing, evidence was introduced showing that police officers found a note book containing 496 numbers bets in the possession of the defendant. Nothwithstanding that evidence, the defendant was discharged by the magistrate. He was re-arrested and later adjudged guilty of illegal lottery activity.

In a second case, the same attorney advised other clients that the magistrate demanded a $200 payment in order to discharge a father and son who were arrested on charges of serving an intoxicated customer. The defendants refused to pay. The father was discharged and the son was held for court. Following the submission of the Summary Report, the attorney executed an affidavit denying any impropriety as detailed in the following chapters.

Two defendants were standing in the hallway of a divisional police court when an attorney approached and told them they better get a lawyer. When the lawyer asked for a fee of $200, one defendant urged the other to retain the lawyer because he was sure this attorney could "get the case discharged."

After the attorney reduced his fee to $150, he was retained. The evidence disclosed that the arresting officer had heard one defendant call in a number over the telephone; and when the officer entered, the defendant placed a slip of paper in his mouth which was then found to contain 24 number plays with repeats and prices. The magistrate discharged both defendants with the assistant district attorney objecting to the discharge of one. That defendant was re-arrested and was ultimately convicted of illegal lottery activity.

Another defendant who refused to retain that attorney did not fare so well. His case was scheduled to be heard before the same magistrate at the same police station. The attorney approached the defendant and advised that he could "take care" of the case and get the defendant "out of this" for $125. That defendant refused to retain the attorney. At the preliminary hearing, the same magistrate held the defendant for action of the grand jury on a charge of writing numbers; but at the trial, he was discharged.

One attorney admitted to Justice Investigators that he used language in talking to his client which could be interpreted to mean that a discharge would be obtained providing the client paid a given sum of money in advance of the preliminary hearing. The attorney explained that he really was talking only about his fee, but another inference might be drawn. In the case under investigation, the defendant believed that the money was necessary in order to pay off others.

The attorney sought to justify that approach because legal fees are not collectible unless they are obtained in advance of the hearing. In order to be certain that the fee is collected in advance, it was necessary to tell the defendant something to the effect that the fee had to be paid in order to secure his discharge.

In some cases the relationship between the magistrate and the attorney led to the inference that influence was used to secure the desired results. In one case a former solicitor to the Board of Magistrates, who was then the solicitor, was retained by three defendants who were charged with receiving stolen goods. After that attorney set his fee at $1,500, one of the defendants complained it was too high. The attorney stood firm on his price "because he had expenses, too." The attorney also said that he knew all the magistrates and had "influence" with the magistrates.

The attorney was present at two preliminary hearings, but did not participate or enter a formal appearance in the recorded proceedings. The evidence disclosed that the defendants had sold a substantial shipment of clothing to a Philadelphia store, which had been stolen from a New York company. An employee of the New York firm admitted sending the goods to Philadelphia after stealing them. The merchandise was later found in the defendants' possession. At one stage of the case, the attorney went up next to the magistrate on the bench. Notwithstanding the evidence, all the defendants were discharged. The defendants were re-arrested and held for the action of the

11

grand jury when the quarter sessions judge ruled that a prima facie case was established. At trial, they were acquitted. The attorney refused to discuss his participation in the case with Justice Investigators so there was no direct evidence of involvement on the part of the magistrate.

Another complaint of improper conduct involved an attorney who participated in a case which was heard by the magistrate who was his father. The attorney was contacted by the brother of the defendant who was charged with robbery and abduction. The attorney appeared at the divisional police court where his father was scheduled to sit and told the defendant's wife, according to his affidavit, that "it would cost $275 to fix the case and take care of everything." The wife rejected that offer. According to the defendant's brother, he gave the attorney $5 to give the victim who supposedly only wanted his money returned. The brother thought the attorney had turned that money over to the victim.

At the preliminary hearing the detective testified that two men grabbed the victim around the neck, pulled him into a car and took $7 from his pocket. At that juncture the detective advised the court that the victim did not wish to prosecute the case. The magistrate permitted the withdrawal of the prosecution and discharged the defendant.

That night the defendant and his brother-in-law drove to the home of the attorney and paid $100 to the woman who answered the door. According to the defendant's brother, the attorney returned the $100 to the brother-in-law, but the brother-in-law stated that the $100 was never returned. When the magistrate's unsworn testimony was taken, he was questioned about this case and stated that nothing improper was done. After the publication of the Summary Report, the attorney executed an affidavit denying any impropriety as detailed in a following chapter.

Politicians

One ward leader was the subject of five complaints that he acted as an intermediary in fixing cases. In one case he told the defendant after his arrest that he would find out who the magistrate was and "see what he could do." The ward leader told the defendant to bring $150 with him to the police station the next morning. Following those instructions, the defendant paid $150 to the ward leader. The defendant had been charged with serving liquor to visibly intoxicated persons and maintaining a disorderly house when police officers observed a fight in progress at his bar. The defendant was discharged at the magistrate's hearing.

Prior to the start of a preliminary hearing in another case, the same ward leader approached a defendant who had been arrested for selling malt beverage in excess of the legal limit. Outside the divisional police court the ward leader told the defendant "it needs $200." The ward leader accepted $150

346

from the defendant and arrangements were made for the balance of $50 to be paid later. At the magistrate's hearing, the defendant was discharged.

In a third case the same ward leader was accused of soliciting the mother of a defendant to pay $25 to have the case "thrown out." The mother refused to provide any information, but another person present executed an affidavit stating that the mother paid $25 in cash to the ward leader. However, that defendant was held in $300 bail for the action of the grand jury.

In another case, he interceded on behalf of a defendant charged with establishing a gambling place and maintaining a disorderly house. On that occasion, the ward leader allegedly talked to the magistrate and advised the defendant that "he could help us but it would cost $100 to do so." The defendant said he did not have that much money so nothing further was done with the magistrate. The defendant was held for court.

The final case involving the same ward leader concerned the arrest of an individual for illegal lottery activity when he was found with one slip of paper listing three number plays. After arranging for the defendant's release on a copy of the charge, the ward leader said it would cost the defendant $60 to have the magistrate discharge the case. According to the defendant he paid the $60 and was discharged at the preliminary hearing.

A member of the Pennsylvania House of Representatives was implicated in a plan to fix a case involving a charge of illegal lottery. The state representative made arrangements with the magistrate to have the case discharged for a $100 payment. He later paid the money in two installments to another intermediary.

Committeemen have also been accused of being implicated as intermediaries in efforts to fix cases. One such case concerned an alleged solicitation of a $200 payment to fix a case after the proprietor of a taproom was arrested on a charge of selling beer to a minor. The defendant provided an affidavit stating that the committeeman secured her release on a copy of the charge and then asked her if she "wanted the case taken care of." When she said yes, the committeeman borrowed her car stating that he was going to see the magistrate. He returned and said it would cost $200 to fix the case, but she refused.

The following day the defendant was held under $500 bail for action of the grand jury. The committeeman denied being involved in an effort to fix the case, stating that he had borrowed the defendant's car so that he could investigate her and her bar. The grand jury concluded that there was insufficient evidence and returned an ignored bill of indictment, thereby dismissing the charges.

Bystanders

Investigation disclosed numerous situations where payments were made to or demanded by unidentified bystanders in the magistrates' courts. In the

11

absence of identification, it was not possible to trace through the evidence to determine whether any payments reached the magistrate. For example, in one case an unidentified man left the magistrate's stand and told the defendant he would have to pay $50 or be held for court. Two other affiants confirmed that demand. Shortly after the $50 was paid, the magistrate discharged the defendant.

Another typical situation was presented by the affidavit of a woman whose husband was arrested for serving visibly intoxicated persons. She received a telephone call from an unknown man who asked if she "wanted the case taken care of." *Following his instructions, she met him at the police station the next day and paid him $100 as demanded.* She then observed him walk into the divisional police court and stand near the magistrate's desk. Her husband was then discharged. Based on that limited information, it is not possible to evaluate whether the magistrate was involved or the unidentified person merely took advantage of the situation to pick up $100.

Another woman executed an affidavit stating that on two occasions unidentified men at the magistrates' courts asked her for money on the representation that they could have her cases discharged. On one occasion, she paid $100 after being approached in the hearing room by a man who said "he could get her case thrown out for $100." She was discharged. On another occasion, three different men approached her and stated that they could get her case discharged with the prices varying between $75 and $100. She declined to pay and was held for court.

In another typical case, a woman was arrested on a charge of illegal lottery when she was found with 118 number plays. She was then contacted by an unidentified man who told her he could get her case discharged for $200. Before her case was called the following morning, the man asked for the money but she and her son refused to make any such payment. According to her son, the man identified himself as a ward leader, stating that "he could have the case busted for $125," but the son refused. After the magistrate discharged the defendant, that man followed the defendant and demanded money because he had "talked to someone and had the case taken of," but his efforts to extract the money were unsuccessful.

Extortion on Copies of the Charge

Questioning of hundreds of applicants for copies of the charge disclosed a general practice among the magistrates to charge for signing copies. Based on a provision in the Magistrates' Act, the only legal charge is $1 in situations where the magistrate takes bail before releasing a defendant on a copy of the charge. A charge in excess of $1 constitutes extortion and also violates an express statutory prohibition against a magistrate receiving any money for the performance of any duty pertaining to his office other than the fees prescribed by law.

Nineteen of the twenty-eight magistrates have imposed illegal charges to sign copies, accoridng to affidavits provided by applicants for those copies. While the cost ranges up to $25, the most frequent price is $5. One hundred seventy complaints of this type were received against one magistrate.

In one case, the applicant stated that he paid the magistrate $10 by check for signing the copy. At the magistrate's request the applicant made the check out to "Cash." In support of the complaint, the applicant produced a cancelled check bearing the date May 7, 1964, which is the precise date when the copy of the charge was signed by the magistrate. That check was made payable to the order of "Cash" and was endorsed in the name of the magistrate. In addition, some complaints were received from applicants stating that payments usually in the sum of $5, were made to magistrates' clerks in order to secure the magistrate's signature on the copy of the charge.

Connections with Gambling Operations

Prior Judicial Statements

Judicial decisions in the past have alluded to connections between the magistrates and organized crime although such ties had not been documented with evidence. The Supreme Court of Pennsylvania in *Rutenberg v. Philadelphia* referred to "vicious practices [which] had developed in the [magistrates'] system" and they enumerated a series of items including:

"... and in general the ineffectiveness and corruption of some of the magistrates in dealing with cases where rackets and organized crime was involved." [4]

In a similar tone, Judge Carr, specially presiding at the trial of Chief Magistrate O'Malley in 1949, commented in his charge to the jury concerning the magistrate's powers:

"In like manner, the temptation is always strong to extend favors and indulgences to organized crime, which in all great cities controls a vast underworld with many votes." [5]

A Few Applicants Obtain Numerous Copies on Gambling Charges

This investigation has disclosed substantial circumstantial evidence indicating conections between the magisterial system and organized gambling. A review of extensive documentary evidence shows a definite pattern of the magistrates' availability to facilitate the prompt release of defendants charged

[4] 329 Pa. 26, at 31 (1938)
[5] *Commonwealth v. O'Malley*, 68 D. & C. 461, at 487 (1948).

with gambling offenses. When an accused is arrested, he remains in custody until a judicial official signs a copy of the charge which authorizes his release until the initial hearing. During a one year period, 11,259 copies of the charge were examined relating to the releases of defendants charged with crimes other than minor ofenses such as corner lounging or intoxication. The statistical analysis showed that a relatively small number of individuals had secured a proportionately large number of the copies of the charge.

In addition, there were other applicants, some of whom were bondsmen, who had obtained numerous copies of the charge with an overwhelming proportion for defendants accused of gambling offenses. For example, one applicant obtained 193 copies of the charge with 174 on gambling charges. Another person applied for 92 copies of the charge with 88 on gambling offenses. A third individual obtained 194 copies of the charge including 124 for defendants charged with gambling crimes. These statistical studies disclosed that about 20 individuals had extensive activity in securing copies of the charge for individuals accused of gambling offenses.

Magistrates Sign Copies in Bondsman's Office

Direct evidence was found linking magistrates to a bondsman's activities which, at a minimum, demonstrates that magistrates facilitate the release of certain defendants on copies of the charge. Two magistrates were observed to be frequent visitors at the office of an active bondsman in center city Philadelphia. Two applicants for copies of the charge executed affidavits stating that those two magistrates had signed copies of the charge for them in the office of that bondsman. Employees of that bonding agency were among the regular applicants who had secured numerous copies of the charge to obtain the release of defendants accused of gambling crimes.

Certain Magistrates Sign Numerous Copies for Special Applicants

The bondsman who had secured 193 copies of the charge (174 on gambling offenses) had 59 of the copies (including 58 on gambling charges) signed by one of the magistrates who frequently visited and signed a copy in the bonding agency's office. The other magistrate, who frequently visited that office and signed a copy there, had signed 23 copies (including 22 for gambling offenses) for the same bondsman. That bondsman was an employee or associate of the bonding agency frequented by those two magistrates. Among the copies of the charge obtained by that bondsman on gambling offenses, two copies were obtained for each of seven defendants who had been arrested twice for setting up and maintaining an illegal lottery; and three copies were picked up for each of four people who were arrested on that charge on three separate occasions. Thus, the proved activities of that bondsman link him closely with those charged repeatedly and many others charged once with gambling offenses. The documents and visits show a close connection between the bondsman and two magistrates.

The applicant who obtained 92 copies of the charge (88 for gambling charges) relied upon one magistrate to sign 54 of the copies (including 51 for gambling offenses). That particular applicant had secured the release on two occasions each for 4 individuals who were charged with setting up and maintaining an illegal lottery operation.

Connections between other magistrates and applicants for copies of the charge were indicated by a pattern of activity when certain magistrates signed numerous copies for the same applicants:

Magistrate A signed 59 copies (58 for gambling) for Applicant 1
Magistrate A signed 54 copies (43 for gambling) for Applicant 2
Magistrate B signed 52 copies (41 for gambling) for Applicant 3
Magistrate C signed 49 copies (44 for gambling) for Applicant 4
Magistrate D signed 34 copies (29 for gambling) for Applicant 2
Magistrate C signed 33 copies (26 for gambling) for Applicant 5
Magistrate D signed 23 copies (23 for gambling) for Applicant 1

Applicants 1 and 2 work out of the same office. Thus, Magistrate A, one of the frequent visitors to that office, signed 113 copies for the two applicants including 101 for gambling offenses. Many other bondsmen relied upon the same magistrates to sign numerous copies of the charge where the most frequent offenses involved were gambling crimes.

Regular Applicants Secure Signed Copies Faster

A time analysis, comparing 2,047 copies secured by regular applicants with 2,047 copies obtained by individuals who made single applications, demonstrated that the regular applicants were able to secure the signatures of magistrates much more quickly. The original-white copy of the charge shows the time of issuance by the police department and the time of signing by the magistrate. The regular applicants obtained more than twice as many magistrates' signatures within 5 minutes of the issuance of the copy at the police district, almost twice as many within 5 to 10 minutes and substantially more in the interval between 10 and 30 minutes after issuance of the copy by the police.

By contrast, the individual applicants took longer to get the magistrates' signatures. Almost three times the number took between 1½ to 3 hours to obtain the signature of the magistrate, and approximately 4½ times as many individuals required 3 to 6 hours to find a magistrate to sign a copy of the charge. While some of the speed by the regular applicants is doubtless accounted for by greater familiarity with the procedure involved, these statistics

11

also tend to show greater availability of the magistrate for the regular applicants.

High Discharge Rate for Defendants on Copies Obtained by Regular Applicants

By tracing the progress of cases through from the copy of the charge to disposition, it was noted that there was a high discharge rate for defendants whose copies of the charge had been obtained by certain applicants. One regular applicant had obtained 84 copies of the charge (including 71 for gambling offenses) during a one year period under study. When the defendants, whose releases he had secured, appeared before certain magistrates, there was a high discharge rate on gambling charges as follows:

Magistrate	Discharged	Held
1	9	1
2	11	0
3	6	1
4	5	0

Similarly, there was a high discharge rate before certain magistrates for defendants whose copies of the charge had been secured by the applicant who obtained 193 copies (including 174 for gambling offenses) as follows:

Magistrate	Discharged	Held
3 (same as Magistrate 3 above)	11	2
5	12	2
6	10	1

The defendants whose releases had been obtained by a regular applicant with 92 copies (including 88 for gambling offenses) had a high discharge rate before two magistrates on gambling charges as follows:

Magistrate	Discharged	Held
9	5	1
1 (same as Magistrate 1 above)	4	0

Other defendants, after being released on copies of the charge by certain applicants, enjoyed a high discharge rate before certain magistrates. Twelve defendants, whose releases on copies of the charge were secured by one applicant, appeared for preliminary hearings before the same magistrate. Eleven were discharged; one was held for court. Similarly, seven defendants, who were released on copies on the application of the same man, were all discharged by a certain magistrate. Numerous other similar patterns were noted.

Re-arrest Pattern

The pattern on requests for re-arrests further indicates a connection between magistrates and organized gambling. Re-arrests are requested where either the police officer or the assistant district attorney at the preliminary hearing concludes the discharge was improper because the evidence established a prima facie case. Of the 578 requests for re-arrests made in all categories in 1963, 396 arose in gambling cases for a percentage of approximately 69. During the year 1964, 375 requests were made for re-arrests on gambling cases out of a total of 520 such requests for offenses in all categories for a 72 percentage rate.

An analysis of individual cases shows discharges in cases where the evidence overwhelmingly proved the defendants were involved in illegal lottery activity. For example, in one case a defendant was observed writing on a slip of paper against the wall. When the officers aproached him, he tried to eat the paper. In a can six feet away, the officer confiscated 16 slips listing 610 bets, 69 lead bets and 57 parlay bets. In the defendant's shirt pocket were 36 blank slips identical to those found in the can. After the defendant was discharged by the magistrate, he was re-arrested, held for court and found guilty of illegal lottery activity at trial.

In another case the arresting officer, armed with a search and seizure warrant, found approximately 2,000 number plays and 12 lead bets in the defendant's premises. She was discharged by the magistrate but was re-arrested and held for court. At trial, she was convicted of writing numbers. In a third case, officers entered the defendant's home on the authority of a search and seizure warrant and found 269 slips of paper listing in excess of 3,000 horse bets, 15 slips listing names and amounts and 69 tally sheets. That defendant was discharged by the magistrate on the statement that there was a "defective warrant." The defendant was re-arrested, held for court and found guilty.

There were many other re-arrest cases which were equally strong and a large volume of cases where the evidence was sufficient to require holding the defendants for court. *Numerous discharges in such extreme cases indicate that the magistrates are either completely incompetent or have some special reason to favor the defendants. While there is good reason to question their competence as analyzed in detail in other sections, even the magistrates' most extreme critics on the subject of qualification would concede that they know enough to recognize a prima facie case when it is so strong.* Thus, the re-arrest pattern in conjunction with the other evidence, including the existence of corruption in the system generally, indicates a sinister connection between magistrates and gambling operations.

Magistrates—Crittendon-Walker

Armed with a warrant authorizing the search of a residence, police officers on August 29, 1963, found in a cellar hallway behind loose wallpaper one slip of paper containing thirty-four number plays. After locating that evidence, William Walker, one of the individuals who lived at that address, was placed under arrest for writing numbers. According to the police report, Walker claimed that the paraphernalia belonged to Andrew M. Crittendon who lived at the same address.[6]

At a preliminary hearing the following day before Magistrate Ruth Marmon at Germantown Avenue & Haines Street, the police officer testified about finding the numbers slips and he further stated that another man and his wife, who lived upstairs, had access to the cellar. Walker was discharged by Magistrate Marmon,[7] who then instructed the officers to arrest Crittendon.[8]

After a hearing before Magistrate Marmon the following day, Crittendon was also discharged.[9] The police requested a re-arrest on the case because there was no assistant district attorney present at the hearing and, according to the police report, the defendant was known to be a pickup man for one of the largest numbers writers in that area.[10] The request for re-arrest was disapproved by the district attorney's office.

While this case has all the surface indications of being properly discharged, a series of affidavits disclose that the case was fixed. In an executed affidavit William Walker stated: After Walker was arrested, he told Crittendon that the police had been at their residence and had searched through Crittendon's personal effects. The following morning Crittendon accompanied Walker to the magistrate's hearing and Walker informed the magistrate that he had been wrongfully arrested since the warrant had been intended for Crittendon. Crittendon then stood up and identified himself which led to Walker's discharge and the subsequent arrest of Crittendon for writing numbers. After Walker was discharged he contacted John Welsh who directed Walker to a magistrate who had his office in the 1500 or 1600 block of Girard Avenue. Walker paid the magistrate $15.00 to sign a copy of the charge and then secured Crittendon's release from jail.

According to Walker's affidavit: The following morning Walker and his wife accompanied Crittendon to the magistrate's hearing where they met Welsh. When Magistrate Marmon arrived in her automobile Welsh left the Walkers and went to talk to Magistrate Marmon. He returned a few minutes later

[6] Philadelphia Police Department Investigation Report: 63–510379.
[7] Notes of testimony *Commonwealth vs. William Walker*, Divisional Police Court No. 8 dated August 30, 1963.
[8] This fact is contained in the Philadelphia Police Department Investigation Report: 63–510379, although there is no reference to it in the notes of testimony.
[9] Notes of testimony *Commonwealth vs. Andrew M. Crittendon*, Divisional Police Court No. 8 dated August 31, 1963.
[10] Philadelphia Police Department Request For Re-arrest Report.

stating that Magistrate Marmon intended to hold Crittendon in $1,000 bail for court. Inside the hearing room Welsh talked to the magistrate's clerk and the clerk in turn whispered something to Magistrate Marmon. Welsh then motioned to the Walkers to go outside with him and once outside, Welsh told Mr. and Mrs. Walker that Magistrate Marmon would discharge Crittendon for $100. Mrs. Walker then advised Welsh that she did not have $100, but that she would give him $50 at that time and would pay the balance in a few days. Mrs. Walker then turned over $50 to Welsh. Welsh and the magistrate's clerk, later identified as Joseph Bardascino, then walked to a far corner of the courtroom, talked for a few minutes, and separated with the clerk returning to the place where the magistrate was sitting. Shortly thereafter Crittendon was discharged. A few days later Walker went to Welsh's office at 15th and Venango Streets and gave him the other $50. Welsh asked Walker to accompany him to meet the magistrate's clerk so that Walker could see that Welsh in fact paid the money over to the clerk, but Walker declined to do so stating that he trusted Welsh.[11]

[11] Affidavit of William Walker dated November 16, 1964.

12

Challenge of the Future
Current Dilemmas

The future of the American city offers a startling prospect, if one stops to consider the predictions that:

—Every month we add to our population enough people to populate a city the size of Toledo;

—Every year we add enough people to make another Philadelphia;

—In twenty years we will double the size of Los Angeles and the San Francisco Bay area;

—In twenty years we will add 6,000,000 to the New York region;

—Since 1940, Baltimore has added to its population a city larger than Milwaukee, and in the next twenty years it will add a city about the size of Miami;

—and, during that same twenty year period Washington will be adding to itself a city the size of Baltimore.[1]

Already half the population of the United States resides in the big cities, and as this population grows, so also must the cities. As the cities grow they will undoubtedly continue to have problems. Perhaps some of the current urban problems will become resolved—yet on the other hand, new and unanticipated problems may emerge. There is a good likelihood that the complexity of the cities of the future will tax the imagination of their administrators, including the police.

A great many of the problems which face the cities are serious problems in their own right, yet at the same time many of them are also *symptoms* of other, deeper problems. One good example is traffic congestion. It is ironic that the traffic in central Philadelphia moves at about twelve miles per hour—the same speed achieved by horse drawn carriages a hundred years ago! [2] Slow traffic with its noxious fumes and noise is indeed a problem in its own right, but at the same time it is symptomatic of other problems: roads and streets which were not constructed to meet the de-

---

[1] "Tomorrow's Cities," *Changing Times, The Kiplinger Magazine,* (April, May 1970 issues), in Clifford L. Snyder, *et al. Viewpoints: The American Cities.* (Minneapolis: Winston Press, 1972), p. 284.
[2] *Newsweek* (January 18, 1971), 44–47, 49.

mand of modern vehicles, the growth of the suburbs which have in turn produced auto-dependent commuters, and the absence of effective mass-transit facilities, to name but a few.

Another serious problem which is also a symptom is the worsening financial crisis being experienced by nearly all major cities. This lack of money is a serious problem in that it can lead to dangerously low levels of service in critical areas which can in turn erode public confidence in local government. It is also a symptom in that it reflects a changing demographic/economic base within the urban area. For instance, as the poorer inner city populations expand the more affluent urban residents have historically tended to move to the suburbs. As this more financially stable group leaves, it takes with it tax revenues while at the same time it continues to take advantage of many municipal services which they no longer support with tax dollars. At the same time, the expanding population of the inner city not only becomes larger, it demands increased city services which it is not fully able to financially support. Since there is proportionally less money to provide for higher demands of service, the levels of service decline (by failing to keep pace with increased demand) thus engendering disenchantment and hostility of the people requiring the needed services. The resulting tension then serves as an additional impetus to the flight from the cities of the middle class resident. This is schematically represented as follows:

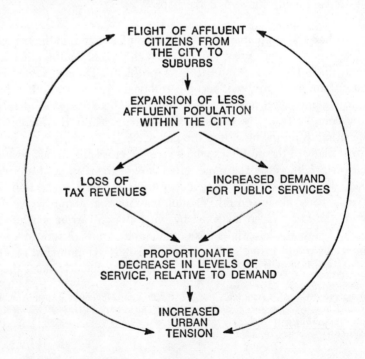

At the same time, other problems continue to plague the cities. These include solid waste disposal—getting rid of the half-ton of garbage produced annually by the average city dweller.[3] Or the continuing poisoning of the air in the cities by a variety of sources.[4] Crime, which continues to generate fear and distrust, is also a serious problem. In fact, crimes of violence are primarily a big city phenomenon: "The 26 cities with 500,000 or more residents and containing about 17 percent of our total population contribute about 45 percent of the total reported major violent crimes." [5]

All of these problem/symptoms affect the quality of life in the cities, and one way or another, they all involve the police. Therefore how the police view their responsibilities and how they discharge them will also play a role in the quality of urban life. The police have indeed become aware of the fact that their relationships with the remainder of the community have not always been the best, and the issue of police-community relations has become important in many communities. Much of this interest was spurred by the 1967 report of the President's Commission on Law Enforcement [6] and the Administration of Justice, especially the task force report on the police, which devoted a lengthy chapter to the topic of the police and the community. Although the report is now several years old, it still contains many valid and current insights.

The topic of police-community relations is usually dealt with by emphasizing its need and by offering suggestions as to how that need should be met.[7] While this approach has considerable merit, certain problems not usually discussed also deserve attention and will be presented in the subsequent paragraphs.

The Symptom/Problem Dichotomy

The preceding discussion of problems as symptoms also applies to the police. Individuals and groups define problems relative to their own perspective—indeed, this is a natural consequence of a society characterized

[3] For a more complete treatment of this problem, see George R. Stewart, *Not So Rich As You Think* (Boston: Houghton Mifflin Co., 1967), especially Chapter 6.

[4] See for example Ron M. Linton, *Terracide: America's Destruction of Her Living Environment.* (Boston: Little, Brown and Co., 1970).

[5] National Commission on the Causes and Prevention of Violence, "Violent Crime: Homicide, Assault, Rape, and Robbery," in "Crime and Violence in the Cities," Snyder, *Violence, op. cit.,* p. 181.

[6] The President's Commission on Law Enforcement and the Administration of Justice, Nicholas deB. Katzenbach, Chairman. *Task Force Report: The Police.* (Washington, D.C.: Government Printing Office, 1967), Chapter 6, pp. 144–208.

[7] See for example Robert C. Trojanowicz and Samuel L. Dixon, *Criminal Justice and the Community.* (Englewood Cliffs, New Jersey: Prentice-Hall, Inc., 1974), especially chapters nine and ten.

12

by a high degree of division of labor. This, as has been noted, is also true of the police. To a law enforcement officer, the problem of a robbery or a homicide is to find out who committed the crime and to prepare a case for prosecution. In a domestic disturbance, the police problem is how to effectively end the disturbance. From the police perspective the problem is not *why* a robber committed his crime or *why* the killer took the life of his victim (other than that such information may help an officer to prepare his case), or *why* a couple decides to have a family fight. In reality the police are specifically called upon to perform a relatively narrow role (enforcement) and individual officers are rewarded for performing that role well (e.g., making a "good arrest" or intercepting a felony in progress). The social forces which play a major role in shaping crime are of very secondary interest to the police.

However, the police have at least verbally committed themselves to "preventing crime and saving lives." Therefore, it should come as little surprise that the police approach to crime prevention has developed out of the traditional manner in which the police have defined the crime "problem" in the first place. Thus police "crime prevention" programs have typically translated into requests for more resources to be devoted to traditional operational tactics. The logic behind this has been multiple: (1) police presence is considered to be a deterrent to crime and therefore more police officers can provide more presence and thus deter more crime; (2) police operations are seen as being the correct approach to the problem but their lack of success is at least partially attributable to the fact that there have simply not been enough men and equipment to get the job done; (3) crime is growing faster than the population (and by inference faster than the police department), thus mandating more policemen and equipment. The validity of these three positions is certainly open to debate. They all unfortunately overlook the simple fact that crime will be prevented only when its *causes* are eliminated, and many of the problems dealt with by the police are in fact *symptoms of deeper problems*. This means that many of the police department's tactics in reality only deal with the surface problem and are totally inadequate in terms of *preventing* crime, although they may be excellent techniques for dealing with specific criminal acts which have already been committed. Since most major police departments state that their primary goal is the prevention of crime, and since they must also acknowledge increasing crime rates, something must obviously be done to resolve the dilemma. In many police departments the answer to this riddle has been found in "community relations."

Under the circumstances described above, many police departments have taken the position that they are doing all of the right things and are doing them properly. Failure most properly can be laid at the doorstep of an indifferent or apathetic public. Operating from this conceptual base, police-community relations efforts tend to develop programs designed to make the public more responsive to *the police department's perception of the problem.* This underscores the philosophy behind the bumper stickers which say "Support Your Local Police," or "Next Time You Need Help, Call A Hippie" (although such stickers are not usually passed out by the police). The department itself is more likely to have "ride-in" programs in which interested citizens ride with police officers on a tour of duty (so that they can develop an appreciation for the complex role played by the police and the difficulties they encounter). Another program has been the "community radio watch" in which individuals with citizen's band radios or private business band radios are urged to report crimes or suspicious events to their dispatchers or directly to the police (many police departments monitor citizen's band frequencies for just this purpose). Some of these programs have had very beneficial results, and the purpose of mentioning them is not to criticize them as programs but rather to show how they may be used in support of a fixed outlook on the part of police.

Basically, the police must realize that the *primary* crime *prevention* agencies within the community are the family, the schools, and the churches. Any realistic effort to prevent crime must include efforts to strengthen and support these institutions. The police can do this in part through the use of family crisis intervention techniques and through effective referral services, whereby social problems can be brought to the attention of the appropriate social agencies. In this connection, it should be pointed out that many of the social agencies have been remiss in accepting responsibility for their own roles and have played a hand in forcing the police into problem areas in which they are ill equipped or poorly trained. The police in the coming decades, if they are to achieve their full potential, must realistically define their roles, especially with respect to the roles of other social agencies. They must carefully examine their enforcement and service activities and become more critically aware of the extent to which their problems are also symptoms. As Ahern [8] pointed out:

If police realize that the overwhelming percentage of street crime in their city is being committed by people from broken families, with

[8] James F. Ahern, *Police in Trouble: Our Frightening Crisis in Law Enforcement.* (New York: Hawthorn Books, Inc., 1972), p. 218.

poverty-level incomes, in areas where housing and education and basic public services are inadequate, and in which the use of drugs thrives, they must insist that society respond meaningfully to these problems. If they do not, they will find themselves battling for decades against the products of the same crime factories. If they realize that the victims of street crime are likewise predominantly from these areas and that these are citizens whom it is their job to protect, they will realize that their task is doubly important.

The Operations/Support Dichotomy

The police department of nearly any large city is a complex organization with numerous internal and external functions. In order to meet the demands which confront them, most police departments are divided into functional units. Broadly speaking, police departments are separated into two main divisions—one which provides the actual delivery of police services (patrol, traffic, investigations) and one which supports them (communications, detention, property, etc.). In many departments "services" actually breaks down into two elements. One deals with administration and the other with direct support services. The "mission" of the police department is seen as being carried out by the operations divisions (patrol, traffic, investigations) which are supported by the remaining elements within the department.

Most chiefs of police are men who have come up through the ranks and most of them have spent a large portion of their careers in direct police operations. One may well suspect that the overwhelming majority of police chiefs see themselves as the highest ranking policeman in the department rather than as the chief administrator of a complex bureaucratic organization. This writer knows one police chief, for example, who wears two pistols in shoulder holsters and who carries a submachine gun in the trunk of his car and another who has a sawed-off shotgun mounted on a swivel underneath his desk. The former chief of the Philadelphia Police Department is reported to have seen himself as a "general in the war on crime."

Since most chiefs have come up through the ranks, one finds relatively few who have a significant degree of higher education—or who are sophisticated in such areas of management as budgeting, personnel, labor relations, or computer technology—or in other areas of prime interest to senior level administrators. A great many of these chiefs continue to focus their attention on problems of traditional police operations, and many of them do so with a dedication based more upon faith than upon hard evidence. Given increasing crime rates, a chief whose primary interest lies in field operations may appear to be just what's needed to deal with the problem of crime; however, as James Q. Wilson [9] has noted:

> ... to close observers of the police at work, there is also some reason to believe that the number and deployment of police have little or nothing to do with the crime rate. For example, there were substantial increases in police manpower in New York and elsewhere during the nineteen-sixties, yet crime continued to increase. Boston and San Antonio report about the same rate of burglaries despite the fact that Boston has almost three times as many police, in proportion to population, as does San Antonio. Though crime skyrocketed when Montreal police went on strike, there were no drastic increases when New York City patrolmen walked off the job.

Perhaps the traditional techniques of police operations require closer examination. Such an examination has been made in several cities and the results have encouraged them to experiment with new concepts in policing.[10] Perhaps one of the greatest problems involving the operations-oriented chief is that he is very likely to view police-community relations as a "support" function which might be of some assistance to the operating line elements. Such a decision might well lead to the formation of a special unit specifically for the purpose of dealing with police-community relations (and which does not interfere with line operations). Thus, according to Ahern (the former chief of police of New Haven):

> Too often ... community-relations squads represent no change in the police department as an institution or in the attitudes of the people in it. If this is true, the community-relations unit becomes a public-relations gimmick that misleads the public. It may be a slick temporary answer to community pressures, but it is more than likely to turn into a fraud. A community-relations unit makes a department no more responsible and no more responsive than it was before. Invariably it is an ornament that distracts attention from a bewildering variety of institutional ills. Often in troubled situations a department's community-relations unit is given a short period to try to 'cool it.' If this does not work, the department reverts to its old ways, and people's heads get cracked. A community that is hostile to police will be increasingly and not decreasingly embittered when on one

[9] James Q. Wilson, "Do the Police Prevent Crime?" *New York Times Magazine,* October 6, 1974, p. 19.

[10] See *Street Crime: Reduction Through Positive Criminal Justice Responses.* House Report No. 93–358, Select Committee on Crime, Claude Pepper, Chairman. (Washington, D.C.: Government Printing Office, 1973).

night a community-relations squad is trying to convince them that the police department is a good thing and the next night the 'real cops' beat a narcotics addict within an inch of his life or arrest someone on trumped-up charges.

For some departments, the 'tactical squad' is the functional opposite of the community-relations squad. A 'tactical squad' is essentially a violence squad whose function is to operate saturation patrols in certain areas or to respond to disturbances with shows of force.

Community-relations units and tactical squads are both admission of the failure of police professionalism. The creation of a community-relations squad says that a police department cannot relate to a community through decent and fair responses to that community's problems as a whole and that it must create a gimmick to gloss over its deficiencies. That tactical squad says that a department is incapable of handling potentially violent situations in non-violent manners and that a single patrolman or a few patrolmen conventionally trained and armed are simply incapable of preventing or controlling significant crime or disturbances. While the community-relations squad as it now functions is usually a distortion of a fundamentally good impulse, tactical squads point toward a militaristic elitism—a kind of shock-troop emphasis—which could lead police departments toward a model even more inappropriate, and in the end more dangerous, than the Dick Tracy crime-fighter image they now promote.

In using an operational approach to police-community relations, a department may run the risk of establishing a unit which in the long run produces a product which actually runs counter to its original goal. If the citizens see community relations as coming from only one element of the police department, they are likely to simply write it off as an attempt to achieve form without substance. In the coming decades the police departments in the larger cities will undoubtedly acquire more competent and professional leadership. With the advent of a more professional group of police executives odds are that police departments will come to see community relations as being the task of all members of the department and that it is to be carried out through the honest, dedicated, and efficient efforts of all members of the department.

Police Secrecy

In a great many incidents involving tension between police departments and the public, allegations of misconduct are made against the police department, or specifically against the actions of individual officers. The usual procedure in such a case (especially if the accusation is serious) is for the department's internal affairs division to investigate and report to the chief. Unfortunately, many citizens "particularly those from minority groups and civil rights organizations, have been dissatisfied with police internal review procedures. They have urged the creation of civilian review boards to investigate and determine the validity of citizen complaints." The issue of civilian review boards has been hotly contested; however, Ahern's position is perhaps one of the best and most concise statements on the subject: ". . . civilian review boards are not an effective solution even to the limited type of brutality or corruption problem that they attempt to deal with. When police departments are bad, the roots of their problems are far deeper than any civilian review board can penetrate." [11]

There are actually two problems involved in this issue. One is "Who shall police the police?" The other involves the official use of secrecy which surrounds so much of police activity and administration. With respect to the first point, critics have claimed that the police are biased in favor of their own and that an impartial internal investigation is not possible. The police, on the other hand, tend to feel that to have "outsiders" involved in official police affairs would be harmful, because outsiders don't understand either the police or their work. In all honesty, neither perspective is without its flaws. The police *can* conduct objective investigations of other police, and non-police citizens *can* be of considerable value to police departments in an advisory capacity.

The real problem is a highly sensitive, emotionally charged gut issue which is fundamentally racial and ethnic in nature. Behind the rhetoric and eloquent phrasing, many outspoken minority citizens feel that the police discriminate against them in their enforcement tactics and administrative policies. They feel that the police should be made to be more responsive to "community needs" and individual examples of police transgressions are often used to illustrate the point. The demand for a citizens review board (with mixed community representation) is thus seen as a means of bringing about the desired changes in the police department. A great many police officers, however, see this as an unwarranted effort to directly interfere with the police in their performance of reasonable and proper police operations. This is an issue which is well understood by its contenders but which is seldom openly and directly discussed: it's a topic which is almost guaranteed to polarize the discussants. This is a matter of major concern which is yet to be satisfactorily resolved in virtually all major cities.

[11] Ahern, *op. cit.*, pp. 220–221.

The second issue—police secrecy—is yet another hotly contested issue. The police are generally "open to view" only under certain closely controlled circumstances. Interested persons can usually arrange to ride with the police and to observe them on the job, and tours through the stations can likewise normally be arranged. Traffic accident reports are usually available for a nominal fee, although other investigative reports are not. A citizen who goes to the police department headquarters intent on obtaining information on a specific offense (or even a class of offenses) can almost certainly be sure of a cool reception. The police operate in a quasi-military style and consider a great deal of their information to be confidential, for a variety of reasons. Ahern challenged this traditional posture when he said that "There is no reason that a police department should not open all but the most necessarily secret of its intelligence operations to the public." [12]

If the police were to "open up" to the public, it is highly unlikely that they would be deluged with citizens demanding to read reports or to otherwise dig into the comings and goings of the department. On the other hand, the knowledge that they could do so if they wanted might create a more open psychological environment. The problem of secrecy is that it not only hides that which ought to be hidden, but it also conceals inadequacies, incompetencies, and maladministration. Perhaps opening the police to greater public scrutiny would help them, much like the case of *Miranda v. Arizona* (384 U.S. 436, 36 Ohio Ops. 2d 237, 86 S. Ct. 1602, 16 L.Ed. 2d 694, 1966) helped the police by forcing them to be more thorough and professional in their investigations.

In the coming decades the police must come to grips with the issue of secrecy. The use of secrecy must be linked to a specific need, rather than simply being a goal in and of itself. When a person makes a complaint against a policeman, and where that complaint appears to be well founded, the police should themselves investigate the charge—and copies of the reports of investigation should be given not only to the police chief but to the complainant and the officer complained against as well. Perhaps the central point to remember is that the police and the community have reciprocal obligations to one another. The police cannot operate effectively in the community if they define all problems on their own terms; nor can the community expect much from the police when it fails in its responsibilities toward them.

The Police as Representatives of the System

The police department serves on the front line: the officers are in the thick and thin of events as they take place. To be sure, they make mis-

[12] Ahern, *op. cit.*, p. 218.

takes—which is only to be expected, given the nature of their task environment and the complexity of the issues which face them. The police, however, represent the *entire* system of justice to a large block of the public. As a consequence, inequities in other parts of the system will also often be laid at the doorstep of the police. Consider the following:

A survey by Boston lawyers divided defendants into those who earned less than $75 a week and those earning more than $100. The poorer defendants went to jail 25 percent of the time and the others 13 percent. A 1972 federal-court study found that 28 percent of white defendants convicted of interstate theft received prison sentences while 48 percent of blacks convicted of the same crime went to prison. The average sentence for blacks convicted of major felonies in seven Southern states in 1968 was 16.8 years; for whites it was 12.1.

This type of inconsistency is keenly felt by those on the receiving end, and it is logical to presume that sentiment in the community will find its expression in attitudes toward the highly visible element of the criminal justice system: the police. Thus even if the police are indeed fair, circumspect, and genuine in their dealings with the public, their relationship with the community as a whole will not achieve its potential until the other elements of the criminal justice system are also just and responsive. This is no small order, for it calls for major changes in many areas and at numerous levels within the entire system. These changes must include substantial court and judicial reform as well as a critical examination of current practices in corrections. One might well suspect that only after these changes are made will large numbers of citizens be willing to re-examine their attitudes towards the police. This is not a new problem; in fact, the President's Crime Commission has previously observed that:

To a considerable extent, the police are the victims of community problems which are not of their making. For generations, minority groups and the poor have not received a fair opportunity to share the benefits of American life. They suffer from bad housing, inferior education, unemployment, underemployment, or low wages. They have been discriminated against and abused by welfare and public housing officials, private landlords, and businessmen. Their frustrations and bitterness are taken out, at least in part, on the policeman as the most visible symbol of a society and its law which have often treated them so unjustly.

The police are sometimes blamed for the evils of the rest of the criminal justice system. When a suspect is held for long periods in jail prior to trial because he cannot make bail, when he is given inadequate counsel or none at all, when he is assigned counsel that

attempts to extract money from him or his family even though he is
indigent, when he is paraded through the courtroom in a group or
is tried in a few minutes, when he is sent to jail because he has no
money to pay a fine, when the jail or prison is physically dilapidated
or its personnel brutal or incompetent, or when the probation or
parole officer has little time to give him, the offender will probably
blame, at least in part, the police officers who arrested him and
started the process.[13]

The Imbalance of Municipal Services [14]

In the area of municipal services, there is widespread agreement that the
political system has failed to correct the inequalities that exist in predictable
patterns throughout the country. Ghetto residents live with the fact that city
governments do not pave, repair, clean, and light the streets and sidewalks
in their neighborhoods as systematically as they do in white, middle- and
upper-income areas. Ghetto residents perceive police departments that permit narcotics traffic, prostitution, and gambling operations to flourish, and
that fail to respond quickly to calls for help in stopping assaults and batteries.
Every day these same citizens experience losses of life, liberty, and property
—losses that are more serious and more widespread than those that occur
in higher income neighborhoods. Moreover, the deficient quality of the essential government services of education retards human development, personal
liberty, and ability to gain employment and acquire property.[5]

These municipal services—adequate police protection and adequate education—are basic government responsibilities. It is imperative, therefore, that
they be allocated to all citizens on an adequate and equitable basis. Until
recently, the allocation of municipal resources was entirely within the purview of local officials, who exercised wide discretion in setting priorities for
service delivery to all sections of a city. Recently, the administrative judgment
of these officials has been questioned by a number of court actions filed by
citizens alleging that, as recipients of inferior services, they have been subjected to insidious discrimination and a denial of the equal protection under
the laws of the United States. Because these issues question the constitu-

13 Donald Dale Jackson, *Judges.* (New York: Atheneum, 1974), p. 367.
14 *Task Force Report: The Police, op. cit.,* p. 150; Gershon M. Ratner, "Inter-Neigh-
borhood Denials of Equal Protection in the Provision of Municipal Services," *Harvard
Civil Rights-Civil Liberties Law Review,* IV (1968), pp. 3–5.
[5] The following text and notes [5–9] * is taken from the report of the National
Advisory Commission on Criminal Justice Standards and Goals, Russell W. Peterson,
Chairman, *Community Crime Prevention.* (Washington, D.C.: Government Printing
Office, 1973), pp. 35–38.
* [footnotes 1–4 omitted]

tionality of local governmental action, the judiciary has been brought into the processes of municipal government administration.

In the most notable case to be decided thus far, *Hawkins* v. *Town of Shaw*,[6] the U.S. Court of Appeals for the Fifth Circuit imposed on the local government an affirmative duty to correct the gross disparities in service delivery demonstrated by unchallenged statistics of inequitable conditions.

The town of Shaw, Miss., is located in the Mississippi Delta. At the time of the suit it had about 2,500 residents—1,500 black and 1,000 white—and almost total residential racial segregation. Evidence introduced in court showed that nearly 98 percent of all homes that front on unpaved streets were occupied by blacks, and that 97 percent of the homes not served by sanitary sewers were in black neighborhoods. Not one of the substantial number of recently acquired medium and high intensity mercury vapor street lighting fixtures had been installed in black neighborhoods. Water pressure was inadequate in two black neighborhoods containing 63 percent of the town's black population. Finally, the record on the placement of fire hydrants and traffic control signs in black neighborhoods satisfied the court that the black sections of town were severely disadvantaged.

The town was ordered to submit a detailed plan to the trial court showing how it would remedy the existing inequities. The Appeals Court indicated that the standard for any remedial measures should be the quality and quantity of municipal services provided in the white area of town—an area which "for the most part, does not significantly differ in needs and expectations from the black portion of town." [7]

The implication of the *Shaw* decision is that, in the area of municipal services, the constitutional concerns of the courts center on the comparative quality of services provided to all citizens in a given jurisdiction. In order to provide, for example, the same quality of fire protection that exists in high income neighborhoods, cities may have to spend more money for fire protection in areas of the city containing the most dilapidated housing. This does not necessarily mean that services provided to more affluent neighborhoods need be diminished. Services should be provided to all communities according to need.

The problem of service inequities is not limited to small Southern towns, as indicated in the 1970 and 1971 local studies of 147 cities and counties in the Model Cities Program.[8] Examples from a cross-section of such cities illustrate these deficiencies.

* [6] *Hawkins* v. *Town of Shaw*, 437 F2d 1286 (5th Cir. 1971). See also Simon, Lawrence, "Equal Protection in the Urban Environment: The Right to Equal Municipal Services," *Tulane Law Review*, 46 (February 1972), p. 516.

* [7] *Ibid.*, p. 1292.

* [8] The Model Cities First Year Planning Programs, U.S. Department of Housing and Urban Development, Library Planning and Development Section, Washington, D.C.

12

Savannah, Ga.

Unemployment in the low-income model neighborhood (MN) is higher than 6.2 percent, as compared to 3.4 percent for the entire city. Ten of the 11 schools in the target area have mental maturity, reading, and arithmetic norms one and two grades below the national average. The high school dropout rate is 16 percent, compared to 9 percent for the school system as a whole. Only 4 percent of the model area housing is "standard." Existence of outside toilets attests to primitive conditions.

Overcrowding is characteristic in the model neighborhood. Since 1960, the population has increased but the number of housing units has decreased. The target area has only three supervised playgrounds with a combined acreage of 2.6. Thus 5.9 percent of the total city-supervised playground area serves 15 percent of the city's population. There are 8 miles of unpaved streets and sidewalks in the MN, in sharp contrast to "historic Savannah" with its beautiful old buildings and well-kept parks and gardens.

Health conditions in the MN are well below the city and county rates. In 1968, infant mortality rates per 100,000 persons were 42.5 in the county and 60 in the MN; tuberculosis rates were 42 in the county and 105 in the MN; infectious syphilis rates were 27.6 in the county and 115 in the MN.

Life in the target area is further threatened by a high incidence of crime. With only 15 percent of the population, the MN experiences 33 percent of the homicides and rapes and 27 percent of the felonious assaults. Juvenile delinquency, as represented by the number of arrests, is also high. The arrest rate of persons under 18 years of age in the target area is 48.2 per 1,000, compared with 33.8 per 1,000 for the whole city.

There is heavy dependence on public welfare, yet few social service agencies are located within the MN or have outreach services there. Residents complain of inadequate coordination between the public and private agencies that provide social services.

Much resident dissatisfaction is directed at the city for its failure to provide adequate municipal services in the MN. Housing inspection, police protection, and problems relating to streets, sidewalks, lighting, garbage collection, storm drainage systems, animal control, and traffic control are inadequate in the MN. Citizen attitude surveys conducted by the Model Cities staff at the beginning of the program and again during its operation indicate a general feeling of hopelessness, apathy, and frustration in the target area; residents have come to accept as inevitable the poverty, crime, and disease that blight their daily lives.

Indianapolis, Ind.

A 1970 Model Cities report revealed that in the model neighborhood there was overcrowding in 16.7 percent of all housing units; 29.3 percent of the households lived in poverty conditions; 11.6 percent of the adult population was unemployed; 19 percent of the city's total major crimes were committed in the MN; 48 percent of the housing in the MN was deficient according to the city's housing code; and the incidence of tuberculosis was 18 percent of all new cases in the city.

Boston, Mass.

Citizen surveys and interviews reveal that services are less effective in the MN than in other parts of the city. Residents particularly express need for improvements in education facilities, crime prevention, legal services, citizen education and rehabilitation, police-community relations, and employment of minorities in the police and other city departments. A 1969 report of the Joint Center for Urban Studies of Harvard-MIT revealed that only 30 percent of Boston's population thought the city government was doing a good job.

Seattle, Wash.

The model neighborhood is typical of many others in the Nation. The following percentages are two to three times higher than in the rest of the city: substandard housing, 24 percent; incomes under $3,000, 17 percent; infant death, 36 per 1,000; welfare families, 3.6 percent; and education, 50 percent of heads of household did not finish high school. Unemployment is three times higher than in the rest of the city and the school dropout rate is 45 percent higher than the city average.

Newark, N.J.

The Model Cities agency reports that unemployment and crime rates are considerably higher in the MN than in the rest of the city. Over 50 percent of all families who live in the MN earn less than $5,000 a year. An estimated 85 percent of the housing units in the MN were built prior to 1940, and 74.3 percent are deficient.

These kinds of extreme inequalities exist in Model City neighborhoods in New York, N.Y., Chicago, Ill., Los Angeles, Calif., and in many cities, counties, and rural areas of the country not in the Model Cities Program. Attitude surveys conducted by the local staffs of almost every Community Action and Model Cities Program indicate deep feelings of resident alienation and despair. Citizens in these areas view local government as unresponsive to their needs and unwilling to expend the funds necessary to correct the situation. They live in an environment that is deteriorated, bleak, congested, and crime infested.

Local government officials should take the initiative necessary to alleviate the conditions of enforced inferiority that place so many Americans in unhealthy and unsafe environments. They can do this by making budgetary

12

allocations that distribute municipal services on criterion of need. Recommen
dation 2.1 presents some of the criteria that should be used in the decision
making process for equitable allocation of municipal resources.

Local government is expected to provide services and operate community
facilities that meet the needs of the entire population. The cumulative cost of
such services places a serious strain on the financial capacity of local government. However, the financial resources that are available traditionally have
been used for the benefit of the relatively affluent sections of most cities.
This has generally resulted in a distribution of municipal services that is
inequitable, as well as disproportionate to the needs and numbers of citizens
living in central city areas.

It is not difficult to understand why the millions of Americans who live in
neglected, deteriorating neighborhoods feel apathetic and alienated. If local
government is to succeed in improving the physical environment and the
quality of life for all citizens, it must begin by making the politically difficult
decision to allocate resources on the basis of actual needs of area residents.
Efforts must be made to provide depressed areas with services equal in
quality to those provided the rest of the community.

In general, central city areas contain the city's poorest residents and its
oldest, most dilapidated housing. These areas are characterized by congested
multifamily apartment buildings with faulty and inadequate plumbing and
electrical wiring, by numerous deteriorated and abandoned buildings, and
by weak or nonexistent housing code enforcement.

Considering the unhealthy and unsafe physical conditions of such neighborhoods, and the fact that they are inhabited by many more people per
square mile than the city's outer fringe areas, it is easy to comprehend why
more resources must be allocated to the inner city merely to raise it to the
same level of quality as the rest of the community.

The high population density of low income neighborhoods, and their substandard housing conditions, may be the two most crucial factors affecting the
level of needed municipal services. It is the inner city resident who must walk
to his destination if public transportation does not reach him or is too expensive. It is he who is inconvenienced or immobilized if sidewalks are not
constructed and maintained and if street lighting is inadequate. Anyone who
loses his freedom of movement and his basic sense of well-being because
of a fear of injury or crime in an inadequately protected neighborhood, and
anyone who suffers a critical illness because of inadequate or unequal sanitation and health facilities, undeniably suffers a serious loss of liberty, and
maybe of life.[9]

Most city codes contain ordinances that authorize sidewalk construction

* [9] Lawrence Simon, "Equal Protection in the Urban Environment: The Right to
Equal Municipal Service," *Tulane Law Review* 46 (February 1972), p. 516.

whenever application for construction is made by owners of abutting property, and when these same owners make a deposit of some portion of the estimated cost of the work. In addition to such authorization, the municipal government itself is generally charged with the duty to construct public sidewalks whenever "the public health, safety, or comfort require it . . ." (7 D.C. Code 608). Owners of most inner city multifamily apartment buildings either neglect to make application for such construction, or refuse to do so. Since the low income residents themselves cannot afford to bear the cost (as can residents in the more affluent areas), the municipal government must take the initiative and fulfill its responsibility to provide for the public health, safety, and comfort of its citizens.

Conclusion

The relationship between the police and the cities is complex and tightly interwoven. The same forces which created the modern cities have also molded the police, and it is unrealistic to consider the police without recognizing this fact. What the police of the future will be must likewise depend in large measure on the forces which will continue to shape the city.

However, the police are not merely pawns in an unfolding urban evolution. They are themselves part of the forces which shape the cities, and to that extent they are also at least co-authors of their own future—or in the words of Thomas Carlyle:

All work is as seed sown; it grows
and spreads, and sows itself anew.

Appendix A

The Community, the Criminal Justice System, and Community Crime Prevention*

Traditionally the term community has denoted territoriality. The community was the place where the householder lived and worked, raised children, and attended church. Today, the meaning of community has changed.

As the population has increased and more people have moved to the cities, the old sense of community has been lost. Today places of living and working often are separated. In large cities, the sense of being part of a neighborhood community has disappeared. Community has come to mean, not a neighborhood, but shared values or a common interest, which may or may not have to do with where one lives. Community then refers to two distinct concepts: in the older sense it is a geographical area, while today it often implies support of common goals.

Everyone in America is concerned with the problem of crime. Crime rates have risen steadily during the last decade; from 1960 to 1970, U.S. total crime rates tripled. But local units of government, from small towns to major cities, are as involved with crime as a national problem as they are with local crime rates. Community crime prevention programs, although implemented locally, must become a matter for national action. Anticrime strategies must be developed for every setting where citizen action against crime can be mobilized —whether the setting is a neighborhood, village, suburb, metropolitan area, State, or the Nation. In the fight against crime, every locality must become a center of action. All the resources of the Nation must be tapped.

While the criminal justice system is a part of American society, anticrime efforts operating in the community and in the criminal justice system rarely are coordinated. Despite the physical closeness of law enforcement agencies and the community, the people and the system often do not work together. In many communities they operate in a climate of mutual hostility. Citizens are not trained to make use of the criminal justice system. When they are the victims of crime, they may not know how to use police assistance or seek legal redress. Law enforcement officials often operate independently of the communities they serve and thus fail to tap community resources in anticrime efforts.

Americans tend to divide their communities into two parts: the official or governmental sector and the private sector. The community is viewed as part of the private sector, while the criminal justice system is considered to be wholly within the official area. The ordinary citizen delegates the responsibility for crime prevention to the official sector—or more specifically, to the criminal justice system.

* Taken from Appendix A of the Report of the National Advisory Commission on Criminal Justice Standards and Goals, Russell W. Peterson, Chairman, *Community Crime Prevention*. (Washington, D.C.: Government Printing Office, 1973), pp. 280–286.

The criminal justice system must continue to play a vital role in crime prevention, as well as in apprehension and rehabilitation. But the criminal justice system, at all levels, is a partner to the community, and at each of its levels of jurisdiction, it must work with community residents for the common goals of crime prevention and reduction. Crime flourishes more readily when these two units do not work together. Thus, it is impossible to delegate crime prevention responsibilities exclusively to the official sector. Crime cannot be reduced unless the public accepts an equal share of responsibility for its reduction. The public must acknowledge that this responsibility cannot be abdicated to government.

The community and the criminal justice system are separate units within the broader system of society. Because they are both parts of one society, they share many values, attitudes, and codes or rules of behavior. At the same time, they operate under many different codes or rules.

The criminal justice system was established to enforce and protect the laws written to regulate behavior in society. Ideally, these laws should express community values. However, this is not always the case.

American society is made up of many subcultures, each with its own values and beliefs about what constitutes proper behavior. The differences between these values often are great. The individuals who make up these various American subcultures are shaped by these values.

Cultural differences, while they provide many benefits for our society, also make the tasks of law enactment and law enforcement complex. Where group attitudes and enacted laws coincide, crime prevention is easier. But where differences exist, individuals and the law enforcement system oppose each other.

One role of community crime prevention is to mediate between the developing attitudes of the community and the responsiveness of the criminal justice system. At present, the criminal justice system and many American subcultures are in conflict. Social unrest and disenchantment with the "system" have grown. It is at this point that carefully designed strategies of community crime prevention can intercede to reconnect the people and the system. The links that can be forged must be built on cooperation and an exchange of ideas. The people must be brought into the process of crime prevention planning. Citizens will support only anticrime programs that are designed for their needs, and with their participation at every stage of planning. Moreover, the commitment of communities to citizen participation is an antidote to institutional inertia.

Community crime prevention is based on the premise that the principal and direct responsibility for crime prevention rests with the total community—the private as well as the official sectors. Government and society must join in this effort. It can take many forms: from providing alternatives to criminal behavior, eliminating corrupt practices in both the private and official sectors, to designing the environment to reduce the opportunities to commit crime. The task is monumental. It can be accomplished, however, if the national ethic with respect to crime is recreated. If the total community is involved in providing the models for public trust and ethical concern, and, if it develops a common set of plans and strategy for change, the Nation can begin to eradicate criminal behavior at every level of society.

Intervention in Social Processes as a Mechanism for Change

There are two basic methods for introducing change into a system: replacement and adaptation. In the replacement method, one attempts to replace inefficient or outmoded techniques with new, more efficient ones. The great technological advances resulting from the scientific and engineering discoveries that have revolutionized agriculture, industry, and medicine are examples of this technique. The second technique, adaptation, is more gradual and involves the redefinition or modification of existing practices.

There are technological advances that can replace outmoded practices in crime reduction and prevention. Generally, however, the major changes needed to produce effective community crime prevention programs require changes in attitudes and behavior both in the community and in the criminal justice system. Changes must occur in public attitudes as well as behavior, and support for the changes must be maintained once they are introduced. Often, it is felt that favorable public opinion is necessary to produce change. Such changes in attitudes are essential but they will not be sustained unless the new ideas or techniques are incorporated in the value systems of new social groups or become items on the agendas of established organizations.

In order to achieve both the necessary climate and the institutionalization of changes in attitude and behavior in community crime control, two difficulties that have characterized previous attempts must be overcome. Past attempts to bring about structural changes in the relationship between the community and crime prevention have been uncoordinated and scattered. In both the private and public sectors, individuals and organizations have developed programs of crime prevention using a variety of ideas and techniques. Some have been successful at the local level and some have won national notice, but generally their effects have been noncumulative and short-lived.

A second difficulty has been the tendency to develop programs that have a direct impact on the individual. Such programs fail because they do not build opportunities for change in the groups, structures, and systems that influence and support the behavior of the individuals who are members. Thus, the individual may be motivated to change his behavior but he is unable to find the necessary reinforcement and support in society. The cycle of recidivism, which has troubled the courts, the corrections system, and society, is testimony to the need for individuals to find some means of joining with others if the structure of their attitudes and behavior is to change.

Given current knowledge of political and social change mechanisms, adaptation, rather than replacement, must be the primary method for developing community crime prevention programs. Broad social changes require time and sustained effort. Planning must begin now. It is possible to begin developing some of the goals of this report as avenues to long-range change. To do so, however, the mediation process between the community and the criminal justice system must be altered in order to maximize social benefits to both. This means establishing communications between the two.

Individuals and groups must sense that they are part of the system, working to solve its problems. They must believe they can work to change the system, not that they will survive by beating the system. If this first step can be brought about, it should be possible to begin to effect changes at the community level. The goals of the community and the goals of criminal justice system will coalesce. To establish a common set of objectives, the community must:

1. Identify the values and goals the community and the criminal justice system share as subsystems of American society.

2. From these common goals, develop a set of objectives that are commonly desired and valued and on which immediate action is possible.

3. Develop strategies and techniques for dealing with those objectives and issues on which there is not common agreement.

4. Find ways to work toward terminating the "we-they" distinction felt and expressed between the community and the criminal justice system.

5. Accept that, in order to produce real change, the law must be responsive to the values shared by both the community and the criminal justice system. The law must mediate between conflicting values. In some cases, this may mean decriminalization; in others, it will require criminalization of acts condemned by society but condoned by law.

But all of this will not just happen. Communities must plan for change and learn from it as well. And, once common goals are established, better Federal, State and local planning of crime prevention programs is essential. Many programs have met with limited success, not because of improper goals but because of poor planning.

Planning and Evaluation

In essence, crime prevention is public business. Citizens' dollars and energies should be spent to achieve results. Creating a successful program requires good timing and careful use of resources. Planning and evaluation are essential to creating successful programs.

If planning and evaluation are applied within a framework of community participation, effective effort can be assured. But creating community structures to implement new programs is a complex task. Large numbers of people will have to be involved, and ways devised to coordinate their efforts to achieve maximum gains

Planning and evaluation are tools. The community must understand their functions and master the techniques for applying them. Planning and evaluation focus attention on the purpose, or stated goal, of an activity. Planners devise ways to achieve this purpose, and evaluations are used to estimate progress in accomplishing it.

Models for Planning

It is easy to misuse the tool of planning. Among laymen, and even planners, many wrong notions of the fundamental procedures of the planning process exist. The method of "predict and prepare" is a planning technique many persons believe is the sum and substance of planning.

The predict-and-prepare model starts with the assumption that the main role of planning is to guess or predict the nature of future events and to prepare to cope with them. At worst, this form of planning takes current and past trends, lumps them together, and comes up with a possible future.

At best, this planning method can provide a reasonable forecast of future trends, based on clear understanding of the laws as well as the facts of past and current processes. But the method does not begin to deal with the real goal of planning: designing a desired future state. Predict and prepare does not allow the planner space to design and create his models.

Good planning emphasizes intervention. Adaptive intervention is the model that should be employed in preparing community crime prevention programs. This technique is based on three assumptions.

1. The value of planning does not lie in the plan it produces, but in the planning process. Process is the most important product of planning: for community crime prevention, it must be a process of enlisting community support. Planning here cannot be done for the community; it must be done with the community.

2. When planning is effective, it is no longer needed. The ultimate fate of good community crime prevention planning will be self-destruction. The techniques it employs eventually should become so much a part of community life that planning can no longer be recognized as a separate activity.

3. Planning must deal explicitly with problems of uncertainty. The planning process must identify what is relatively certain to happen in the future, and plan around these certainties; this is sometimes called commitment planning. Planning must identify what is probable in the future and plan for these probabilities: this is called contingency planning. But planning also must identify what is possible in the future. Planners must intervene to bring about

what is desired rather than what is expected. This is called intervention planning. It is with intervention planning that we are chiefly concerned.

Adaptive planning implies flexibility in program design. Only the flexible plan can deal adequately with unexpected environmental changes. Adaptive planning implies an adaptive organizational structure: a structure that is geared to rapid change. Most important is the ability of this structure to disconnect from other organizational structures and chart its own course. If administrative procedures are emphasized, the organization may be buried in red tape. Where change and stability are in conflict, the adaptive organization opts for change, using techniques of intervention as a strategy for change.

Connection Between Planning and Evaluation

Planning has one main function: to provide a context for more effective analysis of alternative strategies. Thus, evaluation is a part of the planning process. The planner begins by examining the situation for which he is planning to locate the shortest pathways to his goal. When he examines the alternatives, the evaluation process has begun. At the beginning, evaluation focuses on program environment. As the program is implemented, the program itself becomes a focus for evaluation. The ongoing program is evaluated not only to determine whether it should be continued, altered, or terminated, but also to provide information on the enviroment in which the program operates. Even if the program is evaluated as a failure, it can provide valuable information about why the program has failed. The evaluator finds out why the program failed, and uses the information gained from studying these mistakes to design new and better programs.

Planning and evaluation do not provide rules that dictate actions. Their main purpose is to provide a powerful basis for decisionmaking. Intuition and experience are not enough to decide what course to take. Planning and evaluation should clarify purposes, organize relevant information, generate alternatives, focus attention on important positive and negative aspects of proposals, and sharpen the intuition of the decisionmaker. Regular monitoring and evaluation of program performance provides continuing guidance for the decisionmaker, channels our energies effectively and efficiently, and generates new planning efforts and new modes of program implementation.

The Planning and Evaluation Cycle: An Overview

When a community begins to plan, it first must clarify its purpose. What is the problem to be solved and what problems must be overcome to solve it? A clear understanding of the problem and goals must be achieved, or resultant projects may solve the wrong problem. The process is begun by breaking down a given problem or goal into subproblems or subgoals. Then the pur-. pose can be defined.

Next, criteria are defined. Measures of effectiveness are devised to evaluate whether progress is made and if so, how much. The process of defining criteria brings the problem into sharper focus. When standards for problem solving are set, the severity of the problem becomes apparent. At the same time, the purpose becomes clearer.

In planning for community crime prevention, any of the following points can be emphasized:

- Social benefits—diversion of measurable resources to constructive activities
- The public perception of security
- Crime rates
- The relative priority the public gives a particular crime compared to others as a public danger
- Economic benefits—lower theft losses, lower insurance rates, higher local rate of investment

The relative importance of each type of measurement should be indicated by giving each a numerical weight. In this manner criteria can be developed for evaluating the overall effectiveness of each program.

As the community develops a statement of purpose and begins to envision the future it desires, it must develop a model of the problem. In the model, it correlates information on the cause-and-effect relationships that instigate crime. The model can be broken down into two parts: a physical description of the crime, including data on which factors in the physical environment made occurrence of the crime possible and a sociological description taking into account the factors that bring about criminal behavior.

The physical description shows where, when, and how the crime was committed. The behavioral description tells why. Sometimes the two areas overlap. For example, if a jewelry store is left unlocked at night, sooner or later somebody will try the door. On the other hand, some crimes are committed despite overwhelming odds against the criminal. The desperate daytime robberies by narcotics addicts provide an example of the crimes that will be committed no matter what physical problems they present for the criminal.

When the model has been elaborated, the points where community crime prevention effort can intercede effectively may be located. The model can be used to redefine the problem and to restate the program's goals. Thus, the original definition of the problems and the original goals of the program serve to direct the construction of the model, and the model in turn serves to direct changes in the original problems and goals. This type of backtracking and feedback is essential to useful planning and evaluation.

With the model as a basis for the study, a number of alternative means to intervene within society to halt crime can be seen. A large number of alternative means for blocking each type of crime considered can be developed.

Alternatives must be considered in terms of cost. Costs do not refer only to the fiscal expenses of the program. An accurate estimate must include all resources that must be used in the program, such as money, manpower, special equipment, and community goodwill. The community must differentiate between initial investment of resources and the long-term maintenance costs. Cost models can aid in determining the resources required for any given project.

When these models are developed, the decisionmaker can choose among alternatives with an increased knowledge of both the potential short- and long-term effects and the costs of any alternative or combination of alternatives. Once the alternatives are selected, it is necessary to calculate the possible benefits and known costs of the project for a number of years into the future. Long-term cost-benefit planning provides immediate criteria for the ongoing evaluation of the model.

Coordinating goals is an essential part of long-term planning. Alternatives selected separately for their cost effectiveness in achieving separate sub-goals may not be in harmony with one another when it comes to achieving the overall goal of community crime prevention. If, as the program continues, the goals have not been balanced, the planners must return to the earlier stages of the planning and evaluation process. Changes in the statements of goals and criteria and in the construction of the model precede making a new selection of alternatives. This reiteration within the planning cycle is a necessary part of the whole process. Using this method, the contradictions in goals, which more haphazard methods would ignore, are apparent.

As the programs are implemented, they are monitored to provide more information for evaluation. If they fail, their failure may indicate mistakes in the model. Evaluation of the failure should bring suggestions for changes that would make the model more accurate.

Information from ongoing programs, whether the programs succeed or fail, is the major guide to necessary changes and new opportunities. With each repetition, programs should improve as a better understanding of both problems and environment are acquired through evaluation.

The Political Context

Policy decisions are not always made by the technicians or crime prevention program managers who direct programs. Often they are made by the community carrying them out. Planners cannot impose their goals on the community. Citizens choose to participate, and in doing so, they make the actual policy decisions. The public as a whole is one segment of the local political environment. Within this public, many individuals exert great political influence. These individuals can determine the success or failure of community crime prevention efforts by influencing its citizen participants.

Community crime prevention will operate in an environment where politics will be relevant and the interactions of the local program initiator and local citizens will be filled with political overtones. As a result, community crime prevention will present more political than economic problems. Problems of credibility, reliability, and selection of allies will eclipse those of fiscal cost and immediate good effects. A program that uses little manpower may be more efficient economically, but may be dysfunctional in a political sense, because groups not invited to participate may feel slighted, possibly hindering the program.

The planning, implementation, and evaluation strategies proposed here are based on a decentralized operation: usually the local level will actually design and undertake crime preventive programs. The Federal and State agencies will support the community unit with information and limited services. These services could include training, troubleshooting consultation, in-depth research, and the transfer of information from locale to locale.

Some of the services provided to local programs will come from the Federal level and some from the State planning agency. The latter may advise and assist communities when the communities employ field workers (and act as a training unit for other communities). State offices also can troubleshoot for local units when required. And State offices can monitor local programs to insure the implementation of compatible programs in different locales.

The Federal level will have no administrative role, but could be critically important in testing community programs. On the basis of problems and insights encountered at the local level, the Federal agency would direct in-depth research in community crime prevention topics. Possible areas of Federal involvement include construction of large-scale, sophisticated models of the evolution of criminal behavior; studies of the interactions of communities and the criminal justice system; and research into the various methodologies available to the local programs.

The Flow of Information

Because the crime prevention program will be decentralized, good information transfer from locale to locale is essential. Creating an information net, i.e., a device for capturing information, will be a crucial activity at both the State and national levels.

Good information is accurate, relevant, current, and organized. Different types of information from different sources will be needed. The information net should be designed to provide accurate, up-to-date information.

Attempts at gathering and transferring information are hindered by problems of subjective resistance and objective inadequacies in the content of the information. Subjective resistance refers to the indifference or hostility that requests for information evoke, and also to the problem of offering information to people who are threatened by the information. Objective inadequacies in the transfer of information consist of mistakes or misconceptions made in transcribing or interpreting information. Examples of objective inadequacies include irrelevant questions that skirt important issues, unorganized information that blocks usage, and oversights in not delivering information to all those for whom it is relevant.

These problems can be overcome if the State and Federal levels act as clearinghouses for information. Continual monitoring of local programs is necessary to discover successful ones. Ideas should be given broad circulation throughout the State. Publications and symposiums will disseminate information as well as maintain written and spoken contact with individual program participants.

The State agency should be responsible for enhancing the vertical flow of information between local communities and Federal research facilities. This effort will be enhanced if some local anticrime projects are linked informally to the Federal research staff for purposes of experimentation. Such linkage would allow direct acquisition of field information and experience, and aid the researchers in determining which problems and questions are most important in obtaining information from locales across the country.

Goal Achievement Through Organizational Development

Methods that help the community sustain crime prevention activities in a desired direction are needed. The method of organization development applies behavioral science to the "people problems" or organizations for the purpose of improving procedures and work relationships.

There is one overriding principle that guides the techniques of organizational development in responding to organizational problems. This principle is that individuals seek to maintain themselves as individuals regardless of their environment. Their personal goals and needs are the ones they most wish to achieve and satisfy; if there is a conflict between the desires of the individual and the objectives of the crime prevention program, it is almost certainly the program that will suffer.

The importance of allowing all the participants in a community crime prevention effort to share in the control of the program and the shaping of its goals cannot be overstressed. Without this sharing, personnel will not be committed to their unit's proper functioning, and it will become difficult to get personnel to work in accord with their unit's real needs.

Organizational development training includes sessions in communication skills, two-way goal setting, conflict management, alteration of decisionmaking procedures, and the diagnosis and resolution of organizational conflicts.

No attempt should be made to trick the public into a conception of their own goals manufactured by the agency. People may not be committed to decisions they have no part in making. Genuine efforts should be made to keep lines of communication within community crime prevention organizations open, and to distribute influence broadly via decentralized decisionmaking. The integration of the needs of both individuals and community groups with the needs of crime prevention can bring involvement and commitment.

In normal organization settings, the upper echelons of administration control the setting of objectives, often with little or no consideration given either to the demands of the environment or to the thoughts of the other personnel within the system. People involved in a program generally develop some fairly clear conceptions of the goals of the program—by deducing them either from the structure of the program or from what they think the program should be doing—but these conceptions may or may not come close to the objectives that those responsible for selecting the program had in mind. The result is that no one knows what is supposed to be happening in the system, much less what is actually happening.

Investigations of organizations repeatedly reveal that the intentions of personnel often diverge from those that are formally stated for the organization. Subordinates develop notions of their responsibilities to conform with what they are willing to do. They strive to maintain and even assert their autonomy by hoarding information, supplying inaccurate data, and generally providing only halfhearted cooperation. Subordinates who have liberated themselves as much as possible from organization controls have achieved much freedom and autonomy at the expense of both accountability and the proper function of the system. To control the proliferation of objectives in an organization's structure is difficult. When the goals of a system are not those of the people responsible for maintaining the functioning of the system's program, the system is in trouble.

Organizational development demands that personnel actually contribute. Community crime prevention goals should not be established by the high level administrators but by local personnel and citizens guided by Federal and State research. This two-way goal setting is accomplished through the use of techniques developed by organizational theorists. Accordingly, organizational development specifically seeks to open, on a permanent basis, the avenues of communication between levels of administration by which feelings are expressed, openness is encouraged, information is transferred, and the system is changed.

An important point related to the dissemination of information is how it is used. Information forms a basis for analysis, which, in turn, provides a basis for evaluation and decisionmaking. It is important that information be used in this manner, and not for the control of personnel. Real emphasis must be placed on the objective of using evaluation as a means for improving methods and principles, not as a policing mechanism. Proper use of evaluation keeps necessary information flowing from persons who might otherwise feel threatened and obstruct analysis. Or, put more bluntly, if analysis is not explicitly directed towards principles and methods, any evaluation analyst will be seen by crime prevention project personnel as a management spy not to be trusted.

Analysis is often misunderstood by administration and thus is easily sidetracked from its primary purposes of evaluating alternatives and planning future courses of action. This again points to the importance of training personnel at all levels. Each step in planning, implementation, evaluation, and renewed planning has a critical purpose. The educating of the community to this cardinal principle is the first order of community crime prevention business.

Index

References are to page numbers

Index